MORE
THAN
WORDS

5000
Marketing Phrases That Sell

Compiled by
Richard & Lynn Voigt

MORE THAN WORDS
5000 Marketing Phrases That Sell

© 2012 by RIVO Inc – All Rights Reserved!

ISBN-13: 978-1470062040
ISBN-10: 1470062046

First Printing, 2012

Printed in the United States of America

To Access More Of Our RIVO Websites Visit:

www.ActionHeadlines.com

www.Headline.me

www.RIVOinc.com

Income Disclaimer

This book contains educational materials meant to inspire ways to promote personal ideas, products and services that may be appropriate to incorporate or use in or as a business strategy, marketing method or any other related personal or business advice that, regardless of the author's results and experience, may not produce the same results (or any results) for you. The authors make absolutely no guarantee, expressed or implied, that by using or following any of the ideas below that you will make any money or improve current profits, as there are several factors and variables that come into play regarding any level of achievement or success in said personal and/or business venture.

Primarily, results will depend on the nature of the product or business model, the conditions of the marketplace, the experience of the individual, and situations and elements that are beyond your control.

As with any business endeavor, you assume all risk related to investment and money based on your own discretion and at your own potential expense.

If you intend to quote, copy, or use any content herein, in part or whole, it shall be the sole responsibility of the individual to be mindful of all active and lawfully protected copyrights, trademarks, and/or services-marks, by conducting due diligence prior to said usage.

Liability Disclaimer

This book is strictly intended for educational purposes only and was intended to inspire the individual to create ideas of their own design.   This book represents the

Now that all the legal stuff is out of the way, let's begin to have a lifetime of fun by applying, modifying, and customizing the following educational materials to help you creatively promote your own original ideas or marketing niche.

MORE THAN WORDS

5000
Marketing Phrases That Sell

Compiled by
Richard & Lynn Voigt

MORE THAN WORDS
5000+ Marketing Phrases That Sell

In today's world every word has a measurable and emotional impact. Marketing Phrases and Headlines have become the single most powerful marketing tool mankind has ever created. They're the true lifeblood behind every business venture online or offline.

No matter whether introducing or promoting a brand new product or service, teaching a "How To" skill, building a website, or simply sending an email, smart marketers carefully create psychological phrases that are absolutely crucial to successful sales copy and marketing campaigns.

It's been said, don't waste your time and resources trying to reinvent the wheel, just find an easier way to push your marketing cart up hill faster and cheaper, and find more efficient ways to control it on its way down.

This book includes 5,000 great marketing phrases for you to study, alter, and personalize for your next email or marketing campaign.

See what experts do and say that can help you produce some amazing results reaping huge rewards from your videos, products and services.

More Than Words is a powerful collection of great marketing phrases that can effectively teach you to paint dreams, sell ideas, and market your message. It's up to you to use these power phrases wisely.

MORE THAN WORDS
5000+ Marketing Phrases That Sell

1	Double-Check Your Email For Accuracy To Ensure You Receive Access To The Information. Our Privacy Policy Keeps Your Email Safe & Secure.
2	You'll Never Have Trouble Writing Powerful Headlines For The Most Important Aspects Of Your Business. Our Incredible Resource Contains The Right Words That Will Eliminate Your Frustrating Head-Scratching Blanks That Comes With This Marketing Territory. Put An End To Writer's Block Forever!
3	Always Be Yourself Because The People That Matter Don't Mind. And The Ones That Mind Don't Matter
4	I Am Going To Be Delivering A Lot Of Content To You To Help You Be Successful With Our Program.
5	Why Millions Of Internet Marketers Are Too Scared To Do Something About It
6	Well, I Have NOW Realized And Learned That My Failures Were NOT My Fault And You Will Too! It Should Be About You And Building You Up So That You Can Build Others To Be Successful.
7	Lifting A Finger No Not That One Opens Your Eyes With Just One Click
8	Stay Focused Finish A Project And Give It Time To Take Effect
9	Live A Full And Happy Life Filled With The Freedom And Abundance You Deserve
10	The Fact That I'm Exposing 3 Profitable Niches That You Can Invade Almost Instantly By Stealing My Tested And Proven Techniques Is Easily Worth At Least 10 Times The Amount I'm Letting This Exclusive Series Go At.
11	So I've Been Doing Some Crazy Experiments In My "Lab". Basically, I've Put Together A Completely Free, High Powered Business System. I Mean, This Thing Spits Out Money Like Some Kind Of Supercharged Business Monster Truck... And It's Mostly Hands Off Too.
12	Are You Just Going To Sit By While The Pigs Get Fat And Hogs Get Slaughtered

13	We Hope You're Grasping The Big Picture Here. This New Wireless Technology Allows You To Stay Connected To The Internet Nationwide, While Driving, Walking, Camping, Hunting, Fishing, Golfing, Home, Or Office - Connect Anywhere!
14	I Never Blame Myself When I'm Not Hitting I Just Blame The Bat... How Can I Get Mad At Myself? So, If Your Marketing Game Isn't Where You'd Like It To Be Or If You're Not Making Any Real Money After All Your Time And Efforts, Quitting Isn't The Solution. Perhaps You Need Someone To Watch How You're Swinging Your Marketing Bat To Become More Effective.
15	I'm Not Sure What I Could Possibly Do To Make You A Better Offer. So Hit The Order Button Below Right Now And Prepare To Be Transformed Into An Ultra Confident Webmaster!
16	We Have An Excess Of Inventory That Needs To Be Blown Out
17	This Is A Rare No Strings Attached Offer That Even Converts Skeptics Into Believers
18	All It Takes Is Compiling A List Of People Who Share A Common Interest
19	Why You Need To Be Afraid OF Those Smooth Talking Mentors Leaving You Empty Handed
20	Your Time Is A Whole Lot More Valuable Than Money. Time Is Not Something You Can Ever Get Back. Money Is. You Can Always Make More Money. But You Can Never Recover Lost Time. What I'm Going To Share With You Today Is A Completely Different Way Of Thinking Than The "Time Equals Money" Way Of Thinking.
21	Don't Roll Your Eyes Thinking You'll Need To Create Your Own Products In Order To Have An Optin List.
22	Contains 300 Pages Of "No Fluff, No Hype" Tips, Secrets, Resources, Methods, Systems And Information -- So You Won't Waste Even A Minute Of Your Precious Time.
23	By Signing Up You Agree To Our Terms Of Use. Already A Member Then Click Here To Login
24	So Now That You Have This Great Idea How Do You Make Money
25	Buy My System Right Now And Put It To The Test For 8 FULL WEEKS. NO Pressures Or Obligations And Absolutely NO RISKS Involved!

26	I'm Not Here To Sell A Company Or Product. I Coach, Mentor, And Teach Frustrated Network Marketers To Become Successful Leaders And I Do It For Free: Regardless Of MLM Company Affiliation.
27	The Crucial Reasons Why You'll Want To Outsource Building Your Online Empire
28	Add A Picture, Image, Or Work Of Art. Whenever Possible Add A Picture To Your Article. Make Sure The Picture Relates Back To The Article Information And Give Credit Where Credit Is Do.
29	How To Place Your Eyes Inside Your Customer's Brain And Wallet
30	Maybe Your idea Can Solve A Common Problem Simply By Enriching Someone's Life
31	We All Know That Making Your First Dollar Online Is The Hardest
32	That's Why I'm Going To Take All The Pressure Off You Today. You Don't Have To Say, "Yes." You Just Have To Say, "Maybe." Because All You're Going To Put Down Today Is A Single Dollar (Just $1).
33	There Are Several Key Factors That Go Into The Decision Making Process When Anyone Decides To Purchase. It Happens To You Too - Even If You Don't Realize It.
34	If You Were Given $200,000 To Spend, Isn't This The Kind Of _____ You Would Build
35	Avoid These Destructive Mistakes If You Want The Job Done Right
36	How Would You Like To Own Seven Instant Businesses Which Brings In Cash Day-In And Day-Out To Your Account For Less Than You'd Pay For Dinner-For-Two With HOT Products While Making A 100% Profit.
37	Just Imagine - You Have A Website, You Join A Free System, Copy A Small Piece Of Code And Paste To Your Site And Immediately Start Making An Extra $50, 100 Or Even $200 A Day. Doesn't It Sound Great?
38	It's Not Too Late To STOP Shutting Down Your Unprofitable Online Business
39	Your Email Account Has Now Been Verified. We Just Sent You A Couple Of Important Emails. One Of The Emails Will Tell You How This Site Can Help You Advertise Your Link VIRALLY. SO CHECK YOUR EMAIL ACCOUNT.
40	We Live In A World Where Anyone Can Be A Millionaire

41	**In This Economy Isn't It Time You Guaranteed Your Financial Future**
42	**The Cost Of Producing Quality Corporate Videos Has Fallen By 64% Over The Last Five Years... But Most Video Production Companies Are Still Clinging To And Charging 1992 Prices**
43	**Just To Be On The Safe Side We Need Your Help To Verify All Of The Products**
44	**But If A Savings Of $75 Today Doesn't Seem Like That Big Of A Deal To You... Think About All Of The Wasted Hours That You're Going To Be Able To Reclaim As You Automate The Biggest Marketing Chores So You Can Focus On More Profitable Promotions. How Much Is THAT Kind Of Time Worth To You?**
45	**Just So You Know, I'm Not Talking About Promoting Porn To Make This Kind Of Money. I'm Talking About Promoting Legitimate Information, And How To Create The Type Of Site That People Will Flock To-And Pay You Money-For Allowing Them Access To Information That They Want.**
46	**These Experts Are Honor Bound To Hand Over Their Top Strategies But Only Upon Request**
47	**At The End Of The Day It's About Being True To Yourself**
48	**Your Wasting Your Time If You Think You Can Find Something Better**
49	**How To COMPLETELY AVOID The Google Slap All Together Outlining Exact Step-By-Step Processes For Creating Ad Campaigns To Generate You A Virtually Endless, Boat Load Of Traffic To YOUR Websites.**
50	**How Much Should You Pay For A Good Pair Of Marketing Binoculars**
51	**Why You're A Lot More Likely To Be Successful Using This System Than Any Other**
52	**Learn The Truth About Trials And Lead Generation. Not Sure How To Go About Getting Leads, But Still Be Making Sales At The Same Time Without Interrupting Your Sales Process? Not Sure What To Charge For Your Trial, Or How You Can Even Adapt A Trial To Your Business In The First Place? We'll Talk Through These Points Here.**
53	**Instantly Increase Your Sales & Leads By 200% With The Professional Photo In Your Sales page Or Lead Capture Page Without Scratching Head To Figure Out How To Get More Sales Right Now!**

54	You Don't Just Wake Up To Wealth You Have To Earn It
55	Waking Up From This Wonderful Dream Wasn't A Dream After All
56	4 Insider Secrets To A Killer "Pre-Sell" Page. This Is The Technique For Raking In The Bucks...And For Blowing Your Competition Out Of The Water. I'll Also Reveal The Easiest Way To Write A Compelling Headline For Your Pre-Sell Page.
57	How Would You Like To Get Paid For Free Your Ad Is Seen
58	The Point Is, This Can Get You All That And More... The Life You Want Is Waiting For You Right Now. All You Need To Do To Get Started Is Hit That Button, And Then I Can Help You Build The Life You Deserve...
59	You Don't Have To Chase Me Down Or Jump Through Hoops
60	It's Amazing How This Paradox Has Such Broad Appeal And Excites So Much Interest
61	I Want To Help You Get "Unstuck", And Move Into A New Career Path That Will Make Your More Money And Brings You More Enjoyment Than You Have Ever Imagined Possible. I Promise You, It Is Now Within Your Grasp.
62	Once Again This Is Available For The Low Low Price Of FREE
63	Are You Like Me? You Have Your Squeeze Page Or Mini-Site All Setup. You're Getting Traffic And People Are Signing Up But You Agonize Over What To Sell And What To Write About On Your Blog And In Your Newsletter. The Blank Screen Stares At You Expecting A Response, But Your Eyes Glaze Over And Your Brain Begins Thinking Of What Is On TV.
64	If You're Into Affiliate Marketing You'll Find This Profitable Bonus Easy To Promote
65	Once I Added This Crucial Aspect To My Business Building Mindset, It Opened Up An Entirely New World Of Ideas...And A Whole Different Level Of Success.
66	Most Of The Programs Out There Are Worthless, And Most Of The " GURUS' Are Selling Their Programs And Software To You, So That They Can Make Their Millions Without A Care In The World.
67	Have You Ever Played That "My Company Is Better Than Your Company" Game With Another Network Marketer? You Know – Those Conversations Where You Talk All About Your Company's Wonderful Products, Amazing Training And Stunning Compensation Package Only To Then Sit And Listen To The Other Person Go On And On About Theirs?

68	If I Could Help You With That Would You Be Interested In Hearing More About That
69	If You Could Ask Me Just One Question What Would It Be
70	Is It Worth Five Bucks To You To Save Hundreds Or Even Thousands Of Dollars And Months Or Even Years Of Your Life... Avoiding The Crooks And Scammers As You Try To Make Money On The Internet?
71	Free Yourself From All The BS, Dead End Jobs, And Finally Experience The Freedom Of Automatic Internet Income. It Doesn't Take An Einstein-Like IQ, It Doesn't Take Money, It Doesn't Take "Connections, Just This Proven Approach.
72	This Is Not One Of Those Stupid Get Work At Home Get Rich Quick SCAMS You've Seen On Internet. It's Very Serious Business!
73	We Are Going To Provide You With EVERYTHING You Need To Get Started, The Products, The Website Graphics, The Sales Letters, You Name It......
74	Focused Passion Is The Real Secret For Success On Or Off-line
75	If You're Ready To Finally Make Some Fat Cash Online, Then Buckle Up For A Wild Announcement That We GUARANTEE Will Change Your Life. The One Risk Free Opportunity Even A Skeptical Newcomer Like You Has To Say YES To!
76	Automated Built-In Links Page Where Other Websites Can Exchange Links With You
77	An Easy-To-Insert Top Element Most Sales Pages Lack Re-sulting In Lost Sales. You're Probably Losing Sales Right Now If You Don't Have It
78	How Much Traffic Are We Going To Get And How Much Is It Going To Cost
79	Do You Know That You Can Build A Full-Time Income Simply By Promoting Your Web Site.
80	Isn't Time You Stopped Fooling Around And Got Serious About Your Life And Your Business? Chances Like This - To Step Into The Company Of Millionaires And Have Reveal Their Personal Secrets That Made Them Rich...
81	How Do You Use Your Strength To Get To The Goal Right Now
82	Now You Might Be Saying, "That Sounds Great, But I Have No Idea Where To Find 300 Members For My Membership Site.... I Don't Even Know Where To Find The First 50!"
83	I Really Need Your Help Marketing My Proprietary Products & Services

84	Get Your Big Story In Front Of A Lot Of People
85	Why So Many Marketing Ads Turn Out To Be Unprofitably Useless
86	No Matter How Perfect Your Product You Still Won't Sell Steak To A Vegetarian
87	If The Average Affiliate Wants To Expand His Source Of Traffic, He Has To Invest More Time And Effort In Not Only Educating Himself, He Has To Also Do Everything On His Own That He Will Be On The Verge Of Burning Out
88	Wow, I Definitely Need To Clear Something Up Really Quick... There Seems To Be A Lot Of Confusion! Our Office Has Been Getting A Lot Of Questions About Our New (Product) Coaching Program And Asking How It Can Benefit Someone That's Just Starting A New Online Business Or Isn't Making A Lot Of Money Yet.
89	Listen, We All Know That Starting Out Can Be Tough. The "Information Overload" And "Paralysis By Analysis" Plague Claims Many Victims. Plus, It's Scary Going From Working For Someone Else To Being An Entrepreneur. All The Risk Is On You. You Get Afraid Of Doing The Wrong Things Or Making Bad Decisions, So Many Times You Do Nothing.
90	Christmas - What Other Time Of The Year Do You Sit In Front Of A Dead Tree And Eat Candy Out Of Your Socks?
91	Before I Go Any Further... I Want You To Be Completely Certain That I Am Talking From Experience (Not Theory Or Hypothesis) And That I Have Discovered The Key To Real World Success With Email Marketing.
92	That's Your Money Out There, All You Have To Do Is Build A List And Take It.
93	I'd Like To Give You A New Perspective On Creating And Selling Ideas
94	Grab This Private Label Right Collection Of The Industry Changing, Market Revolutionizing Products And Save Thousands Of Dollars In Product Creation, Niche Research & Graphics Design...And Rake In Sale After Sale In Just Minutes.
95	It's All In The Title So Choose Your Title Wisely. You Need To Make Sure Your Title Uses The Keywords You Have Chosen And Is Specific Enough To Be Noticed By Search Engines.
96	A Cool Tool That Can Do Most Anything For Your Business

97	Until A Couple Of Nights Ago I Was Still Searching For The Answer
98	You Said You Wanted To Be Wealthy Well Here's Your Chance
99	What If All Their Hidden Agendas Purposely Kept You From Ever Seeing This
100	Monopolize A Perpetual Niche With Consistent Quality Sales Even In A Down Economy
101	The Lazy Man's Way To Increase Conversions By At Least 75%
102	However, I Understand That It's Difficult Even For The Most Deserving To Part With This Amount Of Money, And While It's Nothing To Me Anymore, I Still Can Remember When It Was A Huge Sum.
103	If There's A Place People Look At Place Your Ads There
104	So I've Decided To Make It Accessible For All Those Who Are Ready And Willing To Make A Smart Decision To Invest Right Now At Only $197.
105	Life Is Too Short To Live That Way. Is $67 Worth Escaping To A Better Life With More Exciting Options Than Your Mind Could Have Ever Imagined Possible?
106	The Little-Known Resource That Lets You Spy On The Market To See What's Selling For What And Who's Buying From Whom...
107	How Many Times Have You Paid Out More Money Than You Had Coming In Trying To Build A Business And An Income For Yourself?
108	Once You Accomplish This Your Life Will Change. You'll Literally Be Able To Write Yourself A Paycheck Whenever You Want. I Do It Every Day. Nothing Beats The Feeling Of Getting Up In The Morning In Your Pajamas, With A Coffee In Hand, To See Your Inbox Overflowing With Orders. It's Simply Amazing.
109	Well, Congratulations. You've Got What It Takes To Make Money Online. And Yeah, I Know It's Tough To Take That In Right Now - You Think I'm Either Kidding Around Or Just Outright Lying Don't You?
110	Supercharge Your Online Business In 15 Minutes With The Biggest...Baddest...Most Complete...Social Network System Built Specifically For YOUR Success!

111	The Internet/Network Marketing Industry Is Moving At Lightning Speed Towards Full Dependence On Blogging, Social Networking, Video Sharing And Search Engine Optimization As The PRIMARY Source Of Traffic To Their Programs. This Can Only Be Effectively Accomplished If You Have Your OWN Website And The Tools And Knowledge Necessary To Utilize These New Techniques To Drive Traffic To Your Sites) 24/7/365!
112	It's Important To Find The Right Niche To Work In. Despite What You May Think, You Don't Want To Look For A Market That Has Absolutely No Competition Unless You Want To Bang Your Head Against A Wall.
113	P.S. There's No Other Viral Marketing Mechanism Online This Powerful. And You'll Certainly Not Find Another Program That Will Allow You To Generate Viral E-books At This Speed.
114	Take Action Right Now Or You Won't Do It At All
115	Now You Can Copy This Exact Million Dollar Blueprint To Give Yourself An Unfair Advantage Over The Competition And Cash In Every Month
116	A New Cutting-Edge Prospecting System Helping Everybody Succeed...The Professional And The Inexperienced Marketer Find New Sign Ups For Their Main Business Or For This New Company
117	But, I'm Still Not Even Charging Half That Much. Yes, $250 Would Be An Unbelievable Bargain To Automatically Build Your Lists And Finally Have Control Over Your Financial Future.
118	How Retired Teachers Created Three #1 Google Websites In Less Than 10 Days
119	Without Online Marketing Skills You're A Lamb Ready To Be Slaughtered
120	You're Frustrated Aren't You? You're Just Sick And Tired Of Struggling To Make Money. You've Waded Through All The Garbage Online - The Lies, The Half Truths... All The Misinformation. Not To Mention All The Scam Programs And Other Baloney That's Out There. And All That Has Brought You Right Here, To This Point...
121	All For Just A Few Minutes Of Your Time...Be One Of The Fortunate Few Who Get In On This Invite-Only Joint Venture That Will Let You Accomplish Everything Mentioned So Far, All By Simply Signing Up Below . . .
122	Suck Out The Cash At The Click Of Your Easy Button

123	Niche Wars Heat Up Internet Global Warming On A Scale Never Before Imagined
124	Get This Wrong And Doors Will Be Slammed In Your Face
125	No Matter How Rich Or How Poor People Are Everyone Wants More Money
126	Remember, Only The First 1,000 People Who Order Will Be Accepted Into "The Language Of Millionaire" Membership This Means You'll Also Be Eligible To Receive All The Extra Bonuses, Training And Fast-Action Incentives. And If You've Read This Far, We Know You See The Immense Value Of This Collection And Are Seriously Considering Joining Immediately.
127	Small Changes That Make A Huge Difference In Using This Invaluable Hot Resource
128	What Could You Do If The Largest Mountain Of Cash Was Within Your Grasp
129	So, It Is Possible To Drastically Change Your Lifestyle FAST, By Tapping Into This Incredible System?
130	Never Again Do You Have To Worry About How To Get Enough Traffic To Your Websites, Because It's All Taken Care Of With This System.
131	Make Your Investment Pay Off, Like It Has For Others. The Profits You Make From Using "YOUR PRODUCT" Could Add Up To Thousands, Tens Of Thousands Or Even Hundreds Of Thousands Of Dollars "
132	Think About It, Why Do People Stop Working On A Program? It's Because They Are Not Getting Anywhere. You Don't Stop Doing What Works, Do You? Of Course Not. Neither Will The People That You Refer. This Is Such A "No Brainer" That Anyone Can Do It And Everyone Who Does Do It Will See Success.
133	Have You Asked Yourself How More Money And Free Time Would Improve Your Life Lately
134	Real Life Changing Events That Average Everyday People Are Now Experiencing
135	Maybe You've Been Previously Scammed, Lied To, And Led In The Completely Wrong Direction. Your Tired Of Cutting Through Fluff And Racking Up Debt For What Sometimes Feels Like A Total Pipedream.
136	If You're Still Not Convinced How Easy This System Is To Operate, Consider This. How Hard Do You Think The Person That Invited You To This Website Is Working Right Now?

137	We've Been Recommending These Guys For Their PLR Content For Ages Now Because They Simply Deliver Great Products And Finger-On-The-Pulse Market Knowledge, And They've Set The Same High Standards
138	How To Generate Traffic To Your Site With Techniques That Actually Work
139	Would You Like To Discover The Safest Way To Automate 95 Percent Of Your Online Business
140	The Art Of Writing An Effective Press Release That Will Gain Results
141	My Coaching Program Will Show You How To Make Money Online In Less Than A WEEK. I WILL PROVE TO YOU By Using My Simple Techniques And 'In-House' SOFTWARE.
142	Discover The Confidence Of Smiling All The Way To The Bank
143	OK, Here's What I'm Doing With My Sales Letter. I'm Going To Tell You Exactly What You're Getting, Exactly What It Can Do For You And Exactly What It Costs.
144	So You Don't Need To Worry About Not Knowing Where To Start. Or What To Do Next. It's All Laid Out For You.
145	I'm Not Charging That Much For The System But The Stuff Worth Your Time Is Pure List Building Gold! You Know What They Say, A Gold Mine Is A Shame To Waste. No Gold Mine Left Behind.
146	Will You Have The Guts To Watch Your Clickbank Account Get Swollen With Cash, As You Sit Back Listening To Others Whine About Click Prices...And Other Problems That You Won't Encounter.
147	The Time Is Now For You To Become One Of The Elite 5%...And You'll Do That Quickly And Easily With Adsense-newbievideos.Com.
148	Isn't It Time To Start Harvesting The Hidden Profit Vault Inside Of You
149	Here's The #1 Way To Increase Conversions By At Least 75% - And I'll Prove It To You
150	Doesn't It Make You Furious That These People Are NO Better, NO Smarter And NO Different Than You? They Do Know A Few Secrets Most Will Never Know That You Are About To Find Out.
151	Just A Click Of The Mouse And You'll Be Ready To Build Your List
152	What Would An Endless River Of Super Hot Leads Mean For Your Online Business

153	You Don't Have To Find People To Give The Guide To. There Is An Endless Supply Of People Online Everyday Looking For Money Making Opportunities. These People Are Using The Traffic Exchanges Trying To Drum Up Business For Their Offer And Checking Out Other Offers At The Same Time.
154	Do You Have Any Idea How Much Money Is Spent Running An Internet Business? There Are Monthly Fees For Autoresponders, Hosting, Management, Advertising, Scripts, And More. There Are Regular Fees For Licensing, Outsourcing, Support, Customer Service, Maintenance, Development, Recruiting And More.
155	Are You Ready To Grab The Brass Ring Of Your New Online Business
156	You Don't Have To Start Out As An Expert To Make Serious Money Online
157	Make More Money In The Blink Of An Eye Anytime You Want
158	Bait N Switch Techniques That Only Destroy Internet Success And Happiness
159	If Any Of That Sounds Difficult Or Confusing, Just Think Back To Your First Day On Any Job, When The Terms Were All New To You.
160	As You Can See, I've Held Nothing Back. Everything You Could Ever Need To... Quickly Build Your List On Autopilot... Jump Into The Deep End Of The Internet Marketing Money Pool With Both Feet.
161	Giving Them A Bit Of Information For Free Up Front Can Help Ease Their Fears. They Will Get A Better Understanding Of The Information You Are Offering And Whether Or Not They Want To Buy It.
162	If You Can't Figure It Out Find Someone And Ask Someone
163	That I Would Have The Big "Ah Ha" Moment That Would Catapult Me From Eating Ramen Noodles To Living In The Lap Of Luxury.
164	Because Most People Have Not Learned The Skills Of Great "Salesmanship." And Being Able To Sell Successfully Is Certainly A Skill. Let Me Clarify. Any Truly Good Sales Person Knows A Transaction Proceeds From Lead To Sale Along A Predefined Route Built Up Of Many Parts – Building Blocks If You Like. And A Good Sales Person Knows The Value Of A Script.

165	The Single Most Important Element Of Any High Value Website - And Why Most Site Owners Are Clueless About It...
166	Limit Ordering To A 2 To 3 Step Process At Most
167	It's Amazing How The Real People Who Run Successful Launches Remain In The Shadows
168	Unless You're Living In La La Land You'd Be Foolish To Pass Up This Incredible Arsenal
169	I Can Get It Done And I Will Find A Way
170	Finally, Just Paste Your Name Onto Our Brand New Series Of High Quality, Professional Videos And You're All Ready To Boost Your Monthly Income, Create Instant 'Sticky Value' For Your Membership Sites,
171	You Can Go As Deep With This Stuff As You Want
172	I'll Send You Home With Either A Ring Worth $4100 Or $1000 Cash Still In Your Pocket
173	WARNING If You Thought Your Affiliate Links Were Safe Think Again
174	For As Long As You Keep This Window Open. Once You Close This Window, I'm Not Offering This Again. Like I Said... I Can't Keep This Offer Up Because It Would Be Unfair To All My Customers.
175	After You Hear This There Will Be Very Little Left To The Imagination Except Lots Of Money
176	The Newest Secret Weapon Is About To Strike An Internet Blaze
177	The 7 Best Ways To Market Your Affiliate Program
178	7 Steps To Increase Your Newsletter Advertising Revenue
179	How To Get More People To Download Your Ebooks
180	Based Upon What You Just Told Me The Next Step Is _____
181	Every Person On The Planet Has To Be Educated In The Skills Of What They're Doing. Whether You're A Doctor, Carpenter, Plumber, Ditch Digger ... Whatever You Are ... You've Got To Be Taught The Skills Of That Business.
182	Lets Take One Of The Most Ridiculously Obscure Micro-Niches You Could Ever Think Of, The Society For Creative Anachronism! In Case You're Wondering Just What That Is...
183	When You Have Traffic Sources That Can Deliver You A Lot Of Targeted Traffic Fast, You Have The Ability To Test Your Offers, Tweak Your Conversions, And Literally Turn A Profit FAST.

184	Not Recommended But You'll Have To Rob A Bank To Get Richer Any Faster Than This
185	A Great Shortcut That Sidesteps The Hard Work Time And Effort
186	I Took Parts Of The Last Few Days Off To Recharge And Basically Pull My Head From In Front Of The Computer For A Bit. I Figured I Haven't Taken A Break In A Long Time So A Few Hours Off Wouldn't Hurt. Guess What Happened?
187	How To Expand Your Marketing Budget Without Using More Of Your Own Money
188	Sure-Fire Ways To Get People To Link To Your Web Site
189	When You're Building Lists Of Subscribers On Autopilot, Money Happens Fast. And Once The Bills Are Caught Up The Debt Is Gone, And You've Taken A Much Needed Vacation Or Two...
190	How To Take Even A Bad Product And Make Crazy Profits With It... Your Promotional Skills Will Be So Good You Can Even Earn From Products That Suck.
191	Even Smart People Don't Even Know How To Succeed On Or Offline
192	Now, If You're Still Here Perhaps You Have Enough Of An Open Mind To Look At Something That Will Finally Make You The Kind Of Money You've Been Dreaming Of Once And For All.
193	Don't Save The Link For Last- The Link Is Your Clincher- It's What Makes Your Prospect Actually Click On Your Website. It Is The Traffic Generator. So, Link Placement Is Vital. Read The Rules Of The Article Directory To Determine The Number Of Links Allowed And Then, If Allowed, Place The Link Throughout The Article, Not Just At The End.
194	Easily Change The Prices And Edit Product Descriptions To Your Own Taste
195	You Are About To Learn The Secrets That Most Internet Marketers Will Never Know About Finding Niche Markets, Low Cost Keywords, And Making Money Online...Finding Niche Markets In Seconds, Without The Hassle And Guesswork Of Normal Niche Marketing Programs.
196	What If I Said I Was Actually Robbing Banks Now (No Not That Way)
197	Is It Worth Five Bucks To Learn In ONE DAY What The Average Person Will Spend YEARS And THOUSANDS OF DOLLARS To Uncover?

198	I Never Set Out To Write Books And Develop Systems For Internet Marketers. I'm Perfectly Happy Raking In Piles Of Affiliate Cash From My Lists And Calling It A Day At Noon
199	I Want To Level With You Right Here, Right Now.....I'm Really Super Lazy! No, Seriously! I Don't Like Putting Out More Effort Than I Absolutely Have To! I've Been Just "Getting By" For Most Of My Life And In All Honesty, It Hasn't Got Me Anywhere Until Recently.
200	First Off I Just Want To Say A Huge Thanks To The Response To Our Free Webinar Training That We Presented Last Thursday Night. When I Seen The Lines Totally Packed I Knew That We Were On To Something Huge And Very Much Needed When It Comes To Training.
201	Do You Hear The Thunder Or Did You Just Pass Gas
202	You Can Keep Doing What You're Doing. Struggling To Make A Few Online Sales. Or Working Full-Time At A Thankless, Futureless Soul Sucking Job.
203	Little Did We Know That This Journey Would Bring Us An Amazing Opportunity With So Much Potential To Dominate The Electronic World Of Social Networking.
204	If You Want Your Life To Change You Must Take Action Today
205	You See, What I'm Trying To Show You Is That Earning 4-5 Figures A Month Is A Realistic Target By Selling A Bunch Of Little Products Online... That Is Once You Discover The 'Backdoor Secret' I'm About To Reveal To You...The Difference Between Me And The Other Gurus Is That I Have Been Flying Under The Radar Making My Money Implementing Strategies... Rather Than Making Money Teaching Strategies...
206	Will You Be Able To Take These Techniques And Mop The Floor With Your Competition With Out Guilt.
207	The Timing Will Never Be Better For Positioning Yourself For This Pre-Launch
208	Keep On Trying But Don't Just Keep Making The Same Mistakes
209	Building Flaws That Can Cost You $10000 In Resale Value If You Buy From The Wrong Builder
210	Because He's Trying To Make A Name For Himself In This Industry He Is Offering Up Something So Over The Top Insane And Ridiculous That It's Really Starting To Build A Huge Buzz Online As Thousands Of People Are Swarming To His Site To Check It Out.

211	Why On Earth Would You Want An Online Business If You Don't Know Where To Even Start
212	Host A "Town Hall" Meeting Or Teleseminar And Use Your Contents To Facilitate The Discussion.
213	This Is A User Generated Content Site That Allows People To Use Affiliate Links Too, And This Site Does Belong To An Affiliate. Like All The Sites Mentioned Above Its Free To Use And Anyone Could Setup A Page Like This With No Technical Experience.
214	Super Affiliates Know Exactly How To Turn A Single Sale Into A Customer For Life
215	Think Of A Roadmap Like Planning Your Trip, But In This Case, Your Trip Is To Get Traffic And Ultimately...Make Sales. This Trip Will Never End And It's More Like Your Pathway To Well... A Successful Business.
216	What If You Found A Way To Break Away From The Rest Of The Pack
217	When Does It Happen What Does It Cost And How Do I Register
218	Tired Of All The Programs That Make You Work And Work And Pay And Pay Without Seeing One Single Dime? - I Am Actually Going To Show You How To "Earn While You Learn" So You Can Turn A Profit Without Becoming An "Expert." My Philosophy Is To Start Doing Something And Perfect It Later So You Can See Results Right Away.
219	Here's All You Have To Do To Instantly Unlock This Time Sensitive Free Report
220	Start Your Own Pack Of Highly Trained Blood Thirsty Marketing Wolves
221	I've Kept The Price Low Because I'm Hoping That Once You've Read This Ebook, You'll Want To Help Me To Get This Vital Information Out To Everyone Who Is Trying To Make Money On The Internet...
222	This Program Can Absolutely 1,000% Help You If You're Just Getting Started. In Fact, It Might Have The Biggest Initial Impact On Someone That's New To All Of This Online Business Stuff. Here's Why...
223	Simple Duplicatable System For Your Members To Follow, Which Will Naturally Eliminate Your Prospecting Anxiety, Training Worries, And Most Importantly Eliminate Attrition In Your Business

224	Upload Your Own Banners To Your Affiliate Programs And Other Websites
225	For Everybody Who's Desperate To Make Money, And Anyone Else Who's Tired Of Being Ripped Off And Sucked In To Lame Schemes That Just Don't Work. And The Crazy Thing Is, It's Probably Easier Than Whatever Work You Do Right Now, And It Can Get You Fast Results And Profits From Day One!
226	How To Pick The Right Web Host For Your Site And How To Save Hundreds Of Dollars While Doing It
227	Reciprocal Link Exchanging Can Expose Your Website To Internet Users On A Worldwide Basis As Link Exchanging Is One Of The Best Methods Of Getting Exposure To Your Site On A Limited Or Zero Budgets.
228	At This Point You Have A Major Choice To Make. You Can Choose To Continue Getting The Results That You Have Been.
229	The ONLY Question That Must Be Answered Correctly If You Ever Hope To Have TRUE Financial Wealth!
230	In An Internet World Full Of Complex Systems Everything Should Be This Simple
231	The Best I Can Do Is Deal With One Word At A Time
232	Learn How To Write Compelling Ads, How To Reach Your Target Market And Attract Hot Prospects Who WILL Sign Up...
233	Add Recent Stats, Figures, Charts, Or Graphs To Your Content To Boost Authority.
234	Laziness Is The Achilles Heel So It's Time To Get Up And Run With The Winners
235	Insiders Really Don't Want You To Know About Placement Targeting, And Raping The Content Network While Everyone Else Is Busy Waging Bidding Wars For The Best And Expensive Keywords On The Search Network.
236	After You Get Through The Products Listed Here, You'll See How You're Going To Get The Inside Scoop On Exactly How And Where I Go To Keep Delivering Fresh Content Every Month And How I Keep My Members Coming Back For More. You'll Be Shocked At How Easy And Profitable It Is To Provide Fresh Content When You Know Where To Look.
237	Watch Me Live As I Use These Powerful Techniques To Dominate My Niche
238	This Ebook Has Been A Consistent Performer For Many Many Months

239	Ever Wake Up In The Middle Of The Night With A Million Dollar Idea
240	Learn The Same Tactics I Use To Create A Small Fortune Online
241	If It Isn't Already This May Soon Be Your Greatest Fear
242	Knowledge Is The Ability To Help And Attract Others
243	You Clearly Understand How Working Less Really Can Make You Much Much More
244	Limited Time Offer To Position Yourself At The Head Of The Opportunity
245	If You Are Working For Someone Else, Negotiate A Commission Or Bonus Structure That Allows You To Be Paid Based On The Value You Bring To The Company. Don't Just Settle For Getting Paid Your Flat Rate Salary. There's No Future In That, No Real Upside.
246	Why Settle For One List Building Tool When You Could Empower Hundreds
247	Are You Ready To Play A Different Game With A Different Set Of Rules
248	Not Only Do You Get To Use It But You'll Have The Right To Sell It
249	Email Metrics Are Nice But You'll Need Much More Than That To Succeed Online
250	Would You Like To Know What Is The Best Time Of Day To Post An Item For Sale
251	You'll Be Stunned How Easy And Powerful This Marketing Method Really Is
252	I Made Myself A Promise Never To Be Vulnerable Again Transforming Debt Into Wealth
253	After Watching The October Tutorial, All I Can Say Is That If That Is The Standard Of Video To Expect Each Month, Then The Sky Is The Limit." It's Not Too Late. You Too Can Get Your Membership Today.
254	Long Gone Are The Days Where Having The Same Keywords, Ad Copy, And Review Pages Are Going To Work Like Gangbusters.
255	The 4 Grim Facts Of Life About Lawsuits Emptying Your Bank Accounts

256	Download Your Package Now. Don't Stay Stuck In The Rat Maze. Grab Yours Now At This Discounted Price And Start Setting Yourself Free And All For About The Cost Of A Night Out.
257	How To Compete With Other Resellers In The Same Market Or Niche You're In.
258	Opportunity Is Not Just Knocking On Your Door...He's Getting Ready To Ram It Down. Will You Answer?
259	Now YouTube Is Awesome. I Love It. Convenient, Free And Easy For You To Get My Video Content. But I Just Got A Message Today From A Well Informed Friend Letting Me Know YT Is Starting To Shut Down 'Make Money Online' Videos. So My Plan...
260	A Step-By-Step Blueprint That Shows You Exactly How To Have Your Own BEST-SELLING HOT Information Product Without Starting From Scratch...So You Can Boost Your Profits ASAP.
261	Give Your Affiliates Five Simple Tools That Create A Feeding Frenzy
262	I Am Going To Bribe You So Hard That You Will Feel Like Peeing Your Pants From The Mental Orgasm And The Spasms In Your Brain's Neurons I'll Spark Inside You.
263	Learn Exactly How To Find And Evaluate Affiliate Programs And Offers So You Can Immediately Spot Which Ones Will Make You The Most Money Fast
264	Generate A Fortune Online More Quickly And Easily Than Ever Before. You'll Be Able To Create A Sizable Income Within Sixty Days!
265	You Have The Option To Earn The Money First For Free, Or Make A Small Out-Of-Pocket Investment To Join And Use Your Profits To Grow At Your Own Pace.
266	How Much Money Will You Need To Earn Each And Every Month FOR THE REST OF YOUR LIFE To Support Your Lifestyle? Be Realistic. Things Always Cost More Than You Think They Will.
267	BREAKTHROUGH! Ridiculously Easy To Use, Yet Incredibly Powerful Software Increases Your Profits By Up to 300% By Converting Your Digital Infoproducts Into Physical Products Almost Effortlessly!

268	Let Me Tell You The Real Story About How I Went From Riches To Rags
269	Just Remember To Pay Your Yearly Renewal Fees For Your Domains Because In Our Busy World It Would Be Devastating To Foolishly Ignore Keeping Close Tabs On Your Investment.
270	Most People's "Greatest Products" Never See The Light Of Day Because They Make The Mistake Of Coming Up With A Product Based On What They "Thought" The Market Wanted, Not What The Market Actually Wanted. In Other Words, They First Develop The Product And Then Try To Find A Market For It.
271	You're Already Doing It So Why Not Build A Real Online Business Around Your Passions
272	Streamlined Method Of Tuning This Campaign Technique Into A Huge Success
273	Have You Wasted Thousands Of Hours And Lots Of Money Trying It On Your Own
274	Human Social Elements Are Far More Powerful Drivers When Asking Someone To Take Action Than Self Interest Or What's In It For Me. The Human Reasoning Behind This Seem To Reflect How People Prioritize Reward. Basically, When Offered The Choice, Social Interaction Offers Immediate Pleasure Instead Of Waiting For A Delayed Pay Off.
275	What Have You Tried To Improve Your Business That Worked And Didn't Work
276	No More Filling Your Tank At $4-A-Gallon Just To Sit In Traffic To Get Somewhere You Can't Stand To Be.
277	Why You Don't Want To Squeeze All The Juice Out Of Your Website
278	Honesty Works And You Don't Have To Lie Or Cheat People To Make Money
279	Invest The Time Now To Renew Your Commitment To Overcoming Past Failures, Including The Fears, Uncertainty And Doubt Placed There By The Conventional Wisdom Of Unqualified, Negative People.
280	Knowing How To Warm Up Your Prospects To A Fever Pitch Can Be Predictable And Shocking
281	Your Life Will Improve Drastically Once You Discover How This Works
282	Build Instant Success Using This Turn key System Without The Technical Hassles

283	Find A Market That Will Trip Over Themselves To Give You Money
284	But To Be Honest, I Really Don't Care Whether You Believe Me Or Not (Sorry If That Sounds A Bit Harsh). Because I'll Still Carry On Making Money, In Fact A Lot Of Money... But What Will You Be Doing In A Month, Six Months, Or A Year From Now?
285	Simply Picking Up The Greatest Product Isn't Going To Work It You Leave It Lying There
286	7 Secrets To How To Increase Conversions By At Least 75% And Grab Yours Today
287	Put All Your Monthly Income On Autopilot And Experience True Financial Freedom
288	For Months I Jumped From Product To Product Trying To Figure It All Out. Hoping Desperately That I Would Soon Find The One Piece Of The Puzzle I Was Missing Out On.
289	Numbered Lists And Bullet Lists Are An Immediate Eye-Catching Device. As Mentioned Above, Most People Will Simply Scan The Article For Useful Information. This Usually Comes In The Form Of Bulleted And Numbered Lists. They Can Attract Viewers And Also Make Your Content Easier To Read And Therefore More Interesting.
290	Ever Consider Doing Just The Opposite Of What The Competition Is Doing
291	In Our Global Economy, Business Is Being Conducted 24 Hours A Day. It Would Be Impossible For You To Personally Follow Up 24 Hours A Day.
292	Would You Be Interested In Having A Conversation About Continuing To Work Together
293	You Really Can't Convince Anyone Of Anything Unless They Really Want It
294	Now You Can Create Amazing Professional Style Banners For Your Own Product, Blogs, Websites, Headlines, And Even Affiliate Promotions In Just Minutes Directly Fro Your PC With Just A Few Clicks Even If Your Don't Have Any Photoshop Skills!
295	Without This You Only Have Less Than 1 Chance In A 1,000,000 To Succeed
296	Set Up A Marketing And Distribution Machine Where Your Efforts Are Multiplied And Duplicated Where You Can Make $10,000 Per Hour, Or Even A Whole Lot More.

297	Amazing 8 Year Old Humiliates The So Called Internet Gurus At Their Own Game
298	If You Are Lucky Enough To Be One Of The 200 To Get Your Copy Of This Training Program, We Want To Give You The Opportunity To Get Paid To Learn The Secrets To Building A Membership Site Empire!...
299	Do Not Invest In Any Training Program If You Think It Will Automatically Make You Money
300	I Don't Know About You But I'd Rather Be Richer With This Than Without It
301	Why Affiliate Marketers End Up Doing More Work Than The Owners Of A Product
302	It's True: You Really Can Increase Conversions By At Least 75% And Here's How
303	How to Create an Offer So Irresistible They'll Eat Rusty Nails and Crawl Over Piles of Broken Glass to Get It
304	How To Attract Search Engine Spiders To Fall In Love With Your Web Site
305	This Is A Promotional Offer That Will End Soon. Once The Number That Have Set Aside For This Promotion Is Reached The Price Will Increase. We Can Only Promise That If You're Seeing This Page Right Now, It May Be Your Last Chance To Lock In This Sneak Preview Price For Only $37.00.
306	I Can't Image How You Could Fail To Increase Sales By Making This Available To Others
307	Your Success Is Dictated Entirely By You – And The Choices That You Make. Not Your Upline, Your Company Or Your Product. Your Own Success Is Ensured With My Easy To Follow Step By Step Videos Tutorials That Leave Out Absolutely Nothing.
308	But Again That's Why I Definitely Have To Limit Copies, Or Raise The Very Insanely Low Price At Least Double After A Certain Amount Are Released.
309	Viral Marketing Is A Brilliant Concept That Allows You To Build A Down-Line Very Quickly With The Help Of Others.
310	Acquiring New Customers Online Is Only The Beginning Of This Amazing Opportunity

311	No Money? Having Something To Invest Can Help Speed Things Along. But Having Money And Investing It In The Wrong Things Can Be Worse Than Spending Nothing. Too Many People Get Caught Up In Buying Every Ebook They See And Then Not Doing Anything Because They're Suffering From Information Overload.
312	If You Want To Live An Amazing Life You Got To Do New Stuff
313	You Can Get Your Hands On The Training That Takes You
314	They Are Doing Some Unbelievable Things To Help Insure Our Success
315	The Almost Scientific Way To Pick A Market Niche That Will Shower You With Cash On Demand. I'll Show You Exactly How To Dig Into One Of The Most Convenient, Free Tools You'll Ever Find, And Pick Out A Market Niche Full Of Rabid Buyers. I'll Walk You Through It Step By Step So You Can't Possibly Miss A Single Thing.
316	Learn How Ezine Articles And Press Releases Give You Targeted Traffic That Converts
317	The 3 Keys To Cutting Through The Hype And Pick Winning Traffic Exchanges (Most Traffic Exchanges Are Complete And Utter Waste Of Time And If You Pick The Wrong Exchanges You Are Dead In The Water.)
318	Shell To DOS Come In DOS Do You Copy Shell To DOS
319	Your Getting The Essential Guides To Making Money Online And Even If You Have No Plan Or Desire To Resell These Products They Are Still Valuable Tools You Can Use And Follow.
320	Access A Powerhouse Of Useful Information To Help Grow Your Business Quickly
321	With The 30 Day Guarantee You Have Nothing To Lose. Hope You See The Value In This Offer And Will Give This Product A Try. To Place Your Order Click On The Link Below.
322	The Feedback Coming In Was So Great I Knew The Response Would Be A Huge Hit
323	Amazing Tips & Tricks For Driving Server Crushing Loads Of Traffic To Your Lead Capture Pages. These Are The Very Same Techniques I Used To Build My Targeted Hyper-Responsive Lists.
324	You May Never Have Heard Of This Guy, But We Bet You Most Certainly Are Aware Of His Creations! He Was In Charge Of Designing And Building The Largest Building And MARKETING Project Ever Attempted By Man.

29

325	You Can Carry On Along The Same Path You're On Right Now... And Your Life Will Stay As It Is. You'll Always Struggle To Pay The Everyday Bills... Loans, Utilities, Whatever... You'll Always Wish You Had Just A Little More Money... You'll Always Dream Of Having A Profitable Online Business... But You'll Never Get Any Closer To Those Things Than You Have In The Past. Or...
326	It Is Possible To Earn A Six-Figure Income Working From Home, For Fewer Hours Than You Currently Work At Your Regular Job. You Don't Need To Be A Computer Tech To Do This Stuff — Just A Basic Understanding Of Using Email And Navigating The Web, Which You're Already Doing By Reading This Blog, So You're All Set There.
327	Experience The Magnetic Power Of Marketing Secretly Below The Money Radar
328	Creates A Clean And Professional Look Reducing New Visitor Bounce Rate Through A Visually Pleasing Presentation. The Longer Your Customer Reads Your Review And The More Chances You Have To Get A Click On Your Affiliate Link.
329	Don't Get Stuck In The Same Trap That So Many Other Marketers Are Stuck In... "Having A Site That Doesn't Convert." Use This 15 Step Guide To Judge Each Site You Build And Make Sure You Are On The Right Path To Turning A Profit.
330	Are You Pulling Your Hair Out Waiting For Your Website To Start Making A Profit
331	But If You Want To Change Your Life And Start Experiencing Massive Success By Watching A Few Videos, Listening To Some Training And Following The Directions, Then This Is Exactly What You've Been Looking For.
332	Only 14 Hours Left To Grab Some Of The Most Valuable Brand New Products Ever Offered
333	Why The Average American Dream Is In Debt 2 1/2 Times It's Annual Income
334	I Can't Promise Your Success. No One Can. But I Can Show You What Worked For Me, And Share The Specific Techniques That Allowed Me To Go From Dead-Broke And Waiting Tables To 7-Figures In Less Than 18 Months.
335	This Is A Friendly Reminder That Your eCard Is Waiting For Pickup
336	Start Building One Way Links To Your Site And Watch Your Page Rank Soar

337	What Scares People More Than Creating A Product Is Building A Website! What In The World Is Html? How Much Does The Software Cost? How Do I Upload Files? Why Isn't It Formatted Correctly? Why Don't My Graphics Look Like The Ones The Pros Have?
338	This Sucks And I Refuse To Make This Same Mistake Ever Again
339	Get Your Brain Storming - Experience The Liberating And Revealing Practice Of Brainstorming By Setting Aside A Specific Amount Of Time Before Starting Any Project To Do It. Even Short, 15 Minute Brainstorming Sessions Can Produce Some Eye-Opening Results.
340	What Every Marketer Needs To Know Before Just Pumping More Money Into Your Business
341	Fortunately We're Living In The Digital Age That Still Appreciates Reading A Great Book
342	Inspire Yourself By Using Inspirational Wallpapers As Your Computer Background.
343	Just The RAW TRUTH On What REALLY Does & Does Not Work In This Industry And WHY, From Someone With Nearly 30 Years Of In-The-Trenches Experience!
344	Six Closely Guarded Secrets Of The Diamond Industry... Revealed At Last
345	It Only Makes Sense When You Understand The Ease Designed Into It
346	If You're Looking For Gimmicks Or Sneaky Marketing Tactics You Won't Find Them Here
347	Gosh, If You Haven't Heard About It, You're Really Missing Out. I Knew It Was Going To Be Big, But It's Really A Phenomenon. Look, Most People Think It's Is Some Kind Of Voodoo Or Crazy Hard To Do. Nope, None Of That's True.
348	You'll Get Personal Video Coaching, So That No Roadblock Will Ever Stand In Your Way, And Every Question You Have Is Answered To Your Complete Satisfaction.
349	Your Autoresponder Can Manage All Of Your Prospects, Remember When It Sent Your Last Sales Letter, What That Letter Was About, And It Can Do All Of This 24 Hours A Day, 7 Days A Week!
350	Times Are Getting Tougher And You've Got To Make Every Marketing Dollar Count

351	You'd Better Try This Out For Yourself And See How Quickly You Get Results. You'll Be Amazed At How Easy It Is To Implement Into Your Business.
352	You Never Risk Anything Because You Pay Nothing To Use The System, The Strategy, Or The Tools And Materials. Your Only Investment Is Made AFTER You Are In A Position To Profit.
353	You Can't Become Something You Hate In Order To Be Successful. This Model Works For The 8% Who Are Real Salespeople. It's A Disaster For The Rest Of Us ... A Very Bad Business Model.
354	7 Years Later And Still The Best Way To Make Money Online
355	In Addition To A Website Exactly Like This, You'll Also Receive Your Own Password-Protected Back Office Where You Can Track Your Sales In Real Time!
356	I Can't Think Of Anyone Who Couldn't Have A Successful Launch With A Little Help
357	Double Your Money Back If You Don't Increase Conversions By At Least 75% With Our Amazing System
358	I'll Be Honest With You. What I'm Offering You Is Affordable For Most. It's Valued In Excess Of $197, But You Won't Need To Pay That Today. If You Take Advantage Of This Special Offer, You Will Only Need To Pay $20 For This Entire System.
359	Website Under Review. You See This Page, Because The System Administrator Is Currently Checking This Website For Malicious Content. This Redirect Will Be Removed Once We Will Finish Manually Checking All Files On This Account.
360	Creating An Auto Income System Can Make All Your Dreams Come True
361	This Is Your Private & Personal Invitation To Join One Of The World's Most Rewarding Financial Associations. Now You Can Collect Your Share From Over $4,000,000 In A Matter Of Days.
362	I'm Going To Give You One Of My Best Selling Programs For Free
363	Find Out EXACTLY What Your Customers Want To Buy From You Next...Without Guessing Or Leaving It To Chance.
364	Building A Network Marketing Business Over The Internet Just Got A Whole Lot Easier
365	Delivers Sales Driven Results Because The System Has Proven Itself Reliable
366	Baby Steps Is A Great Way To Gain Confidence In Building Your First Online Business

367	What I Have To Say Will Be Music To Your Ears
368	For Travelers Who Want To Make Money While Enjoying Every Vacation
369	Before I Share This Information Let Me First Explain The Basic Concept
370	A Lot Of What He Says Is Very Good. But One Point Of His I Take Issue With Is His Advice That We Should Think Of Each Hour Of Our Time As Worth A Certain Amount Of Money.
371	How To Avoid Those Nasty Market Niches Where People Don't Want To Spend Money
372	The One Thing Most Internet Marketers Don't Do And Why It Costs Them A Ton Of Money
373	Approach Your Audience With A Non Conventional Lesson They'll Absolutely Love
374	All You Need To Do Is Pin Up The Target You Intend To Reach
375	If You Had The Chance Wouldn't You Like To Work From The Comfort Of Your Own Home? You Could Spend More Time With Your Family, Which Is Really What Life Should Be All About.
376	I Know How To Generate 6 And 7 Figures With These Types Of Sites...And I Know How You Can Easily Avoid All The Pitfalls That Usually Stop People In Their Tracks Before They Ever Get Out Of The Starting Gates.
377	This Is Definitely The Next Best Thing To Winning The Lottery
378	If You're Struggling Trying To Make Money Through Affiliate Marketing...Struggle No More! I've Dissected Affiliate Marketing And Built It Up Piece By Piece From The Ground Up With My Own Experience! I Know What Works And What Doesn't And I'm Gonna Tell You Exactly That.
379	How A New Kind Of Clay Improved My Complexion In 30 Minutes
380	I'm About To Reveal How You Can Make Up To Hundreds Or Even Thousands Of Extra Dollars A Week Taking Pictures And Submitting Them Onto The Internet In Your Spare Time!
381	This Will Definitely Benefit You For The Rest Of Your Internet Life
382	Every Keystroke Click And Action Is Being Stored And Tracked Right This Minute

383	It's The Software That Will Have You Building Complete Sites, Quickly & Easily. Sure You Can Continue Doing Things The Way You've Always Done Them, And Continue Getting The Dismal Results You've Experienced, Or You Can Do What The Experts Do.
384	Why Your Time Is Better Spent Submitting Articles Rather Than Just Reading Them
385	FIVE Ways To Write Copy And Avoid Being Clever And Critical
386	How Would You Like A List Building System That Will Explode Your Sales, Signups And Build Your List At The Same Time Without You Spending A Single Cent?
387	You Can't Help But Learn Something That Will Change Your Life For The Better
388	Virtual Real Estate Is The Equivalent Of Southern California Ocean Front Property? Because Of The Recurring Income Model, These Sites Are Valued At The Top For Online Properties And Are Bringing Top Dollar Every Single Day.
389	How To Work With Clickbank, The Largest Online Affiliate Network. I Made Over $305,682 With Clickbank Last Year And This Video Shows You How.
390	God Loves You Because Of Who God Is, Not Because Of Anything You Did Or Didn't Do
391	Why Marketers Think They're Winning While Losing Half Of Their Profits
392	Think About It. When You Have A Problem, You Want A Solution Right? You Don't Want To Wait. You Want A Quick Fix And You Want It Now. You'd Want It And Guess What So Do Your Prospects!
393	It Takes So Little Time For A Child Who's Afraid Of The Dark To Become A Teenager Who Wants To Stay Out All Night
394	We're Talking About Making Money Over And Over Again For The Rest Of Your Life
395	Accumulate Wealth And Financial Independence Using The Power Of Exponential Growth
396	Imagine Getting Paid Handsomely For Simply Publishing Your Own Thoughts And Ideas
397	And At The Risk Of So Totally Over-Delivering That My Husband Won't Speak To Me For 2 Weeks, If You Act Now, I'm Also Going To Include These

398	It Stands To Reason If You Target These Overlooked, Under-The-Radar Keyword Phrases You Will Stand A Much Better Chance Of Both Diverting The Traffic To Your Offer AND Converting That Traffic Into Profits!
399	Link Away- It Is Okay To Link To Other Sites. Link To Your Heart's Content- Links Do Not Have To Just Be Certain Words. You Can Also Make Title Links And Anything Else You Want Links. People Are Automatically Drawn To Links, So Switch It Up And Make Your Content Stand Out.
400	I Have An Excuse Because I Work Hard All Day, And Have To Fight The Endless Traffic Jams Just To Get Home And Then Cook Or Serve The Meals, Wash The Dishes Drive The Kids Here And There, Etc.
401	You Can Always Refine You Goals Once You Write Them Out
402	Internet Marketers Are Always Looking For Fresh New Ways To Increase Their Sales And Expand Their Business. With Time At A Premium And Money Available For Advertising Getting Slimmer By The Day More And More People Are Turning To Double Opt-In Submitters To Market To The Masses. Email Empire Was Designed With The Premise That You Do Not Need To Spend A Fortune To Get The Word Out On Your Offers And Opportunities.
403	Note: "On Topic" Links Hold More Value Than "Off Topic" Links. For Instance, A Link To Your Dog Training Site From Another Pet Care Site Is Going To Be More Relevant Than A Link From An Automotive Parts Website.
404	All You Have To Do Is Just Pay The One-Time Fee And You Get
405	So Do You Want To Depend On Someone Else's Newsletter Being Read And Hope That You're Picked Out Among The 12 Other 3-Line, Black-On-White Text Ads To Make A Sale?
406	This Business Will Produce An Awesome Income For Anyone Who Puts A Little Effort Into Promoting It. Not Overnight Though. This Is Not A 'Get Rich Quick' Scheme. It Does Produce A Steady, Growing Income. How Quickly It Grows Depends On How Much Time And Effort You Put Into It. One Hour A Day Produces Good Results. If You Have More Time, Your Business Will Grow Faster.
407	What If I Taught You Some Very Important Basic Tactics I Use To Grow My Own Business
408	Why Is It That Most People Don't Skydive Off Of Mountain Tops

409	I Also Realized That The Best Way For Me To Help You Isn't To Only Teach You Every Single Way To Succeed As An Online Marketer Like I've Done. I Realized That For You To Achieve True, Lasting Success In Life (Both Financial And Otherwise) You Must Understand The Exact Success Principle That Will Get You There In No Time Flat.
410	If Words Have Little Effect In Marketing Consider Including This Well-Known Word In Your Next Header: SUPERCALI-FRAGILISTICEXPIALIDOCIOUS And See What Happens.
411	Thinking Of Adding Pay-Per-Click Ads On Your Site? Make Sure It's The One Source Buyers Look For On A Site (Probably Not The One You're Thinking Of)...
412	Unknowingly If You Actually Spend Time On Searching High Targeted Keywords With Huge Demands
413	Why Selling High Ticket Items May Be A Total Waste Of Your Time
414	Specialize In Niche Content For Moms, Students, Teachers, Or Baby Boomers.
415	The Nuts And Bolts Of Why The House Always Wins And Why 96% Of Americans Are In Debt
416	Now, Building A Product Is Easy. You Can Hire Someone To Write You An Ebook Or Software. Even Easier... You Can Just Become An Affiliate For Someone Else's Product.
417	You Will Now Have The Ability To Add Or Delete Your Own Programs To Display To Your Downline, And Even Create And Display Your Personal Bio To Them... This Is Personal Branding At It's Best.
418	Make This The Subject Line Of Your New Reality $1000 Commission Earned
419	Here's To The Chosen Few Who Are Really Ready To Stop Working For Peanuts
420	Someone Who Can Stop You From Making Those Deadly Wrong Turns
421	I Stuck It In The Closet And Pretty Much Forgot About It - I Thought I Wasn't Destined To Write And Publish A Book.
422	This Question Made Hundreds And Thousands Of Entrepreneurs Go Through Several Sleepless Nights. I Remember When I Made My First Affiliate Site. I Thought I Had Just Hit A Gold Mine.
423	In Relation To Your Business Success, What Corrective Actions Have You Put Into Effect?

424	Think You Have To Swindle Website Owners To Get Them To Hear Your Offer? WRONG! I'll Give You The Exact Script That Gets Their Greed Gland Working Overtime That Puts You In The Driver's Seat.
425	You Know When You Have A Great Product When You Your-self Want To Buy It
426	You Really Need To Sneak Your Way Into Your Customers' Head And Speak To Their Needs, Their Wants, Their Prob-lems, Their Frustrations, Their Fears & Their Desires.
427	We Help Our Clients Capture More Visitors And Make More Money Now Using A Private Million Dollar System. Do You Know Anyone Who Can Benefit With Such A System?
428	If You Think You Can Go It Alone You're Either A Genius Or A Fool
429	Disclaimer: Clickbank Reserves The Right To Change Their Policies And Procedures At Any Time Without Notice.
430	I Am Counting On You Not To Follow Any Links In This Email, However, You Will Find Something Only Offered To My Sub-scribers If You Do.
431	I Mean It When I Say We're Missing An Integral Part Of The Team
432	Want To Know How Being #4 #5 Or Even #10 Puts You In A Great Online Position And Doesn't Even Cost You Any Money
433	Isn't It About Time You Started Letting The Good Times Roll
434	So How Much Is This Worth To You? I Wanted To Make This Affordable For Everyone, So The Price I Came Up With Is...Not $67 Not $47 Not $27 Only $21 For The First 30 People! I Also Have A Money Back Guarantee, Just In Case That Price Is Not Low Enough…
435	Discover How To Keep 100% Of Every Penny Earned
436	Do NOT Promote Your Referral Link Directly In Your Ads. Send People FIRST To Your OWN Website And GIVE Them Valuable Information That They Need So They Can Make A Fortune On The Internet Just Like You.
437	Tracking And Analysis Seem Like 4 Letter Words To Many Marketers, Because They Just Aren't Into 'Metrics'.
438	The Main Reason I Charge $1 Is That It Focuses On Those Who Really Value My Services
439	I Know What You Might Be Thinking By Now!! Why Would I Help You Get Your First Few Sales - Its Plain And Simple - I Get Paid When You Get Paid.

440	Now It's Even Easier To Reduce And Even Eliminate Refund Requests
441	Japanese Scientists Have Created A Camera With Such A Fast Shutter Speed They Now Can Photograph A Woman With Her Mouth Shut
442	Why Say NO When YES Can Get You Everything You Dreamed About
443	The Best Investment You'll Ever Make To Reduce And Even Eliminate Refund Requests
444	Seeking Success The Hard Way Is What Happens When You Don't Know What To Do
445	When Starting A New Online Business Focus On Just That First Sale
446	Sharpen Your Focus - Using Action Machine Pro Regularly Helps You Get Into The Habit Of Eliminating Productivity-Killing Distractions So You Focus Your Concentration And Energy To The Task-At-Hand.
447	Now That We've Worked Out All The Bugs We're Ready To Launch This Baby
448	Start Saving Time And Money While Increasing Your Income With This Powerful And Easy To Use Tool. You Can Be Set-ting Up Your Rotating Links In Less Than 3 Minutes!
449	Why You Don't Have To Be Elegant To Be An Effective Eye Stopper
450	Isn't It About Time You Take Total Control Of Your Earning Potential
451	Why You Need To Optimize Title Tags For Each Web Page
452	They Were Not Able To Fail. I Wouldn't Let Them. And I Won't Let You.
453	More Of The RIGHT Backlinks To Give You MASSIVE Jumps In Search Engine Rankings AND Increased Traffic At The SAME Time! STOP Gambling On Expensive Backlink-Sellers Who May DOOM Your Sites To The Sandbox! Use Our Simple Step-By-Step Plan to Finally Compete With the Big Boys For FREE.
454	I Often Receive Emails From People Just Like You Who Are Struggling To Make A Living Online. You've Bought Existing Systems And Courses But You Just Can't Seem To Make It Work.
455	How Your Next Launch Could Set Off A Chain Of Events That Shocks The Internet World

38

456	I Want You To Hear A Message From My Personal Mentors. These 2 Gentlemen Have Truly Shown Me The Art And Science Of Adding Dozens Of New Distributors Into Business Every Single Week.
457	Make A Killing In The 65 Billion Dollar Affiliate Marketing Industry
458	The Book Is A Quick And Easy Read, That's Straight To The Point With Real-Life Case Study Examples Showing Our Exact Plans That Have Worked 100% Of The Time.
459	Yes, Having Now Put This Proven Plan Into Action, And Witnessed It's Tremendous Success. I Wholeheartedly Recommend It To All. It Is Easy And Straight Forward To Use.
460	The Fast Start Guide To Quick Affiliate Cash You'll Be Able To Use In The Very First Hour You Get Your Hands On This Limited Series.
461	In Marketing, It Pays To Know About These Teeny Little Bits Of Information, And Sometimes It's These Bits Of Information That'll Allow You To Flank And Outperform Your Competition.
462	Some Of What We Learn Is Forward While Others Are Backwards
463	You Can E-Mail Random Members With Your Offers. Depending On Your Membership Level You Can E-Mail Other Active Members Using Our System If You Have Enough Advertising Credits.
464	The Ability To Live A Life Where Opportunities Fall At Your Feet, Relationships Are Easy And Beautiful And Success Just Comes Easy... And Really, That's What We All Want Isn't It?
465	Don't Get Hold Of An Email Address And Let It Go Cold. Work Your List By Providing Useful, Relevant Information And Tips And Then When You Do Have Something To Sell You're More Likely To Get A Positive Response.
466	The Easy And Incredibly Simple Way To Choose A Profitable Topic Or "Niche" For Your First Affiliate Promoting Website (In Order To Increase Your Profit Potential, You Must Make Your Site Is Targeted At A Certain Topic...The More Targeted It Is The More Profitable It Will Be!)
467	To Do It Any Faster You Really Would Have To Turn To Crime. (This Is A Lot Easier, And There's 100% Less Risk!)
468	What If This Incredible Site Could Help Thousands Of People Earn Thousand By The Weekend

469	You Can Get A Free Copy Of The Book Here, As Well As Get Access To Some Other Awesome Bonuses That Come Along With The Book.
470	How Would You Like To Start Saving Yourself Stress, Time, Energy, And Money All At The Same Time From The Use Of A Simple, Duplicatable System?
471	Ask A Bunch Of People For Their Opinion And They Will Respond
472	Are Your Ready To Leave The Herd And Become A Leader
473	Do You Consider Yourself Lucky To Still Have Your Job. But The Boss Is Working You Far More Hours And Your Pay Is Never Going To Go Up. Just Today New "Productivity" Figures Were Released, Showing Workers All Over The World Are Working 3 Times Harder, 3 Times Longer, And Still Getting Paid The Same Just-Get-By Salary.
474	You Won't Believe How Much You Can Make With Just One Hour Of Effort
475	How Any Website Can Have Non Stop Pleasure While Making A Lot Of Money
476	20 Up And Coming Profit Sectors You'll Want To Keep For Yourself
477	You Will Learn Exactly How To Build Your Own Profitable Sites And You Will Then Have A Quality Product To Sell Online.
478	You Beta Watch Out You Beta Not Cry Cause We're Testing This Offer Before Many Will Buy
479	If You Like What You See Here Wait Till You See The Real Money In Your Bank Account
480	Start An Online Business That Becomes Self Funding Without A Lot Of Money
481	At The Time I Didn't Understand There Was So Much Money To Be Made With Websites And NOT So Much Working For Some Stiff Company That Squeezed Out My Just-Above-Water Salary Every 2 Weeks – I Knew This Was No Way To Live...Though My Bosses Would Have Me Believe Differently.

482	If You're Promoting Crap Products, No Magic Can Help You. And If You Haven't Yet Noticed, It Is The 21st Century Out There, Then This Is Not For You Either. Stick With The Good Ol' 872 Pages Of Hard Selling Copy And You'll Be All Set For Failure. And Finally If There's No Way You Could Pay A Bit Of Money For An Ad That Would Help You Pull Off The Next $100,000 Product Launch, Then Please Hit The 'Back' Button Immediately!
483	We're Putting Out The Fires Of Disappointment Once And For All
484	Want To Know The Easiest And Quickest Way To Create Your Own Financial Dynasty
485	The Information Contained In This Guide Just May Be The Most Important Information That You'll Read. After All, If Your Affiliates Aren't Happy, You Won't Be Able To Motivate Them To Promote Your Products No Matter How Hard You Try.
486	How To Grab Their Attention For More Than A Couple Of Seconds
487	It Ain't Rocket Science All You Really Need To Know How To Do Is Copy And Paste Because There Are Tons Of Videos Showing You How To Do Every Step. I Am Not Kidding When I Say, Even Homer Simpson Can Make Money With Affiliate Marketing.
488	Ready To Accept Online Credit Card Orders With Popular Payment Methods
489	How Many People Want To Learn How To Make More Money
490	Of Course, You Can't Just Jump On The Bandwagon And Try To Make Money On Instinct. It Just Won't Work. You Need Guidance From Somebody Who Has Been There And Succeeded.
491	In The Blink Of An Eye And A Click Of Your Mouse You'll Access The Ultimate Answer
492	Ways To Increase Your Traffic And Sales By Giving Away Software
493	How Would You Like The License To Clone My Entire System
494	But I'm Going To Foolishly Attempt Teaching A Concept That Usually Requires Hours And Hours To Get A Visitor To Grasp, In A Few Paragraphs. I Should Probably Have My Head Examined, But Here Goes…
495	Create A Million Dollar Business You Can Sell Or Pass Down To Your Children

496	I'm Not Sure Any Secrets Exist Once Exposed Except For Those Very Few People Use
497	It's Rumored That The Husband And Wife Couple Who Operate The Sites May Either LIMIT How Many People Are Allowed In, Or At The Very Least "Choke" Down The Flow Of New Members So As Not To Let Just Anybody Get In.
498	Why All You Need Is A Dirt-Simple Website. You Do NOT Need Anything Fancy. Attractive, Yes. Fancy, No. I'll Tell You The Quick And Easy Way To Set Up Your Site, And Clearly Explain Some Of The "Technical Lingo" Behind It In Simple Layman Language.
499	I'd Be Up Until 2 Or 3 In The Morning - There Were Days When I Didn't Even Sleep, I Just Stayed Up All Night Searching Online, And Went Straight To Work. That's How Desperate I Was... You See By Then I'd Racked Up A Monster Credit Card Bill Buying Up Just About Everything I Could Find About Making Money Online...
500	How To Cram Eight Hours Of Classroom Computer Training Into One Easy 75-Minute Session...At Your Home Or Office
501	If You Really Love What You Do This Will Make You Rich
502	See How Good It Feels To Be Widely Respected And Viewed As The Expert Within Your Niche. Develop Relationships With A Loyal Following That Will Secure Not Only Your Expert Positioning Within The Niche, But Your Financial Future As Well, If You Play Your Cards Right.
503	We'd Rather Gain Your Trust First By Allowing You A Sneak Peak Into Our Open Vaults
504	Even Better, You'll Be Collecting Steady Cashflow From Those Lists. Not To Mention The Gurus Who'll Be Offering You Even Fatter Commissions To Promote Products You're List Will Love.
505	Because I Don't Make Outrageous Claims I May Lose A Few Orders.
506	Discover The Street Smart Secrets I Use Online To Make $27,000 A Month And More Working Less Than 30 Minutes A Week And You Don't Even Need A Web Site. You Don't Even Need A Product Of Your Own And Most Internet Marketers Don't Have A Clue As To How To Do This.
507	Send Out A Printed Newsletter To Your Clients Using Your Contents.

508	Have You Ever Wondered What Your Customers Are Thinking Of When They End On Your Website. Think About It, If You Knew Exactly What They Were Thinking About Or Looking For, You'd Be Able To Provide Them What They Really Want.
509	You're Out Of A Job Right Now. You've Been Looking Your Butt Off, But There Are NO Jobs Out There. Every Time You Find What Looks Like A Job It's Either A Thinly Disguised Scam, A Part-Time Deal, Or They're Looking For Someone Who Is Already A Star In The Industry.
510	How To Get An Unfair Advantage Over Your Competition To Put You Ahead Of The Pack
511	How To Create A Search-Engine Friendly Post On Your Blog. I Will Take You Through The Different Things You Need To Do To Make Your Blog And Posts "Optimized" For The Search Engines, Meaning You Will Rank High In The Search Results For Topics Or Keywords Related To Your Niche. This Is Really Important Stuff To Get Maximum Exposure In Your Market!
512	You'll Be Happy Footin' All The Way To Your Bulging Bank Account
513	If You've Noticed, I'm Sending Fewer Emails That Only Featuring Truly Valuable Content These Days. I've Decided Its Important To Show You The Tools And Resources I Actually Use In Order To Help You Build Your Business. Here's One Of My Favorites…
514	Have Faith In Yourself And Don't Let ANYONE Tell You Otherwise
515	Select A Task, Start A Timer (Like An Egg Time), And Focus On Nothing But Accomplishing That Task. This Means You Don't Answer The Phone, You Don't Get Up For A Drink, You Don't Log Onto Facebook - None Of That. You Remain Focused On The Task-At-Hand!
516	The System Will Work For You… If You Let It. The Question Is – Do You Prefer To Reinvent The Wheel Yourself? Or Do You Enjoy Sitting Back And Letting Others Save You The Time, Money And Hassle Of Doing It Yourself?
517	If You Want Something You Have To Go After it Now Not Just When It's Convenient
518	How To Spot The Hidden-Value Websites And The Simple Methods That Turn Them Into Cold Hard Cash In Your Pocket....

519	I Am Sure You Are Starting To See How All This Will Add Up Quickly. If You Do Your Daily 'Work' You Will Soon Have A Huge Organization Of People Under You, Working For You, Making You The BIG Paychecks That You Desire.
520	We'd Like For You To Understand That Building A List Can Be Very Time Consuming And Boring..
521	You're Really Never Ready That's Why They Call It A Leap Of Faith
522	I'm Known By Millions Of People Around The World And Have Sold So Many Products That I've Lost Count. I've Written Ebooks That Have Been Downloaded Hundreds Of Thousands Of Times, Developed Courses That Have Helped Thousands Of People Make A Living Online, And Mentored Hundreds To Reach Their Wildest Dreams.
523	This Site Was Created To Reach Other Entrepreneurs Out There With A Burning Desire To Live A Lifestyle Of Privilege And Comfort. Do You Fit The Profile?
524	You're Going To Need To Be Fast To Catch This One
525	Why Millions Of People In The United States Are Living Near Or At Poverty
526	Key Factors To Avoid So That Your Product Isn't Going To Be Dead On Arrival
527	4 Shockingly Easy Ways To Get Scads Of Drooling Buyers To Whatever You're Selling. Best Of All, Three Of Them Are Completely Free. And They're So Easy To Do, You Might Think I'm Kidding...But Your Competitors Can Only Wish That Were True.
528	Today It's Your Turn For Me To Bribe You Into Becoming A Lifetime Fan
529	The Two Most Valuable Skills Are How To Write A Great Sales Letter And How To Automate All Your Selling And Marketing. Mastering These Two Skills Are The Keys To Building Wealth And Growing Your Business.
530	Build Any Business With This System Watch Your Mailing List Grow By The Minute
531	We Will Be Limiting Distribution To This Incredible Package To Only 500 Affiliates

532	The True Concept Of A Sales Letter That Kills. There A Lot Of Rumors And Myths About Writing Sales Copies And I Clear The Fog Of Doubt Once And For All By Slicing Through The Nonsense And Give You All Of What You Need To Know And Understand About Writing Your Very Own Powerful Sales Copy.
533	Own A Gold MasterCard? A Premier Visa? Not After You Read This, You Won't
534	What If You Could Find A Way To Give Yourself More Time? What If Small Adjustments To Your Daily Routine, And Small Changes In Your Habits, Could Free Your Schedule, And Allow You To Focus On What's Most Important?
535	You Don't Need To Manage, Pay Or Deal With Employees. You Don't Need Any Special Education, Skill Or Experience To Profit Wildly From - Your Online Business!
536	We Do Not Pretend To Offer It At A Low Cost Or For Free And Then Make You Pay A Monthly Fee To Upgrade, It Is A One Time Only Payment.
537	So Much So, You Could Realistically Build A Livable Income For Yourself And Your Family And Say Goodbye To Your Job Forever!
538	There Are Dozens Of Factors You May Have Overlooked That Greatly Limit Your Success Online
539	Do You Want To Know The SECRET Of The TOP PRODUCERS? The One Little Secret That You Can Apply And Master
540	This Is What Web Marketers Dream About Traffic And Sales With Virtually No Effort
541	There's One Thing I Didn't Mention Yet That You Really Need To Know To Avoid Failure
542	Everyone May Know That Time Equals The Money Trap Few Know How To Break Free
543	You'll Get A FREE Step-By-Step Marketing Plan And Strategy, Marketing Sources, And FREE Pre-Written Ad Copy And Messages That You're Free To Use Or Give Away.
544	They Completely Ignore The Fact That The Only People On Your List Who Are Worth Anything To You Financially Are The People Who Actually BUY What You're Selling.

545	I Don't Have To Remind You That Times Are Tough Right Now. Good People Losing Their Jobs, Businesses Shutting Their Doors. You Know The Story. And There's Only One Thing That Can Turn This Grim Situation Around... You! That's Right, You. Because When You Help Others Change Their Lives, Your Life Changes Too... At Break Neck Speed!
546	Don't Stand At The Threshold Of A Brand New Life And Fail To Exercise A Leap Of Faith
547	You'll Be Like A Fly On The Wall In My Top Secret Hideaway
548	You Don't Need To Be In Business For Yourself To Start Thinking This Way. You Can Start Thinking This Way Even As An Employee Of A Company. Start Thinking, Not "What Is My Time Worth?" Start Thinking, "What Is My Contribution Worth To The Company?" "How Much Value, How Much Profit Am I Bringing In?"
549	Finding This Answer Was A Discovery That Would Forever Change The Way I Would Approach Online Business, And One That Has Transformed My Life To A New And Wildly Prosperous Direction.
550	It Is A Fact That People Are On The Go These Days. Many Of Them Want To Learn While "Waiting". Many Others Like To Set Their iPod's Up Beside The Computer And Follow Along. This Keeps From Having To Open, Close And Move Windows Around.
551	Why You Must Divorce Yourself From Your Personal Connection To The Project For It To Be Successful
552	It Simply Requires A Smarter, Fresher Approach. Fortunately There's A New Tool That Addresses All These Problems With Traditional Article Marketing, And Knocks Your Article Marketing Efforts Right Out Of The Ball Park.
553	7 Tips For Skyrocketing The Effectiveness Of Your Email Marketing Efforts
554	If You Can't Follow Up With Potential Sales Leads, You're Losing $1,000's In Future Profits... You MUST Collect The First Name, Last Name, And E-Mail Address Of Every Person Who Reads Your Ad. Second, It's CRITICAL That When You Capture This Contact Information, You Get Permission To Send These Sales Leads E-Mail In The Future Using An Opt-In Offer.

46

555	One Of Those "Multi-Level" Schemes. You Know The Stuff Where You Have To Persuade All Your Family And Friends To Join Up Underneath You? It Sucked.
556	Don't Be Mislead By A Social Web 2.0 Because Article Traffic Remains Key To Free Traffic
557	This Product Is Instantly Downloadable After Purchase And Is Delivered In PDF Format Which Is Viewable With Adobe Reader On Most Popular Operating Systems Including Windows, Mac And Linux.
558	You Do Not Need Any Technical Knowledge At All, As Long As You Can Copy And Paste Into Your Web Page.
559	See One Of The Greatest Launches Ever Created With Absolutely No Money
560	Things Changed...Competition's Fierce And Making A Profit As An Affiliate Marketer With Google Adwords Was Literally Impossible. It Actually Came To A Point Where The Only One Making Money From Google Adwords Was Google Itself!
561	If You Seriously Want To Know How To Generate Thousands Of Dollars In Hard Cash In Record Time, Starting From Scratch And With No Previous Experience... This Is Definitely For You!
562	The ONLY Thing Required Of You, Is To Give Away The Business System By Following The Instructions In Our Simple Step-By-Step Marketing Plan.
563	Problem I'm So Great I'm So Smart I Don't Need To Do Marketing
564	If You Just Take Action, And Use Even A Fraction Of What We Teach You In This Program, There Is No Doubt In My Mind That You'll Start To Experience The Same, Amazing Results That We Have Been So Blessed Over The Years To Experience.
565	Explode Your Profits With Our Easy Ad Placement Tool – Allowing You To Profit From Multiple Advertising Revenue Streams Including Google Adsense, Affiliate Products And Your Own Products... The Ads Are Targeted Automatically Based On Member Profiles... And It Requires No Technical Skill On Your Part To Make All This Happen.
566	How A Simple Press Release Turns Into One Of The Surest Ways To Influence Sales

567	Success Is An Extremely Complex System Of Both New And Age-Old Teachings, Practices And Wisdom That Has Been Passed Through The Centuries In Dozens Of Different Forms. In Fact, It's So Complex That Only 1% Of The World's Population Truly Understand What It Is And How To Apply It To Their Own Lives. Most People Who Are Introduced To It Are Immediately Overwhelmed By The Complexity Of It And Quit Before They Every Get Started!
568	The Information Marketing Business Is The Fastest, Easiest, Most Lucrative And Most Cost-Efficient Business There Is. But Just Jumping In Is Not Enough! There's A Better, Faster And Easier Way -- And Several Times More Profitable, Too!
569	You Will Learn How To Sell E-Products (Electronically Downloadable Products) To Hungry Niche Markets. No Multi Level Marketing, No Pyramid Schemes, No Forex Trading Etc.
570	Use Your Content As A Topic Of Conversation For Coaching Calls.
571	Chances Are You're Involved In A Great Organization Yourself Now, Whether You're Making Money In That Company May Be Another Issue. You See, I'm Not Here To Sell You My Primary Opportunity - I'M HERE TO HELP YOU DOMINATE YOURS!!!
572	That Way You'll Never Have To Take Money Out Of Your Pocket. From There You Can Finance The Rest Of The Business Building Process Out Of A Small Portion Of Your Profits!
573	Apart Than Wishing You A Wonderful And Prosperous New Year, I Also Want To Thank You For Being My Subscriber And Customer. Thank You. Happy New Year!
574	Writing A Great Sales Letter Just Became A Whole Lot Easier
575	Start Profiting From A Largely Untapped Mega Trend Poised To Generate Millions
576	For Newbies Who Want To Clearly Identify Great Digital Internet Business Opportunities
577	Rewrite To Create Squidoo Lenses.
578	Closely Guarded Secrets Have Been Stolen And Now Revealed For Everyone To Read
579	Everyone, And I Mean Everyone That Makes A Full Time Income Will Tell You That Traffic Is One Of The Most Important Aspects, If Not THE Most Important Aspect, Of Online Marketing.
580	But Then I Saw The Light And Got Myself A Coach
581	They're Going To Go Inside Of Their Head To Understand It

582	It's A Special Offer That Won't Last Much Longer Because If The Community Becomes Too Large We Won't Be Able To Provide Adequate Support. The Doors Will Close Soon.
583	New Federal Law Requires That All Nail Clippers, Screwdrivers, Fly Swatters And Rolled-Up Newspapers Must Be Registered By January 2030
584	Why The Hard Way Is The Right Way To Riches Online
585	They Thought I Was Crazy When I Told Them My Plans
586	7 Powerful Tips For Building A Highly Successful Affiliate Marketing Group
587	Think About This...Any That Showed Supposed Real Members Holding Fans Of $100 Bills, Claiming That This Was What They Made In 24 Hours Or A Few Days - Or Whatever...
588	Tweet With Twitter- Tweet Tweet, You Have Mail. Twitter Is A New Social Media Revolution That Combines Text Messages With The Internet. It May Seem A Little Confronting, But It's A Great Way To Advertise Your Website. Get A Following And Send Them A Tweet.
589	Open The Floodgates To Thousands Of Targeted Visitors Waiting With Cash In Hand
590	Discover How To Take Your Company Into The Midst Of Incredible Success
591	This Guide Tells Exactly What I Do, All The Mistakes I've Made, And How You Can Get Started With Your Own "Very Small Business." I Didn't Hold Anything Back, And Some Of The Information Is Fairly Personal.
592	Step By Step Blueprint To Turn Millions Of Cash Paying Visitors Into Buyers
593	You Need To Be Here To See And Believe It For Yourself
594	What Has Changed In The Blink Of Your Eye Is Everything
595	It's Rare To Find Someone Who Can Properly Teach The Basics
596	Imagine If You Can Position Yourself As The 'Go-To' Person With All The Tools And Information That People Want. And Having The Rights To The Most Lucrative Products That You Can Sell In The Hottest Niches.
597	Take Some Time And Go Through The Basics Of SEO On The Main Search Engines. Understanding The Do's And Don'ts Of SEO Is Critical When It Comes To Generating Traffic. After All, You SEO Strategy Can Either Make, Or Break Your Website.

598	How Would You Like A Solution With Every Element Needed To Get Started Online
599	Your IP Address, Billing Information And Connection Information Will Be Recorded, Traced And Checked For Fraud. All Fraudulent Transactions Will Be Investigated And Prosecuted In Accordance With Applicable Law.
600	Learn From Master Marketers Who Can Turn Nearly Any Product Into A Serious Money Maker
601	Success Can Be Yours Don't Miss Out And Fail Over And Over
602	Different Types Of Offers You Can Promote And How Much They Pay Out
603	In A Couple Of Weeks We're Going To Change The Rules And Make History -- Seriously! So, Let's Make History (And Money) Together. Here's The Scoop...
604	You Are Just Moments Away From Downloading A Truly Amazing Free Guide That Can Help You Find A Quicker And Easier Path To All The Real Solutions You'll Need To Help Your Business Expand And Grow.
605	Add Just This One Live Code To Your Thank You Page
606	Something Needs To Be Done About This. So We Are Firing Back Up The Webinar Service And The Passion To Profit Power Point Training And We Are Going To Dig Back In. We Have Updated The Training With Fresh New Content And Methods Of Finding Your Niche. It Is Time To Help Get This Settled Once And For All.
607	Then, If They Can Ever Make It Through The Technical Setup Of Their Site, They Have To Go Out And Shell Out Another Pile Of Money To Hire A Graphic Designer To Create The Look And Feel Of Their Site.
608	No Hype No Fancy Words Just Down To Earth Laymen Terms
609	Sorry For The Short Notice, But This Is Kinda Urgent. There's This New Site Offering Super High Quality Websites With Master Resell Rights All For A Crazy Low Price.
610	You Have Incredible Potential Hidden Within You At This Very Moment. Now There's A Proven Method – Based On Studying And Modeling The Most Successful Leaders And Teachers In The World - That Can Allow Dramatic Improvement In Your Quality Of Life.

611	Unlike Other Money Back Offers, I Won't Even Ask You To Prove You Followed My Plan. Anyone Who Asks You For Proof Is Really Just Trying To Figure Out A Way To NOT Give You Your Refund. I'm That Confident What I Have For You Is Better Than Anything Else You've Ever Purchased!
612	If I Don't Get The Results I Need Then I Must Change My Behavior
613	It Takes Less Than A Minute To Read This Entire Page. This One Minute Will Be The Most Precious Minute Of Your Life!
614	Everything You Need To Know To Create And Sell Your Own Info-Products
615	If You Use Too Many Keywords Then You Could Be Banned From The Article Directory And Your Articles Not Accepted. This Is A Complete And Total Waste Of Time So Follow The Rules Of The Directory And Don't Try Any Sneaky Stuff!
616	I Could Even Try To Show You How You Are Going To Unlock Secrets Even Google Doesn't Want You To Know... How To Spend NOTHING On Adwords And Still Make A Total Killing.
617	Explore The Secluded Regions Of The Gallery, Populated With Powerful Massive Scripts, Cool Software, And Exclusive Books That Defy Nature In Both Size And Cunning
618	Here Are 5 Things To Know. Forget About Past Failures. Use Them As A Benchmark. Commit To What You Want To Achieve. Be A Positive Thinker. Your Mind Will Influence Your Actions. Don't Whine And Blame, Have A Plan. Do It Now.
619	As Soon As You Have Purchased, We Will Send You Your Login Details Instantly, Even If It Is 3am!
620	The Hidden Truths Of The MONEY TREE Formula! Understand These Jealously Guarded Secrets, And You're Financial Problems Will Be Over For Good!
621	Make Sure You Take Advantage Because You May Never See This Phenomenon Again
622	This Payment Processing And Shopping Cart Software Script Allows The Following Payment Methods: 2Checkout, Paypal, Payment, Wire Transfer, Cash, Check, Money Transfer, COD And Billed Orders.
623	Why You Must Pre Qualify Your Marketplace Before Wasting Your Money
624	Finally, You Can Start Selling A Product That Everyone Needs & Wants. This Allows Anyone To Get Started Online Easily, Because It's Never Been Explained So Clearly Before, Step-By-Step. Now It Truly Is So Easy!

625	I Can Give You A Technique That Will Really Help You
626	Thank You For Your Recent Purchase Order#: XXXXXXX. We Encourage All Customers To Leave Feedback For Their Transactions. Please Note That Your Feedback Will Not Be Edited Or Removed. Please Make Sure That You've Given The Seller Every Chance To Resolve Any Issue First By Leaving Feedback From Your Account Area On The Following Link.
627	Think About Why Most Of Us Use The Internet Each Day And The Billions Being Made
628	What Do I Know That You Don't Know About Internet Marketing
629	Is Your Marketing Running On Empty Simply Because You Don't Know What To Do Next
630	How Much Time And Effort Are You Already Sacrificing For A Paycheck And A Boss That Controls 40, 50 Or 60 Hours Of Your Life Each And Every Week? You Aren't In Control Of Your Life... Your Boss Is!
631	The ONLY Thing Most So-Called Gurus Care About Is Lining THEIR Pockets NOT YOURS
632	If You've Been Putting Off Creating Your Own Products Check This Out
633	I Understand That By Placing My Secure Order Today, I Will Be Getting Instant Access To This Powerful Application That Is Capable Of Putting More Money Directly In My Pocket With Very Little Effort.
634	How To Properly Market Your Resell Rights Products For Maximum Profit.
635	Forget Everything You've Read Or Seen About Making Money Online Using This System
636	Get Real Referrals And Confirmed Signups For All Of Your Programs
637	Anyone With Access To A Computer Can Make A Killing Online If You Know This Secret
638	OK You've Been Flooded With Biggest Firesale Promo Emails In The Last 6 Hours. But, Guess What, There's More To Come :-), So Here Are Some Thoughts That Could Help You Handle The Situation.
639	Some Of The Things You Are About To Learn Might Not Make Sense To You - I'd Hope You Can Just Trust Me... I've Done A Lot Of Testing And We Operate In A Lot Of Niches.
640	It's A Shame When Even College Graduates Can't Make Money Online

641	Unique Methods To Dominate The Search Engines... So You Own Multiple Listings On The First Page... Imagine The Traffic You'll Get From Owning The Front Page!
642	How To Easily Set Up Your Own Forum, And A Little-Known Killer Technique To Make Your Forum Come Alive. Setting Up Your Forum, And Filling It With Lively Discussions And Content, Is A Snap... If You Know The Secrets. And I'm Revealing Them All Here.
643	My Main Offer Followed By My Continuity Program And Then My Value Trojan
644	My Money Making Skills Aren't Free But I Do Offer Them For A Very Reasonable Fee
645	The #1 Element Proven To Siphon Customers Into Any Sales Funnel Across Any Market!
646	I Believe There Are Two Legitimate Ways To Make Money Online: Create Your Own Product And Sell It, Or Find Someone Else's Product And Sell It. Either Way You Have To Sell. Period. No Way Around It.
647	Good News Is: You Won't Be Getting A Lot Of Competitors And You're Enjoying Near Unadulterated Advertising. The Not So Good News? Spots Are Truly Limited. Book Your Solo Ads Now!
648	Because For You Select Few Men And Women, I Guarantee The Same Kind Of Results I Get... Will Be Yours If You Just Follow This Easy To Implement Plan!
649	Wouldn't You Like To Be Able To Generate Income By Simply Providing Your Honest Opinion? Wouldn't It Be Nice To Finally Tell People What You Think And Turn That Into A Residual Income Stream?
650	Say Goodbye To Your Day Job And Hello To The Lavish Lifestyle Fit For A King Or Queen
651	It's Incredibly Rewarding To See A Person (Like You) Who's Experiencing The Same Frustration I Did Years Ago, And Personally Show You The Path To True Personal And Financial Success.
652	Market Yourself, As Well As Your Product. You Could Write Articles, Ebooks, Do Free Consulting, Do Speaking Engagements, Etc.
653	You'll Be Able To Watch Over My Shoulder As I Proceed To Dig Into Niches That I've Selected From My Own Personal Portfolio. I'm Going To Set Up Money Streams From Start To Finish

654	What Could You Accomplish If You Could Instantly Customize Your Professional Content
655	This Devilish Device Drives Visitors Mad With Curiosity And Boosts Opt-In Rates Like Magic
656	The Big Hairy Secret That Big-Name Brokerage Houses Don't Want You To Know About Their Mutual Fund Selection Process
657	In A World Of I Come First It's Refreshing To Find Remarkable People Who Care About Me
658	We'll Show You More Than Just How To Be A Better Writer. With Our Superior Techniques, We'll Help You Surpass Your Competitors And Learn About Other Authors Who've Had Success With Us.
659	Just Submit This Simple Form To Claim Your FREE Email Mini-Course And To Learn About A System That Costs Almost Nothing And Contains Ready-Made Capture Pages And Everything You Need To Start Building Your List And Making Money Just 10 Minutes From Now.
660	Here Are The Secret Stepping Stones For Your Ultimate Success For Any Niche
661	Now Is The Time To Take Action And Sign Up For This Free Offer Right Now
662	Affiliate Links Are OK But Wait Till You Read This Reality Check
663	Now You Can Shoot An Email To Early In The Morning And See Cash In Your Clickbank Account That Same Evening.
664	Most People's "Greatest Products" Never See The Light Of Day Because They Make The Mistake Of Coming Up With A Product Based On What They "Thought" The Market Wanted, Not What The Market Actually Wanted.
665	It's All Right Here In The Breakthrough Automated List Builder System. And It Comes With 10 Easy-To-Follow Video Modules So You'll Be A List Building Master In No Time.
666	We Do Things Differently Than Everybody Else Out There And This Really Works! Like Me, You've Probably Wasted Time And Money Struggling To Figure Out How To Succeed With Your Own Business, Or Even If It Was Possible In The First Place.

667	First Off, This Is Definitely Not For Everyone. You Must Meet Certain Requirements To Be Considered. Because You Will Be Working Directly With Me And My Team. The Same Team I Talk To On A Daily Basis. The Same People That Are My Most Trusted Advisors.
668	A Swipe File Is A Collection Of Sales Letters And Ideas That He/She Has Saved To Give Him Inspiration And/Or Ideas When He Needs It.
669	Imagine Being Able To Fire Off Emails To Someone And Say Please Design This Type Of Blog For Me And Set It All Up Because I Don't Know How Or Please Create This Landing Page For Me So It Will Have An Opt-In Form That Will Start Building Opt-Ins So I Can Make Affiliate Commissions..."
670	You Have Usually Just One Chance To Grab Your Prospects Attention And Make A First Impression.
671	How High Will You Allow Your Financial Flood Waters To Rise Before Accepting Help
672	I Know You're Busy, So I'll Make This Message Ultra Quick. If You've Ever Wished You Could Make More Money From Less Effort, You Need To Drop What You're Doing And Read This Message IMMEDIATELY.
673	As Long As You Own People Money You Will Always Be A Prisoner Of Debt
674	Unlike Google You Get Paid On Results, Not Clicks. And The Result Is The Chance To Earn Far Greater Commissions.
675	You May Even Use Some Of Them Currently, But Have No Idea Why - Imagine What You Can Learn By Reading Through ALL Of These Strategies!
676	But... None Of That Will Happen Unless You Secure Your Place Right Now. You See, Everything You've Done In Your Life So Far Has Lead You To This Point... And If You Want To Get Past This Point, You Need To Take Some Action And Shake Some Stuff Up.
677	Some Of You Are Thinking, "I've Got Bills To Pay This Week, This Month. I Have A Mortgage To Pay. I Need My $50 Per Hour Job. I Have Kids To Feed. I Can't Afford To Invest The Time In Building A Machine Or Developing A Product That Might Pay Off In Six Months Or In A Year."
678	7 Moral Ethical And Perfectly Legal Ways To Increase Conversions By At Least 75%
679	You Qualify For An Immediate Discount On Our Best Selling eBook

55

680	Feel The Emotions Behind The Goals You Really Want To Achieve
681	Jump On These Rare And Exciting Opportunities In An brand New Exploding Market
682	Use Your Content As A Free Giveaway For Your Long-Time Customers.
683	I Came Up With This Idea To Show You Exactly What I'm Doing Not Just Tell You What You Should Do.
684	BUT - I CAN Reward You With A HEAD START As A "Thank You" For Following Me Through The Entire "Outsource Force" Video Series. I Want To Send You An EARLY Notification BEFORE THE PUBLIC, With A Private "Back Door" Link To Reserve Your Coaching Spot With Me.
685	Your Living A Pipe Dream If You Think A Successful Business Is Built Only On Free Traffic
686	Ways To Increase Your Traffic And Sales Using Free Follow-Up Autoresponder Courses
687	My Only Question To You Is Are You A Doer Or A Perpetual Wannabe
688	Have You Completely Under Estimated The Lifetime Value Attached To Your Customers
689	Why "Slow And Steady" Is The Wrong Way To Think. "Get Rich Quick" Is Just As Wrong, But "Slow" Doesn't Cut The Mustard Here (I'll Even Show You Proof Of How I Went From $0 To The High Five Figures With A Brand New Site In 30 Days!)
690	WARNING: No One Really Cares About You Because They Just Want Your Money
691	If You Don't Apply This Information It's You That Gave Up
692	The First Step Toward Making $10,000 Per Hour Or $100,000 Per Hour Is To Stop Thinking "How Much Your Time Is Worth?" And Start Thinking "How Much Value Are You Creating?" When You Buy A Computer Or Software, Are You Thinking "How Much Did I Just Pay Bill Gates Or Michael Dell?"
693	Rent A Booth At A Trade Show And Sell The Physical Products You Created Using Your Content.
694	Forget About Your Stuff You Want To Get Into Their Minds
695	This Will Have Your Site Looking Like It Was Built By A Professional Web Designer And It Will Be A Site You Can Be Very Proud Of.
696	Wealth Building Program For Those In It For The Long Run

56

697	Ultimately You'll Want To Create A Network Of Powerful Products And Services
698	The BEST Place To Sell Your Product. Sure, You'll Have A Website Where People Actually Download Your Product, But How Will You Take Credit Card Order? How Will You Accept Payment? How Will You Handle Refunds.
699	Why A $27 Investment Can Be Worth A Small Fortune On Even A Small Squeeze Page
700	If You're Planning On Spending $2500 On A Diamond Engagement Ring
701	No Prospecting No Phone Calls No Selling Required And No Inventory
702	How Many Times Have You Invested In A "Work-At-Home" Opportunity After Reading A Splash Page Or Website That Never Fully Explained What The Program Was All About.
703	You Don't Even Need Your Own Product Other People Will Pay You Just For Recommending Their Products. When You Pick The Right Products And Promote Them The Right Way, There Is No Reason You Can't Make Enough Money To Quit Your Day Job.
704	Follow Up Designed To Position You As A Leader And Expert
705	In Just Minutes You're Going To Discover Everything You Need To Know To Build Your Own Ultra-Responsive List Of Subscribers That Will Send You Mind-Boggling Profits Each And Every Month.
706	Create A Print-On-Demand Book.
707	I'll Never Go Back To A Suffocating, Mind-Deadening, Low-Paying Insecure Cubicle Job Again. You'll Soon Feel The Same Way After Getting A Taste Of This Lifestyle.
708	I Have Been Praying For A Tool Like This That's Not Only A Great Product But At An Unbelievably Great Price.
709	Own A Gold MasterCard Or A Premier Visa Not After You Read This You Won't
710	Secret Weapon Loads An 'Army' Of Ideas With Killer Content On Autopilot That Explodes Your Profits And Unleashes A Never Ending Supply Of Free Targeted Traffic Directly To All Of Your Sites!
711	What If I Gave You A Powerful Technique That Would Change Your Life Would You Try It
712	The More Screwed Up Our Economy Gets The More Opportunities You Have To Profit

713	Over 100 Top Marketers Will Come Together To Bring You The BIGGEST And BEST Firesale Ever -- Jammed With Tens Of Thousands Of Dollars Worth Of Best Selling Products For You!
714	Real Secrets Behind Developing Your Own 15 Second Elevator Pitch For Your Big Idea
715	As Part Of An Insane Marketing Test, Shawn Casey Is Offering His Best Selling Internet Business In A Box For Absolutely Free! All You Have To Do Is Act Now!
716	Publicists Can Create A Swipe File Of Great Press Release Headlines. Swipe Files Are A Great Jumping-Off Point For Anybody Who Needs To Come Up With Lots Of Ideas.
717	How Working Closely With 2 People Can Produce More Results Than Working With Hundreds
718	Been Guilty Of Not Staying Focused Long Enough To See The Fruits Of Your Labor
719	The Fact Is, People ACT On Your Messages Because They Are Drawn Into Your Words/Thoughts And, Even If They Do Not Accept Them 100%, They Do Not Want To Give Up A Potential Advantage By Continuing To Read Your Message.
720	I'm Sure You've Heard Of Network Marketing Multi-Level-Marketing Viral Marketing And Affiliate Marketing?
721	Even If You're A Lazy Couch Potato And Only Follow A Quarter Of What You'll Learn In This Course, When You Run The Numbers It's Truly Unbelievable What You'll Be Able To Accomplish.
722	An Easy-To-Follow System For Creating Your Own High-Demand Products To Sell Online
723	Don't Waste Your Time And Your Traffic Credits Promoting Things In Traffic Exchanges That Nobody Wants!
724	As Busy Webmasters, Do We Do Or We Forget About A Reciprocal Link Exchange Strategy Or Do We Find A Way To Get It Done...And Reap The Rewards Well Into The Future?
725	No Longer Agonize Over Your Unproductive Efforts Online Because Help Is At Hand
726	Even With A Poorly Written Sales letter You Can Still Make Money Online
727	Think About This - Once In A While, Something Comes Along That Can Really Change Things For The Little Guy. This Is One Of Those Things. If You Don't Want To, Or Can't Afford To Pay For High Quality Traffic, This Is For You. If You Don't Want To Wait Months Or Years To Make Money, This Is For You.

728	If You're One Of The First 100 To Buy In This Is Exactly What You'll Get
729	Create Attractive T-Shirts And Badges And Sell Them.
730	No More Sleepless Nights And Endless Hours Struggling To Squeeze A Few More Lines Of Copy Out Of Your Exhausted Brain -- It's All Been Written For You Already.
731	PS: Sorry No Regrets - The Price Can Go Up At Any Time. Please Don't Let This Amazing Deal Pass You By. Order It Today Before It's Too Late Or You'll Kick Yourself Later.
732	Please STOP For A Moment If You're Thinking Of Creating An Online Business
733	You Should Also Spread Your Links Throughout Your Article So That It Looks Natural To The Search Engines.
734	It's This Simple - Those Who Keep Going Eventually Reach Success
735	I'm Not Going To Sit Here And Waste My Time With Anyone Else's Excuses Or Theories When I Already Know What Works.
736	Full Private Label Right Are A Great Inexpensive Way To Grow Your Internet Business
737	A Good Marketing Strategy Is To Start With An Entry-Level Product That Sells Very Inexpensively, Say Around $10-$20. Then Ideally You Should Have A More Expensive Product In The Same Niche To Offer Those That Purchased Your First Product.
738	All You Need Is A Piece Of Paper And A Pen
739	Your Autoresponder Without Thinking, Or Your Shortened URL, Could Be Killing Your Click Through Rates.
740	Money Is Only A Small Component Of Success, You Need To Understand That Right Away. Once You Realize That Fact The Money Will Start Flowing To You Faster Than Ever Before!
741	Why You Always Plant Your Virtual Garden One Seed At A Time
742	Quick Results Is What You Should Expect For Every Viral Campaign With These Tactics
743	Come On Get On Board Before You Miss The Gravy Train
744	Some Guy Writes What SHOULD Be An E-Book Or A Video Course, But Instead Of Charging You Once, He Sets Up His Content As A Membership Site.
745	Do You Really Want To Live The 2-Hour Work Week You've Always Dreamed Of

59

746	This Report Will Show You How To Run A Successful Marketing Campaign
747	I Don't Care If You're A Meat Eater Or Not, This Will Save Your Bacon! I'm Telling My Friends And Family To Get On This Too. Trust Me, You Don't Want To Be Left Behind.
748	Remember That I Will Be Removing This Special Free Offer Very Soon ... Then It's Are Gone FOREVER!
749	I'm Going To Expose Every Bag Of Tricks The Gurus Use
750	If You Are Serious About Becoming Financially Independent, Now Is Your Chance, Don't Be Part Of The 90% Who Don't Do Anything With An Opportunity.
751	Want Priority Access? Get Early Access To Rewards By Inviting At Least 3 Friends. The More Friends You Invite, The Sooner You'll Get Access Plus Exceptional Cash Back Rewards.
752	There Can Only Be 4 Possible Reasons For Holding You Back
753	Are You Willing To Do Whatever It Takes To Make It Online
754	If You're Interested In Making Money And Building An Online Business With The (Product), We Provide Our Members With An Opportunity That Is Un-Paralleled.
755	How To Create Irresistible Offers And Sell More Stuff Than You Ever Thought Possible
756	Spy On The Competition And Find Out What Is Working For Them
757	Major Diet Plans: Which Ones Actually Work...And Which Ones Are Guaranteed To Torture You, Cost A Fortune, And Leave You Fatter
758	The One Thing All Effective Landing Pages Have In Common. Plus, The Most Important Part Of Any Landing Page That Can Significantly Increase Your Conversion Rates! Why Giving Your Prospects Too Much Of A Certain Something Can Overwhelm Them And Ultimately Lower Your Conversion Rates. Find Out How To Prevent It Using This Simple Strategy.
759	Your Life Will Improve Drastically Once You Discover How This Works.
760	How To Create A Hop Link And How To Disguise It So That It Looks Like A Normal Domain Name. You Will Learn Some Clever Little Tips That Will Help You To Build Your Online Income.
761	How To Create A Unique Voice And Convey Your Own Information Products

762	If You're A Tire Kicker Please Pass On By Now Because At This Price There Are NO Refunds
763	I'm Not Telling You To Quit Your Job. You Might Need To Keep Your Job -- At Least For A While. I'm Trying To Show You How To Think Differently -- To Stop Thinking Of How To Get Paid A Little More Per Hour, Or A Little More For Your Time.
764	I Can Help You Fine Tune Your Email Piece For Optimal Response. After All, Being The Owner Of This Mailing List And Sending Thousands Of Unique Emails Over The Years I Know What Works And What Does Not!
765	You're About To Learn 'Secrets' That Most Network Marketers Will Never Know About How To Really Build A Huge Network Of Productive Distributors And Happy Customers! Give Us. Just 22 Minutes And We'll Teach You How To Make More Money In Network Marketing Than Ever Before, No Matter Who You Are And Where You Live!
766	If You Keep Doing What You're Doing Right Now, Will You EVER Meet That Monthly Income Goal? In Other Words, If You Keep Going Just As You Are Now, Will You EVER Have The Life That You TRULY Desire?
767	For Every Day That Passes Is Another Day You Choose To Give Up Making More Sales From Your Web Sites And The Opportunity To Make A Real Difference In Your Future But Only You Can Choose To Make That Happen.
768	Will You Email Me Everyday And Let Me Know That You Did That
769	So Why Am I Giving This Powerful Information Away For Free? Quite Simple. I Want To Gain Your Trust And Build A Long And Prosperous Business Relationship With You.
770	Resourceful Things You Can Do With A Product That Doesn't Sell
771	You'll Find It Stimulating And Invigorating Working With These Internet Movers And Shakers
772	I Wanted To Get This To You Before The Weekend Hit So That You Were Able To Still Get Free Access Before It's Not Available Anymore.
773	How To Avoid Common Work Problems. Covering These Details Before You Start Will Help Make The Process Easier And Boost Your Productivity.
774	Doing Joint Ventures Is Probably The Most Important And Profitable Thing That You'll Learn To Do.

61

775	It Helps A Lot To Have A Template To Follow — Both To Get Your Business Started And To Make Products To Sell. I've Found One Good Step-By-Step Program That Does An Excellent Job At A Reasonable Price.
776	Build A Substantial Monthly Income Without Having To Recruit Family And Friends
777	I'm Not Even Charging $500. Even Though My System Gives You Immediate Access To All The List Building Knowledge You'd Pay Hundreds Per Month To Be Spoon Fed Along With Other Systems.
778	It's 100% Free! Absolutely NO Pressure And You Can Opt Out At Any Time. No Need To Beg. Every Email Has A Link At The Bottom, So Get As Much Free Stuff And Quit If You Like.
779	How To Set Up A Free Blog. You Don't Need To Buy A Domain Name And Hosting, I Will Show You How To Set Up A Free Blog That Will Do A Fantastic Job Of Promoting Your Affiliate Product.
780	That's Why It Is So Important To Find These Tiny, Unexploited Niches And Just Take Over. You Locate Opportunities Where Competition Is Non-Existent Or Minimal -- And Demand Is Great -- And You Sweep In With A Shovel And Start Mining The Gold. That's How You Really Make Money With Information Products...
781	Are You Able To Envision Having No More Troubles Or Financial Woes
782	Learn To Write Sales Copy! Why? Because If You Can't Write Sales Copy, It Doesn't Just Affect Your Sales, It Affects Your Lead Generation, The Response To Your Ads, Your Resource Building, Your Profits, And The Quality Of Your Products - Everything!
783	His Idea Was For You To Use The Marketing Methods To Sell YOUR Product. What If You Don't Have One? What If You Do, But It Is Not A Million Dollar Product?
784	Are You Really Ready To Have Your Conversion Rates Fly Off The Charts
785	I Could Sell It To One Person, But That Limited The Number Of People Who Could Actually Afford It. So I Decided To Make My Business Available To A Few People And Make It Affordable To Almost Everyone. Some Close Internet Marketing Friends Were Concerned That Selling Too Many Packages Would Devalue It.

786	Still Stuck In The Stone Age? Listening To Ebooks Written Years Ago, That Give You Bogus Information That Might Have Worked Back Then But Are Dangerous To Your Wallet Now? Don't. Here's What Works.
787	Why Choosing The Right Domain Name Will Ensure Long Term Success
788	Your Web Business Relies On One Thing And One Thing Only ...Your Headlines. That's Right, Headlines Above All Else Grab And Peak Curiosity Before A Single Word Of Your Million Dollar Ad Copy Offer Is Ever Read...Period!
789	Greatest Gold-Mine Of Easy "Things-To-Make" Ever Crammed Into One Big Book
790	You've Made It A Very Easy Decision With Your 100% Iron-Clad Money Back Guarantee And I'm Ready To Start Right Now, So I'm Clicking The Secure Order Button Below.
791	Unemployment May Be Peaking But You Would Never Know It In This Niche Market
792	For Years, Many Programs Have Attempted To Implement A No-Sponsoring System. Sadly, 100% Of Them Failed In Days.
793	We Know Why Will You'll Want To Tell All Your Friends About This One
794	After Seeing All Of This Value I Know You Are Just Itching To Invest In Rights To These High End Products Plus Lock In Your Fast Mover's Bonuses. You Can Now Completely See How Owning The Rights To These Products Can Give You A Major Headstart On Your Competition.
795	Create Videos And Audio Content On CD Or DVD.
796	I'm Going To Help You Got From Point A To Point B
797	Internet Street Wars Have Broken Out As Affiliates Scramble To Survive The Outcome
798	Why Have A Business Without A Great Keyword Domain That Automates Free Traffic
799	If You Have Any Questions Or Need Help With Anything, Just Submit A Ticket From Within The Affiliate Center And We'll Get Right Back To You.
800	Each Issue Is Quick, Easy To Read Yet Provides A Wealth Of Practical Information About How To Overcome Objections, Create Buyer Urgency And Close The Sale. As The Owner Of A Financial Services Firm Here In Chicago I've Learned The Importance Of Being Aware Of Important Buying Signals That Enable Me To Close At Precisely The Right Time."

801	If You Still Don't Understand The Power Of The Internet You Need To Read This Now
802	When It Comes To Going After What You Love In Life, Don't Take NO For An Answer
803	With Affiliate Internet Marketing, Anyone... And I Mean Anyone... With Access To The Web Has The Capability To Earn Hundreds Of Thousands Of Dollars Every Year... (Many Do It Every Month).
804	Imagine Income Flowing Into Your Bank Account On A Regular Basis
805	Pays You A Commission Runs On Complete Auto-Pilot And Then Repeats Again And Again
806	Has The Magic From Your Internet Business Been Destroyed By Limited Profits
807	That Means Cold Hard Cash In Your Pocket With Each Click Of The Mouse
808	Now You Can Eliminate Your _____ In Under _____ Days With This _____
809	A Computer's Attention Span Is As Long As It's Power Cord
810	It Isn't A Matter Of Right Or Wrong That Keeps You From Succeeding Online Is It
811	Think Of This As The Last "Internet Marketing Course" You Will Ever Need To Buy, Not Only Am I Going To Teach You Everything You Need To Know Right Now Today, But As The Internet Changes And Evolves I Will Be Updating The Videos In The Program And You Will Get All This Information For Free!
812	Want To Know How You Can Milk Google For Penny Clicks That You Can Recycle Over And Over For 1000% Returns?
813	Don't Continue To Settle For Scraping The Bottom Of The Barrel Anymore
814	You'll Have To Move Fast If You Want Total Access Meant For Only The Few Invited
815	Learn How To Squeeze Your Subscriber List Into A Buyer's List
816	Do You Feel Like Your Cheating Them If You Charge For It
817	Are You Really On Your Way To Becoming An Internet Millionaire
818	I'm Contacting You To See If You Have A Squeeze Page Website Set Up Yet For Your Affiliate Programs. If You Have Affiliate Programs And You're Using The Page The Company Gave You, You're Missing Out On A LOT Of Business.

819	Listen, We Both Know That Guarantees Like That Are Pretty Rare. A Guarantee Like That Backed By A Product This Good Is Pretty Rare In The IM Industry. It Just Doesn't Happen. But Earlier, I Promised You A Crazy Price... And I Really Wasn't Joking. If You Move Fast On This, I Mean Right Now, You Can Grab It For Just $77. $77 For A Complete No-Brainer.
820	All I Used To Do Is Work Until I Met This Amazing Person
821	Better Than A Poke In The Eye With A Sharp Stick
822	Put It This Way: If You Found This Page, You're Smart Enough To Earn A Profit Online. It's That Simple. Heck, Let Me Put It Another Way... If You Can Check Your Email, You Can Make Money Online. Insane Amounts Of Money. More Than You Could Possibly Spend.
823	Our Squeeze Page Works With Any Program That You Have. The Squeeze Page Website Is YOURS And Allows You To Customize Your Offers, Which Your Affiliate Program CAN'T.
824	When You Look Through Your Strengths Then The Outcome Is Obvious
825	If You're Not Sure What Content To Offer-I'll Show You What To Offer, And Where To Get It. I've Literally Created A Fool-proof Method That Has Worked Time After Time On My Own Sites, And I'll Teach You How Easy It Really Is To Set Up Your Own Income-Generating Site. I'll Even Show You How To Find Affiliates, Who Will Promote YOUR Site.
826	Be Somewhat Subtle About How You Drive People To Action, But Make Sure You Do Drive Them To Action.
827	After All The Hard Work Is Done Did You Get Paid Enough
828	Quit Crying Out Of Frustration Just Because You Haven't Yet Achieved Success Online
829	If You're Not Providing Solid Information As A Trustworthy Resource You're Doomed To Fail
830	Ever Get Upset Thinking About Where You'd Be By Now But Then You Realize You Weren't Ready For It Yet?
831	When The Economy Goes Down Business Owners Spend More Money On What
832	You Probably Won't Be Able To Sleep Tonight After You Check This Out
833	Most People Give Up On Their Current Offer And Jump To Another And Another And Another Because They Are Not Seeing Results Quick Enough. That Sets You Up For A Huge Amount Of New Sign Ups Real Fast Because My Splash Pages Get A Higher Than Normal Response.

834	Rewrite Your Content From The Perspective Of Your Child, Dog, Parrot, Or Mother - If It's Funny Enough, It May Go Viral!
835	No Marketing Magician Here Just Access To Perfecting This Startling Discovery
836	Ready To Break Free Of The Debt Conspiracy And Actually Experience The American Dream
837	The Path Of Least Resistance Was My Direct Path To Profits
838	7 Basic And Simple Ad Tips To Immediately Increase Your Effectiveness
839	Why Settle For A Few Peanuts When I Can Make A Fortune Selling Peanut Butter
840	What Actions Do You Need To Take Immediately To Further Your Success?
841	Learn How To Deal With Each Search Engines Quality Score So You Can Get Visitors Way Cheaper Than Your Competitors. (I've Used This To Get Clicks For Less Than $0.05 In Markets Where People Are Paying $0.60 - $0.75)
842	All Of My Work Is Designed To Save You Time And Effort So You Can Begin Making Money
843	Affiliate Marketing Is Probably The Best Way To Start Off If You Have No Experience But You Want To Make A Living Online. You Don't Need Any Inventory, You Don't Even Have To Have Your Own Product.
844	Make Your Skill Set Take You To The Top Of Your Game
845	If You Can't Focus Your Efforts You Won't Make Money Online
846	As You Can See There Are Some Pretty Interesting Concepts Here
847	The First Step, Is To Stop Thinking How Much Time Is Worth And Start Thinking, "How Can I Use Leverage Automate And Multiply My Actions? Then Find Something You're Doing That Brings In A Little Money And Multiply Your Efforts 1,000 Fold Or A Million Fold.
848	It Just Seemed Like The Perfect Way To Teach And Guide You No Matter What Level You Might Be At, To Really Make An Affiliate Income The Fastest Way Possible. I Figured It Was One Of My Most Brilliant Ideas To Date.
849	Avoid The Mistake Beginning Affiliates Make Only To Have Their Links Bounced Unknowingly
850	Want To Buy Every Luxury Toy Imaginable During The Next 12 Months

851	Discover All You Need To Know To Create Your Very Own High End Profitable Article Directory And Garner Hoards Of New Pages So You Can Get Massive Free Organic Search Engine Traffic To Your Website.
852	If You Want To Increase Conversions By At Least 75% And Have All But Given Up Here's Hope
853	That's A Real World $552 Value (Not Just Numbers Pulled Out Of The Sky)... And It Doesn't Include Unlimited Email Support You Get In Case You Run Into Any Snags That The Course Doesn't Cover (Not Likely)...
854	Without One Cent Of Your Money You Can Test Drive This Amazing System
855	It Doesn't Matter If You're Just Looking For An Extra Couple Hundred Bucks A Week To Pay The Bills, Or If You Want To Go The Whole Hog And Make Enough To Buy Sports Cars And Live The High Life. You Know, Hire A Yacht, Sail The World, That Kind Of Thing. Or Maybe You Just Want To Make Enough To Quit Your Job And Have A Little More Freedom. Whatever, It's Your Call.
856	You'll Have All The Time You Need To Do It Right
857	That's What They'll Say If You Get Caught Using The Wrong Marketing System
858	Learn How To Write A Killer One-Page Sales Letter... Because This Skill Can Literally Make Your Fortune And Help You Achieve Financial Freedom
859	Are You Still Throwing Away Dollars After Dollars Just Sifting For Gold Dust
860	Want To Learn How To Create Free Advertising That Works For You Automatically
861	One Mistake Leads To Another...Then Another...Then Another. Months Have Gone By, Thousands Of Dollars Have Been Spent, And They Still Have Not Made Money -- And They Give Up.
862	Are You Smothered By Tasks That Waste Your Time And Money
863	I First Learned About Success From Studying "Think And Grow Rich" By Napoleon Hill About 25 Years Ago. For A Number Of Years After That, I Only Used A Few Affirmations And Only Used Them Occasionally. I Got Great Results When I Used Them, But Found I Didn't Have Time To Use Them Consistently.
864	If You've Tried And Failed Now You Can Access A Winner

865	There's Another Woman Waiting For Every Man And She's Too Smart To Have "Morning Mouth"
866	It's No Wonder You Are Tired And Don't Have Any Time Left To Build A List Or Getting Started With Building A List If It's Not On Your "List" Of Things To Do.
867	You Won't Be Able To Sleep For A Week After Hearing This
868	Why Most Sites That Promise To Bring You Targeted Traffic Are Truly Bogus Offers
869	How He Turned Several Ordinary People Into Successful Internet Marketers In Just 2 Weeks
870	Discover How YOU Can EXPLODE Your Social & Business Contacts PLUS Build An On-Going Residual Income Through This Amazing, Simple-To-Use Add-On Product
871	This Book Is Crammed Full Of Useful Tricks And Tips On How To Make Money On The Internet, It Is Ideal For Those Of You Who Are Relatively New To The Internet Marketing.
872	You'll Leave Sales On The Table If You Don't Use Guarantees
873	Don't Believe Me? Here's A Personal Challenge. Pick Up The Phone And Call The Smartest Guy In Your Office, Business, Or Whatever Your Place Of Employment Is. Ask Him To Give You Just One Millionaire Strategy.
874	How Can I Support You To Help You Get What You Want
875	Our Internet Friends Think We're Certifiably Nuts To Offer Such A Great Deal And Incredible Guarantee. We Can't Promise We Won't Be Raising The Price Soon.
876	There Are Hundreds Of People Claiming To Be Experts Who Want To Teach You How To Make Money Online. However, Very Few Of These So Called "Experts" Actually Succeeded Using The Products They Sell.
877	No Other Sponsor Will Disclose The Quick And Easy Ways They Use To Generate Quick Money Which Helps Them Market Their Main Programs.
878	If You're Just Working A Regular Day Job Will Your Dreams Come True
879	Learn How A Struggling Entrepreneur Discovered How To Use Analytic Tools And Data To Run A Business Online And Significantly Increase Profits And Decrease Advertising Costs, Or Even Eliminate It
880	How To Find Profitable Affiliate Programs Fast. If You Want To Be A Successful Super Affiliate, You Need To Capitalize On The Best Affiliate Programs And Hit Them Like A Ton Of Bricks.

881	Just Let Me Know Within 30 Days And You'll Get Your $ Back
882	Everything You Do Each Day Will Multiply Over And Over Again. You Will Start Receiving Large, Weekly And Monthly Checks For All The Efforts Of Other People.
883	Adoptions Needed Immediately In Order To Find A Lot Of Great Homes
884	My Entire Purpose Is To Share This Information And To Learn From You More Ways Of Reducing Or Eliminating Debt. In Turn This Information Will Then Be Shared With Still Others.
885	How To Get Free Advertising By Participating In E-mail Discussion Lists
886	Think About It... Major Online Search Engines Generate Billions Of Dollars In Ad Revenue Every Single Year. This Gets Passed On To People Just Like You And Me Who Run Simple Little Websites That Help People Find What They Need.
887	This Tool Is So Simple Anyone Can Use It! You Can Now Quickly Rebrand These PLR Products To Make Them Unique To You That Would Normally Cost Hundreds Of Dollars Just To Outsource, But It Won't Cost You Anything Extra.
888	What If You Could Crack The Marketing Code With A Mouse Click
889	By Acting Today You'll Also Receive Access To My Private Membership Group Which I Just Started About A Month Ago. Its Purpose Is To Help One Another Make More Money.
890	Make MORE MONEY Easier. Your Friends Might Resent You. Money Will Pour In While Your Out Golfing, Or Shopping At Your Favorite Store And They Are Slaving Away For Wages At Their Soul-Sucking J-O-B.
891	It Is A Statistical Fact That Over 95% Of Network Marketers Never Make A Dime In This Industry. The Odds Aren't Very Pretty.
892	How To Keep 100% Of The Profits From Each And Every Copy You Sell
893	How To Avoid Making The Same Devastating Mistakes That 97% Of People Consistently Make
894	How To Double Your Online Profits Using This Easy One Step Approach
895	Well You're Not Alone. I Would Bet That Not 1 In 500 People Have Ever Heard Of The Society For Creative Anachronism. But, Do You Think You Could Find Those 300 Members We Were Talking About In A Tiny Micro-Niche Like This?

896	The Quickest Way To Increase Sales By 28% With A Simple Trick Near Your Order Button
897	I Was Shocked And Embarrassed When I Found Out That Home Remodeling Was Labeled America's #1 Most Complained-About Industry
898	I'm Not Pointing Any Fingers. But Very Few (Greedy Underground Super Affiliates) Want You To Know These Insider Secrets, Because Then You'll Be On A Level Playing Field.
899	Create A FAQ Or Q&A "How-To" Page Based On Your Content.
900	How A Selfish Experience Can Instantly Create A Strong Flood Of Recollections
901	Here Are 13 Powerful Tips For Improving Your eMail Marketing Campaigns
902	If All Those Little Known Methods Were So Powerful Why Aren't You Filthy Rich
903	Now... They Are Certainly Valid Techniques, But What Separates The Cream Of The Crop Marketers From The Rest Of The Bunch, Is The Successful Marketers Are In Control Of What Traffic Gets Delivered To Their Sites
904	Grab A Notepad And A Timer... I'm Going To Reveal To You A Simple System Of How To Finally Get Things Done! Quit 'Spinning Your Wheels', Going To Bed Feeling Guilty You Wasted Your Day, And Seeing More And More Stuff Pile Up In Your Life.
905	Here's A Hint Of What Your Buyers Will Uncover After They Pay You For This Course That You Soon Will Have The Rights To Sell. How To Select The Top Affiliate Products That Pay You The Highest Commission And Convert The Best To Put More Money In Your Pockets Faster. What Website Allows You To Point-And-Click And Create, Cash Sucking Turn-Key Search Engine Friendly Websites In Minutes, FREE!
906	Click Here To Download The Master Set Of Keys For Success
907	The Truth About Blogging That Can Add Up To 64% Value To Your Site Just By Using The Right FREE And Stupid-Simple Software!
908	Earn Fantastic Commissions Just For Giving My Solutions Away. You Soon Realize That Some Of The Details I Share Are So *Hush Hush* They Can Only Be Revealed To My Affiliates.

909	It All Comes Down To The Offer And The Quality Traffic It Generates
910	Highly Entertaining Online Video Shows How A Couple Of Teenage 'Airhead' Girls Are Making Over $9,000+ Per Month Online With A Wacky, Fun And Insanely Obvious Idea That Anyone Can Do Too.
911	Would You Jump At The Chance To Earn Multiple Streams Of Residual Monthly Income
912	Working At Home For Yourself Does Not Have To Be Difficult. In Fact, Once You're Up And Running You'll Often Find That You Have More Free Time Than You Ever Imagined Having!
913	We Help Our Clients Quickly Find Secret Business Opportunities Online That Can Automatically Make Money While They Work, Sleep, Or Go On Vacation! Do You Know Anyone Who Could Benefit By Learning How To Make More Money Creating Multiple Streams Of Passive Income?
914	A Constant Stream Of Traffic Flows Into Your Site, Day And Night, With Literally NO EFFORT On Your Part.
915	Consistently Rake In Hundreds Of Hungry Visitors Eagerly Wanting To Join Instantly
916	And In The Process Get People So Excited, Curious, And Interested In A Product That They Go Ahead And Purchase It Through Your Affiliate Link!
917	I Think I'm Going To Take The Rest Of My Life Off From Work
918	Want To Know Where I Find New Business Ideas At Virtually ZERO Risk
919	You Can Learn On Your Own Through Trial And Error Like The Woman In The Story Above Insists On Doing, Or You Can Learn From Someone Else Who's Already Paid That Price Which Is What I Like To Do.
920	Access Our Members Area And Download Your Concise Report Loaded With Strategies That Will Allow You To Build Your Niche Marketing Empire, From Scratch.
921	Want To Grab Yours Today Here's How To Increase Conversions By At Least 75%
922	Free Comprehensive Real Estate Property Survey Allows You To Compare & Price Out Every Single Possible Available Site... Without Talking To A Broker
923	When It Comes To Making Money If You've Not Uncovered These Critical Facets, Well, You Guessed It... You're Going To Fail.

924	The "Inside Scoop" On Exactly How The "Big Boys" Play With Mass Traffic And How YOU Can Too Starting Today (Taught By Virtually No One) To Generate Traffic That Will Dwarf What You May Be Using.
925	It's No Longer Enough To Have Just A One Way Communication Between Product Owner And Customer. In My Opinion It Needs To Be A Multidimensional Conversation.
926	However, I Feel That I Should Warn You That This Is Not A Get-Rich Quick Scheme. You Will Have To Put In Some Work – Fun, Easy Work But Still Work Nonetheless.
927	Even If You're Not A Copyrighter You Can Use These Ideas To Spark Winning Sales Letters
928	Why Most Viral Marketing Campaigns Fail But Not With These Simple 12 Strategies
929	Siphon Some Of That Flood Of Traffic Off Into Your Direction Right Now And Don't Even Lift A Finger To Do It.
930	It Saddened Me To Do This But I Had No Choice
931	The Best Way To Get Your Niche Audience To Your Site Is To Target Them In Article Marketing. Article Marketing Is A Revolutionary Way To Use Your Words To Generate Traffic. Essentially You (Or Hired Content Writers) Can Write About A Topic Directed At Your Site And Include A Bio And A Link To Your Website.
932	Learn How To Write Ads That Will Generate Tons Of Traffic, How To Increase The Amount Of Clicks To Your Site, And How To Make Sure When You Do Pay Per Click... You Only Pay For The Clicks That Will Make You Money
933	This Report Was Written For Both The Newbie And Advance Internet Marketer In Mind. So No Matter Where You Are, If You Implement My System Properly, You Will Make More Money Than You Are Making Now.
934	Set Clear And Measurable Goals Then Commit To A Course Of Action
935	Don't Start A Business Just Because Everyone Else Is Doing It
936	Remember What It Took To Learn How To Ride A Bike
937	I'm A Personal Business Coach. I Help People Make MONEY On The Internet Doing Things They Already Love To Do! I'll Help Them Figure Out What They Really Want Out Of Life And Keep Them Focused On Achieving Results Every Step Of The Way. Do You Know Anyone Who Could Benefit By Learning How To Make More Money Right Now?

938	If You're Like Me (And I Suspect You Are), Your Inbox Got Bombarded Today With Pitches For The Latest Marketing Strategy, And Tomorrow It'll Be Filled To Overflowing Yet Again. It Happens EVERY DAY!
939	When You Read The Testimonials We Receive Daily You'll Understand Why We Make Money
940	Time Heals Almost Everything So Give Everything Time And Even More Time
941	Can You Invest The Next 30 Days To Learn How To Generate Leads And Turn Web Site Visitors Into Customers?
942	Are You Missing The Big Picture On Really Making Money Online
943	What If You Could Give Away Unlimited Products And Earn Recurring Commissions For Life
944	Earn Up To 75% Weekly Fixed Interest & 5% Referral Commission
945	A Really Winning Online System That Has Helped Thousands Succeed Online
946	In Case You Want To Modify The Templates And The Graphics Elements Further, You Also Get Full PSD Source Files To Everything, Which Gives You Complete Control Of How The Templates Look And A Lot Of Flexibility.
947	Time-Crunched Marketer And Father Of Four Teaches You How To Turbo-Charge Your List, Blast Your Conversion Rates, Triple Your Double Opt-Ins, And Do It Over And Over In Any Niche You Choose - Guaranteed!
948	Print Out The Professionally Designed Materials And Include It When You Ship Physical Products As A Bonus.
949	You Could Continue Going It Alone, Spending Big Bucks On Copywriting & Templates, While Going Broke In The Process, Or You Could Continue At Your Dreary Job, And Flush All Your Dreams Down The Toilet. With Those Options, My Heart Goes Out To You. But Thankfully There Is A Third Option.
950	Ever Watched An Infomercial And Felt Every Button They Pushed Like What They Were Selling Was The Perfect Answer To All Your Problems And You Just Couldn't Wait To Get Your Hands On IT.
951	Subscribers Will Instantly Be Taken To Your Pre Sell Page With This System
952	Is Your Website A Hidden Goldmine That Simply Needs An Experienced Prospect Manager
953	They Want To See You Can Help Them Solve Their Problem

954	Scroll To The Bottom Of The Order Page And Click Your Free Download Link
955	I Will Be Concentrating In Helping You Become Profitable With Your Store And Anything Less Than Full Concentration From You May Hold You Back From What I Think We Can Achieve For You Working Together.
956	You've Got To Find A Way To Get Out Of Whatever You're Stuck In
957	Capitalize On The Biggest Trends Facing These Multi Billion Dollar Industries
958	Package Your Content As A Complete Home Study Course.
959	WARNING! Don't Let This Pass By. I'm Telling You Again. If You Miss This Once In A Life Time Opportunity, You Could Die Regretting It. What IF This Is Just The Opportunity That You've Been Waiting For?
960	You Can Qualify For A Brand New Home In Just 6 To 18 Months
961	This Is Your Once In A Lifetime Chance To Understand Exactly What To Do
962	Get All The Targeted Traffic You Know You Need To Succeed Online
963	The 10 People You Referred Will Work To Refer 10 Others - Now You Would Have 100 Random Members To Mail.
964	Mark My Words When It Happens It Will Happen Like This
965	We'll Show You A Couple Of Different Options On How To Use These Effectively
966	Just Tell How Something Helped You, Made Something Better, Faster, Easier For You And How Someone Else Can Get The Same Results.
967	Cash In On The Red Hot Video Revolution And Harness The Massive Appeal Of YouTube
968	Sure, I Know You're Tired Of All The Bs Claims You See With Most Of The Online Businesses Out There... That's Why I Decided To Not Waste Your Time, And Give You Undeniable Proof Of This System Right Here... You're About To Have Your Entire Life Changed - Permanently.
969	Which Of This Disastrous Marketing Roadblocks Do You Want To Successfully Overcome

970	I Start Almost Every Day With Affirmations. When I Am Faced With A Problem (Of Course Problems Still Appear--They Always Will) I Almost Always Respond Positively And Find Solutions Quickly. And The Reason? Because I Have Trained My Mind To Respond This Way Through The Repetition Of Positive Thought.
971	I'm Contacting You To See If You Have A Squeeze Page Website Set Up Yet For Your Affiliate Programs. f You Have Affiliate Programs And You're Using The Page The Company Gave You, You're Missing Out On A LOT Of Business.
972	Now That He's Making All This Money It Wasn't Such A Dumb Idea After All
973	It Starts From Figuring Out How To Create Profits On Demand (Just Like Turning A Tap). Then That Gives You Freedom To Do What You Want And When You Want.
974	Since The Internet Is Such An Active Place, People Have Found Methods To Deal With Over-Stimulation. One Way Of Getting By Is Called Receptive Input Filtering.
975	Discover For Yourself How To Finally Pay Off Your Bills, Get Out Of Debt And Run Your Own Successful Online Business.
976	Tired Of All The Techie Mumbo Jumbo Adsense Speak That Requires A PHD In Engineering To Understand... And That Only Sucks Money Out Of Your Wallet Instead Of Stuffing It Full Of It?
977	Lack Of Knowledge Can Limit A Person's Marketing Approach In The Same Way Information Overload Confuses People From Taking Any Profitable Action.
978	The Primary Goal Each Day Is To Figure Out How To Automate Another Piece Of Your Business. Most Of Your Selling Can Be Done With Machines And Systems. To Build An Asset, To Build A Machine That Throws Off Income Automatically, Without You Being There, Is Your Ultimate Goal In Business.
979	Do You Want To Get My Next Product For Free? You Can As My Bonus When You Pick Up My New Course That Just Opened Up Today. I'm Sure You'll See A Ton Of People Talking About It Today, And For Good Reason.
980	You'll Be Saving Yourself Time, Effort, And Getting A Whole Heap Of Valuable Back-Links For A Small Monthly Subscription... It Really Is A No-Brainer. I Suggest You Check It Out

981	I Think You Would Agree There Is No BETTER Way Of Being Trained On Screen By Video Capture. See How Things Are Done Before Your Eyes. It Will Take You By The Hand Visually Showing You How To Take The Necessary To Become Successful Super-Fast.
982	Powerful New Software Tool Uncovers Hot Untapped Niche Markets That Have Been Completely Overlooked By The Masses And Allows You To Swoop In And Absolutely Dominate These Niche Markets In Google!
983	It Might Give You Some Ideas About How You Can Tell A Story About A Product Or An Ebook.
984	Let Me Show You How To Close The Toughest Customers By Putting Them Completely At Ease With Creative Sales Closing Techniques For FREE!
985	Keywords Are An Important SEO Factor To Consider When You're Creating Headlines, Ad Copy, Blog, Or Web Site.
986	Today I Would Like To Take A Moment To Discuss The Importance Of Exchanging Links With Other Sites.
987	Have Exclusive Access To A Variety Of Software Tools To Help Your Business Run Smoother And Be More Efficient. (And Save You Much Time!)
988	Why Cash Flow Is Like An Internet Addict To Nearly All Marketing Experts
989	You Can't Look At The Future In Your Rear View Mirror
990	What If I'm New To The Internet And Internet Marketing? Once Again - No Problem
991	Where To Place Your Text Ads To Attract Grab And Hold Your Visitor's Attention
992	Links To 4 Special Websites Where You Can Get Paid To Do Almost Anything...Immediately! Whatever Your Skill Or Knowledge May Be, Someone Out There Is Willing To Pay You For It. Heck, You Can Even Make Money Even If You Have No Special Talent Or Ability, As Long As You're Willing To Take Action.
993	Find The Smartest People He Knew And To Invite Them To Partner With Him. He Thought If He Brought In The Smartest Most Competent People He Could Find And Gave Them A Share Of The Business, The Business Plan Would Pretty Well Take Care Of Itself. That Plan Certainly Worked Well For Bill Gates.

994	And When You Get Hordes Of Visitors All You Need To Do Is Present Them With An Irresistible Offer And Suddenly Your Part Time Business Has Become A Giant Money Making Monolith.
995	Why Not Pull The D A Y J O B Trigger
996	I Got A $250 Bonus From My Day Job And Now I Want To Pay It Forward To 25 People And Grow A Huge Business.
997	You've Got An Important Decision To Make Success Or Continual Failure
998	Your Education, Your Job Or Even Your Economic Circumstances, You Can Generate Thousands Of Dollars Online, Quickly And Easily.
999	I Will Explain What I Do And Show You Exactly What You Must Also Do To Discover How To Make More Money Than You Probably Ever Dreamed Possible Using A Digital Camera!
1000	If You're A Green As Grass Newbie Who Got Your First Computer Yesterday, You Can Follow This Stuff. But Also, If You've Made Money Online Before, And You Wish You Could Make More... Well There's Some Super Hot Stuff Here For You Too... Stuff That I Guarantee You Don't Know. Check Out Some Of The More Advanced Stuff:
1001	How Will You Begin Justifying All This New Money To Your Spouse
1002	The Fastest Way To Pick Something Up Is To See It, Hear It, And Repeat It, Then You Can TRULY Be Up And Building Your List And Generating Profit In Mere Minutes.
1003	What Would You Do If You Knew Exactly What Kind Of Information People Buy Online
1004	Warning: Coarse Language Used "I Am Pissed Off...And I'm Not Holding Back From The Bastards That Did This To Me" You Wont Believe What's Happening Right Under Our Noses...And I Am About To Put A Stop To It!
1005	They Laughed When I Sat Down At The Piano But When I Started To Play
1006	You To Spend More Than An Hour Or So A Day On This
1007	Be Sure To Be On The Lookout Tomorrow For A Unique And Personal Offer
1008	Costly Pitfalls Of Not Writing A Profitable Ad That Will Drain Your Bank Account

1009	Once Your Marketing System Is Set Up, Your Capture Page, Your Lead Capture Form, Your Email Auto-Responder Campaign...Generating Auto-Pilot Income Comes Down To Just ONE Thing...Driving Quality Traffic To Your Website.
1010	It Sucks When You Write A Sales Or Squeeze Page That Only Ends Up With Measly Conversions.
1011	When Your List Sees This They'll Be Foaming At The Mouth Eager To Instantly Order
1012	You Spoke We Listened And Together We Made A Ton Of Money
1013	Do You Think You Can Wake Up One Morning And Say, "I'm Going To Be A Doctor!" And You Go Down And Join A Company, Get A Distributor Kit For 50 Bucks, And You're A Doctor? f Course Not. That's Ludicrous.
1014	While Others Are Worrying About The Recession, Credit Crunch, Falling House Prices And Job Insecurity... By Successfully Using My System, I've Been Stuffing Thousands Of Dollars Into My Bank Account Each Week, Over The Last Several Years.
1015	You Will Probably Just Skim This Email And Not Read The Entire Thing. But I Promise If You Read The Entire Message You Will Be Glad You Did Once You Get To The End. I Guarantee It Will Be Worth It For You.
1016	In Addition To Getting Your First Two Paid Sign-Ups, I Will Reveal Some Of The Easy Ways To Generate Quick Money And Market This System At The Same Time
1017	If You're Not Making Money In Your Own Business, What Makes You Think You Would Do Any Better In Mine? This System Will Show You How To Put Money In Your Pocket NOW By Revealing How To Profit From The 98% Of People Who DON'T Join Your Business!
1018	How To Use What You Already Know About Internet Marketing To Make A Killing Online Without Building A List, Affiliating For Products, Or Spending A Dime On Traffic...
1019	Regardless Of The Ingenious Methods Of Making Money You Still Gotta Get Started
1020	We Also Have A Monthly Mastermind Call Where We Talk About Different Aspects Profiting With Google Adsense.

1021	Learn What Others Are Doing Wrong So That You Can Do It Right. Are Your Sales Being Effected By This? I'll Bet At Least On Of These Negative Points Is Present In Your Material Right Now And You Need To Remove It Now, Because You're Losing Sales.
1022	Now Here's A Product You'll Be Proud To Promote And Buy For Yourself
1023	For The Very First Time, These Cutting Edge Techniques Are Gathered Into One Place. And The Best Part Is They Are So Simple And Easy To Use. While We've Done All The Hard Work, All You Need To Do To Tap Into Your Own Inner Success Mechanism Is "Plug And Play."
1024	People In Many Countries Across The Globe Are Just Now Beginning To Realize Full Time Incomes That Can Grow Each Month. Are YOU Going To Pass This Up Without Seeing And Hearing What It's All About?
1025	These New Marketers Didn't Play By The Rules Of The Game. Instead, They Laid Clever Marketing Traps And Captured As Many Surfers As They Possibly Could. What Amazed Me Was How They Did It On All Complete And Total Auto-Pilot.
1026	Believe It When We Say We All Look Forward To Seeing You On Top
1027	Only 100 People Will Get Private Label Rights To This Offer
1028	Any Chance You Ever Get I Recommend You Grab This One With Both Hands
1029	How Much Would You Pay For A System That Makes Money
1030	The Real Benefit To Your Business Substantially Increases Beyond The Launch Date
1031	These Are Some Of The Things That Attracted Me To Partner With Them
1032	The Secret To Writing Autoresponder Emails That Pull In Cash Like Crazy Even If You Flunked High School English.
1033	Pay-Per-Click Is So Expensive If You Aren't An Expert You'll Go Broke In A Week
1034	I've Just Found The Greatest Viral Marketing Idea Of All Time
1035	Produce Illustrations, Comics, Or Graphic Novels Based On Your Content.
1036	Confusing Powerlines Uplines Downlines Leading You Down The Path Of Online Poverty
1037	Earn Daily Earn Often You Keep 100% Of What You Make

1038	Why Keep Fighting It When You Already Know Being Successful Is Far More Enjoyable
1039	If You're Impatient Like Me Then You're Going To Love These Marketing Strategies
1040	These Strategies Are Absolutely Fool Proof, So It Doesn't Matter If You Have Absolutely No Experience Or Have Never Been Successful Building Your Online Business. These Proven, Ridiculously Simple Strategies Will Work For You. All You Have To Do Is Pull The Trigger.
1041	You're About To Discover How To Make At Least An Extra $150 FOR FREE By The End Of Today... And Multiply That On Complete Autopilot Each Day After
1042	No Matter What Your Income Goal It's Easier To Hit Your Numbers
1043	Create And Sell A Training Guide To Corporations Or Small Businesses.
1044	The Feedback Has Been Astonishing. People Say, "I Could Have Written That Book! That Was My Story. Why Did You Steal My Story? How Could You Know Exactly What I Went Through?"
1045	You Can Choose From Our List Of Recommended Programs, Where You'll Find Some Of The Best Income Generating Programs, Or You Can Plug In Whatever You Are Already Marketing.
1046	How To Properly Set Your Product Apart From All The Rest Of Your Niche Competition
1047	How Your FROM Name Triggers Recipients Whether Or Not To Delete Your Email
1048	If You Were Given $200000 To Spend Isn't This The Kind Of Future You Would Build
1049	Write Down All The Things You Want To Get Done For The Day. Everything From Writing, Creating Content, Or Planning Your Next Project To Answering Your Email And Balancing Your Checkbook. Assign A Specific Time To Each Task Or Group Of Tasks. Anything From 15 Minutes To 2 Hours. Chunks Of 30 Minutes Or Less Work Best
1050	They're Excited About Their Home Business And What It Allows Them To Accomplish
1051	This Entire Course Is Contained Within One Ultra-Convenient, Downloadable Module Where You'll Get Instant Access To Fabulous Material.

1052	I Don't Want To See You Wasting Your Time Doing Things The Wrong Way, That Is Why I Created This Video Training Series.
1053	Zip Zilch Nada That's Right It Won't Cost You One Single Cent
1054	See, All That Stress Was For Nothing. I Was Picturing All These Bad Things Happening. The Real Payoff Is Picturing All The Good Things That Can Happen. If You're Serious About Changing Your Life Then You Must Understand How To Control The Power Which Makes Your True Desires Come To Life. That's The Real Secret You're Seeking.
1055	What Smart People Know And Why They Buy Virtual Real Estate For As Little As $10 A Year
1056	Often Many Webmasters Overlook The Benefits Of Reciprocal Link Exchange. Those Serious About Website Promotion Know Well That Reciprocal Link Exchange On Well Placed Websites Rank Higher.
1057	We All Know That We Live In Tough Times Right Now. We Live In Times Where You May Have A Hard Time Paying Your More Basic Bills, And You May Be Struggling With High Credit Card Payments, Or Are Having A Hard Time Just Staying Afloat Financially.
1058	Don't Waste Your Valuable Time Creating Products Without Knowing This First
1059	WARNING: Many Entrepreneurs Get So Wrapped Up In Their Work They Forget To Take Care Of Their Lives. And The Results Are Neglected Families, Loss Of Friends, And Declining Physical And Mental Health.
1060	Still Not Any Closer To Your Dreams. Still Not Making Money. Haven't Quit Your Day Job. Not Sure What To Do Next. Don't Know Who To Believe. Well That All Changes Right Here Right Now!
1061	You'll Be Highly Impressed With Our Incredible Knockout Blow You've Been Desperately Seeking In Other Ebooks And Guides That Haven't Delivered
1062	How Do You Use Your Strength To Leverage What They Want
1063	Let Me Cut To The Chase Here, If You Follow These Simple Steps And Start Experimenting With Facebook Marketing, You Will Have An Unlimited Supply Of Traffic At Your Fingertips, Just Waiting To Be Converted Into Sales
1064	Staring Crowds Are Waiting For New Products That Pin Point Their Needs

1065	It's BRAND NEW, So, If You're Quick You'll Access A Huge Library Of Software, CDs, Ebooks And Video Tutorials Designed To Help You Become More Successful At Making Money Online.
1066	How This Content Driven Subject Line Is More Effective Yet Seldom Used
1067	Do You Have The Discipline It Takes To Spend 4 Hours A Day From Home Starting New Campaigns That Can Make You More In A Day Then You Earned In A Week At Your Safe
1068	It's Already Working For Other People. All You Have To Do For It To Work For You Is To Follow What They Are Already Doing!
1069	Discover The Easiest Way To Profit Online With A Brand New Step-By-Step Guide That Reveals The Secret Techniques We Use To Generate Over $1,000 A Day Without Even Having A Website Or Product!
1070	Get My Secret Tips And Tools On Where To Find The Best Offers, Best Payouts, And Find Out Exactly How To Tell If An Offer Is Worth Running. (This Will Save You Time And Money... Not To Mention Getting Rid Of The Frustrations Or Finding Good Programs.)
1071	I Have Found Some Great Videos That Will Guide You Through This Whole Process And Show You Step-By-Step How To Get Your Affiliate Marketing Business Off The Ground And Is Really Easy To Follow.
1072	Pays You A Commission, Runs On Complete Auto-Pilot And Then Repeats It Again And Again 24/7/365.
1073	These Same Grocery Stores Have Invested Millions Of Dollars In Total On Researching Buying Triggers Like These To Boost Profits. It's This Form Of Marketing That Works Like Magic On Almost Everyone.
1074	Link Exchange Is Where You Feature Other Websites Links On Your Own Website And In Exchange, Your Partners Will Display Your Web Site Hyperlink On Their Own Web Pages.
1075	Plain And Simple... They Make Money! And Once They're Setup... They Keep Making Money Over And Over... With Little Or No Additional Effort. The Good News Is That No Matter What You Have Been Doing, Your Life Just Got Easier And More Profitable...
1076	Here's Someone Willing To Break Down Powerful Ideas Into A Series Of Simple Lessons

82

1077	You Could Start To Make Money Online Today! This Website System, A $399.00 Value, Is Yours FREE If You Act Now.
1078	Create Pamphlets Or Brochures Advertising Your Business Philosophy.
1079	Identify Your Uniqueness And Stake Your Claim Your Claim To Virtual Real Estate
1080	If You're Not On The Top 10 List You May Never Get The Traffic You Deserve
1081	Discover How To Setup And Manage Your Very Own High End Article Directory In Literally Minutes, And Have The Article Directory Already Receiving Content On A Daily Basis. Show People A Proven System For Profiting Automatically From Other People's Content Over And Over Again.
1082	Here's Something Of Great Value even Your Money May Not Be Able To Buy
1083	You Only Need A Tiny, Tiny Slice Of A Huge Market To Make A Very Comfortable Income. It's A Truism In Marketing That There's No Point In Re-Inventing The Wheel. You Can Knock Yourself Out Trying To Convince People To Buy Something Totally New In A Market Where No Money Is Being Spent...
1084	Are You Ready To Be Inspired By A Wealth Of Experience
1085	We Believe Everyone Online Should Have The Opportunity To Make A Lot Of Money
1086	Find Out Exactly How To Read Your Web Stats And Find Out Which Ads Are Making You The Most Money... So You Can Make Even More Profit While Cutting Your Costs
1087	Stop Being A Victim And Start Your Own Scam Free Zone
1088	The Instant Sale Secrets System Is The Closest To "Connect The Dots" And Make Money Online WITHOUT Any Marketing Experience And Technical Know-How."
1089	I Really Hope You Have What It Takes To Become A Millionaire
1090	How Are You Finally Going To Show A Real Profit For All Your Online Efforts
1091	There Is Absolutely No Risk, Whatsoever On Your Part. The Burden To Deliver And Satisfy Is Entirely On Us. If You Fail To Create The Review System That Works For You - Then We're The Losers, Not You.
1092	What Faster Profits Do For Your Business Will Change Your Life
1093	You Stare For Hours On End At Your Monitor Just Wondering How It All Works

1094	For Most People Trying To Get Real Traffic To Their Web Sites Is Like Trying To Part The Red Sea... It'll Never Happen For Them Without A Miracle...
1095	Six Closely Guarded Secrets Of The Diamond Industry Revealed At Last
1096	But The Truth Is, I've Found More People Confused, Perplexed, Puzzled And Just Plain Baffled About Internet Marketing. And Who Wouldn't Be?
1097	Don't Allow People To Intrude On Your Working Blocks Of Time
1098	Advice To Wives Whose Husbands Don't Save Money For Their Wife
1099	The Amazing "One-Click" Trick To Link Blasting Every Major Social Bookmarking Site For 20% Traffic Increases Every Time You Do It...
1100	Do You Have The Guts To Trample Your Competition And Legally Steal Their Traffic
1101	The Fast Track To Getting You Up And Running Toward Super Affiliate Status
1102	After Knowing The Methods And How To Pull It Altogether, There Was Still One Piece Of The Puzzle That Was Missing - This Is The One Piece That Is The Main Reason More People Fail To Duplicate His Success - A Product.
1103	I Won't Try To Fool You. It Wasn't Easy, And I Spent Many Frustrated Nights Trying To Figure Out What I Was Doing Wrong. But Once I Learned The Key Ingredients To Promoting A Website, All Of That Hard Work Paid Off.
1104	They Will Never Create Something Like 'Nasty Dirty Money'. In Fact, 'Nasty Dirty Money' Was Produced In Total Secrecy...Not Even My Closest Marketing Buddies Knew What I Was Up To. Because If They Did, The Backlash Would Be Almost Unthinkable...
1105	It's Been Said Links Are The Currency Of The Web, And An Honest-Gotten Inbound Link Is Like A Tip For Good Work.
1106	So It Stands To Reason If You Target These Overlooked, Under-The-Radar Keyword Phrases You Will Stand A Much Better Chance Of Both Diverting The Traffic To Your Offer AND Converting That Traffic Into Profits!
1107	We're Just Scratching The Surface Of The Full Profit Potential Here...If You've Been Living Anywhere Near The Us Over The Past Year, You Know The Real Estate Market Is In A Steep Decline.

1108	You Deserve A Beautiful Smile Even When Your Web Site Frowns
1109	The Desire And Willingness To Take Action Is The First Step
1110	If You've Tried To Make Money From Other Forms Of Advertising Before And Failed Then It Really Isn't Your Fault. Unleash The Power So That You Can Start Making More Money Today!
1111	Every Program In The System Offers You Rewards For Referring Other People. Either Monetary Rewards Or Advertising Credits. Everything Your Referrals Do Will Result In One Of The Above Rewards For You.
1112	What To Do When Thoughts And Ideas Pop Into Your Head
1113	How You Can Access A Million Dollar Tool For Less Than A Big Mac
1114	Traffic's Great, The More The Better... But It Won't Pay Your Rent On Its Own... That's Where This Comes In: You Have To Convert That Traffic Into Money. Whether It's Through A Squeeze Page Or A Direct Link To A Sales Page, You Need A Page That Basically Spits Out Money For Every Single Visitor You Deliver.
1115	However, I Will Be Available To You...And You Also Will Be Offered A Special Chance To Be Part Of A Very Exclusive Community Of Like Minded Affiliates Kept Secret From The World Until Now. I'll Tell You About That Later...
1116	You Will Receive An Instant Email Containing Your First Niche Suggestion - Including Keyword Statistics, Powerful Monetization Strategies And Some Emails Even Contain Full Packages Of Ready To Use Articles!
1117	Create A Full Fledged Website And Flip It For Profit.
1118	As A Dedicated Subscriber This Is My Way Of Saying Thank You
1119	You Gave Up On The Job A While Back And Now You're Trying To Make A Living Online. Thank Goodness If You Have A Partner Who Has A Job, Because Otherwise It's Pretty Bleak. Because The Whole Internet Business Thing Is Looking Harder Every Day.

1120	Now, If You're Like Me – And I Think You Are – You Only Want The Best Things In Life For You And Your Family...You've Seen Yourself Sipping Dom Perignon...Dining At The Best Restaurants Around...Maybe Even Shuffling The Streets Of The Latin Quarter In Paris On The Last Leg Of Your European Vacation Thinking To Yourself, "I Can't Believe I'm Here"...Living Without Worrying About Money – Or The Lack Of It.
1121	Social Bookmarking Will Get You Some Fake Friends And Jokes That Really You Didn't Need To Know, But It's Not Going To Send Hungry Customers To Your Site.
1122	P.P.S. Sorry Affiliate Links Are Reserved For Those Who Purchase Only, Those Willing To Invest In The Tools And Education That Makes It Possible To Stay On The Bleeding Edge Of The Game.
1123	Where To Get High-In-Demand Resell Rights Products That Will Bring Your More Sales.
1124	What Would It Take To Really Build A Wildfire Under Your Butt
1125	If You're Looking To Start A Home Business To Make Some Extra Cash, Or You're Exploring Your Options Because Your Current Home Business Isn't Making You The Money You're After...Beware...You're Definitely Swimming In Shark Infested Waters
1126	Why You Need To Stop 'Selling' And How A Few Subtle But Powerful Changes Can Have A Dramatic Impact Upon Your Profits - I Laugh When I Read The Over-hyped Emails That Hit My Inbox Every Day. Learn How Lowering The Sales Volume Will Actually Explode Your Sales.
1127	Of Course This Is An Affiliate Program With Really Big Benefits
1128	Become My Affiliate And I'll Give You 75% From Each Of Your Sales
1129	Surefire Ways To Find And Secure The Top Spots On The Search Engines
1130	These Powerful People Movers Will Help You Build An Irresistible Business
1131	Use PLR Wallpapers To Create On-Demand Physical Products Like Mugs, Magnets, Stickers, And Other Items.
1132	Purchase Can Only Be Downloaded Once So Customer's Can't Pass Link Around
1133	They Realize I've Left Nothing Out And That's Why They've Sent You Here To Benefit From These Strategies

1134	Use The Phrase "Invest In Our Product" Instead Of The Words Buy Or Purchase. This Makes Prospects Feel They're Investing In Their Future If They Buy.
1135	Keep On Doing What You've Always Done And You'll Keep On Getting What You've Always Got!!.... NO One Time Offers And NO Time Pressure Tactics. I Will Assist You 'One On One' To Put You On Track To $200 Per Day Within 30 Days.
1136	This Is A System That Is SO EASY That Anyone With Work Ethic, Regardless Of Experience, Can Get Big Financial Results Starting Their First Week And Month Into The Business.
1137	Whether You Are Offering A Product Or A Service, People Have To Understand What It Is, Why They Need It And Why They Should Get It From You.
1138	How To Develop The Anti Credit Mindset That Controls Knowledge Power And Money
1139	Track Clicks On Text Links In Your Emails Newsletter Or Ezine
1140	I Don't Need To I Don't Want To I Don't Have To Hmm
1141	How On Earth Can You Offer These Incredible Masterpieces For Less Than $75
1142	Create Eye-Catching Lead Capture Pages That Virtually Force Your Visitors To Opt In, Sending Your List Nuclear In Size And Profitability... Even If You Don't Know A Single Thing About HTML.
1143	Have You Pre Identified Your Visitor's Desire To Purchase From You
1144	Carving Out Your Own Niche And Keeping It Is The Problem
1145	Profit From Your Knowledge: During This Powerful Webinar Series And Coaching You Are Going To Learn So Much About Traffic Generation That You Could Literally Take Away Everything You Have Learned And Offer To Do A Service For Local Businesses.
1146	First The Offer Then The Traffic Then The List Then Money Dah
1147	What's The Most Powerful Way For You To Make Money Online In Today's Economy
1148	You Might Have The Best Idea In The World, If You Can't Make A Profit From It, And/Or If You Can't Optimize It, Then This Idea Might Be Useless (Or Should Be Replaced By A More Valuable One).
1149	Simple Yet Misunderstood Tricks That Can Easily Triple The Response To Your Ads

1150	What's The Next Action You're Business Needs To Take Right Now?
1151	Next Week I'll Have At Least One Killer Deal Alert For You That You Won't Want To Miss, And I'll Also Talk More About How To Use These Programs To Your Advantage. Expect That Email To Arrive After The Weekend.
1152	Some Of My Killer Launches Have Been For Products That Had A Very Limited Life Span.
1153	New Federal Law Requires That All Nail Clippers Screwdrivers Fly Swatters And Rolled-Up Newspapers Must Be Registered By January 2030
1154	Please Check Your Email For Login Details. You Will Then Be Directed To Your Individual Members Login Page
1155	How To Use Your Website As A Magnet For Capturing Leads
1156	The Reports In These Packages Are Crammed Full Of Extremely Useful Information. Any One Of Them Would Be A Valued Asset In Any Marketing Or Business Membership Site. If You Break These Down Into Article Format, You Can Have Years Of Content Ready To Add Week After Week.
1157	I Not Doing Anybody A Favor By Getting Sales For Them...Instead I'd Only Be Helping Myself...As Simple As That!! Now Is That What You Really Want Me To Do?
1158	As You Can See People Just Like You With Very Little Prior Experience Are Already Seeing Results. Even Top Gurus Are Singing The Praises.
1159	If This Email Image Is Missing Please Click Here To View An HTML Page
1160	Just When You Are Starting To Get A Grip On What The Whole Web 2.0 Thing Really Means, We're Already Hearing About Web 3.0... Web 4.0... And Web Insert The Next Number Here...
1161	Understanding What Motivates People To Buy is The Key To Your Success
1162	I Can't Give Away Too Much About This New Site But The Couple Of JV Partners That I Have Shown It To Have Been Blown Away By How Cool It Is. Here Is All You Have To Do:
1163	Right Now There Are Literally Thousands Of Affiliates Struggling To Make Their First Sale
1164	Hope Your Week Has Been Good So Far And This Will Make It Even Better
1165	If You're Not Here Soon Watch Out For The Avalanche Destroying Everything In It's Path

1166	Marketing Experts Paid Tribute To The Amazing Formula As (Directly Or Indirectly) Having Played A Role In The Success Of Their Online Business
1167	Unlimited Ways To Succeed Online Even If You're Currently Hard Pressed For Money
1168	Can You Really Afford Not To Buy This Right Now? If You Are Not Harnessing The Power Of Facebook Marketing, You Are Missing Out On A Literal Gold Mine. Don't Put That Kind Of Power Into The Hands Of Your Competitors!
1169	Now You Can Find The Most Profitable Affiliate Programs To Promote In Any Niche Market
1170	Two Great Approaches That Expose Your Product To Thousands Of Affiliates
1171	Uncover The Real Profits You Were Never Meant To Know About
1172	If You Downloaded This Unique Software When I Recommended It, But You Haven't Got The Full Package Yet, You Need To Act Now. That Link Bypasses The Opt-In And Gets Straight To The Point. It May Be Your Last Chance To Get Your Hands On It Before It's Gone Forever.
1173	I Agree That This Series Is Easily Worth That And That This Would Weed Out Those Who Really Are Just Fooling Themselves And Don't Deserve The Chance To Employ These Samurai Style Tactics.
1174	How Are You Going To Spend The Rest Of Your Day Today
1175	I Have Something That I Know Might Just Hold The Answer For You
1176	Simply Change Your Website's Stinky Socks And Start Smelling The Sweet Smell Of Success
1177	And, We Want To Show You That Our Site Can Pay You Thousands For Only A Little Work!
1178	I'm About To Hand You The Keys To Your New Niche Blog Empire . . . And All Of The Content That Goes With It! All You Need To Do Is Set Up Your Blogs Each Month And Suck In The Profits
1179	Prove You Are An Expert. You Need To Prove This With Your Words And With Your Bio Line. After The Article, You Will Most Likely Have A Chance To Explain 'About The Author.' Demonstrate Your Knowledge By Providing Background Information.
1180	In Just 7 Minutes And 23 Seconds You Can Achieve An Internet Miracle

89

1181	The Wonderful Thing About Hiring Virtual Workers To Help You Get Your New Online Business Going Is That You Don't Necessarily Have To Hire Someone Full-Time, You Don't Have To Pay Them A Lot - In Fact, You Can Get Someone To Help You For Many Hours A Week For The Same Amount You're Going To Have To Pay To Host Your Web Site Each Month Anyway.
1182	Maybe You've Been There, Too. Frustrated... Knowing You Have As Much Knowledge And Talent Of Any Big Shots Living In The Fancy Houses You Drive Past, And Still Having To Struggle Just To Get By Every Month.
1183	You Could Spend More Time With Family And Friends, Take A Much Needed Vacation And Even Pay Off Those Bills! You Could Get Out Of Debt And Be Free From All That Stress
1184	You Know How Some People Have This Problem - Well I Offer This Solution
1185	PS - You're Going To Make Massive Cash Fast When You
1186	This Product Breaks Down The Process For Launching A Profitable Online Business Into Bite-Size Tasks That Anyone Can Implement.
1187	We Provide People With A FREE Wealth Creation Strategy That ANYONE Whose Short On Time, Money Or Internet Experience Can Use To Create A Better Lifestyle For Themselves And Their Family.
1188	For The First Time We're Unveiling A Proven Technique For Converting New Leads
1189	Who Can You Turn To That's Willing To Help Your Financial Success
1190	This Is Something So Relevant It Should Be Taught At Every Level In School
1191	What I Will Do Is Offer The Product To Them For Half Price, But Also Tell Them That They Must Wait Six Months For Delivery Of The Product. I'll Explain Exactly What I Am Doing. I'll Explain That The Product Is In Production And That They Are Getting The Product For Half Price Because They Are Part Of A Test-Market Focus Group.
1192	You're About To Learn So Much You Can't Help But Make Money
1193	LIST BUILDING: (Arguably The Second Most Important On The List) . List Building Brings You Residual Income Day After Day, Year After Year, For All Of Your Eternal Life, If You Do It Right.

1194	People Ask Me All The Time, "Can't I Just Promote Affiliate Products Without Building My Own List?" Sure, You Could. You Could Also Push Your Car Instead Of Driving It. But, Why?
1195	74% of Children In The US Have People Taking Care Of Their Children
1196	Follow Certain Rules Over And Over And You'll Soon Product Results
1197	You'll Never Make As Much Money As If You Learn How To Play In The Big Leagues Where Multi-Billion Dollar Companies Who Spend Millions Of Dollars Month In And Month Out To Get New Customers.
1198	You'll Absolutely Love The Step By Step, Hold Your Hand, Approach. What's So Cool About This System Is That Even If Someone Had No Idea What Any Of The Terms Actually Mean, They'd Still Be Able To Follow The Steps And Potentially Make Money. And For Those Who Are Already Familiar With These Internet Marketing Terms, It Really Is An Idiot Proof System.
1199	Don't Get Stuck With Nothing To Show For All Your Efforts
1200	How To Generate As Many Pre Qualified Leads As Your Business Can Handle
1201	Use Your Content To Create Adsense Sites.
1202	Creating Freedom Online Is The Greatest Thing About Being Self-Employed. You Can Start With A Few Bucks And A Good Idea To Make Lots Of Money Online! I Did, And I'll Teach You How!
1203	For Less Than A Fraction Of The Cost Of Lesser In-Depth Programs
1204	High Definition Video And Audio Recordings Of The Entire Process Were Created, From Learning The Simple Methods, To Understanding The True Power You Have Within Yourself, To Putting Your New-Found Knowledge Into Immediate Action To Create Success In Any Part Of Your Life.
1205	You'll Never Be Left In The Dark With Our Customer Support
1206	Did You Ever Figure Out Exactly What May Be Holding You Back
1207	Lay The Foundation Now Build Your Dream Upon A Solid Proven System
1208	In My Opinion Perhaps The Most Important Lesson I've Learned Is To Stay Focused

1209	If Words Have Little Effect In Marketing Consider Including The Longest Word In Your Next Header And See What Happens.: PNEUMONOULTRAMICROSCOPICSILICOVOLCANO-CONIOSIS
1210	What Should You Be Looking For Ahead Of Time With Your Next Ad Campaign
1211	In Half The Time It Takes You To Read This You Could Have Made Your First Sale
1212	Why Are You Still Getting In The Way Of Your Own Dreams
1213	You Must Have The Right Boat To Swim In This Market
1214	Keep The Bonuses As My Way Of Saying Thank You For Giving It A Try
1215	OH The Things We Take For Granted In Life Now That We're Into Internet Marketing
1216	Most People Think They Need To Invent Things From Scratch In Order To Be Able To Create Products. It's Wrong. Most Of The Time You Only Find New Ways To Achieve Things To Differentiate From Your Competitors.
1217	If You Were Handed All The Missing Elements On A Silver Platter Would You Take It
1218	If You Have Been Scratching Your Head Trying To Crack The Code Of How To Create A Successful Online Income, This Could Easily Be The Most Shocking Tool You Have Ever Encountered...
1219	The True Concept Of A Sales Letter That Kills. There's A Lot Of Rumors And Myths About Writing Sales Copies. Slice Through The Nonsense And Understand How To Write Your Very Own Powerful Sales Copy.
1220	If You've Been Looking To Seriously Boost Your Online Income Then Becoming A Well Respected Expert In Your Market Will Help You Achieve That. Nothing Says "Pro" More Than Someone Who Is Constantly Producing Fresh Content That Their Market Loves. If You're Providing New Information For Your Subscribers Every Week Or Two They Will View You As Being On The "Cutting Edge" Of The Market.
1221	Wishing Things Were Different Will Not Change Your Life Action Will
1222	The Key Is Satisfaction! If You Have Any Issues With An Item You Purchase From Me All You Have To Do Is Communicate And I Will Gladly Make Things Right. Isn't That Better Than Leaving Negative Feedback And Getting Stuck With Something You Don't Like?

1223	What You Really Need Is Learning How To Get The Things You Want Out Of Life
1224	But You'll Need To Be Waiting By Your Computer For It So You Can 'Jump' To Register Before The Public Gets Their Shot At Any Remaining Spots. Just Tell Me Where To Email Your "Early Bird" Invitation Below, And You'll Be Hearing From Me Soon – BUT BE READY!
1225	Good Or Bad I Will Post Reactions And Feedback On My Web Site. Your Feedback Can Be Completely Anonymous... I Simply Want Your Thoughts And Reactions.
1226	Customers Want The Answer To Their Problems. A Quick Fix For Their Woes. A Simple Solution That Will Make Their World A Better Place And They Want It Now!
1227	Learn How The Best And The Brightest Market Their Products And Services. How To Close Like A Confident Sales Pro That 'Gets The Deal Locked Up' Every Time. How To Turn Your Bright Idea Into A Successful Company.
1228	This Requires Some Work But Proven To Be Well Worth It
1229	I Believe In An Honest Day's Work So Is This Legal
1230	Ride The Wave Of Internet Profits By Giving Away Hot In Demand Products
1231	You Need To Hear From Somebody Who Knows The Ropes And Can Teach You How To Start Earning Money Faster Than You Ever Dreamed It Was Possible!
1232	You're About To See How You Can Make A Comfortable, *Hands Off* Income, From Simple Websites That Take Less Than 2 Hours To Setup And Generate You Cash For Months, And Even YEARS To Come.
1233	Are The Grammatical Errors On Your Website Destroying Your Professional Image
1234	How To Quickly Research The Subject Of Your Next Book Or Article To Know If It Will Sell.
1235	I've Been Getting Excited Here So Let Me Just Slow Down A Moment
1236	They Will Knock Down Your Door With Credit Cards In Hand
1237	Steps To Build Businesses Online WITHOUT Chasing Family And Friends, Without Buying Leads, Without Hotel Meetings, Without Cold Calling, Without Handing Out Flyers, Without Prospecting.
1238	How To Streamline Your Online Money Making Ventures So Effectively That It Runs On Autopilot. Meaning Once The 'Nuts And Bolts' Are In Gear ... Sit Back And Let It Do It's Thing!

1239	It's A Search Engine That Spiders The Entire Clickbank Marketplace And Makes Those Thousands Of Infoproducts And Software Programs Available To Your Searchers. You Simply Add One Line Of Code To Your Web Page.
1240	Find Out If There Is A Market For My Product Before I Go To All The Effort And Expense Of Creating It. If People Buy, I Move Forward Full Bore And Produce The Product. If No One Buys, Or Too Few People Buy My Product At Half Price, I'll Know There's Probably No Market For It.
1241	How To Write Articles Quickly Even If You Know Nothing About The Subject
1242	This System Is Unlike Anything Else Available Out There, And The Power Will Completely Blow You Away.
1243	Build, Or Have Yourself Built, A Website Of Your Own. Find A Niche That Will Fit Your Desires. Or Become An Affiliate, And Promote Other Peoples Products.
1244	After This Video Your Site Will Be Ready To Go And You Will Be Able To Take Money Online.
1245	What Is What They Do And How Can I Do It Too
1246	Imagine Being Able To Set Up A Single Traffic Campaign And Sitting Back While It Continues To Go To Work For You Day In - Day Out, Without Ever Having To Give It Another Minute Of Your Attention. No Tweaking, No Extensive Testing, No Monotonous And Repetitive Split Testing Involved. These Strategies Have Already Been Rigorously Tested And Proven To Work!
1247	It Seemed Like Everything Out There That Was Supposed To Teach Me "How To Make Money Online" Was Full Of Hype, Lies, And Garbage, You Know... Nothing That "Really Worked" For "Real People"... I Felt Completely Stuck
1248	Why Adding Your Signature To Ads Can Double Even Triple Responses
1249	For Every Visitor There Exists The Irresistible Offer They'll Eagerly Purchase Instantly
1250	This Strategy Will Even Show You How To Self-Finance The Business Building Process So You Won't Go Broke BEFORE You Earn A Profit. And Because The System Is Free, YOU RISK NOTHING!"

1251	The 6 Golden Rules That You Must Follow To Create A Cash Spewing Squeeze Page That Converts Like Crazy - I'm Going To Show You The Fastest Way To Squeeze Page Profits And How You Can Build Your Own High Converting Page Today. I'll Even Show You Some Of My Squeeze Pages And Give You The Low Down And Why They Convert At 40% + Every Time.
1252	You're Going To Get To See Inside Another One Of My Simple Sites. This Time Its One That Has Tons And Tons Of Sub Niches. Who Knows... Maybe One Of You Will Use One Of Those Sub Niches And Build A Site.
1253	What You Need To Do Today To Out Fox The Competition
1254	This Page Is Going Offline TODAY... Because I'm Only Going To Allow The First 100, 87, 62, 46, 23 marketers who are tired of struggling and want to make the easy money to get this $97 Blueprint For FREE..."''I Doubt You Need Any Convincing To Click The Link Below And Get Your FREE Copy Of (Product).
1255	Don't Let Them Steal And Lock You Out Of Your Own Domain
1256	The Six Types Of Profitable Product You May Want To Do Yourself And Some Real Cash With It Now.
1257	The Only 3 Web Pages You Need To Create. Yep, Only Three, And I'll Tell You How To Set Them Up In A Flash.
1258	Today I Will Share A Very Powerful Strategy That Will MAKE Your Website Visitors To LIKE YOU, TRUST YOU And Buy MORE Of Your Products Even If They Have Never Seen You Before In Their Lives.
1259	The 4 Questions You Must Answer Before Setting A Price And The Simple Way To Answer Them (Get This Wrong And You Could Be Losing Thousands Of Dollars In Potential Revenue.)
1260	I Knew That What I Was Learning Could Change My Business So Radically And So Quickly That I Could Barely Wait To Get Home From The Seminar And Put It Into Practice.
1261	Now Own Florida Land This Easy Way $10 Down And $10 A Month
1262	You Can Have Your Own Affiliate Marketing Business Up And Running In Minutes
1263	Hear What The Latest Buzz Around The Marketing Campfires Have Uncovered
1264	Why Struggle To Create A Winning Ad When Someone Else Has Already Done It For You.
1265	How To Get People To Almost Always Click On Your Ad And Read Your Description

1266	The Headline Resources Alone Are Worth A Hundred Times The Cost Of This Course
1267	The Best Part Is Every Single One Of These Products Pays Your Commissions Directly Into Your Paypal Account Immediately When Someone Buys...Even Better — You Can Re-Sell The Report Itself... This Can Be A Gold Mine For You If You Take Action...
1268	I've Basically Said To Heck With That. I'll Create My Own Products And Marketing Programs. And I'll Control The Entire Process. No More Clients Really To Deal With. Well, I Still Have Some Clients -- Those That I Like.
1269	If I WERE To Teach You All I Know Right Now
1270	Do You Have Any Idea How Wonderful It Is To Go To Sleep Every Night Knowing That Your Family Is Happy, Your Mortgage Is Paid, There's Food In The Pantry, You Have All The Fun Toys In Life You Deserve, And You Have Your Next Vacation Planned.
1271	And Just In Case You're Wondering, The Automated List Builder System Comes With A 100% Unconditional Money Back Guarantee.
1272	When Are You Going To Join The Inner Circle Of The Big League
1273	90% Of Businesses Fail Not Because The Owner Lacks Skill And Knowledge
1274	You Need To Buy It Now Because Time Is Running Out
1275	If You Are Not Happy With The Results You Are Getting From Hour After Hour Of Surfing, It's Time For A Change. You Can Keep Doing What You're Already Doing, Hoping Beyond Hope For Different Results...
1276	But I Must Warn You - There Are 3 Qualifications You Need To Meet, In Order To Experience The Results You've Dreamed Of. Before I Reveal To You Those 3 Qualifications. So, Let's Take A Look At The Following:
1277	Quickly And Easily Create Profit Pulling Information Products To Accelerate Your Online Success And Double Your Existing Sales Without Ever Creating A New Product While Finally Shedding Feelings Of Frustration, Information Overload, And Lack Of Direction Once And For All.
1278	All The Traffic In The World Doesn't Mean You'll Get A Sale

1279	Let Me Introduce You To Trance Inducing Language In Your Messages Gets Your Readers' Attention And Puts Them Into A Highly Receptive State Of Mind. That's All It Does. But The Results Are Spectacular! It Takes An Expert To Craft That Kind Of Copy... That's Why The Most Successful Online Marketers Hire The Best To Write This Kind Of Copy For Them.
1280	Take Advantage Of The Same Secrets Used To Generate Incredible Amounts Of Income Online. More Than 135,000 People Are Already Using It!
1281	The Sky's The Limit When You And Your Team Bring In Even More New Team Members And Participate In As Many 100% Free Money Programs Found In The Members' Area As Possible.
1282	Simply Copy What These Brand New Top Money Earners Are Doing Right Now
1283	You'll Also Receive In-depth Training On Hidden Features Of The Site Not Being Offered Anywhere Else. Free Advertising Packs Are Given Away Daily To Active Members. You Need Look Nowhere Else But Right Here For The Latest Tools And Resources To Grow Your Business!
1284	We Also Provide You With All The Support You'll Need To Help You Succeed. If You're SERIOUS About Building A Better Lifestyle For Yourself, Then You'll Do The Little Bit It Takes To Succeed With Our System.
1285	You Can Hire Someone Part Time To Help You With Your Book Keeping And All The Clerical Functions That Must Be Done In Any Business. Maybe You Can Hire Someone To Help Clean Your House And Shop For Your Groceries In Order To Free You Up To Focus More On Your Business."
1286	If You're Renting A Home Or Apartment With A Payment As Little As $550, You Can Qualify For A Brand New Home In Just 6 To 18 Months
1287	Running A Successful Online Business Is NOT A Purely Selfish Endeavor? Yes. You'll Be Able To Take Care Of Your Family And Enjoy Life Like You Never Have Before. But, You'll Also Be Doing So Much More. It's A Business And Lifestyle You Can Be Proud Of. Then You Help Improve The Economy Of Your State And Country By Having More Money To Give To Worthwhile Causes You Believe In.
1288	Why Most People Want It Regardless Of Whether Or Not They Will Ever Use It

1289	He Did The Whole "Big Launch" Thing And Gave Away Tons Of Valuable Information Already, And Is A Guy Now Earning Millions Of Dollars.
1290	What's The Abstract Thing They Want Behind Your Product Or Service
1291	P.S. The Quicker You Sign Up, The Higher On The Matrix You'll Be! Don't Let Any More Opportunities Slip Through Your Fingers, Get Started Today!
1292	I'm Exposing Some Unique And Very Hidden Strategies That Will Make It Easy For You To Get Started With A Very Low Budget, Little Or No Tech Experience, And You Really Don't Even Need Your Own Website.
1293	Be Part Of The 10% Elite Who Actually Want To Improve Their Lives For The Better And Take Action.
1294	Feel Like Giving Up Go Out On A Limb Or None
1295	If You Let This Cat Out Of The Bag Prepare For The Avalanche
1296	How We Made More Money At The End Of One Day Than At Both Our Day Jobs All Month
1297	Here's The Good News: You Can Set Up Your Automatic, Internet Wealth Machine And Have It Ready To Generate Cash In Less Than 48 Hours Even While You Keep Working At Your Current Job, It Is Not Just A Dream,
1298	Are The Pillars That Support Our Financial Future Starting To Crumble
1299	Why Waste Your Time And Money On Building Someone Else's Business? Even If You Never Get A Single Signup, They Will Benefit Greatly From Having Thousands Of Reps Like Yourself Advertising Their Business.
1300	You Are Going To Learn A Very Powerful Business Model That Can Be Replicated Over And Over Again. You Just Need To Be Willing To Learn And Believe In Yourself And Your Success.
1301	Sorry No Regrets As The Cut Off Time For This Offer Is Midnight Tomorrow
1302	Which Would You Rather Have Paper Clips Or Pay Per Clicks
1303	Good Luck As This Is Impossible To Find At Any Price
1304	We Come From Different Backgrounds And Different Ideas Of What Success Looks Like
1305	Tell A Story Be Specific And Give Them A Great Reason To Buy

1306	There Are Spineless People Out There Ripping Off All Your Products And Sharing Them With All Their Low Life Friends. And It Doesn't Matter If You Have Protected Your Downloads With A Special Script Or A Password Protected Area. Because...Once They Have "Legitimately Downloaded" Your Product, They Can Do Whatever They Want With It. And They Do It With A Big Grin On Their Face!
1307	Zero To Wealthy Is A Realistic Possibility Especially When You Have These Tools
1308	How A Free Software Program Can Create Cash On Demand Whenever You Open It Up And Use It... And Why This Underused Free Software On Your Computer Will Give You The Edge To Dominate Your Competition.
1309	Why 99% Of All Internet Marketers Still Don't Have A Clue About This Missing Link
1310	Despite My Best Efforts To Warn My Hosting Companies About The Launch And My Insistence That We Get The Maximum Amount Of Bandwidth Allowable, We Still Managed To Crash Not One But TWO SERVERS.
1311	It's A Great Feeling To Be Able To Spend Time With Your Family, Relax And Read A Book, Or Even Take Off For A Mini-Vacation Whenever You Feel Like It. The Feeling Of Freedom And Getting Rid Of That Habitual Stress Is Worth Whatever It Takes.
1312	Whose Dreams Are You Going To Build Yours Or Someone Else's
1313	Bonus Timer - If You Order Before The Timer Expires You're Guaranteed All Of The Following Bonus Offers. After That, I May Remove These Bonuses At Any Given Moment. Contact Me For Further Details...
1314	Build Massive Lists Of Highly Qualified Prospects By Using A Little Known Technique
1315	P.S. We Want You To Feel Proud For This Purchase Because We Know The Value Of This Solution Offered.
1316	How To "Ethically Steal" Winning Ideas And Top Secret Information From Your Most Successful Competitors. Discover Their Hidden Strategies On Selling, What Questions The Audience In Your Market Are Asking, And Other Confidential Data That Could Skyrocket Your Earnings.

1317	In Fact, Some Of His Strategies Were Returning Over 300% Or More. When He Decided To Partner Up And Bring His Knowledge To You - On A Silver Platter - Revealing Literally Everything He Knows About Traffic.
1318	The Psychological Danger Of Permanently Pigeonholing Yourself Into The Path of Poverty
1319	Don't Let This Amazing Deal Pass You By. Skip All Your Product Development Chores And Start Exercising Your Creativity In Producing Profits From Them!
1320	Takes Equal Effort To Sell A $9 Product Or A $4,995 Product
1321	SO...Before This Starts To Sound Like An ALL OUT Sales Pitch, Let's Get Back To The Story.. You Name It, I Tried It. It Wasn't Very Long Ago That I Was Probably In The Exact Same Situation That You Are In Today.
1322	People You've Never Seen Will Want To Put Money In Your Hand
1323	The Truth Is, These Stores Rely On The Fact That Most Buyers Will Buy More Than They Intended To, Buy Much More Than What They Have On Their List And Be Seduced Into Buying Sale Items Because They're On Sale.
1324	How To Make 24% - 68% Of Your Customers Immediately Increase Their Orders 25%-35% Just By Adding One Simple Page. (Very Slick And Powerful.)
1325	These Methods Have Never Been Taught Like This Anywhere, By Anyone, Which Makes It So Much Easier For New People Getting Started Like You To Start Succeeding Right Away. There Aren't Any Fancy Tricks, Software, Or Difficult Techniques That You'll Have To Learn. You Don't Have To Have Any Previous Experience.
1326	In Our FREE Heavy Hitter Report, We'll Show You How To Systematically Add Reps Into Your Business Right Now
1327	Now Tell Me, How Can You Grow A Quality List Of Subscribers If You Cannot Create A Professional Lead Capture Page? If You Don't Know How To Get Past List-Building Success, How In The World Can You Succeed?
1328	My Accountant My Friends And My Family Think I'm Insane For Doing This
1329	Tips That Make It Easier For Your Customers To Access Your OTO
1330	Wouldn't You Like To Know The Invisible Pirates Of Internet Marketing
1331	But I'm Not Going To Even Come Close To That Price

1332	If You're Looking To Start Your Own Home Based Business, I Have The Perfect One For You. Big Time Marketers Use And Generate Hundreds & Thousands Monthly With This Little Know Wealth Generating System
1333	Discover For Yourself How To Finally Pay Off Your Bills Get Out Of Debt And Run Your Own Successful Online Business.
1334	With This Success Cookie Cutter You Can Do It Over And Over
1335	This Information Can Truly Change Your Life Now It's Up To You
1336	What Ever Your Interest Passion Or Hobby We'll Show You How To Turn It Into Money
1337	When You Are Working Late The Boss Will Never Be Around When You Are Surfing The Net The Boss Will Always Drop By
1338	You'll Get Free Lifetime Upgrades Meaning Each Time A New Course Version Is Released You Can Download It Right From Your Member's Area Without Paying A Dime.
1339	Why A Title Tag Is The Single Most Important SEO Element
1340	How To Jump Start Your Brain When You Have Website Blockage
1341	The Paradigm I Want To Share With You Here Does Not Aim To Double The Value Of Your Time. It Aims To Increase The Value Of An Hour Of Your Time 1,000 Times Or More. In Fact, Your Time Is More Valuable Than Money. Time Is Not Something You Can Ever Get Back. Money Is. You Can Always Make More Money. But You Can Never Recover Lost Time.
1342	I Actually Give A Damn About Your Success And Won't Take No For An Answer
1343	Maybe All You Really Need Is A Swift Kick In The Rear
1344	Let's Face It, Blogs On The Topic Of Internet Marketing Are A Dime A Dozen. I'll Be The First To Admit It Takes A Lot To Impress Me. But Then There Are Some That Make Me Want To Come Back Again And Again Like This One.
1345	The Most Important Thing You Need To Know To Make Your Website Profitable
1346	Fill In The Blank Headline Formulas You Can Copy And Paste
1347	You'll Be Adding Powerful Content To Your Web Pages In No Time With This High Quality Audio Tutorial.
1348	Are Bills Filling Your Mailbox Want To Get Rid Of Them
1349	Get A Head Start On Everyone Else And Reap The Rewards

1350	Discover How I Increased The Sale Price Of My First Product By Ten Times And Still Made Four Times More Sales Than I Had At The Lower Price. Are You Charging Too Little For The Products You Put Your All Into Creating?
1351	Ready To Turn On The Light Switch That Guides You To Your Online Fortune
1352	7 Unique Ways To Make A Consistent Profit From Your Ezine
1353	If You Make It Easier To Pronounce It Will Be Easier To Re-member
1354	Have You Finally Reached Your Last Ditch Hail Mary Internet Marketing Moment
1355	Lead Capture Page Creator Turns You Into A List Building Monster Capable Of Generating Enormous And Ultra-Responsive Subscriber Lists, Hungry For Whatever You're Selling...All At Warp Speed!
1356	You're Future Starts Here But Only If You Take Action Now
1357	Get the Latest Marketing Information Delivered Right To Your Email Inbox
1358	The Contents Of This Package Were Originated And Created By Us
1359	This Is A Final Reminder That The Special Pre-Launch Early Bird Discount On 'Privileged Memberships' Ends Today - Friday (DATE) Midnight. Price TRIPLES Tomorrow - PLUS If You Join Today You'll Be Guaranteed Some Extra Unadvertised Bonuses (You Won't See These On The Site)
1360	Not Just What To Do But How To Do It Profitably
1361	What Will You Be Thankful For When You Wake Up Tomorrow
1362	When We Say It's Fast Easy And Affordable It's Our Name That's On the Line
1363	Just For Trying Out System We'll Send You 1,000 Targeted Leads
1364	Flip The Action Switch In Your Head From 'NO' To 'YES' - No Longer Will Overwhelmingly Big Tasks Paralyze You From Taking Little To No Action. Use Action Machine Pro To Break These Monsters Into Smaller, Bite-Sized Pieces You WANT To Eat!
1365	The Point Is, You Can Do Whatever You Want. And You Can Do It Whenever You Want. And More Than That, You Can Do It In Style. So If You Want To Hang Out On Yachts, You Can. You Want The Big House, You Can Have That Too... Or Maybe You're More Conservative? You Just Want To Put Your Kids Through The Best Schools, And Save A Little For Later In

	Life?
1366	Why He Needed To Speak Out And Reveal The Raw Truth About Internet Marketing
1367	Don't Have A Clue As To What You Should Do Next
1368	But I'll Tell You What This Is One Piece Of Software That You DO NOT Want To Pass Up Checking Out...I'll Be Using It For Sure. It's An INSANE Way To Build Buyers Lists With An Important Twist All On Total Autopilot...
1369	No Objections When You Tie The Benefit To The Solution You're Offering
1370	Use Your Content To Promote An Ebay Store.
1371	Learn To Write An Effective Online Press Release To Drive More Traffic
1372	Blog Empire And All Of The Content That Goes With It
1373	Today Add $10000 To Your Estate For The Price Of A New Hat
1374	Find Yourself Making Less Money Now That You're Working For Yourself
1375	If You Can Dream It We Can Help You Build It
1376	We May Not Change The World But We Can Help A Lot Of People
1377	Boost Your Conversion Rates With Pre-Sell Pages And Time Sensitive Bonuses
1378	Even New Retirees And Recent College Graduates Are Now Running Successful Businesses
1379	And They're Looking To You For Help. THAT Is The Basis Of A Long-Term Relationship, And THAT Is The Effect You Can Create With "Success In 10 Steps."
1380	High Quality Search Engine Friendly Directories The Ensure Natural Link Growth
1381	Apply This To Your World Of Dreams And Watch What Happens
1382	I'll Set Up New Campaigns From Start To Finish So That You Can Literally Just Watch Me Approach It The Correct Way.

1383	Most Importantly, Take Control Of Your Lifestyle And Financial Future... Is Right Here In This Package. And You're Mere Seconds Away From Tearing It Open And Seeing It Glow Before You
1384	If You're A Newcomer, Running A Business Can Be Taxing On Your Budget! But, With Affiliate Marketing, You Don't Need A Big Budget To Make It Work! You Can Simply Use A Variety Of Free And Low-Cost Marketing Methods To Generate Clicks To Your Affiliate Link.
1385	How To Eliminate Costly Mistakes Before You Make Them Virtually Guarantees You Stay On The Right Path!
1386	This Powerful Software Script Makes It Easier AND Cheaper Than Ever Before. You Can Now Effectively Advertise Your Products To A Group Of Prospects With A Simple Click Of Your Mouse.
1387	Sick And Tired Of All The Hype And Hassles Yet Need To Start Making Some Real Money
1388	I Stumbled Across A Very Simple Formula That Sells Products Like Crazy. If You're Interested In Selling Your Products By The Hundreds Or Even Thousands, Check Out This URL I Ran Across
1389	Create Viral Quizzes With Your Content To Test Your Audience's Knowledge.
1390	Write A Manifesto To Spread Your Ideas And Name All Over The Internet.
1391	We Buy Something We Want Based On Emotions, Then Justify And Rationalize Our Decision With Explanations In Our Mind. So When Writing Your Sales Copy For Your Products And Services, You Should Reach Out To People, Appeal To Their Emotions, Make Them WANT What You Have To Offer And Justify It With The Rest Of Your Copy.
1392	It's Difficult Enough To Make Money Through Momentary First Impressions If It's Not Exciting
1393	The Sales Letter Is Converting Between 2-9% Depending On The Focus Of The List... In Other Words, This Letter Is Doing *Very* Well At Converting Visitors To Sales!
1394	I Want To Personally Welcome You For Joining A Membership Where People Really Get It
1395	P.P.S. You Have 30 Days To Decide If This Solution Is THAT Good As Described Here Or Not. If At Any Time In Thirty Days You Decide This Script Was Not What You Needed Then You Will Get Your Money Back ASAP.

1396	Don't Forget To Leave A Comment If You Liked The Article / Free Report :) Or If You Have Any Questions If You Post Them Below I Will Be Happy To Answer Them Take Care Kind Regards (Your Name).
1397	Free eBook Exposes All The Lies Myths And Hype To Help You Finally Success Online
1398	For A Limited Time Only, You Can Advertise To My Private List Of Over 50,000+ Marketing Subscribers & Get New Leads And Customers For Your Business.
1399	Agree To Disagree Because You Don't Have To Win Every Argument
1400	Giving Up Now Could Be The Worst Decision You'll Ever Make. We Didn't Give Up And Look Where We Are Now... And Think Where You Can Be On Your Way To Just 10 Minutes From Right Now.
1401	Please Take Out A Piece Of Paper And List All The Benefits Of Being Completely Debt Free
1402	Isn't it Time For You To Hear The Whole Truth And Nothing But The Truth
1403	Why No Other Opportunity Can Hold A Candlestick To What We're About To Offer You
1404	No Long-Term Commitment! Set Up Your Account Today Absolutely FREE. Try It For 30 Days With Zero Cost And Zero Risk. Once You See How Powerful This System Is And How Easily It Can Save You Time While Increasing Your Sales, You Can Select The Option To Continue Using Our System For Just $17.95 Per Month.
1405	Why You Need To Learn How To Market To The Masses
1406	Want To Uncover Amazingly Simple Strategies To Spread Your Viral Reports Like Wildfire
1407	You'll Have The Know-How Required To Take Care Of These Sites And Tackle Basic "Techie" Problems Without Being At The Mercy Of A High-Priced Internet Nerd!
1408	The Reason 95% Of People Are Poor Is Because They Do This Backwards
1409	Big Problems With Duplicate Content Even If You Create Ten Versions Of Your Article For Ten Different Article Directories. You Still Only Really Have Ten Chances To Have Your Article Appear In The Search Engines.
1410	How To Take Control Of Your Financial Future And Turn Your Debt Into Real Wealth

105

1411	You Can Make Money Even If You Have Absolutely No Training To Speak Of Because My Proven And Tested System Introduces You To Several Opportunities So Easy - Even "Newbies" Can Make Money With Them.
1412	When Articles Aren't Unique They Don't Get Picked Up By The Search Engines. This Is Called The "Duplicate Content Penalty".
1413	Aside From The Extra Money I Earn I Love My Work Again
1414	If You're Like Us, You're Sick And Tired Of People "Showing" You An Income Opportunity And Then NOT Showing You How To Earn An Income With It.
1415	Its A Complete No Brainer... And The Best Part Is That This System Is So Easy To Follow And Implement That 'Rinsing & Repeating' It Every Time Is As Easy As Taking A Stroll Through The Park.
1416	This Means Not Only Do You Have A Good Size List To Email, You Also Have A Passive Residual Income From (Product) For As Long As They Maintain Their Upgrade Status.
1417	Things You Should Know Before You Bid On A Business Product From An Online Auction
1418	The Response To The Last Email I Sent Has Been Great. We Knew That The People Who Went Through The Course Were Excited About It, But We Could Never Have Guessed How Excited Everyone Else Was Who Heard About It!
1419	There's A Brand New Membership Site That Has 5 Websites You Get That Make Money For You Automatically - And You Can Get Them In Just 6 Minutes From Now - All With Just 1-Click!
1420	When You Learn How To Become A Good Marketer... You Will Never Be Out Of Work - No Matter How Bad The Economy Gets, How Competitive The Market Gets, Or How Much The Internet Changes
1421	Don't Just Dream About It Get Up And Make It Happen
1422	7 Moral, Ethical, & Perfectly Legal Ways To Increase Conversions By At Least 75%
1423	Don't Make The Foolish Mistake Of Ignoring Psychological Triggers That Make Money
1424	Someone Just Got Wind Of This Rumor And It's Spreading Like Wildfire
1425	We're Looking For Quality People Who Want To Improve The Quality Of Their Lives

1426	This Is By Far The MOST Important Thing I've Ever Taught. It's Literally As Easy As Saying..."Send It To www..." And Almost Instantly People Will Start Flooding To That Site!
1427	But, The Price Can't Stay This Low For Long... So, Get It Right Now While You're Thinking About It. Even Though It's A Steal At Twice The Price, Why Pay More Later When It's This Low Right Now?!
1428	Become A Benefactor To Many People By Using My Money Tools
1429	Men Who Know It All Are Not Invited To Read This Page
1430	Don't Believe All That Unadulterated Crap… That's Right, There's So Much Junk Polluting Our Internet These Days, And Many Of The Programs Dedicated To Adsense Fit Squarely In The 'Crap' Category.
1431	How This Simple Word Instantly Transformed Into My New Found Fortunes
1432	Most People Are So Caught Up In The Day-To-Day Mechanics Of Making It Through The Day; They Just Don't Have The Time Or Resources To Devote To Working On Their BIG PICTURE Of The Life They REALLY Want.
1433	Purchased Visitors And Bulk Emails Are So Generic, Untargeted, And Rehashed You're Better Off Trying To Win The Lottery Than Expect Results From Them
1434	But Once You've Witnessed What's Waiting For You On The Inside
1435	Why Site Review Authority Dot Org Notes 81.6% Of These Websites Were Found To Be Scams
1436	How Would You Like To Yank The Profits Right Out From Under Your Competition
1437	Here's The Only Way Left For Regular Guys/Gals Like You And Me To Increase Conversions By At Least 75%
1438	As You'll See In The Video, We've Given You An Easy To Use Traffic Generation Software That Is Powerfully Simple To Help Automate Your Traffic Generation. You'll Be Able To Upload Videos, Press Releases, And Submit Articles To Some Of The Best Sites On The Net. And Then You'll Be Able To Virally Spread Them Using Your Twitter And Digg Accounts At The Push Of A Button.
1439	Discover Blog And Ping Marketing And Learn How To Use It Effectively
1440	Quit That Dead End Job And Walk Away Making More Money Than Your Boss Did

1441	How A System Of Empty Boxes Can Be Stuffed With A Lot Of Money
1442	Rethink Your Future Online Before You Waste More Time And Money
1443	You Never Have To Purchase A Thing, Because What's The Point Of Starting An Online Business If It's Hard To Understand, It Costs You More Than You're Earning And It Interferes With Your Current Job And/Or Lifestyle?
1444	Sure, You Probably Don't Believe Me, And That's Fine. In Just A Second You'll See Evidence Of Exactly What I'm Talking About. And I've Got To Warn You - It's Going To Hit You Hard, Like A Straight Shot Right To The Gut. But Before We Get Into That, Let's Talk About You For A Sec...
1445	We Hope You're Grasping The Big Picture Here. This New Wireless Technology Allows You To Stay Connected To The Internet Nationwide, While Driving, Walking, Camping, Hunting, Fishing, Golfing, Home Or Office - Connect Anywhere!
1446	Free Book Tells You 12 Secrets To Increase Conversions By At Least 75%
1447	No Matter What Product Or Service Your Sell Here's An Honest Roadmap For Your Success
1448	7 Rapid Fire Tricks To 'Shortcut' Success That Will Have You Dancing All The Way To The Bank. And SO MUCH More!
1449	This One Idea Is Key To Making A Lot Of Money
1450	You Earn Multiple Streams Of Monthly Recurring Income As Members In Your Growing Organization Automatically Feed Into The 6 Progressive Level Core-Business After You.
1451	Grab Your 100% Free Home Business Secrets Report Now And I Will Show You How To Increase Your After Tax, Take Home Income By As Much As $200-$800 Or More Per Month.
1452	Are You New To The Internet And Don't Know How To Get Started In A Home Business Of Your Own?
1453	7 Must Haves For Your Site To Get Your Customers To Trust You
1454	The Point Being, These Websites Really Focus On The Huge Income Being Made And That YOU TOO Can Make That Kind Of Money, Just Like Those Pictured On Their Website.
1455	Each Member Of Our Team Of Experts Brings Their Unique Contribution To The Table And - With Profound Clarity - Explains How Easy It Is For You To Activate Your Own Personal Power.

1456	P.S.S. I'm Also Running A Contest Only During The Pre-Launch And Launch Period, In Addition To The Regular Commission, You Can Also Win Several Cash Prizes Even If You're Not The Top Affiliate.
1457	How Would You Like To Be Part Of The Solution And Not The Problem
1458	The #1 BIGGEST Mistake That Prevents You From Ever Reaching Real Success Online. Stop Falling Prey To This Trap Once And For All With A Simple, Yet Powerful Profit Pulling Strategy That Eliminates The Guesswork And Gives You A Step By Step Blueprint To Profiting Online.
1459	But If You're Interested In An EASY -- NO RISK Way To Build An Income Large Enough To Dramatically Improve The Quality Of Your Lifestyle... Sign Up Right Now And Get Started.
1460	How To Fix A Dead Website By Testing And Tweaking Your Advertising Campaigns
1461	No Matter What You Decide At The End Of Your 30 Day Trial, You Will Absolutely Better Understand How To Use Autoresponders To Increase Profits, Save Time, And Boost Efficiency. You Win!
1462	Would You Say We're Correct In Our Impressions Of Your Commitment So Far
1463	We Are Excited To Introduce To You A Revolutionary FREE MONEY Team System That Will Exponentially Increase Your 100% FREE INCOME By Utilizing The Power Of Internet Today.
1464	In Other Words, I'm Committing That Anyone Who Reads The Guide, Listens To The Audio, And Puts In A Good Faith Effort.
1465	This Software Is Your Complete Easy To Use Roadmap To Making Money Online...And If You Ever Have A Question Or Need Help...Just Click On "Ask A Question" And Contact Me!
1466	Each Of These Incredible Items Offer You A Highly Marketable Product. You Can Begin Selling Them As They Are Right Away, And Can Claim Authorship And Immediately Turn Them Into Your Own Original Product.
1467	It Was Just One Of Those Hit Me With A Ton Of Bricks Moments
1468	If You Want To Get Better, Faster And More Dependable Results From Being In Business, You'll Hear Him Discuss And Explain The Following In Terms Anyone Can Instantly Understand And Use.
1469	I Have Weird Friends Who Think I'm Weird And They're Nor-

mal

1470	I Could Try To Describe How You Are Taken By The Hand And Literally Walked Through Each Step Of The Process From Start To Finish.
1471	Product AD: Triple Discount Sale Take Our Super 70% Off, Bonus + 20% Off + Final Triple Discount + 10% Off
1472	Business Is About Profiting On Every Time Money And Investment Made
1473	Join Our VIP List -- 100% FREE. Who Else Wants To Discover The Secrets To A Massive, Passive Income. Give Us 60 Minutes And We'll Force Some Of The World's Top Marketing Experts To Reveal Their Most Profitable Methods For Building YOUR Business That Instantly Makes You Money.
1474	And Not Only Do I Tell You Exactly What To Do But I Also Give You The Reasoning Behind Every Step.
1475	Quick Questions Will Reveal An Operating Philosophy That Saves A Lot Of Money
1476	Golf, Fish, Hike, Kayak Or Boat To Your Heart's Content. Stay Home With The Kids Or Even Home School Them. Live Like A Bum, Buy A Beach House And Read, Lounge By The Pool. Sun And Relax By The Ocean – Everyday.
1477	Need A Steady Increase Of Quality Web Site Links Pointing To You Web Site
1478	Get Instant Access To Everything You've Seen Laid Out Before You Here, And Within Minutes You Can Be On Your Way To Life On Your Terms.
1479	You Can Add Your Programs To The Downline Builder Page So That The People You Refer Will Be Exposed To Your Businesses Or Affiliate Sites. This Is Unlimited Exposure To Anyone You Refer!
1480	Want The Best Marketing Tactics Without Having To Re-Mortgage Your House
1481	Pardon The Dust As I Install And Tweak A New Theme
1482	If You Want To Make More Money Put It Higher On The Page
1483	Are You Constantly Looking For New And Better Programs To Join
1484	Today I Want To Offer You An Incredible Selection Of Software & Scripts That Will Help You Achieve Success With Your Online Business At A Fraction Of The Regular Price... In Fact,
1485	Are You Finally Ready To Get Started And Make Real Money Online

1486	Are All Your Google Adsense Ads Still Residing All In One Basket
1487	Lastly, Our Team Has A Co-Op Like Nothing You Have Ever Seen In Your Life. The Only "Outdoor" Co-Op In The World. Wait Till You See It! This Is On Top Of All Other Ad Avenues In Place And In The Works.
1488	It's Time To Dig Deeper On This Very Important Subject Our Guests Will Be Talking Specifically About The PERSONALITY TYPES Of Your Potential Business Partners And How This Greatly Affects Your Business. If You Can Master This Skill It Will Send Your Business Into Hyperdrive.
1489	Surely There Was Something I Could Do?? I Really Felt Like I Could (And Should) Make A Difference. BUT I Knew From The Start It Wouldn't Be Easy...It's Just Me - One Person Against The Whole Well Oiled Machinery Of The Guru-World (Which, Admittedly, I Am Also Part Of!)
1490	Never Have To Worry How We're Going To Make The Next Car Or Mortgage Payment. It Means Not Worrying About Bills Or Debts. What Does Financial Freedom Mean To YOU?
1491	A Super-Secret (But Crazy Obvious) Way To "Spy" On What's Selling Like Hotcakes... And Grab Your Share Of The Over-flowing Profits. It's 100% Free, But Most People Completely Overlook It.
1492	Stop Throwing Your Money Down The Back Hole Of Internet Bankruptcy
1493	Amazing! Just Point And Click And You Can Be On The Way To Having Kick-Butt Sales Letters Because There's A Cus-tomer Born Every Minute.
1494	I Stopped Playing These Games LONG Ago! I'm Part Of (In My Opinion) The Single Best Company On The Market Today – Training To Die For, A Creative And Ingenious Product Line And A Compensation Package That Is Making Me A VERY Wealthy Man...But I'm Not Going To Tell You About It...
1495	Once You Have Taken This Step And You Have Your First Domain Name, You Are On The Road To Success All You Need Now Is The Website And The Product - Which He Will Show You In The Next Videos.
1496	Is It Really Enough To Just Have A Product? Of Course Not! You Need A Website To Sell It On! Unfortunately Most People Think They Have To Know Everything About HTML And Web Design Before They Can Do This.

1497	The 7 Critical Things Any Affiliate Website Needs To Have To Be A Winner. Miss Just One And Your Profits Will Go Downhill Faster Than A Landslide.
1498	Unless You Win The Lottery The Fact Is You're Not Going To Be A Millionaire Overnight
1499	Making Money Online Is Simple If You Still To The 3 Essential Basics. Number 1: You Must Drive Traffic To Your Site. Number 2: You Must Have A Sales Letter Or Lead Capture For Higher End Products. Number 3: You Must Follow Up And Make Repeat Sales.
1500	While Veterans In Niche Building Will Get A Lot Out Of This Book, This Has Been Written For Those Who Haven't Figured It Out Yet, Those Who Want A Clear Defined Path. Most Books Give You The Theory, But Leave Out The 'Here's The Exact Steps You Need To Go Through', We've Made Sure That You Can Follow This Through, Step By Step.
1501	Still Have Nothing To Show For Your Blood Sweat And Money Online
1502	You're Just Moments Away From Starting Your Quick Start Instant Training That Allows You To Set Up A Profitable Online Business Right Away… Plus A Ton Of Other Amazing (And Free) Bonuses To Help You Succeed Fast…
1503	Every Day 100,000's Of People Are Looking For Ways To Make Extra Money. They Voluntarily Enter Their Names And Contact Information Onto 1,000's Of Web Sites Around The World Hoping To Find That One Golden Opportunity.
1504	Experience The Easiest Least Resistant Way To Generate Tons Of Targeted Traffic
1505	What If I Could Scramble Your Brain And Suck Out Unlimited Money Ideas
1506	Tired Of Waiting Around For Your Marketing Campaigns To Become Profitable
1507	There Is An Empty Chair At Our Table With Your Name On It
1508	Are Customers Running From Your Site Like A Skunk In The House
1509	Every Day We Bring Together A Remarkable Array Of Amazing Products At No Cost. Our Powerful Proprietary Systems And Techniques Scour The Earth, Searching Out An Incredible Range Of Hidden Freebies.

1510	Hey, I Am Not Going To Use Some Phony Scarcity Tactic And Tell You That I Am Only Making So Many Copies Available Or I Will Pull This Offer Sometime In The Future Because You Will Get Lifetime Updates Every Six Months Or So As The Traffic Exchange Community Grows And Evolves.
1511	I'd Like To Give You Some Golden Nuggets Of Crucial Information
1512	If You're Easily Offended By Stories With Adult Themes, Including Talk Of Obscene Amounts Of Cash…You May Want To Click Away Right Now. But If You Can Stomach The Offensiveness Obscenity The Ride Will Be Worth It.
1513	We Would Like To INVITE You To This Special Event Where You Are Going To Receive A Minimum Of 2,500 Unique Visitors To Your Site Every Single Month By Just Joining Us In The Biggest Event Of The Self Improvement Industry. All You Have To Do Is Follow Our Procedures Below Taking ONLY 5 Minutes.
1514	Use Scientific Marketing Methods To Find Out What People Need Or Want To Find Out What People Are Willing To Pay For. "Scientific Advertising" Is The Term Used By The Great Claude Hopkins, The Father Of Modern Advertising When He Basically Invented Direct Marketing About A Century Ago.
1515	While I Might Be A Little Crazy For Exposing Some Profitable Niches, I Can Make Money In Others, And I'm Sure I've Got A Decent Foothold Already.
1516	Optimize Your Real Potential Of Current Skills Level Of Expertise Or State Of Your Business
1517	Work As Hard As You Want Or Let This Site Sell Itself
1518	The Most Important Element REQUIRED Near The Bottom Of EVERY Sales Page Guaranteed To Increase Conversions
1519	We Couldn't Have Been Able To Do This Six Months Ago
1520	Displays Random Featured Products Every Time The Front Page Is Visited
1521	Let Me Fill You In On Another Inside Secret Mistake I Made Early In My Career
1522	First, So As Not To Waste Each Others Time Any Further, If Adult Content Offends You, Then Just Delete This Right Now And Best Of Luck To You!
1523	How Much Are YOU Earning From Your Adsense Account Right Now? I Think You Will Agree, You Don't Get Ads To Convert Like That From Pay Per Click.

1524	As A Fellow Marketer I Can See Why This Collection Is Going Fast
1525	Every New Website Needs To Be Burped Along The Path To Prosperity
1526	It's Really Is That Easy To See If You're A Winner Or A Loser
1527	People You Don't Know Will Want To Be Knocking On Your Door
1528	Internet Marketing Success Is A Numbers Game. In Other Words, For You To Make Online Riches, You Need A System Or An Idea That Propels You To Online Success, Something That Will Be A Revelation To Your Bank Account.
1529	Make Sure You Attend The Live Welcome Orientation Webinar With Me Tomorrow (DAY) At XX PM Pacific / XX PM Eastern. Here's How To Login: Registration Web Link: (Example) https://www1.gotomeeting.com/register/XXXXXX
1530	How You Can Address Your Prospect And Qualify Them To Read Your Sales Letter. Find Out How You Can Be Personal, Be In Touch, And Understand Your Prospect To The Fullest - Even If You Don't Know Him! This May Sound Absurd, But I Will Show You How You Can Understand And Confirm Your Prospect's Challenges By Addressing What He Is Already Going Through That Would Encourage Him To Read Your Sales Letter From Top To Bottom!
1531	Take Action Steps To Create Your Product In The Next 30-Days
1532	Collecting And Counting Cash Is The Most Difficult Part Of My Business
1533	I Think This Does An Excellent Job Of Explaining Things Step-By-Step Even If You're The Rawest Of Beginners In This Field. Of Course, If You Do Have Some Experience, You Simply Skip Over The Parts You Know Already, But Everything You Need To Know Is In There.
1534	Making Money Isn't Hard IF You Know What When Where & How
1535	Awesome - What More Can I Say I Will Use This Exact Strategy To Drive More Traffic To My New Membership Website. This Is Just One More Tool In My Arsenal.
1536	Have You Waited Too Long Only To See Sorry We Are All Sold Out
1537	This Is What My New Coaching Program Is Designed To Help You Do. I Honestly Believe It Can Make The Biggest Difference In Someone's Life That's Start A New Online Business.

1538	As You Can Clearly See, This Training Program Delivers The Goods! Every Tip, Tactic, And Strategy That We Have Personally Used To Consistently Bank Fat Paychecks Month After Month, After Month Has Been Included.
1539	Tweak Your Conversions To High Profits For DIRT CHEAP, Even If You're On A Shoe String Budget. You'll Discover How To Get The Greatest Discounts On Traffic Sources And How To Literally REMOVE ALL RISK For You.
1540	After More Than 4.5 Years Of Intelligence Gathering, Testing, And Sweat, We've Finally Completed 'The Language Of Millionaires...It Contains Years Worth Of Expert Knowledge And Insider Information You Will Never Find Elsewhere!
1541	I Can't Name One Marketer Online Who Isn't Passionate About What They Do... And Thankful Every Day That They Put Their Hesitation Aside And Just Went For It.
1542	Why So Many People Quit When Walking On The Hard Path
1543	You Should Be Asking - Can I Really Afford This Ignore Information
1544	The Interesting Challenge We All Have Is In Recognizing Our Own Strengths
1545	We Challenge You To Find Any Other Product On The Market That Covers This Business Course As Comprehensively And Systematically As We Do. You'll Be Wasting Your Time, Because No Other Course Is Available With The Detailed Explanation And Insight As This One. You Simply Cannot Find Another A To Z Course On This Subject.
1546	Allow Affiliates To Custom Brand Their Affiliate Link In The PDF.
1547	By Invite Only! The Video Training Program Is Closed To The General Public And Is Now By Invitation Only
1548	How Many Years Will It Take Before You Hear This Wake Up Call
1549	Create Greeting Cards With The PLR Graphics, Quotes Or Affirmations.
1550	Trigger Headlines You Should Be Aware Of And How You Can Use Them In Your Favor. It Is Said That A Headline Is The Most Important Component Of A Sales Letter, So Important That It Decides Whether You Make Or Lose A Sale. All Professional Sales Letter Writers, Knowing Or Unknowingly, Use Any Or All Of The 5 Different Headlines In Their Sales Copies. Discover What They Are, And You Wouldn't Find Yourself Guessing What Qualifies As A Great, Attention-Grabbing Headline!

115

1551	What Will It Take For Your To See The Big Picture Before It's Too Late
1552	Building Your Own Website Is The Cornerstone Of Any Online Business. If You Can't Do It You're Potentially Handing Over Thousands Of Dollars Each Years To Your Competitors Who CAN Build Their Own Websites.
1553	Do I Need To Create A Product To Really Be Successful
1554	Here's Everything You Need To Get Your Information Marketing Business Off The Ground
1555	A Complete Guide To Take Your Affiliate Earnings To The Next Level... Using Cutting-Edge, Timely Techniques To Create A Huge Income Stream For Yourself...On Autopilot.
1556	Well, I Knew That If I Wanted To Make Real Money Online Then I Had To Do Something That Nobody Else Was Doing... I Needed To Find A Niche. So I Spent The Best Part Of The Next 18 Months Scouring The Internet And Trying All Kinds Of Stupid Ideas, While Desperately Looking For The Ideal Online Business... And Thankfully, Just Before All My Money Had Run Out, I Eventually Found It.
1557	Use Videos To Get Hundreds Of Visitors A Day For Free
1558	The Guide Is NOT Designed To Help You Get Rich Fast Or Become An Internet Millionaire - Mostly Because I Have No Idea How To Do That.
1559	Once You Understand How This Works You'll Wonder Why It Took You So Long To Get Started
1560	What Is Going On In Your Prospect's Head? Why Does A Person All Of A Sudden Want To Look At Network Marketing As The Hopeful Answer To All Their Prayers? There Isn't One Right Or Wrong Answer Here, But I Can Tell You One Thing... People Are 100% Predictable.
1561	Most People Are Always Looking For A Way To Make Money Online
1562	Perhaps The Biggest Bargain You'll Ever Get Your Hands On If They're Still Available
1563	Don't Put All Of Your Marketing Eggs In One Basket, Unless They Just Won't Stop Pushing The BUY Button.
1564	It's Really Unfair How Someone So Unethical Can Consistently Make So Much Money

116

1565	Want To Know How You Can Milk Google For Penny Clicks That You Can Recycle Over And Over For 1000% Returns? Learn The Different Aspects Of Profiting With Google Adsense That Can Help Make You Serious Income For Life.
1566	Ever Wonder Why One Person Succeeds And Another Fails Or Why Someone Has Massive Success In A Company, Then Leaves, Goes Someplace Else, And Starts To Duplicate That Success Over And Over With Another New Idea?
1567	Everyone Is Dead Wrong About List Building...Including How To Create An Instant Cash Producing Squeeze Page Which Puts Money Deposited Directly Into Your Paypal Account In Just Hours From Scratch.
1568	We Are Not Human Beings Going Through A Temporary Spiritual Experience. We Are Spiritual Beings Going Through A Temporary Human Experience. This Is What We Are Put On This Earth To Do Anyway. Have A Great Day And Bless Someone Else In Some Little Way Today!
1569	What If You Never Had To Worry About Duplicate Content Again
1570	You Don't Need A Lot Of Money To Get Started Rolling Up Your Online Sales
1571	Bottom Line – This Works But Only If You Apply Action
1572	For People Who Want To Increase Conversions By At Least 75%
1573	These Amazing Resources Will Allow You To Put This Information To Use Immediately In Your Own Business! Where Else Can You Get An Internet Marketing Education With PLR Rights For A Fraction Of The Cost Of The Products Themselves?
1574	The Answer Was As Clear As A Bell Right In Front Of Me
1575	Since It's Your Product You Can Set The Price Of This Huge Course To Whatever You Want. Video Courses Like This Can Easily Go For $37 To $67 And More If You Made It Into A Physical DVD Product.
1576	Even If You're A Newbie You Can Become Extremely Successful With This System
1577	By Concentrating On One Aspect Of Growing Your Business Per Learning Session, You Will Accomplish Far More, And Enjoy Much Greater Success In A Shorter Period Of Time.

1578	Thousands Of People Just Like You Are Using The Internet, Right Now, To Live The Lives They've Always Wanted - And You Can Too ... Even If You're An Absolute Beginner, Even If You Don't Have A Technical Bone In Your Body, And Even If You've Never Managed To Make A Single Cent Online!
1579	If You're Ready To Plow Internet Fields Plant The Seeds You'll Enjoy Reaping The Harvest
1580	When You Take Time To Really Think About It, And Take A Hard Look At The Numbers, You'll See That Making The Kind Of Income You've Been Dreaming About, Is Actually Much More Within Your Reach Than You Thought.
1581	P.S. With This Incredible Matrix Feature, You'll Get A New, Random List Each And Every Day! You Could Wake Up To-morrow And Have Access To The Entire List!
1582	There's Such A Thing A Spillover Your Reason To Join Now
1583	What Are You Going To Do With All The Extra Cash flow
1584	Let's Think About It For A Second... What Are Your Alterna-tives? What Else Could You Buy For $77? Another Lame Get-Rich-Quick Ebook, Couple Of Video Games Or DVD? Maybe Even A Couple Nights Out With Your Friends. None Of Them Will Make You Buck One. And That's Why You're Here Right? You Finally Want To Make Some Serious Money Online?
1585	Click Here To Get 1 Million Guaranteed Real Visitors For Free
1586	Not Really Committed To Success? Then You Should Be Honest To Yourself, Stop Wasting Your Time And Leave This Page Right Now.
1587	Continue To Alter Your Words Until You Get The Response You Want
1588	I'd Like To Personally Invite You To My Next Live Call
1589	You Wouldn't Drive To Prison If Freedom Was A Choice, So Why Feel Like A Prisoner At Work?
1590	Click This Link To Find Out Who He Is And See The Actual Program He Taught Me That I Used To Create My One-Page Sales Letter!
1591	How Many Times Have You Tried Following Some "System", Only To Find Yourself Stuck, Not Able To Get It Working? Frustrating Isn't It?
1592	All You Need Is A Proven System One That Works For The Average Joe And Jane.

1593	Not Everyone Wants To Work For Themselves, And I Understand That - But For Those Who *Are* Interested In Creating A Life Of Freedom, This New Guide Will Help You More Than Anything Else We Offer.
1594	Once You Understand It You'll Decide How Best To Profit For It
1595	They Can Be Distributed To Anywhere In The World And They Can Be Automatically Downloaded Without You Being There So You Can Make Money Even While You Are Sleeping.
1596	What I'm About To Share With You Should Probably Be Considered Illegal But It Isn't Yet
1597	Today Add $10,000 To Your Estate For The Price Of A New Hat
1598	You Going To Have To Ask What Are Their Perceived Options
1599	Learn The Diseases Every Online Marketer Should Know About Before They Strike
1600	I'll Look At Your Fundamental Business Building Components, Your Current Profit Performance, Your Company Purpose (Or Lack There Of). I'll Separate The "Theories" From The Truth. The Opportunities From The Problems. We'll Clearly Discuss What All This Analysis Reveals As I Interpret My Findings, For You --- Again, You Won't Be Charged A Penny For Me To Do This.
1601	Video Is An Extremely Powerful Tool And Is Something That Every Website Should Be Using In One Way Or Another.
1602	While Everyone Was Failing Miserably How Did We Continue To Keep Reaping In The Profits
1603	Don't Need To Know - No Time - Not Interested Enough To Care
1604	You're Getting A Chance To Ride Co-Pilot With Him As He Asks What Really Works When It Comes To Reaching The Dreams You Never Thought You Could Accomplish!
1605	Remember Not To Use Outrageous Or Unbelievable Claims In Your Ad Copy. People Are Too Savvy Online And Won't Believe You.
1606	Are You Spending Too Much Of Your Money Just For Your Website's Ads
1607	Never Be Stuck Again For Fresh Ideas Even If You Think You're Not Creative, Hate Writing, Or Have Difficulty Coming Up With High Converting Ads, Headlines, Subject Lines, Bullet Points, And Article Titles With The Ultimate Swipe File 3.0.

119

1608	Break Free From Your Constant Web Traffic Struggles With This Amazing New Technology That Gives You Viral Advertising, Web Traffic, And Solo Emailing All In One!
1609	If You're Interested In An EASY -- NO RISK Way To Build An Income Large Enough To Dramatically Improve The Quality Of Your Lifestyle... Sign Up Right Now And Get Started.
1610	You Can Be Well On Your Way To Making A Great Part-Time Or Full Time Income Online Or... You Could Be In The Exact Same Spot You Are Right Now. It's Your Choice!
1611	Like To Get Paid Big Time Every time Someone Sneezes Or Blinks
1612	How To Burn Off Bloated Website Fat Cells In Less Than 1 Minute
1613	Figure Out The Words They Are Saying To Find Their Button
1614	Full International Master Resale Rights (MRR), You Can Sell The Rights To Others To Sell The Package, And They Can Sell The Right To Others To Sell The Package Any Where In The World.
1615	How To Develop A Portfolio Of Simple Little Websites That Create More Streams Of Income
1616	This One You'll Want To Print, Frame And Hang On The Wall - It's That Good!
1617	All Of This, Comes With A 100% Satisfaction Guarantee...And For The Ridiculously Low One Time Investment Of Just $47 If You Act Right Now!
1618	All You Have To Do To Become Rich And Successful Now Is Save This And The Following Pages And Read Them Through Carefully.
1619	If You Know Where And What To Look For You Won't Get The Shaft
1620	I Really Want You To Make A Lot Of Money With This
1621	Non Reciprocal One Way Linking Pointing Directly To Your Web Site
1622	Discover The Niches And Keyword Phrases That Give You The Greatest Odds Of Making The Most Money Possible In The Shortest Amount Of Time.
1623	When You Are Finally Done With All Of Your Chores, All You Want To Do Is Plop On The Sofa, Kick Off The Shoes And Relax,

1624	2 Simple Marketing Tactics To Implement And Incorporate Into Your Business Today To Have Prospects Approaching You – Instead Of You Approaching Them.
1625	Are You Sick And Tired Of Being Lead Down More Dead End Wild Goose Chases
1626	Why Your Promotional Materials And Templates Should Look And Feel Similar
1627	It Doesn't Matter How Great Your Product Is Or How Talented Your Affiliates Are ... If They Are Not Motivated, You Are Not Going To Make The Money You Need To Live The Wealthy Lifestyle You've Been Dreaming About.
1628	Yeah, The Above Paragraph Came Out Easy Because I Have Had To Write And Say That For Years To Explain The Simple System. It Works - Period
1629	Maybe This Sounds "Corny" But I Truly Care About Your Success. So, Here's How We Get Our First Win-Win, And How You Can Get This Powerful Package In Your Hands Right Now... With An Extra $50 Off.
1630	Getting The Maximum Amount Of Traffic In The Least Amount Of Time (It Took Me Ten Years To Develop This Plan. I Recently Had To Change It Because Of Innovative Software Designed For Surfers. That's Just One Reason Why I Am Going To Be Constantly Updating This Book.)
1631	As The Internet Grows And Develops, One Thing Is Becoming Evident. We Cannot Ignore The Fact That Social Media Is Taking Over The Internet.
1632	I Still Wanted To Get Away From My Job, And Out Of My Tiny Apartment, So I Didn't Stop Looking For Other Ways To Make Money. Every Night I'd Finish Work, Rush Home, And Be Glued To My Computer - Just Scouring The Internet, Looking For The One Thing That Could Actually Make Me Some Money...
1633	Hi! It Would Be Really Cool If You Could Leave Honest Feedback About The Product - It Helps Me Know If I'm On The Right Track. If I'm Not, I Often Record New Content Covering Any Omission. It Also Helps Other Buyers Decide If The Purchase Is Right For Them. You Can Visit The Sales Thread Here:
1634	Listen, This Is Not Some Run Of The Mill, "Old Fashioned" Coaching Program. This Is Not About Theory Or Reading A Bunch Of PDF's. This Is About Working With My Team On My System Which Has Been Proven Time And Time Again To Bring In Boatloads Of Traffic And Sales For Me.

1635	A Compete And Proven Business Model You Can Follow To Build An Affiliate Empire That Runs On Virtual Autopilot.
1636	The Medium Of The Message Changed. Instead Of Billboards, It's Banner Or Text Ads...Letters Are Now Emailed...Web Sites Replace Brochures And Full-Color Catalogues...And Live Chat With Customer Service Replaces 800 Numbers, Etc
1637	I Really Don't Hold Anything Back. This Is The Real Deal. This Is The Hard-Hitting Stuff I Personally Used To Build An Online Empire. I Don't Dummy-Down Any Of The Information Like Many Other Products Do. I Don't Waste Time Explaining Basic Principles. I Assume You Already Know Them And Dig Right Into What You Need To Do To Make Money. There Are Also A Ton Of Other Killer Bonuses Included In This Package That Could Be Worth A Fortune.
1638	With The Extra Cash Flow You'll Be Able To Hire Experts
1639	Own A Wide Collection Of Automated Sales Agents And Have An Army Of People Promote Your Business 24 Hours A Day, Non Stop.
1640	She Was Also Lamenting The Fate Of Thousands And Thousands Of Other Internet Marketers Who Weren't Privileged (Nor Had The Money To Afford) To Have A Good Mentor.
1641	Whether You Are Looking To Increase Sales Of An Existing Product, Or You Are Planning To Launch A New Product And Want To Ensure Your Sales Will Be As High As Possible.
1642	Looking Back On Last Year There Are Many Things I Wish I Had Done Better, And Many Things I Am So Glad I Did Do, And That I Will Most Certainly Do Again And Expand Upon This Year.
1643	Manual, Slow And Tedious Traffic Generation Strategies Are A Thing Of The Past. If You Want To Get In On The Cutting Edge In Traffic Generation Tactics, And Solidify Your Position In The Marketplace, You Need To Begin Implementing These Surefire - Instant - Free - And Revolutionary Traffic Strategies Today!
1644	And If You Haven't Already, You Can Download My New Report," Affiliate Marketing" While You're There.
1645	Have You Heard About It? I Am Not Kidding. This Is Really Possible And It's Happening! What If You Can Get More Than One Sign-Up A Day? You Do The Math!

1646	Control Your Time Instead Of It Controlling You - Use Action Machine Pro Helps To Become More Aware Of How And Where You Spend Your Time Each Day. As You Become More Aware Of Your Habits, You Easily Discover Ways To Use Your Time More Productively, And Eliminate Previously Hidden Time-Wasters.
1647	Don't Worry About Getting This Perfect Just Let It Start Making Money
1648	So If You've Already Got Blogs That Are Struggling To Earn A Few Dollars Or You're Sick Of Spending Thousands Of Dollars On Google Adwords Or Other Paid Advertising Then You Need To Read Every Single Word On This Page.
1649	When You Consider That A "Baby Boomer" Will Retire Every 8 Seconds Over The Next 20 Years, The Stage Is Set For The Greatest Economic Opportunity For Home Business Owners The Internet Has Ever Seen.
1650	Why They Will Want To Fight Even Harder To Avoid Losing The Opportunity To Buy
1651	Are You Ready To Turn Your Failure With Adwords Around, To Finally Discover The Clickbank Code That Until Now Has Eluded You?
1652	I Truly Believe You Can Make As Much Money As You Wish Providing You Have The Desire
1653	It Doesn't Have To Be Either Or It Can Be Both
1654	Why On Earth Have You Settled For Just Sitting On The internet Sidelines
1655	Hot To Use Your "Marketer's Eye" To Spot The Hidden Value In Websites—And Turn Them Into Cold, Hard Cash In Your Pocket...
1656	Get The Script Right Now (Just Click The Link Below) And Start Using It. If You're Not Thrilled Just Ask For Your Money Back.
1657	I Further Understand This $100 Off Coupon Won't Be Around For Long, And If I Take Action Now I Ensure I Can Buy This Product At The Special Price Of Only $97 Before It Is Too Late! With That Said I'm Clicking On The Add To Cart Button Below To Secure My Private Label Rights Package At The Discounted Price!
1658	Yes! I Also Understand That If I Invest In This FREE Course Right Now
1659	For A Limited Time, I'm Dropping The Price Below $100 And Charging Just $67 For The Entire System.

1660	Thank You For Visiting This Website To Learn About An Amazing System And How You Can Earn Over $4,000 In 7 Days Without Ever Recruiting, Joining Any MLM's, Matrixes, Building Downlines Or Talking To A Single Person At All. This Exact System Has Been Utilized For The Last Three Years To Make Big Bucks Real Fast For Lots Of People Just Like You...So Be Sure To Read Every Single Word On This Page...It's That Important!
1661	Step Away From Lame Replicated Affiliate Sites And Make More Money
1662	Create Simple Little One Page Articles To Promote Affiliate Products That Pay You Regular Commissions.
1663	Not A Tech Nerd? Not A Problem, Either If You're Reading This, Then You Know How To Navigate The Web And Use Email. If You Know More Than That, Great. But You Really Know All You Need Already.
1664	I Used To Help All The Other Internet Marketers Get Rich
1665	With All Of The HYPE That Is Out There On The Internet To-day, You Want To Believe That JUST ONE PROGRAM Could Actually DO What It Promises. This Is Where We Come In To The Picture.
1666	The Coolest Way To Heat Up Your Marketing Approach While Be Energy Efficient
1667	How To Find An "Information Hunger" You Can Feed. This Is So Easy To Do, It'll Shock You. No More Wondering What Your Product Needs To Satisfy...It's All Right In Front Of You, Just Begging To Be Exploited For Big Bucks.
1668	Affiliate Marketing Can Give You The Ability To Cash In From Anywhere, Anytime, And Gives You The Ability To Fire Your Idiot BOSS And His Crappy J-O-B.
1669	We Know The Commission Potential Here Is Pretty Good Al-ready But There Is Potential To Earn Even MORE.
1670	New Discovery Reveals How To Increase Conversions By At Least 75%
1671	If It Wasn't A Matter Of Money What Kind Of Business Would Make Your Life Happier
1672	Are You Ready To Stop Searching, And Finally Get Some Real Answers To Your Questions About How To Generate A De-cent Income Online?
1673	As The Economy Makes Corrections So Should Your Bank Account Be Prepare For Prosperity

124

1674	If You're Not Testing And Tracking Your Results You're Ignoring The Gold Under Your Own Feet
1675	Relationships Are How Money Is Made Online...The Internet Moves So Fast Sometimes It's Hard To Keep Your Fingers On The Pulse Of What Is Happening Online.
1676	Make Time For Your Dreams - Are You Neglecting Your Dreams And Letting Everything Else Gobble Up Your Limited Time, Energy, And Resources? Use Action Machine Pro To Make Time Every Day To Take Even A Little Action To Move You Closer To Things You Want In Life!
1677	How Many Of These Marketing Mistakes Have You Made Just Today
1678	It's Amazing When You Work Towards Something With All Of Your Heart And Intention And Truly, Magic Happens.
1679	What You Can Or Can't Do With Different Types Of Resell Rights Products. This Is An Important Part You Don't Want To Miss. Not Abiding With The Rights Of Resell Rights Products Will Lead To Serious Legal Cases.
1680	All The Things You Should Watch Out For When Buying Content For Your Website To Make Sure You Get The Best Content Possible And Your Moneys Worth.
1681	How Many Programs Have You Joined That Didn't Pay You A Penny
1682	Ultimate Testimonials. Discover How We've Taken The Number One Method Of Improving Customer Faith In Your Product Into The Future, And How You Can Do It Too With Very Little Effort On Your Part. (This Has Shown To Double Our Sales With Specific Products And Services).
1683	How Much Should You Pay For A Good Pair Of Binoculars
1684	Don't Try To Talk Them Into Buying Something They Don't Want
1685	A Revolutionary Modernized Money Making Program For You. Get Ready With Your Optin Email Lists To Due Battle For Unlimited Orders In Crusade Mode Via Your Site Right Now
1686	You Have The Ultimate Power In Your Own Hands And You May Not Even Know It
1687	SEO, Or Search Engine Optimization Is The Be-All-End-All Of Traffic Generation. The Two Go Hand In Hand. This Is Because, In Order To Gain Traffic To Your Site Your Articles, Your Advertisements And Your Website Must All Be Search Engine Optimized.

1688	Turn Your Interests, Hobbies, Passions, Or Knowledge Into A Six Or Seven Figure Income! That's Right, We'll Give Your Everything You Need To Know In Order To Quickly Start Bringing In 5-Figure Per Month Paychecks!
1689	The Top 10 Ideal Resources For Every Online Business Committed To Becoming Wealthy
1690	How To Create The Perfect Autoresponder Follow-Up Messages To Turn Browsers Into Buyers
1691	This Report Will Show You How To Instantly Enhance Your Conversion Rates
1692	Would You Like To MULTIPLY Your Web Traffic...And Your CLICKS And CONVERSIONS? If You Want More Targeted Visitors To Your Website But Think It's Too Difficult Time Consuming Or Expensive You're Not Alone. In Fact Nearly 70% Of The Internet Marketers We Surveyed Said That Generating Web Traffic Is Their #1 Challenge.
1693	Revolutionary Traffic Report Reveals Secrets That Most People Will Never Now About Making Money With Traffic Exchanges!"
1694	Critique Your Content Or Write Your Own Commentary By Playing The Devil's Advocate.
1695	If You Can Fill Out This Simple Form You Can Easily Customize This Program
1696	Let's Take This Next Step Together Through A Series Of Adjustments Providing Peace Of Mind
1697	I Know What This Is Going To Do For Your Business
1698	Looking To Make Hordes Of Easy Cash Selling Other People's Products Online And Dreamt Of A System That Totally Automates And Accelerates The Difficult Task Of Building Your Marketing List?
1699	Your Download Information Will Be Sent To The Email Address You Entered Above, In The Next Few Minutes. If You Don't See It, Please Check Your Spam Folder.
1700	How To Clearly See The Truth Beyond The Smoke And Mirrors Of Their Lies
1701	Meanwhile, I'll Be Sitting Back Grinning As The Chaos Ripples Through The Online Money Making Industry.
1702	Remember You're Getting To Try Out The First 30 Days For Free RISK-FREE
1703	Working For A Living Doesn't Work Anymore Unless You Want To Be Poor

1704	It's Best To Use First Person Point Of View. If You Are Offering Advice, Second Person Point Of View Is Often A Wise Choice. Third Person Point Of View Can Seem A Little Too Impersonal And Academic; However, It Certain Articles, This Actually Works Well.
1705	P.S. I'm Not Kidding When I Say This Won't Be Free For Long. If You've Been Listening To All The Marketing Talk Lately They Keep Talking About "Moving The Free Line".
1706	And What If We Told You That We've Already Cornered This Research For You And Hand You The List Of Keywords On A Silver Platter... For Each And Every Product You Promote?
1707	Are You Living The American Dream Or Just Playing The Victim Card
1708	How To Make Money Writing, Even If You're Not A Great Writer. You May Be Surprised At How Easy It Is To Make Money Writing. You Don't Even Need To Have Scholar-Level Writing Skills.
1709	You're Going To Discover Exactly How I Made A Million Dollars
1710	What Would Happen If I Shared One Neat Trick That Would Get You Loads Of Visitors
1711	1:14 a.m. - Caller Reports Hitting An Intruder In The Head With An Axe. Notes That Intruder Was In The Mirror
1712	Just Like A Quality Home Your Website Needs A Strong Solid Foundation To Prosper
1713	Believe Me... The Training Alone Is Worth One Hundred Times The Price Of Your Subscription. Will Have Unlimited Access To Our Members Area Where You Will Learn:
1714	The Internet Is About To Change Again So You Better Well Prepared
1715	Because I Know This New Guide Won't Be For Everyone, I'm Creating A Special Guarantee To Make Sure People Can Use It.
1716	You Can Wish For Anything But Without Your Action It's Only A Dream
1717	It's Really That Simple. Not Selling Products = No Check. Yes, Even The Big Wigs Have To Sell Lots Of Products To Get The Big Checks.
1718	Let Me Cut to The Chase Here, If You Follow These Simple Steps and Start Applying SEO to your Websites, You Will Be Automatically Ahead of 90 Percent of your Competition

1719	Got An Affiliate Program? Recruit Affiliates And Build Your Affiliate Army! As You Know, The Nature Of My Mailing List Is Mostly Internet Marketers And What Faster Way To Grab Affiliates Than To Mail Blast Out To Them Here!
1720	The 7-Point Checklist For Getting Advertisers To Your Ezine
1721	Touch Your Readers, Not In A Corny Way, Or Unethical Way, But With Powerful Triggers That You Can Use To Create A Strong Bond With Your Audience. If You Won't, Your Profits Will Go In Your Competitions Pocket Instead. It's Entirely Your Choice.
1722	Grab It For A Tiny Fraction Of What I Paid For It
1723	Why Easy To Remember Keyword Domains Make A Lot More Money
1724	No Matter How Many Un-Profitable Google Campaigns You Have Now ... We Will Show You How My Secret "Glitch" Quickly Adapts Them To Wildly Profitable Yahoo! Money-maker...
1725	The Ultimate System Of Setting It Up Correctly One Time And Getting Paid Over And Over
1726	Are You Listening To This Guy And That Guy And Still Confused
1727	Go Ahead! Order Using One Of The Options Above! Get A Jump Start On ANY Competition By Utilizing A Product Designed From The Ground Up To Help You Out Earn Your Competition...
1728	The 2 Essential Skills You Must Absolutely Develop If You Expect To Succeed On The Internet. Ignore This Crucial Advice And You'll Fall Flat On Your Face Just Like 95% Of Online Marketers.
1729	I Do Not Refund To Those That Refuse To Let Me Know I Made A Mistake And Feel Better For Lashing Out Rather Than Being Humane About Things. Life Is Too Short To Go Around Pissed Off.
1730	Consider The Psychological And Demographic Attributes Relating To People's Interests Or Lifestyles. Knowing This Data Helps You Understand The Psychograpics Of Your Prospects Better And Gives You The Ability To Trigger Their Emotional Hot Buttons.

1731	Your Ultimate Goal Is To Build A Business That Essentially Runs Itself, Without You Even Being Present. The Sales Are Just Made And The Jobs Just Get Done Because You Have Great Employees Who Are All Great At Their Jobs, Who Are Well Trained, And Who Know Exactly How To Do Their Jobs.
1732	There's Something We Think You Need To Know Of Vital Importance
1733	The Only Way I Was Going Back Online Would Be If I Could Be Profitable Without Surfing For Ten To Twelve Hours A Day And Most Importantly, Everything I Did Was Going To Be Above The Board. No Underhanded Cutthroat Marketing Tactics For Me.
1734	What Actions Could You Choose To Make Your Business Even More Successful?
1735	It's True. People Have Been Feeding You The Wrong Information About List Building For A Long Time, And It's Time We Set The Record Straight Right Here
1736	Search Engine Optimization Is All About Making Your Website As Attractive As Possible For Search Engines. The Most Successful Sites Are Those That Turn Up Early In The Search Results.
1737	How To Win The Marketing Wars With Your Own Team Of Affiliate Warriors
1738	Former Barber Earns $8000 In Four Months As Real Estate Specialist
1739	You're Buying 10 Years Worth Of My Experiences And Over $100,000 In Lessons Learned The Hard-Way So You Can Skip All The Crap And Instantly Dive Right Into What Works.
1740	No Need To Hire A Professional Copywriter, Who Will Charge You Anywhere From $100 To As Much As $500 For A Single Email Message
1741	Please Setup This Web Site And .com Domain Name For Me So I Can Just Email You Some Of What I Want On The Homepage And You'll Get It All Online For Me And Ready To Go Or Please Make This Page Rank High In Google So I Can Start Getting Free Traffic From It And...*Presto* That Work Is Done. Well, This Is Exactly What Having A Virtual Worker Assist You Can Do For You!
1742	A Simple Trick That Re-Uses Testimonial Content Which Increases Conversions By 19%

129

1743	You Get To SEE Me And Watch Exactly How I Make Massive Cash Fast
1744	Pick A Good Name For Your Business And Product. Your Names Should Be Memorable And Describe The Kind Of Product Your Offering.
1745	You Will Learn How To Create A Video That You Can Put To You Tube And Other Video Sites For FREE. This Is A Great Way To Get Traffic To Your Website.
1746	Everything That All The Other So Called Trainers, Teachers, Taught Me Was All Wrong They Didn't Know What They Were Doing. I Guess You Can Say They Teach What They Learn, But Thing About It I Trusted Them
1747	How Will Your Company Survive When Email As We Know It Is Dead
1748	If Making Money Online Was So Easy Why Isn't Everyone Wealthy
1749	Child Reveals A Simple Short Cut That Increased Conversions By At Least 75%
1750	The Paradigm I Want To Share With You Here Does Not Aim To Double The Value Of Your Time. It Aims To Increase The Value Of An Hour Of Your Time 1,000 Times Or More.
1751	How Do You See Your Life Unfolding Click Here For Incredible Options
1752	Learn How To Do This Or Walk Away From Internet Marketing Now
1753	The Best Places To Get Your Reliable Web Hosting And Domain Names For Your Network Of Affiliate Promoting Websites (You'll Need This To Get Online And Get Started On The Road Of Long Term Affiliate Success)
1754	Now, Don't Get Me Wrong, There Are A Few Of Them Out There That Are Completely, And Honestly Selling Good Products, But When Was The Last Time You Either Used What You Bought, Or For That Matter, "Read" It?
1755	Learn These Five Steps To Choosing A Winning And Most Profitable Affiliate Programs
1756	Don't Let Technology Get It The Way Of Making Money Online
1757	The Way I Am Paid For My Direct Mail Packages Is A Flat-Fee For The Writing, Plus Some Kind Of A Royalty, Which Usually Totals 5% To 10% Of The Gross Income Produced By My Direct Mail Package -- The Percentage Depending On What I Think The Potential Might Be For Repeat Mailings Of The Same Direct Mail Package.

1758	Looking For A New Way To Line Your Pockets With Money
1759	Primitive Instincts Bite In A World Where The Size Of Your Bank Account Matters
1760	But I Vowed To Never Give In, Give Up, Or Let Anyone Defeat Me, I Had A Clear Vision Of Where I Wanted To Be And One Day It All Finally Clicked And I Found My Way.
1761	Finally, Live The Lifestyle That You Have Always Been Dreaming About. You Can Create A Fortune In As Little As 60 Days. Just Imagine What You Can Do With The Money.
1762	When My Friends Started Emailing Me Asking Me How I Was Doing And Wondering If I Would Ever Go Back Online; I Came To Realize For Me To Be Truly Happy, I Had To Know, One Way Or Another; Could I Still Have A Profitable Business And Still Enjoy My "Second" Retirement?
1763	Profitable Reasons To Add A Discussion Board Or Chat Room To Your Web Site
1764	Don't Leave Your Day Job Until You Know It's Time To Walk Away
1765	Targeted Results For Your Product Or Service. Imagine Being Able To Reach 45 Million People With Your Offers In A Matter Of Minutes Rather Than Spending Countless Hours Submitting Ad After Ad Until Your Fingers Rub Raw!
1766	Words Paint Pictures And Pictures Create Stories Helping People Solve Problems To Regain Control Of Something They Want Very Badly. So Badly, They'll Instantly And Eagerly Pay To Own The Solution Without Hesitation.
1767	Controversial New Ebook Reveals Why Prospecting And Recruiting Is Actually Destroying Your Business...And... How To Make Money REGARDLESS Of Whether You Sponsor Anyone Or Not!
1768	Put This In Front Of A Million People Watch What Happens
1769	Take These Secrets And Apply Massive Action And You Will Succeed Anywhere
1770	But Like All Great Things, The End Product Turns Out To Be So Amazing That It Can Be Applied To Other Tasks And Other Industries As Well.
1771	Remember, This Offer Is Only Good For The First 200 People Who Take Action Now. Once They're Gone, They're Gone Forever.
1772	But You'll Have To Wait To Find Out What They Are
1773	It'll Take Work But You Can Become Financially Set For Life

1774	Maybe You Know Someone Else Other Than Me Who Knows How To Help
1775	Now! Own Florida Land This Easy Way $10 Down And $10 A Month
1776	The SIMPLEST Way To Turn-On Your Very Own Automatic Income System That Pays Non-Stop Cash To You 24/7...Even If You're A Complete Newbie!
1777	Check Out Why All Traffic Is Simply Not Of The Same Quality
1778	Want To Kick Some Serious Butt Using Some Profoundly Effective Shortcuts To Success
1779	If You Can Follow Simple Directions Here's How To Increase Conversions By At Least 75% In Your Spare Time And Have Fun Doing It
1780	Work For Minimum Wage For Life Or Start Making Money Online Now
1781	If You Love Football Then You Know That If You Can't Block And Tackle You Can't Play. Well, This Is Your Blocking And Tackling Video Basics, How You Get Paid, And What To Watch For.
1782	This Free Report Will Cause You To Work Less And Earn More
1783	When Like-Minded People Who Want To Increase Their Income Join Together, They Effectively Build The Numbers Of Prospects Into The Thousands That They Can Send Their Promotions To Quickly.
1784	It's Been Said That Ideas Are A Dime A Dozen. Yet Without Fresh Ones All Marketing And Sales Would Stagnate. So What If I Allowed You A Sneak Peak Into My Private Collection, My Personal Bank Full Of Great Ideas, How Many Could You Really Handle At One Time...10...50...1,000...50,000? Interested In Taking A Peak?
1785	Once You Get Settled In We'll Begin The Adventure Of A Lifetime
1786	Biggest Myth: It Takes A Lot Of Money To Use Outsourcing For Your New Business. So Many New Folks Think That They Can't Outsource And Get Others To Help With Their New Online Business Because It's A "Catch 22" -- I.E. Their New Business Isn't Making Money Yet So They Don't Have The Money To Pay Someone To Help Them Make More Money.
1787	How Often Do You Hear Yourself Saying No I Haven't Read It But I've Been Meaning To

1788	How To Write About Your Product Or Service That Represents The True Value Of Your Offer
1789	I Had Never Really Given It Much Thought. I Was So Caught Up In My Own World. The World Where I Had A List And Just Assumed It Was Normal For Everyone To Be Doing Exactly The Same Thing.
1790	Detailed Instructions For Creating Your Product. I'll Show You What Do And How To Do It, And You'll Know The "Why's" Behind Every Step.
1791	Test Drive This Step By Step System Entirely At My Risk
1792	Not Sure If You've Heard Yet, But These Guys Have Just Released A Tremendous New Product Which Shows YOU Exactly How To Take Advantage Of "Mass Traffic" To Your Websites. But First, Real Quick...
1793	Watch Your Business Grow From The Comfort Of Your Favorite Chair
1794	Internet Marketing Takes A Completely Different Approach Because People Who Conduct Business Online, Search For Credible Companies With Which To Do Business Online.
1795	Looking For The Latest-Greatest Program That's Going To Make Me A Million Overnight. Guess What? It Doesn't Exist. If You're Not Focusing Your Attention On ONE Thing You're Falling For EVERYTHING And Accomplishing NOTHING.
1796	Avoid These Viral Report Mistakes That Most Marketers Commonly Make Every Day
1797	Ways To Get People To Visit Your Web Site Again And Again
1798	You Can Join One Or More Of The Free Money Making Programs That We Offer And Earn The Investment Fee BEFORE You Join The Core-Business.
1799	Once A Person Signs Up And Gets Started And Takes Their New Business Seriously, They Rarely Quit. This Is Because They Are Making Money Very Easily. You Don't Quit A Good Paying Job That Only Takes One Hour Of Your Time Each Day.
1800	How A Flat Broke Mother Of 3 Stumbled Into The Internet Hall Of Fame Of Success
1801	With NO Risks Involved, It's Totally Up To You If You Want To Use The FREE System To Make Money.
1802	Why Subscribers Willingly Whip Out Their Wallets To Give You Money Every Month

1803	You Will Learn Step By Step How To Build Your Own Powerful Website From Scratch. In A Matter Of Minutes, You Will Cry Laughing When You See How Simple This Is.
1804	To Ensure That You Get Just The Right Package For You, We Provide 2 Different Options You Can Purchase. Simply Read Details For Each And Order By Clicking The "Order Button".
1805	See You Inside The Members Area In A Moment From Now
1806	Brand-New Private Label eCourse Lets You Easily Teach Your Customers and Subscribers The Basics of Running Their Own Successful Viral Marketing Campaigns.
1807	Why You Need To Outsource Your Grunt Work So That You Can Take Your Money To The Bank
1808	Making Money Online Isn't Rocket Science. Email Marketing Is The Fastest Way To The Top, Even If You've Never Even Tried It Before. Once You Cut Your Teeth On This Amazing Strategy That Will Literally Hand Over The Keys To Building Your Online Email Marketing Empire, You Will Never Again Struggle To Make Money Again.
1809	Is 5 Minutes Worth Learning How To Pay Off All Your Bills
1810	Making Money Isn't Easy But There Is A Real Alternative That Makes It Easier
1811	This Is An Instant Download And It Cost Me Nothing In Terms Of Time And Delivery Cost And I Really Want As Many People As Possible To Afford This So They Can Benefit From It.
1812	Tired Of Dealing With The Pain Time And Expense Of Creating A Profitable Website
1813	This May Be Your Last Chance So Please Don't Blow It
1814	I Will Be Giving A 30 Minute Head-Start To Those That Sign Up For The Notification List. I Have A Funny Feeling That This Will Sell Out Within That 30 Minutes.
1815	Discover A Simple System You Can Start Using Right Away To Generate More Leads, Position Yourself As A Leader, Create Immediate Cashflow AND Build Your Primary Business On Auto-Pilot Without ANY Of That "Old-School", Out Dated, Silly Pitch And Chase Stuff Still Being Taught By Uplines Stuck In The 90's
1816	With Just A Few Clicks You'll Instantly Jump Start A Profitable Business
1817	Readily Search Engine Optimized To Help Your Website Rank In The Search Engines

1818	No Longer Do You Need To Stay Up For Days At A Time, Drinking Cases Of Red Bull And Consuming Pots Of Coffee Through Your IV Drip While You Foam At The Mouth,
1819	Where I'll Give You My Honest And Unbiased Review Of The Newest Adsense Programs On The Market, So You Know What Works...And Better Ye, How To Use It.
1820	It's Time To Dig Into The PSYCHOLOGY Of YOUR Prospect. A Million Dollar Skill Which Is Funny Because This Industry, More Than Any Other Industry, Is All About People And Building Relationships. Knowing A Bit About Human Behavior Could Make Or Break You In Your MLM Business Yet No Company Provides Any Training On The Subject.
1821	Show Me What I Want To Buy And Tell Me Why I Really Need It
1822	That Dream Is Long Gone..." Everyone Is Frantically Searching For Security And Freedom. Turns Out The Dream That Was Promised Was Nothing But A Hoax. Let's Not Forget Existing Businesses. Some Markets Are Actually Booming Right Now! But The Ones You See Waist Deep In The "Stuff", Desperately Need Your Help. Doesn't Matter If They Are Online Businesses Or Brick And Mortar.
1823	P.S. The Greatest Thing About 'Working For Yourself' Is Not Money. It's Freedom. I Value Freedom More Than Anything Else, And I've Been Able To Create A Life Of Freedom (And Travel) Over The Past 10 Years.
1824	Sell Something People Want, Need, And Are Actually Looking For Online. We Prefer Information Products And Ebooks Because There Is Nothing Physical To Deliver Or Ship.
1825	How To Kill 2 Turkeys With One Stone. I Am Sorry About The Title...It Doesn't Mean To Kill Real Turkeys ;-) It's About How To Get 2 Targeted Offers Exposed By Sending Visitors To ONE Website Only.
1826	Take The Time To Download This Life Changing Book, It Will Save You Years Of Failure And Frustration!
1827	7 Order-Pulling Ways To End Your Sales Letters To Generate More Purchases
1828	To Carve Out A Beautiful Life As An Internet Mogul...Filled With Freedom, Wealth, And All The Time In The World To Actually Enjoy It. This Is About You. Your Fate, Your Future...Your Freedom.

1829	Here's The Full Layout On Everything You Get To Start Generating Your Own Multiple Streams Of Affiliate Commissions And Stuff Your Mail Box With Fat Paychecks...
1830	An Incredible Product Guaranteed To Multiply Your Profits And Explode Your Customers List. FREE For The Next 100 Customers Only! The Most Powerful Tools To Maximize Your Profits From The Work From Home Internet System.
1831	Add Your Own Keywords And Meta Tags And Help Your Search Engine Ranking
1832	Take Your Time. Review This Program At Your Leisure To Absorb Every Last Proven Secret, And Put Them To Work For You. And After A Year, If, For Some Reason, You Don't Want To Use These Secrets – Or If They Disappoint You Somehow – No Worries. Just Let Us Know Within A Year And We'll Give You A Full Refund.
1833	You Also Get Free Updates! For One Whole Year You Will Receive Updates At NO-COST.
1834	The Hard-Driving, Closing Salesperson Is About 8% Of The Population. And Those 8% Have Convinced The Other 92% That The 8% Are Right And The 92% Are Wrong. How Did They Do That? Because That Is What They DO.
1835	No Matter How You Feel, Get Up, Dress Up And Show Up
1836	You Can Take My Money But You Can't Take My Dream
1837	Take Action And Do Something To Get You Towards Your Goal, And Trust That You'll Find A Ways To Figure Everything Out As You Go Along.
1838	OK - I Wasn't Gonna Share This... But I Really Want You To Do Well So... This Bonus Chapter Will Teach My Secret 'Flipping The Market' This Is Good Stuff Never Before Revealed - This Is The Secret Is Responsible For Making Me Over $3,000,000 Online!
1839	Do Something Once And Be Paid On It For Many Years To Come
1840	You Can't Buy This Until After You Try It For Free
1841	Why You Need To Be Marketing To Pebbles Rocks Boulders And Mountains
1842	This Report Will Show You How To Avoid Common Marketing Disasters

1843	The Internet Is The Number One Source For Shopping, For Researching Term Papers, For Chatting With Friends, For Catching Up On Celebrity Gossip, For Buying Consumer Products, For Watching The News And For Generally Staying Informed With The World
1844	Stop Allowing Yourself To Get Robbed Every Day While Your PPC Ads Spin The Cost Meter At High Gear, Ringing Up Credit Card Bills And Driving Up Costs Without Even Providing You With A Guarantee That All Of That Money Will Actually Help You Grow Your Online Business!
1845	After More Failures Than I Can Remember, I Picked Up The Internet Marketing Bug. This May Be Your One And Only Chance To Get Your Hands On This Exclusive Affiliate Series.
1846	You Need All The Ingredients If You're Going To Bake A Cake
1847	If You Wait, The Final Price Will Be $37 But You Can Get Everything Now For Just A One-Time Low Payment Of $9.97 Backed Up By Our 30 Day Full Money Back Guarantee! Order Now Before The Price Goes Up!
1848	Let's Be Honest, Having A Large Number Of People Expecting To Read Your Emails Is Practically Priceless And If There Was A Way To Tap Into That Opportunity, Wouldn't You Be First In Line?
1849	This Is Your Opportunity To Finally Take Full Control Of Your Success Online
1850	I Spent The Money. I Perfected The System, Now I Want YOU To Reap The Rewards. Why? Because it's The Promise I Made Myself Years Ago And It's Finally Coming True! Don't Fall Into The Other Traps And End Up Falling Where I Did. Just Let Me Give You My Exact Blueprint And Run With It!
1851	Something About Those Triple Digits Just Skewers The True Value Of Things. So, To Make This The Easiest Choice You've Ever Made.
1852	Is Your Head Still Stuck In The Clouds Trying To Make Money Online
1853	How To Make Money Online Even If You Never Made A Penny Before
1854	I'm Going To Be Very Blunt With You Because Neither Of Us Have Time To Mess Around; If You Truly Want To Be Successful Online, You Absolutely Need To Know Exactly How To Drive In An Absolute Flood Of Traffic To Your Website, On Command.

1855	Have You And Your Website Received The Google Slap Of Death
1856	If, After 30 Days, You Decide To Keep The System, Your Credit Card Will Be Charged A One Time Fee Of Only $97 (Instead Of $197). Or You Can Return The System Within 30 Days And You Will Never Be Charged An Extra Penny!
1857	One They Taste Your Offer You'll See Why Customers Keep Coming Back To Feast
1858	NOW Is The Time To Get Them When They Are Bundled Into A Special 78% Discount Offer Like This And YOU Will Save 78% Off The Regular Price!
1859	Remember, If You Sell ANY Of My Products Now, You'll Get Credit For ALL Future Products That Customer Buys!
1860	Life Doesn't Just Happen To You... It Is What You Make It. Good Or Bad. Right Or Wrong. Hopeful Or Miserable. The Future Is In Your Hands. But This Offer Is Only For A Limited Time...
1861	You'll Never Be Able To Find Another PLR Package That Will Make You More Money Than This Period!
1862	OK, Get On The Webinar With Me Tomorrow, And I'm Really Looking Forward To Helping You Build Your Business!
1863	Start By Giving Someone The What And The Why Not To How
1864	Burn Candles, Use Nice Sheets, Wear Fancy Lingerie And Don't Save Them For A Special Occasion Because Today Is Special
1865	Then They Each Refer 10 More - Then They Each Refer 10 More And Pretty Soon You Have A List Of Thousands Of Random Members To Email To Who Are Eagerly Awaiting Your Information.
1866	Things You Can Tweak To Give Your Site The Recognition It Deserves
1867	Generate The Income That You Want, And That You Deserve. It Doesn't Matter Who You Are. No Matter Your Age,
1868	Why You Need To Finish Your Homework Before The Next Step
1869	Hands That Look Lovelier In 24 Hours Or Your Money Back
1870	Eliminate Wasteful Advertising Excite Customers And Drive Quality Customers To Your Site
1871	You Can Now Do It With Ease. Automatically Generate Ad Links, Track Their Responses And Compare Their Results. Improve Your Ad Campaign Now By Identifying Which Ads Work And Which Ads Don't.

1872	You Should Only Have One Question To Ask Yourself... Are You Willing To Take Your Future Into Your Own Hands And Change Your Fortune. Take Our "Review Blogs" System To The Test Now For Free.
1873	Over 70% Of Marketers Don't Know How To Properly Install A Complete Resell Rights Package By Themselves! Now You No Longer Have To Be Worried Or Frustrated.
1874	This Can Be Your Last Chance To Set Your Own Schedule And Work Whenever You Want To – You Can Work As Much As You Want Or As Little As You Need!
1875	The Key To Making Money On The Internet Is A Two Step Process I Call Divert And Convert. Every Profit Seeking Website On The Internet Uses This Process Whether They Realize It Or Not.
1876	Why Some People Almost Always Make Money In The Stock Market
1877	Getting A New Website Isn't Easy Because In Order To Be Successful, You Have To Understand Web Development, SEO, Linking Campaigns, And Of Course, You Need A Marketing Strategy.
1878	It's A Minefield Out There! Driving Traffic To Your Website Can Be An Absolute Nightmare. Narrow The Search With The Internet Marketer Who Has Honed It To Perfection! Follow These Footsteps And Dramatically Increase Traffic.
1879	The Question A Lot Of People Have Is, "Is The Marketing Of Digital Goods Any Different Than The Marketing Of Physical Goods?" Let Me Say That The Professional Methods Of Marketing Never Change. It's The Mechanics Of Marketing,
1880	YES! Give Me My Free Site Now! Set It Up For Me For Free So I Can Get Started RIGHT NOW!
1881	The Formula I've Honed Over Time That Works No Matter What You're Trying To Sell. Writing Your Ads This Way Are Worth 3x More Per Click Almost Guaranteed
1882	Watch Out Your Business Might Not Be Able To Handle This
1883	How To Get Your Site Reviewed For Free And Win Customers As You Do It
1884	The Four Things Every Viral Report Should Feature To Ensure A Successful Launch
1885	Doesn't It Feel Like Life's Passing You By While Other Marketeers Are Getting Filthy Rich
1886	Want THE Boat To Get You Where You Want To Go

139

1887	For Those Who'd Like The Report To Be Compiled Into A PDF Already, Without Any Author Name Associated, This Is For You.
1888	Are You Constructing Your Marketing Campaign On The Scale Of The Hardron Collider
1889	You've Set Up A System That Looks And Performs Exactly Like Our Expensive, Professional Sales Systems For Our Own Products. Except Now Anyone Can Have Killer Video Squeeze Pages And Look Like A Pro.
1890	Just Find A Fairly Simple Thing To Do. Billions Of Dollars Are Made Every Year By Envelope Companies That Do Nothing But Make And Sell Envelopes -- Envelopes That Might Only Produce A Penny Each In Profit For The Company -- Or Less. How Many Envelopes Are Used Everyday In America Or In The World?
1891	The World's Most Incredible Direct Response TV Media Minds Are Now Combining Their Resources To Form What Many Say Will Be The Next Billion Dollar Home Business Success Story And You Have A Chance To Profit From It.
1892	Do You Really Want The Lowest Bidding Temp Agency To Provide Employees For Your Million Dollar Project
1893	One Question That Probably Is On Your Mind Is, If I Purchase This Can I Get My Money Back If It Fails To Provide The Bene-fits That It Guarantees?
1894	You Need To Know What It Is You Want To Market
1895	If You Are Not Thrilled By The Number Of Targeted Visitors You Receive With This Software, Let Us Know And We Will Issue You A FULL REFUND. No Questions Asked
1896	I Would Recommend That You Get Started Today And Learn How To Tag Your Blog Post Correctly.
1897	Actually, You'll Think Of This As Your "Cookbook" To Internet Marketing By Simply Following The Step-By-Step, Day-By-Day Instructions For 33 Days And We Guarantee You'll Turbo Charge Your Online Sales
1898	You Woke Up This Morning To Realized This Wasn't A Pipe Dream
1899	I Don't Even Want To Take Your Money If You Have The Smallest Doubt. I Don't Need Forum Whiners, Tire Kickers, Habitual Refunders, Or Any Other Cry Babies.
1900	Re-Insert A Simple Graphic Near The Top Of Your Sales Page And Watch Sales Boost By 19%

1901	Discover Fresh New Tactics That Have Proven Themselves To Make Millions
1902	Having Said That, As With ALL My Products, I Do Not Represent You Will Experience Profits As I Have Nor That The Typical Or Ordinary Buyer Of This Or Any Of My Products Makes Substantial Income.
1903	Don't Just Create Silly Products When You Can Be My Affiliate
1904	Live The Life You Deserve Today And Be Completely Covered For Any Kind Of Emergency
1905	Position Yourself For Maximum Profits By Giving Away Hot Turn Key Products
1906	Each Of These Complete, In-Depth Training Programs Is Worth $1,000. But I'm Giving Them To You To Make Sure You've Got Everything You Need -Because I'm Committed To Your Success.
1907	It's Not Your Fault Someone Got You To Buy Into That Trap
1908	I May End Up Kicking Myself For Telling You But I'm Finally Ready To Spill The Beans
1909	Create Scarcity Fear Of Loss And A Deadline With Limited Quantities
1910	His Passion For Helping Others Succeed Led Him To Establish One Of The Fastest Growing Online Distance Learning Organizations On The Internet Today.
1911	What I Didn't Know When I Started Turned Out To Be A Great Journey I'll Share With You
1912	Free Things Like Youtube, Ezine Articles, Squidoo And Such Are Great. They All Serve Their Purposes. Though At The End Of The Day, They Are NOT OURS. They Can Be Taken From You At Any Time. Then What? What Happens To All Your Marketing Efforts When That Day Arrives? It's Time To Start Developing Plan B C & D.
1913	Never Stop Learning! Never Stop Trying! Never Stop Doing Things And Experimenting With Ways To Make Your Business Better.
1914	The Three Reasons Why You Must Guarantee Your Products And How To Word Them To Reduce The Number Of People Ready To Abuse It.
1915	What Would If Mean To You If You Got The Outcome You Wanted

1916	One Under Used Method Of Premium Product Creation. Did You Know You Could Take A Product You Were Planning To Sell For $20 And Turn It Into A $500 Monster Without Much Effort? I'll Show You Exactly How I Do This For 90% Of My Business Ideas Without Overvaluing Myself To The Point Of Low Sales Figures.
1917	Be Warned Once 500 Copies Are Sold Out They'll Be Taken Off The Market Forever
1918	The Dirty Little Secret That Affiliate Marketers Don't Want You To Know About
1919	Regardless Of What You Want To Do With The Web, There Is The Potential To Make A Lot Of Money And Market Your Product Or Service To The Right Clientele And More Market-ers And Every Day Joes Are Discovering The Potential Of Targeted Traffic.
1920	We'll Guide Through Every Step Of The Installation Process And Basic Configuration As Well As Outline The Usage Of Your New Review Blog For You To SEE Exactly How Things Are Done To Ensure You Do It Correctly.
1921	This Is The Ultimate Opportunity To Obtain The Skills Needed For Running A Highly Successful Web Venture Of Any Kind, And Remember With My 100% Guarantee There Is Absolutely No Risk!
1922	This Is Not A Recurring Payment So After One Year If You No Longer Need The Service, You Do Nothing And Your Account Will Automatically Close.
1923	The Greatest Collection Of Over 15,000 Swipe Files And Moti-vational Words And Make A Huge Fortune Selling These In A Hungry, 13 Billion Dollar Market!
1924	You Can't Lose With Our 100%, Ironclad, 60 Days Money-Back Guarantee! Yes You Read That RIGHT! Your Satisfaction Is Assured Through Our No Risk, You-Can't-Lose, 100%, No Questions-Asked, Iron-Clad Money-Back Guarantee.
1925	The Perfect Solution For Internet Marketers Selling Books, Reports, Manuals, Audio Products, Video Products, Images, Public Domain Works, Scripts And Software, Digital Services Such As Web Design And Hosting, And Much, Much More...
1926	If "The Secret" Isn't Working For You, You Should Really Check This Out. Again, There Is No Charge For This. Just Some Great Content That I Feel Will Help You Make The Most Of Your Online Business.
1927	Created For People Who Want To Write But Can't Get Started

1928	Tired Of The Recent Flood Of Giveaways Rehashing The Same Old Products
1929	You'll Be Astonished At How Quickly You Can Transform These Ideas Into Cold Hard Cash
1930	Our Action Headlines Combined With Your Drive, Creativity And Persistence Is The Key To Your Dreams Of Financial Security, More Time With Your Family, And Most Of All, The Freedom That You Desire.
1931	If You Were Offered The Ultimate Opportunity How Long Would It Take For You To Grab It
1932	Why Having One Product Will Make You Some Money But Never Wealthy
1933	This Is What Your Inbox Looks Like When You Have A Winning Product That Sells Like Hotcakes!
1934	First, I Want To Address The Rumors. Which Rumors Are Those? The Ones Flying Around Out There Making You Think That PPC Is Dead.
1935	Of Course The Down Side Is The Poor Pay, The Wage Slave Mentality And Worse Of All (Remember We Are On Earth For A Limited Time Only) You Are Selling What Little Amount Of Glorious Time You Have Left.
1936	If You Have Been Looking For A Smart And Quick Way To Earn FREE Daily Cash Online, This System Will Automatically Let You Earn Much More Than You Could Ever Do It Alone All By Yourself!
1937	Strike Win-Win JV Deals To Sell Your Product And Grow Your List In One Slick Move Or Outsource Everything In Half The Time And Cost Of Doing It All Yourself.
1938	Specifically Designed For Those Of Us Unable To Write A Coherent Sentence
1939	Free Internet May Come To The U.S. Allowing Regulators To Auction Off Unused Spectrums
1940	It'll Continue To Earn Your Money Month After Month And You'll Continue Pocketing Thousands Upon Thousands Of Dollars Applying Our Tactics And Techniques.
1941	Why American Cottage Industries Are Popping Up All Over The Internet
1942	If You're Sick And Tired Of Worrying About How Much Money You Have In The Bank, Fed Up With Everyone In Your Life Constantly Doubting You, And Finally Ready To Turn Your Internet Marketing Dreams Into A Profitable Reality, Then You Need To Do Everything In Your Power To Be Here.

1943	You'll Never Be Stuck For Words Again Because You'll Have Access To The Greatest Headlines And Mini Phrases Ever Written To Jog Your Imagination And Spark Your Natural Writing Brilliance.
1944	If We All Threw Our Problems In A Pile And Saw Everyone Else's We'd Grab Ours Back
1945	You Do Not Want To Put This Off. You Can Get It Now, Or You Can Get It Tomorrow And Pay 3x's More, Why Pay More Later? Just Hurry On Over Because Your First 30days Of Access Is Free Even! We've Made Millions Of Dollars Online And We Want To Show You How To Do The Same.
1946	I've Only Used This Method So Far To Personally Train A Few Coaching Clients And As You Have Seen Earlier, They Are Well On There Way To A Solid Six Figure Business.
1947	Focus On The Specific Niche That Clearly Relates To Internet Marketing
1948	A Decision Has To Be Made. But Don't Make A Hasty One. This Compete And Proven Business Model You Can Follow To Build An Affiliate Empire That Runs On Virtual Autopilot.
1949	People Don't Care About The Process They Only Care About Solutions
1950	Go Ahead... Get The Tool And Learn The Secrets, You At Least Owe It To Yourself To Take A Look. Get The Tool Now And Let Me Know What You Think
1951	You Could Spend Countless Dollars And Thousands Of Hours Trying To Find This
1952	Experts Tell Us That It Takes An Average Of 7 Different Contacts To Close A Sale. If You Are Not Following Up With Your Prospects On A Regular Basis, You Are Losing Sales!
1953	Necessary Supplies That You Need To Make Money Online. These Are Simple Things You May Need To Make You More Efficient And Maximize Your Income.
1954	I'm Gonna Just Let The Truth Fly...And Maybe It Will Finally Open Your Eyes To A Nasty Super Affiliate Conspiracy.
1955	We Decided To Set The Record Straight Once And For All
1956	It's A Shame For You Not To Make Good Money When These Men Do It So Easily
1957	Why Settle For Less When This Idea Can Explode Your Sales Overnight
1958	Are You Ready To Tear The Internet Game Apart Once And For All

1959	You May Decide To Acquire A List Of These Opportunity Seekers Who Are Hungry To Make Money Online. You Will Be Given Access To A Virtually Unlimited Supply Of These Leads. Are You Intrigued?
1960	How Many People Are On The Internet Right Now Buying Stuff
1961	Limiting Numbers Without Limiting Your Profit. There Are Many Reasons Marketers Will Limit The Number Of Customers Allowed To Buy Their Product. Done Right, This Is One Heck Of A Marketing Tool, But Done Badly, It'll Ruin Their Sales Figures (Not To Mention This Has The Potential To Actually Allow The Site Owner To Lose Money). Learn To Limit Numbers Without Ruining Your Businesses Potential.
1962	This Will Help Get You Started In The Right Direction Right Away
1963	How To Find The Type Of Work Suitable For You. I'll Give You Sound Advice On Choosing The Ideal Type Of Work To Do.
1964	There's Nothing Magical About Making Money Online So Why Are You Still Struggling
1965	The Falling-Off-A-Log Way To Pick A Market To Sell To. You Can Do It All With 100% Free Tools And In Just A Few Minutes. I'll Show You Exactly How...
1966	Read Our Incredible Free Report And Discover When People Are Most Likely To Buy Through Your Affiliate Link Including The Best Places To Advertise Affiliate Products And What Type Of Affiliate Programs Convert Best.
1967	Even If You Do Not Want To Use The Full Potential Of Our Site, You Can Join For Free And Start Using Just One Feature Or Follow Our Step-By-Step Instructions To Start Building Your Business Immediately.
1968	Now All That's Left For You To Do Is Watch Your Commissions Skyrocket. It Really Is That Easy.
1969	Generating An Avalanche Of Pre-Qualified Targeted Leads Is Crucial To Your Success
1970	By Just Tagging Your Blog Post You Can Actually Increase Your Exposure To Search Engine By 300%!
1971	Listen, It Wouldn't Be Fair To Give You The Perfect Tool To Create Subscriber-Sucking Web Pages Without Letting You In On The Wicked Techniques I Personally Use To Build Enormous Ravenous Lists At Will.
1972	The Golden Rule Is To Not Overuse The Yellow Highlighting, So What I Do Is Limit Myself To Two Highlights In The Body Of The Email.

145

1973	In This LIVE Web Class, You'll Discover How To Create Brand New Products Fast And Discover How To Sell Them Even Faster. Plus, You'll See My Top Eyeball-Grabbing Headliner Collection.
1974	Continuity Is Being Considered The "Holy Grail" Of Internet Marketing Because Who Wouldn't Want To Get Paid Month After Month For The Same Amount Of Effort To Make That First Sale.
1975	If You Want To Start Generating Some Serious Cash In Record Time, Be Sure To Read Every Word On This Page Very Carefully. Because I Have Recently Uncovered And Been Testing (With Great Results) One Of "Google's Best Kept Secrets" And I Will Show You How To Use It To Make Even More Money With My System.
1976	You Will Be Billed At The Low Rate Of Only $97 Month
1977	There Are Only A Few Days Left At This Sales Price. Why Pay More If You Don't Have To. The Best Thing Is You Can Use These Tricks And Tactics And Be Up And Running In Minutes That's How "Quick" It Is.
1978	When Writing Your Sales Copy For Your Products And Services, You Should Reach Out To People, Appeal To Their Emotions, Make Them WANT What You Have To Offer And Justify It With The Rest Of Your Copy.
1979	Well, To Be Blunt, It's Not Crazy At All. It's Perfectly Feasible To Start Making Money On The First Day Of A Business. You Just Think It's Crazy Because Of All The Bad Information You've Been Fed. All The Guys Selling You Their Dumb, Overrated Products Want You To Think It's Hard To Make Money Online
1980	You Can Get A Lifetime Membership To Adsensenewbievideos.Com With Access To Everything Mentioned Above, For A Very Low One Time Investment Of Only $47, If You Act Right This Instant.
1981	Once You Optimize This Single Page Be Prepared For An Endless Flood Of Customers
1982	Everyone Is Running Around Trying To Teach You How To Build A List Of People Who Want To Get Your Free Emails.
1983	Still Spending Sleepless Nights Making The Same Errors Day After Day
1984	We Give You The Tools And Teach You The Skills To Help You Be Successfully In The Network Marketing Industry.

1985	By Now I'm Sure Your Aware That I Have Something To Offer And I'm NOT Going To Subject You To Some "Hyped Up" Marketing Spiel That Your Probably Fed Up Of Reading...I've Simply One Goal....To Exterminate All YOUR Past Failures By Taking You By The Hand And Showing You The Devastating System That Quite Simply Put, Will Enable You To Crank Out The Moolah...
1986	But Then You Get That Sinking Feeling In The Pit Of Your Stomach
1987	Site Maps Help Search Engine Robots Find Every Page On Your Website In Just Two Clicks. What This Means Is Better Search Engine Results For All Your Web Pages. Make Sure You Link All Pages Properly For The Best SEO Results.
1988	Give Me A Dollar And I'll Give You $1,369.00 Of Proven, Jealously Guarded Internet Money Making Tools Which You Can Keep Even If You Ask For A Refund Of Your Dollar!
1989	WARNING: The Sad Truth Is That The Dishonest People Set You Up To Always Win
1990	The Real Trick Is Holding Your Reader's Attention Long Enough To
1991	I Stopped Buying A New Money-Making System Every Other Week. I Stopped Reading The Business Opportunity Section Of The Paper. I Started Focusing On Forming The Foundation That I Would Build All My Future Success On.
1992	There's No Two Ways Around Really Making Serious Money Online Without This Approach
1993	There Isn't Going To Be A Stupid 'One Time Offer' When You Click The Button Above. I Have Nothing Better To Offer You. There Isn't Any Upgrade Or Platinum Package. There Is Only One System And It Is Free For Anyone To Try. You Will Not Have To Commit To Any Payments Until You Are Sure This Is The Right Program For You.
1994	This Free Offer Will Self Destruct In 5 4 3 2
1995	Imagine Putting A System Into Place That Once Unleashed Continues To Work For You! So You Don't Have To Put Any Extra Effort To Make It Run. It Continues To Build And Grow On It's Own!
1996	Do I Pay You Directly Or Should I Pay Someone Else
1997	This Video Lays Out The Little-Known Methods Of How The Super-Elite Marketers Dominate Niches Like A Walk On The Beach.

1998	Now I Know That Sounds Bold Maybe Even A Bit Cocky But It's True
1999	This Can Accelerate Your Success Because It Teaches You To 'Bypass' Spending Weeks Or Months Of Your Time To Learn All The Technical Stuff And Things It Takes Just To Get Web Pages Online And Other Elements Just To Get Money Coming In -- Because You're Learn How Easy It Is To Get Someone Else To Setup Everything For You; So You Can Focus On The Marketing Part.
2000	Exactly How And Where To Find Great Content For Your Website If You Don't Feel Like Spending Hours On Creating It Yourself (This Is A Great Shortcut That Will Enable You To Focus More On Making Huge Sums Of Money Rather Than Writing Articles :)
2001	The Reason Why You Must Step Out Of The 'Builder Mindset' To Create Awesome Products That Will Take The Marketplace By Storm.
2002	It's Time To Take Action Because Hoping For Something Better Isn't Enough
2003	If You Aren't Willing To Invest A Puny Amount Of Time Or Effort To Watch Over My Shoulder As I Actually Show You Live Case Studies Of Campaigns In Real Time Then Do Yourself A Favor And Stop Searching.
2004	Even With Little Money Knowing How To Leverage It Will Make You More
2005	At What Point Will Reality Sink In So That You'll Change Your Approach To Internet Marketing
2006	What Could You Do If You Could Cut Your 60 Hour Work Week Down To Only 6 Hours
2007	It Doesn't Matter How "Technically Challenged" Or "Untalented" You May Think You Are Because My Brand New Software Program — Complete With Step-By-Step Onscreen Video Tutorials
2008	When I Saw This Chicken Running Around With His Head Cut-Off, The First Thing I Thought Of Was How I Use To Market My MLM Business (Weird, I Know, But That's How Determined I Was To Be A Success In This Industry...
2009	It's Easier To Achieve Millionaire Status Today Than Ever In History
2010	Don't Waste Your Money Buying Anymore Promises Until You've Proven This To Yourself

2011	They Laughed When I Said I'd Increase Conversions By At Least 75%
2012	I'm Sure You'll Give It Your 110%. But If Something Is Not Working Out, Tell Me Exactly What The Problem Is And I Will Clarify It More Precisely To Ensure You Follow Through And Make Money Online For Sure.
2013	Which Do You Want To Overcome First Fear Lack Of Money Or Lack Of Knowledge
2014	Take Action Over The Next 30-Days To Find Or Create A Great Product To Sell
2015	The Cool Thing Is That Not Only Are You Invited To A Really AWESOME Celebration But There Are So Many Prizes Available For You To Win, Odds Are Very Good That You Will Easily Walk Away A Very Happy Winner Today. And, I Just Know You Are Going To Have Tons Of Fun!
2016	And We're Not Talking About Just Any Kind Of Untargeted, Unresponsive Freebie Seekers! No, No. Those Will Just Waste Your Time And Money. This Is About Individuals Who Have Either Shown Interest In Your Kind Of Product Or Have Actually Purchased Similar Products!
2017	A Swipe File Is A Collection Of Tested And Proven Advertising And Sales Letters. Keeping A Swipe File (Templates) Is A Common Practice Used By Advertising Copywriters And Creative Directors As A Ready Reference Of Ideas For Projects.
2018	We Have Built Affiliate Memberships Over And Over Into The Tens Of Thousands Of Members With A "System" That We Have Perfected That We Call THE SIMPLE SYSTEM FOR SUCCESS.
2019	I Test Everything I Do. I Test Not Only Products, To See If Anyone Wants Them. I Test Ads. I Test Headlines. I Test Offers. I Test Everything -- And I Find Out Through Trial And Error What Works And What Doesn't Work. I Find Out What People Want. And Then I Give It To Them.
2020	Instead Of Wanting To Run Away, What If You Were So Full Of Domineering Confidence That You Desired To Charge Into Action Head On? What Is Sad Is That This Way Of Thinking Is Not Only Possible - But Inevitable - If You Follow The Process We Outlined Here.
2021	There Is Simply No Faster Or Easier Way That I Know Of To Generate A Passive Income Of Five Figures Per Month Or More...Every Month...Than With Membership Websites.

2022	Why You Have Less Than 6 Seconds To Capture And Hold My Attention
2023	Strap Yourself In For One Hell Of A Ride With A Big Frickin Bang
2024	This Secret Has Made It Possible For Me To Drive Hundreds Of Thousands Of Visitors To All Of My Sites On Complete Auto-Pilot, And It Doesn't Matter If I EVER Come Into The Office Or Even Turn On My Computer!
2025	How Would You Like To Personally Pick The Brain Of A Stellar Marketing Genius
2026	Make Your Marketing And Selling Automatic And Robotic So That You Are Not Out There Having To Make Cold Calls And Selling Yourself. You Set Up A System That Allows Machines And Systems To Do All Your Selling For You.
2027	It Is Not Hard To Build Your Own Facebook Empire, As Long As You Know What You Are Doing. Allow Me To Give You The Benefit Of My Expertise And Experience. I've Sold Countless Products Online, And Have Learned Through My Successes And Failures What Works. I Created This Video Series Specifically To Help People Learn The Right Way To Practice Facebook Marketing.
2028	Are You Being Suckered Into Scam Shortcuts And Loop Holes To Make Your First Million
2029	Don't Give Up – Not Now – You're Only One Step Away
2030	I Want To Earn Your Business The Old Fashion Way Through Trustworthy Quality
2031	Is Fear Holding You Back From Accomplishing Your First Really Successful Online Business
2032	You See, Unlike Most Online Opportunities, I Don't Have To Fool Or Deceive You To Get You To Sign Up For My System.
2033	Keeps An Easy To Manage Record Of All Customers And Orders Online
2034	When You Really Come Right Down To It, The Foundational Principle Of Building A Business Is Duplication. When You Find Something That's Working For You, Even If It's Just Turning A Tiny Profit At First, Just Figure Out How To Duplicate It . . . Over And Over Again.
2035	Never Think Your Customers Are Satisfied With Their Purchase. You Should Be Constantly Finding New Ways To Better Your Product And Service.
2036	Make Sure Life Begins To Happen The Way You Want It To

2037	Even If You Have Screwed Up A Million Times Before And Struggled In The Past...Once You Are Shown By An Expert How To Do It, In A 'Baby Steps' Way And In A Language You Can Understand, It Will Make Earning These Commissions Easier Than Shooting Fish In A Barrel...
2038	If It Really Is This Simple There Must Be A Very Good Reason Why
2039	Create A Discussion Forum Where You Post New Content To Be Discussed Every Day.
2040	Why There Is Way More To Being An Affiliate Than Just Click-bank... Big Affiliate Opportunities Are Staring You In The Face Everywhere On The Web... I'll Show You How To Capitalize.
2041	Imagine Waking Up One Morning And Checking Your Email To Find Dozens Or Hundreds Of Payment Notifications. Now That's One Thing I Sure Don't Mind Flooding My Inbox. This Is Happening Right Now And I Can Prove It To You.
2042	Finally! A Quick And Easy Way For YOU To Painlessly Set Up Your OWN Moneymaking 'Mini' Websites... Without Being A Computer Geek, Buying Expensive Software, Or Paying Out-rageous Fees To A Webmaster!
2043	Questioning Techniques That Will Tell You Exactly When They Will Buy
2044	I'm Going To Share With You The Exact Same Secrets To Achieving The Same Results That I Am. You Will Be Doing The Exact Same Things That I've Been Doing Each And Every Day. And No Stone Will Be Left Unturned. I Promise. If You Follow My Instructions Exactly, You're Going To Make Money, Lots Of It...And In 7 Days Or Less!
2045	Advertising Credits Are Earned From Our Site By Clicking On E-Mail Credit Links Or Text Ads Within Our Site.
2046	Clickbank Is The Internet's Largest Digital Marketplace, Where Thousands Of The Web's Most Popular Products Are Sold Every Day.
2047	Revolutionary Breakthrough System Reveals Million Dollar Loophole That Will Make You Hundreds Up To Thousands Of Dollars A Day Quickly And Easily...Without Selling A Single Thing...100% Guaranteed
2048	Are Your Prospects Resting On The Fringes Of Your Target Market

2049	You'll Never Get Rich That Way, And More Important You'll Never Get The Life Of Freedom And Abundance That You Deserve.
2050	I've Been Meaning To Give You This But Business Has Been Crazy
2051	I Also Have A Few More Bonuses For You On The Inside, But You'll Have To Wait To Find Out What They Are. But I'm Basically Giving You Everything You Need To Get Your Blogs Going Each Month
2052	Why Marketers Are Saving Their Best Products For Release This Day
2053	Due To Double Entries There Is Three More Spots Left In The Give It All Away System. It Is Possible That They Will Be Gone By The Time You Receive This Email. The Only Way To Now For Sure Is To Go To The Link And Check It Out.
2054	In Less Than 3 Hours I Am Opening The Doors To My New Total Business Package Offer, Which Only 10 People Will Get. You Can Get All The Details Here:
2055	Now You Can Finally Cash In From The YouTube Gravy Train... Turn Casual Viewers Into Frenzied, Wallet-Waving Buyers... Keep Reading. There's Something You Need To Know...
2056	Be Professional And Courteous In Your Final Correspondence With Them, Thank Them For Trying Your Product, Apologize That The Product Did Not Meet Their Needs, And Promptly Refund Them. After That, You Have No Obligation For Any Further Correspondence.
2057	BUT, It's Nearly Free. Trust Me, When You See What You're Getting You Won't Believe Your Eyes. Check It Out Right Now, And Grab Yours While You Can At
2058	A Powerful Technique To Make Sure You Stay Focused On Your Prospect With Laser-Like Precision, Creating A Win-Win-Win Situation For You, Your Client, And Your Prospect And Why It's Actually Okay For Your Client To Lose Money On The First Sale ... Just To Keep The Prospect Happy!
2059	How To Stop Prospects Dead In Their Tracks And Force Them To Read And Devour Every Single Word Of Copy You Write.
2060	Work Your Way Into The Deepest And Darkest Corners Of The Inner Circle

2061	We Have All Been There. You Get An Email Or Read An Ad That Drives You To A Website Where You Are Met With Incredible Claims Of Untold Wealth, Your Emotions Run Wild.
2062	Feel Like You Never Left The Office Every Day Of The Week
2063	How To Make Money With Blogs. Search Engines Love Blogs As Well. Even If You Don't Have Any Technical Knowledge Or Experience, That's Ok. I'll Show You A Very Useful Site That Walks You Right Through Setting Up A Blogging Account.99
2064	You'll Receive Free Upgrades For Life – You Are Guaranteed To Always Have The Latest Software Running Your Site... And Unlike Many Software Providers Who Charge Yearly Fees For Upgrades... You Won't Pay A Dime When A New Version Is Released.
2065	Now, Do You Know Someone That Would Benefit From Having Their Own Copy? Tell Them About It With The Form Below! As A Thank You For Referring Friends, We'll Send You A Special Bonus Gift Via Email.
2066	Good For You...But Let Me Tell You A SECRET! There Is A BIG Percentage Of People Out There That Before They Buy ANYTHING From You, They Will Go To Google Or Yahoo And SEARCH For YOU And Your Products.
2067	There Is Nothing Worse Than Reading Through An Article That Has Grammatical And Spelling Errors, Unless, Of Course, You Are The One Writing It. So Take The Extra Time And Actually Re-Read Your Work. This Does Not Mean Simply Pressing The Spell Check Button. It Means Reading It, Top To Bottom And Catching All Of Those Hidden Errors.
2068	Don't Let Your Wildest Dreams Be Limited By Anyone Or Anything
2069	Let's Take A Look At How We Can Make That Happen
2070	If Making Money Is So Easy Why Are You And Your Friends Broke
2071	There's Too Much Information Tons And Tons And Tons Of It
2072	How To Create Quality Free Gifts That Will Have Your Visitors Scrambling For More
2073	Why You Need To Immediately Protect Your Own Identity Theft Now
2074	Get Paid To Do Your Own Traveling As A Legitimate Tax Deduction
2075	Are You Tripping Over Your Own Internet Feet And Falling Flat On Your Internet Face

153

2076	Or You Can Take Action Today And Grab Our Free Report And Discover What It Really Takes To Grow A Colossal Organization.
2077	Copy And Paste These Into Your Sales Copy To Spice Things Up A Little, And To Add Visual Aids To Make Your Copy More Noticeable. These Graphics Elements Will Come In Different Colors And Styles. And They're Already In PNG And JPEG Formats, So You Don't Need Any Special Software, You Can Use Them As Is. Here Are Some Samples...
2078	How Can You Leverage That Strength To Create The Result You Want
2079	Why Can A Lazy SOB Succeed In Business When Others Can't
2080	You Will Look At Today As The Day That Put You On The Path To The Level Of Income And Type Of Lifestyle That You Have Always Dreamed Of...But Wondered If You Would Ever Really Experience.
2081	Eventually You Will Have A Huge Organization Of People Working For You As They Work For Themselves. You Will Get To The Point When Your One Hour A Day Is Actually Producing Results That Could Only Be Produced If You Worked 24 Hours A Day. Still Doing Your Simple, One Hour Job.
2082	Blogging And Affiliate Marketing - What Type Of Blog Works Best
2083	Think You've Heard It All When It Comes To Web 2.0? Think It's All A Tedious Waste Of Time? You're Right... MOST Of It Is.
2084	What's The Thing They Do To Get This Amount Of Traffic
2085	The Following Invite Is ONLY For List Owners. If You're Only Interested In Learning More About What I Have Up My Virtual Sleeve, Then Stay Tuned -- We'll Have More Details For You ... Pronto.
2086	People Will Buy Them All If Each Seems Incomplete Without The Other
2087	A Dead Simple Trick Applied To Your Headline Proven To Boost Conversions By 17%

2088	This Is Not A Limited Time Offer. The Problem With Waiting Is You Are Passing Up A Great Opportunity To Start A Real Online Business Today. If You Decide To Wait, You Will Probably Lose This Page Or Forget About It. If You Are Lucky Enough To Find Your Way Back Here In A Few Months Or A Year Later And Then Get Started, You Will Be Kicking Yourself For Not Starting Sooner.
2089	How To Turn Curious Surfers Into Loyal Life Long Customers Without Spending One Penny
2090	Do Not Add Extra Spaces To The Username And Passwords When Submitting Them To The Download Form (Especially If You Cut And Paste Them From This Email). If Your Login Doesn't Work, Please Make Sure You Have Removed All Spaces When Submitting The Username And Password.
2091	You May Not Know It Yet But You're Sitting On The Edge Of Incredible Success
2092	It Was Designed To Give ANYONE A Realistic Chance To Earn A Life Transforming Income In Their Spare Time Regardless Of Any Limitations They Currently Face!
2093	Content Rich Web 2.0 Warrant Fresh Content That Improves Your Page Rank And Traffic
2094	Answer Questions On Discussion Forums Using Your Content.
2095	Wake Up And Smell The Coffee But Make Sure You Get In While The Getting's Good
2096	With One Giant Turbo Kick You'll Be Well On Your Way To The Bank
2097	These Are Just A Few Reasons For The Large Scale Failure Of Marketers Entering The Adsense Space And Trying To Make A Go Of It...
2098	How Would Your Website Love To Have The Power Of MySpace Or Facebook
2099	Affiliate Marketing Needn't Be So Stressful! That Is Why This Affiliate Marketing Manual Is Different From The Rest...It's So Easy To Follow, You Won't Be Pulling Your Hair Out Figuring What To Do!
2100	This Is The Best Program Online For People Sick And Tired Of All The Hype And Empty Promises...That Want To Finally Achieve Success Online And Make Big Cash Working From Home!
2101	Tips To Writing A Compelling Headline To Get Your Page Opened And Read

155

2102	Are You Continually Being Seduced Into Debt By The Wizards Of Debt Manipulation
2103	Why Are So Many So Desperate To Buy These Just From Me
2104	Once You See Exactly What I'm Doing You'll Understand This Powerful Marketing Lesson
2105	You're Only A Few Simple Steps Away From Securing Your Copy
2106	Just As I Was About To Give Up The Answer Clearly Appeared
2107	You Don't Have To Go It Alone Anymore I'm Here To Help
2108	The Only People Who Will Fall Behind Are Those That Don't Join
2109	I Hope You're Not Going To Make The Same $5,000 Mistake I Just Made
2110	Contact Me Before The 30 Days Are Up And You'll Pay Nothing
2111	Is It Worth Five Bucks To Be Able To KNOW What They're Up To BEFORE They Get Their Hooks In You?
2112	How And Why Some Marketers Rarely Ever Fail To Make Money Online
2113	You'll Will Be Able To Earn An Extra $2,400 A Year Through Your Own "Very Small Business" That You'll Create In The Next Few Weeks.
2114	Join The Hungry Marketers Who Proactively Prowl The Internet Seeking Their Fortunes
2115	Smash Those Nagging Small Tasks With A Sledgehammer - You Know The Kind; They're Important, And They Need Done, But They're Small And You Never Seem To Find Time Get Them Done And Cross Them Off Your List. Use Action Machine Pro, Set Aside A Measly 30 Minutes, And Don't Just Whittle Away At Your List - Set It On Fire!
2116	Eliminate Debt Once And For All While Creating Permanent Financial Freedom
2117	I'm Offering You A Way Out, The Chance To Shun Your Corporate Hell, Your Idiot Boss, The Suit And Tie, In Exchange For A Hawaiian Shirt, Flip-Flops And A Laptop.
2118	What Is The Best Allocation Of Your Time Money And Resources
2119	This Offer Will Sell Out Fast Because Of The Incredible Results It Has Already Achieved

2120	I Am Going To "Show You" Exactly How You Can Copy What I Do And Make Yourself Thousands Of Dollars A Month. This Is All About Making Serious Money By Following My Simple Step By Step System, Implementing My Unique And Proven Methods And Using My System's Undercover Techniques.
2121	Create An Unstoppable Flood Of Laser Targeted Traffic Eager To Start Swarming Your Site
2122	When You Add In That Bonus It's Easy To See How This Is An Absolute No-Brainer Of A Deal. But, At The Same Time, This Deal Is So Incredibly Good That It's Going To Be Gone Before You Know It.
2123	Stunning Squeeze Pages That Will Blow Your Competition Away With Incredible Ease
2124	Now Baby Boomers Are Making Big Money Online And So Can You
2125	Again And Again You'll End Up With The Same Question Unless You Have These
2126	I Knew I Needed To Build A List But Had No Idea How. I Struggled To Figure Out The Fastest Way To Make A Decent Living From Home But Just Couldn't Seem To Get It Right.
2127	Finally Turn A Decent Profit. Find Profitable Products To Promote With Ease. Pinch Google For Penny Clicks, And To Receive A Full-Time Income For Part Time Work From Home.
2128	A Constant Stream Of Traffic Flows Into Your Site, Day And Night, With Literally NO EFFORT On Your Part. This Is What Web Marketers Dream About. Traffic And Sales With Virtually No Effort.
2129	It's A Powerhouse. I Make Serious Cash Using This Very Same System I'm Practically Giving Away To You. I'm Confident You Will Too With Me Here To Help Guide You To Success...
2130	Only 3 Kinds Of Websites That Will Ever Make A Huge Fortune Online
2131	How To Tell The Difference Between Features And Benefits. Most Novice Writers Write Sales Letter That Make Them Broker Than Yesterday And One Of The Main Reasons Are Found In Their Failing To Understand The Distinctions Between Features And Benefits. I Define Them In Simple English And Show You Multiple Examples Of Benefits Vs. Features Which You Can Use For Your Own Sales Copy!
2132	I Love Internet Marketing For The Same Reasons I Hate It

2133	Here's Our Free Thank You Gift That 97% Of Our Subscribers Have Used To Generate More Revenue Online Today!
2134	Sure Beats The Heck Out The Hassles Of A Day Job
2135	I Recently Emailed You And Gave You Links To Some Videos About A Guy Selling $29,000,000 PER YEAR Online Worth Of Info-products (And His Business Is GROWING Every Year.) If You Haven't Figured It Out Yet By Now, Selling Information Products Online Is One Of The BEST Business Models You Can Use.
2136	The Only 2 Keys You Need For A Successful Internet Business
2137	The ONLY Thing Required For You To Earn An Incredible Income Is A Small Investment Of Your Time And Effort To Give Away The System To Others. That's It!
2138	Plus On Top Of Everything Else, You're Getting 2 Powerful Bonuses Valued At $1247...And These Aren't Your Standard Fare Crappy Ebook Bonuses...No, These Are Real.
2139	Prepare A Media Kit Promoting Your Business.
2140	Let Me Show You Exactly How To Find Hot Trends Using Google® And Make Some Easy Money On A Daily Basis. You May Already Know All About Trends, But I Will Take The Learning Curve Out Of Making The Easy Money And Get You Started In The Next Hour.
2141	With A Push Of A Button, This Revolutionary, Easy To Use, Affordable System, Will Promote, Distribute And Syndicate Your Message To The Billions Of Internet Users Worldwide In Minutes And Start Appearing In Search Engines In Hours.
2142	Did You Know That In 2010 Alone Info-Product Sales Are Expected To Exceed $448 Billion? That's Billion - With A B. It Has Doubled In The Last Several Years Alone ... So, Are You Gonna Catch This Wave Or What?
2143	Life Is Pretty Neutral Allowing You To Reach Any Goal You Desire
2144	Only Serious Motivated Marketers Are Willing To Take Immediate Action Because Of This
2145	You Really Won't Mind Writing Small Checks When You're Getting Paid Big Checks
2146	There Are No Better Healers Than God And Your Angels. When You Use Angels In Every Area Of Your Life, Life Becomes So Much Better. The Greatest Thing About Angels Is They Heal From The Inside Out So When You Heal The Inside, The Outside Is Sure To Follow.

2147	Social Media Sites And Social Opportunities To Target Your Niche Market And Network With The Right Prospects. So Why Not Take Advantage Of The Social Nature Of The Net By Using Social Media As A Way To Generate Traffic And Target Your Niche. Below We Have Listed Some Of The Top Tips In The Subject Of Social Media Traffic.
2148	FREE Quick Simple And Effective Strategies Without Any Hidden Agenda Or Obligation
2149	When All You Need Is A Break.. A Chance... A Shot... It Doesn't Seem Fair That Some Get The Breaks While Others Wait Forever - And Maybe Never Get It At All.
2150	You Can Read About It But Until You Join And Start Making Money You'll Won't Believe It
2151	It Just Makes Total Sense To Use The Work Of Others As A Starting Point For What You Do With Your Business. This Way You Save A Ton Of Time And Effort And Find Yourself Constantly Coming Up With New Ideas Every Day.
2152	These Are Just A Few Of The Reasons That I Have Decided To Start My Own Business
2153	Nobody Ever Said Life Would Be Fair, So I Became Determined To Make My Own Break. I Began Where Everyone Searches For Answers These Days—The Internet.
2154	With Customer Testimonials Like These We Don't Have To Sell Anything
2155	Listen To The Herd, They Say The Content Network Is Crap, Meanwhile Savvy Marketers Like Myself Are Cleaning Up Building Huge Buyers Lists For Pennies.
2156	Use PLR Affirmations, Quotes, And Snippets From Articles To Create Coasters, Business Cards, Or Post-It Notes With Your Contact Details.
2157	As I Continued To Answer Questions And Help People Through The IM Obstacle Course, I Began To Enjoy It. A Lot.
2158	Ozone Created By Electric Cars Now Killing Millions In The Seventh Largest Country In The World, Mexifornia, Formerly Known As California
2159	I Love Teaching And Now Even More I Love Teaching Others How To Make Lots Of Money
2160	I've Been Working On This Incredible Collection For Many Years And Need Your Feedback
2161	How To Build A Customer Base That Will Eagerly Love To Do Business With You

159

2162	The Most Important Questions You Prospect Will Definitely Have In Mind That You Must Answer Well. You Don't Have Mind-Reading Abilities, But I Show You The Most Important Questions Your Prospect Would Definitely Want To Have Answered And How You Can Answer Them Well In Order To Close The Sale.
2163	If You Don't See How This System Can Help Your Business, Do Nothing. Your Account Will Automatically Expire At The End Of The 30 Day Trial. Keep All The Training Information As My Personal Gift.
2164	But What If I Told You There Was A Shortcut Available …That There's A Way For You To Build Your List Much Faster Than You Probably Ever Imagined Possible … While Making Cash Profits At The Very Same Time.
2165	Imagine Waking Up Some Weekday In The Near Future… There's No Alarm Clock, Just A Few Birds Singing Into The Late Morning.
2166	Discover The Four Most Profitable Months In Which To Spend Your Advertising Budget
2167	Maybe It Wasn't Your Fault Just A Matter Of Bad Timing
2168	How To Get Quality And Effective Articles When Outsourcing The Work. Not Knowing This Information Could Leave You Broke Before You Even Make A Single Cent From Your Articles.
2169	I'm Ready To Take Charge Of My Life And Start Making REAL Money Online. I'm Prepared To Reach New Financial Heights And Improve The Quality Of Life For Me And My Loved Ones.
2170	This Is A Very Simple Process That Can Be Repeated Over And Over Again Creating Many Multiple Income Streams.
2171	You're Probably Wondering How This All Works? Well, We've Scoured The Globe To Bring You The Finest Lessons In Human Development. This Includes The Areas Of Emotional, Physical, Spiritual, Financial, Relationships, Career… You Name It And We've Got It Covered. We've Left No Stone Unturned To Create A Program That Helps You Live A Happy And Fulfilling Life.
2172	You're Getting Everything You Need To Get Started And Actually Having Success Online
2173	A Simple Guide To Search Engine Optimization, Which Is An Awesome And Very Cheap Way To Get Free And Extremely Targeted Search Engine Traffic That Will Generate Sales!

2174	How To Build A Loyal Following Who Will Buy Almost Anything You Promote (The Best Part Is Even Raw Beginners Can Start Using This Method On The Very First Day; It Is That Simple And Easy To Do.)
2175	You Can Easily Get Ranked In Search Engine By Just Repeating The Keywords You Are Target In The Title And Body.
2176	I'm Not Looking To Become The List Building Guru, I Don't Want To Hang Around With Rich Elitists. But I Do Want To Make A Great Second Income Working For Me 24/7/365.
2177	Avoid The Cost, The Hiring Headaches, The Training, The Turnover...Enough Said. Although We Will Talk About Outsourcing With Virtual Employees Once Your Sites Profits Start To Roll In.
2178	If You're Not Using A Sweet & Sexy "Grab Your Customer By The Eyeballs" Trigger Phrases And Action Headlines Then There's No Doubt You're Losing Thousands Of Dollars In Extra Profits Each Month.
2179	The Simple Untold Secret Clearly Explains What You Should Never Do Online
2180	You'll Kick Yourself Really Hard If You Don't Order This Today
2181	I Can't Promise You'll Build A Huge Downline Just By Reading The Book, But I Can Show You How I Built The 2nd Largest Team In My Company In Less Than 1 Year.
2182	When Is The Last Time You Had Fun Without A Computer
2183	You Do Not Have To Use This Software To Build Your Sites, But You Can Learn How To Build Your Own Instead Of Having To Outsource Your Website Design Paying Upwards Of $400 A Time.
2184	Why On Earth Would You Want To Handicap Your Earning Potential By Forgetting This
2185	Take Advantage Of The Hottest And Most Profitable Online Trend Since The Dawn Of The Internet – It's Super Easy To Set Up Your Own Social Networking Site And Cash In On Multiple Streams Of Revenue Instantly.
2186	How Long Is It Since You Realized That The Job You're In Won't Free You Up From Financial Worries For The Long Term, But Will Just Keep You At It, Day After Day, Week After Week And Year After Year Until You're Simply Out Of Time?

161

2187	If Demand For The Product Is Too Weak, I'll Just Refund The Money For Anyone Who Has Paid In Advance For It. But If The Orders Start Coming In, And Come In Strong, I'll Have A Pretty Good Idea That The Product Will Be A Hit. And That Will Motivate Me To Move Forward Full Speed To Get The Product Ready For Distribution.
2188	Why Should I Trust You When I've Been Burned So Many Times Before
2189	Use PLR Wallpapers To Add Some Flair To Reports.
2190	Why 93% Of What You Learn Is A Bunch Of Bull
2191	To Sell Something Successfully, You Should Always "Sell The Problem Before You Sell The Solution!" Unfortunately, Most Marketers Jump Right Into Selling The Features And Benefits Of Their Product, Without Taking The Time To Understand If Their Prospect Believe They Even Have A Problem.
2192	Why Minisites Are Still A Fantastic Yet Very Simple Way To Make Money Online
2193	Stop Listening To Those Blowhards Who Tell You It's Easy To Make Money Online
2194	That's Right... For Every One Of These Ebooks That Is Sold From YOUR Webpage (I'll Give You A Website Exactly Like This And I'll Even Pay To Host It For You)... I'll Make NOTHING And You'll Keep The Five Dollars!
2195	We Learned Early-On About Target Marketing. Only Talk To People Who Have Raised Their Hand And Want What You Have.
2196	If You Aren't Getting At Least 45% Conversions On Your Pages, You Need To Get Serious By Adding Some Of Outrigger Keywords And Action Headlines To Your Next Ad Campaign, As Well As, Your Website.
2197	You May Not Know Me Yet But Given The Chance I May Be The Very Person You Need Most
2198	Send Snippets Of Content As An Email Tip To Encourage Customers To Return To Your Website.
2199	What's The Value Of Having A Program That Puts At Your Fingertips All The Effective Marketing Strategies And Power Promotional Tools That Will Increase Your Website Traffic And Generate Massive Website Profits For You?
2200	How To Make Sure Your Autoresponder Messages Are Being Read And Not Being Deleted

2201	And Because The Program Is Self-Funding, You'll Be Able To Afford To Move Through Each Step In The Pay-Plan At Your Own Speed By Using A Portion Of Your Profits Instead Of Money You Don't Have.
2202	Sites Like Myspace, Youtube And Facebook Have Hundreds Of Million Of Users EACH - And Yet You Have To Be ON Their Websites To Use The Social Networking Features.
2203	You Must Agree To Everything I Say And Do If You Want To Succeed
2204	Rise Up And Take Full Command Over Lost Sales And Lost Commissions Forever
2205	Mastering The Art Of Writing A Million Dollar Ad May Have Become Easier Than You Think
2206	How To Write Ads With Tested Proven Formats That Almost Always Get Clicks
2207	Simply Fill In Your Details Below To Claim Your Free Gifts Worth $189
2208	How To Show The Importance Of Your Readers In Online Copywriting
2209	When I Read This The Inner Light Bulb Simply Blew My Mind
2210	This Is By Far The Most Important Thing You Need To Understand If You're Ever Going To Break Free From The Grind. Break Free From Just Doing "Okay And Break Free From Seeing Tiny Paydays.
2211	I Can't Be Held Liable For Your Repeated Failure If You're Not Willing To Take Immediate Action With A Tested And Proven, Answer To Your Prayers.
2212	Stop Prospects Dead In Their Tracks And Force Them To Read And Devour Every Single Word Of Copy You Write.
2213	As I'm Sure You Are Aware, The Mobile Browsing Market Is Taking Off At Extreme Proportions. People Love Browsing The Internet Via Their Smart Phones, Ipads, Tablets And Other Mobile Devices. But Only A Very Small Percentage Of Websites And Blogs Are Actually Optimized For Mobile Browsing And This Means You Could Be Losing Lots Of Traffic And Money
2214	A Dozen Dirty Tricks Of New Car Dealers. Some Are Totally Undetectable -- Unless You Know What To Look For
2215	We Didn't Re-Invent The Wheel, But We Did Re-Invent A Pay Plan! Now Is Your Chance To Be A Part Of Something HUGE!

163

2216	You Won't Spend Precious Energy Worrying About Whether One Of The Most Important Linchpins Of Any Product Launch -- The Copy -- Is Strong And Effective
2217	Are You Interested In Living The Care Free Lifestyle In The Land Of Milk And Honey
2218	How Do You Get A Job Working From Home? But How Do You Do This? You Start Your Very Own Internet Marketing Business, That's How!
2219	You Have None Of The Risks Facing Other Business Owners Lets Face It. Most New Business Fail In The First Year, Starting A Traditional Business A Risky Proposition. You Don't Have To Worry About Losing Your Shirt, Income And Home When You Are An Affiliate Marketer.
2220	I Want To Empower You To Be Able To Live The Life You Always Wanted
2221	Works With UK Pounds, US Dollars, Euros, Australian Dollars Or Canadian Dollars
2222	Exactly How You Can Easily Make Your Websites Extremely Easy To Edit And Link With Other Websites You Own.
2223	It Took Lots Of Trial And Error To Filter Through All The Fluff And Garbage Being Sold Out There Before I Found Real Success.
2224	Don't Allow Your Marketing Fate To End Up In The Pocketbook Of Strangers
2225	These Videos Will Lead You Step-By-Step To Affiliate Marketing Riches - From Selecting Your Product To Promoting It For Monster Profits... All Without Spending A Single Dime.
2226	Think About It...How Many Internet Marketing Products Have You Bought To Date? A Few Hundred Dollars Worth? A Few Thousand Dollars Worth?? Have You Bought The Car, The House, That Vacation They Always Seem To Promise You On Their Sites?
2227	Ultimate Set And Forget System That Keeps Humming All The Way To The Bank
2228	Are You Finally Ready To Pop The Bubble On This Myth
2229	This Time You'll Be Able To Instantly Take Action Headlines From Our Online Arsenal Lists And Use Them To Your Own Ends With Virtually Zero Effort – Simply Copy And Paste.
2230	Protect Yourself From Being Burned By Candidates Who Over-Represent Their Skill Level

2231	You're About To Learn Secrets That Most _____ Will Never Know About _____!
2232	Informational Education Is What People Are Willing To Buy So Sell It
2233	WARNING: You Do Realize That People Will Lie Just To Get Your Money
2234	Start From Scratch Instead Of Scratching Your Head Trying To Reinvent The iWheel
2235	So Good I Just Had To Tell You About It Before I Explode
2236	In Terms Of Generating Wealth And Enormous Income, I Almost Can't Think Of Worse Advice Than The "Time Equals Money" Paradigm. That's The Kind Of Thinking The Leads To A Lifetime Of Slavery. Instead, Start Thinking About The Value You Can Create.
2237	This Free Book Could Be Worth Thousands Even Millions To Your Company's Bottom Line
2238	Great Giveaways Here. (Save Link And Use As You Wish, More Gifts Added Regularly) For You Now... I Would Like To Invite You In To The Launch Of A Unique One-Way Link Building System That Works BIG TIME!
2239	Our Affiliate Program is one of the greatest ways that online network marketers can uncover concealed cash for advertising, cash flow, or education.
2240	How To Completely Eliminate Visitor's Hatred For Your Opt In Page
2241	I Never Thought I Could Increase Conversions By At Least 75%
2242	Have You Had Success In Your Life, But Are Looking For Something New That Will Pay You What You're Worth And Allow You To Spend More Time With Your Family And Friends?
2243	Did You Know The Average Consumer Can Eliminate All Debt Including The Mortgage With The Money Currently Earned In An Average 7.5 Years? It's True.
2244	YES, What Your Seeing Is Real, I've Probably Lost My Mind But I'm Going To Show You 3 Niches I Am Already Working.
2245	To Build A Million-Dollar Internet Business, Plan It Out And Know What Are The Steps That Will Get You Closer To Your Goal. You Can't Get To Your Destination If You Don't Know What And Where Is Your Destination. Make Sense?
2246	Why Do So Many Home Businesses Fail In Attempting Their Product Launches

2247	Develop A Companion Worksheet, Checklist, Spreadsheet, Or Cheat Sheet.
2248	And By This Time Next Week You Could Have A Whole Bunch Of Them... And By This Time Next Month... Man The Sky's The Limit. You Could Have Tons Of Sites, Each Ripping You Down Some Serious Profit. You Could Be Making Thousands A Week, Just Like I Do.
2249	How To Apply Viral Leveraging And Cause A Ripple Of Extra Affiliate Commissions From Areas Of The Internet You Never Dreamed Existed (With The Right Programs...You Can Do This Several Times Throughout Year. And Here Is The Best Part; You Can Do This With Several Programs At Once.)
2250	We Show People Who Know Little Or Nothing About The Power Of The Internet, How To Attract A Lot Of Visitors, Using A Step-By-Step System That Teaches Them How To Make A Lot More Money Online Doing Things They Love Doing. Do You Know Anyone Who Could Benefit By Learning How To Make More Money Right Now?
2251	By Following This Marketing Approach, Your Recurring Commissions Could Easily Grow Beyond Your Expectations By This Time Next Year!
2252	What Are You Planning To Do As You Read All The Reports Of The Stock Market Falling, Bank Failures, Retirement Plans Crumbling, Plant Closings, Unemployment On The Rise, And Foreclosures Around The Country.
2253	What Business In Their Right Mind Wouldn't Want To Cut Their Costs In Half
2254	If What The Self-Proclaimed Gurus And Internet "Experts" Were Telling You Was Working... Why Are So Many People Still Struggling To Make A Self-Sustaining Income Online?
2255	Don't Wake Up To A Hacked Or Down Website During The Holiday Buying Season Or Just When You're Relying On Revenues From Your Website More Than Ever To Help You Through Tough Financial Times!
2256	So Do You Want To Know How Much This Will Cost You
2257	Discover The New Wave Of Budding Traffic Sources Before Anyone Else Knows About
2258	It Must Be So Compelling They Go Through Anything To Get IT
2259	Savvy Clickbank Affiliate Is Not Afraid Of A Little Competition By Those Inferior And Lacking These Table Turning Skills.

166

2260	Focus On Not Getting Distracted Once You Set You Business Goals Into Action
2261	If You're Like Many Of My Readers, You Watch And Listen To What People Are Saying About How You Can Make Thousands On The Internet As And Not Even Have To Leave Home With A Mixture Of Envy And Disbelief.
2262	There Are More Self-Proclaimed Gurus And 'Wannabe' Gurus Out There Than You Can Shake A Stick At.
2263	Start By Selling Just One Low Cost Report And Test The Market
2264	How To Write An E-book And Then Give It Away For FREE!
2265	While The Internet Marketplace Is Filled With Millions And Millions Of Prospects, You Still Won't Make Any Money If Nobody Knows About You. The Solution To Attracting People Like Ants To A Picnic Is To Get Your Site Listed On All The Major Search Engines, Such As Google, Yahoo And MSN.
2266	What If I Could Make It A Lot Easier For You To Succeed Online
2267	Take Your Knowledge To A Local Talk Radio Show.
2268	Are The Wizards Of Manipulation Still Sucking Your Bank Account Dry
2269	You Have Nothing To Lose! I Am Offering A 30 Day No Questions Asked Refund. Take It, Try It Out. If You Are Not 100% Satisfied With It, Then Return It. That Right There Is 'No Risk'
2270	Are You Listening To People Who Still Don't Have A Clue As To What They Are Doing Online
2271	The One Element Of Any Website That Buyers Care The Most About (It's Probably Not What You Think) – Plus The Simple, Quick And Easy Way To Get It On Your Site...
2272	If We Want To Make More Money We Need To First Start Thinking Our Time Is Worth More. So If You've Been Making $50 Per Hour, He Says, Start Thinking Your Time Is Worth $75 Per Hour.
2273	Owning A Membership Site Offers Tremendous Opportunities And Profit Power That Can Be Spelled In Two Words: Recurring Income. Yes, A Lifetime Income If Membership Website Owners Only Knew How To Do It.
2274	Since I Have Been Doing Business Online I Have Never Seen An Offer This Good For New Products That Are Being Sold Each And Every Day. It Truly Is A One Time Opportunity Of One Of The Best Deals I Have Ever Seen.

2275	Times Have Changed, Did You Keep Up? Pricing Strategies Are Changing, And They're Changing Faster Than Ever Before. Most Can't Keep Up, Or Don't Know Whether They're Too Expensive Or Too Cheap. I'm Going To Show You Exactly Why You Can Almost Never Be Too Expensive And How To Spot It Before Taking A Sales Hit When You Are.
2276	What Makes This Offer Different Is That These Claims Are Extremely Credible And We Can Prove It.
2277	Why Leave Success To Chance When You Can Guarantee A Successful Launch For Free
2278	This Is All Included With Your 30 Day Free Trial Along With Full Access To All Of Our Powerful Promotional Tools AND The Training To Make It All Work For You.
2279	Why This Simple Punctuation Mark Becomes The Most Read Copy Of Your Entire Offer
2280	Are You Ready To Stand Behind The Curtain And Master A Few Simple Strategies
2281	They Tell You To Go Here And Do This... But Then When You Try It Yourself, You Hit A Huge Hump. You Find The Page Is No Longer Live... Or You Need To Buy A Piece Of Software, Or Sign Up For Some Kind Of Monthly Payment Program... There's Always A Catch.
2282	Never Again Have Writer's Block!, You'll Never Have Trouble Writing Powerful Headlines For The Most Important Aspects Of Your Business. Our Incredible Resource Contains The Right Words That Will Eliminate Your Frustrating Head-Scratching Blanks That Comes With This Marketing Territory.
2283	Have You Focused All Your Internet Efforts The Hard Way Without Results
2284	Laugh At Procrastination - Take Any Task You've Been Putting Off, Give Yourself 30 Minutes To Get It Done, Start Your Timer, And Watch What Happens. This Simple Process, Which Action Machine Pro Automates, Creates A 'Virtual' Space In Your Brain For That Task That You Feel Unexplainably Compelled To Fill With Its Completion!
2285	You Really Only Have 2 Options And Option 1 Is Far Too Risky
2286	It's Really All About Automating Great Products And Creating Residual Daily Income

2287	I'm Sure That Makes It A Real No Brainer, Right? I Will Be Limiting The Amount Sold So May Pull This Down Anytime. I Pulled A Previous Offer The Market And Was Drowned By Emails From People Asking Me To Reopen, They Missed Out So Make Sure You Don't.
2288	I Should Have Seen It Coming. Company Loyalty Is A Thing Of The Past, So, I Decided I'd No Longer Trust My Future To The Corporate World. Instead, I Took The Advice Of Donald Trump And Robert Kiyosaki And Found A Good Direct-Sales Network Marketing Company.
2289	You're The Only Person Who's Not Managed To Find The Answers
2290	Can You Get Just One Visitor To Your Website Each Hour
2291	We Can Also Set Up An Automated Advertising And Follow-Up System For You With All The Ads And Follow-Up Letters Pre-Loaded Into It Which Will Help You Build Your Own Personal Mailing List.
2292	What If Everything You've Been Taught Was A Lie To Ensure Your Failure
2293	Think Of A Ferrari. It's Got All The Fancy Styling And Beautiful Lines. Gorgeous Paint Job And Unheard Of Aerodynamics. But, Without The Engine It's Not Going Anywhere. You've Got To Have The Right Foundation To Build That Beautiful Car.
2294	What Result Could I Achieve That Would Make Me Feel Successful
2295	Powerful Promotional Tools Than Can Dramatically Increase Traffic Sales And Profits
2296	In Fact, We're So Absolutely Positive Of This – We're Willing To Give You One Of The Most Daring Guarantees You'll See In Print.
2297	Urgency And Scarcity Are The Two Most Important Reasons To Buy Now
2298	I Encourage You To Read Over The Testimonials From People Just Like You, Who I've Helped Overcome Their Fear Of Asking For The Order, And Taught How To Become Relentlessly Effective Closers With A Combination Of The Right Attitude And Knowing Precisely What To Say In Any Selling Situation.
2299	In Terms Of Generating Wealth And Enormous Income, I Almost Can't Think Of Worse Advice Than The "Time Equals Money" Paradigm That's The Kind Of Thinking The Leads To A Lifetime Of Slavery. Instead, Start Thinking About The Value You Can Create.

2300	I Spent Months Reviewing Dozens Of Books, Audio Programs, And Seminars And Translated The Most Important Ideas Into Affirmations. Some Of The Authors I Studied Are Napoleon Hill, Tony Robbins, Zig Ziglar, Dale Carnegie, Brian Tracy, And Many Others. I Wanted To Master The Inner Game Of Success.
2301	Get Noticed: Go In With A Bang By Launching Your New Site, Or New Content On Social Bookmarking Sites. Many Social Bookmarking Sites, Such As Digg, Reddit And Netscape Are Read On A Daily Basis And A Perfect Place To Start Your Traffic Generation Debut.
2302	Our Business Helps People New To The Internet Learn How To Attract A Constant Flow Of New Customers Helping Them Make More Money With A Program Called "The Language Of Millionaires. " Do You Know Anyone Who Can Benefit By Making More Money Now?
2303	Congratulations On A Smart Business Decision. There's Only One More Thing To Do And That's To Look In Your Email Box To Find Your Confirmation Link. Click On That To Make Sure You Don't Miss Out On The Crazy PLR Deals That I'm About To Send You.
2304	What I'm Offering Here Is A Proven Unique System That Will Allow You To Build Yourself An Automatic Income That Never Dies. As I Said, It's Like Having Your Own Cash-Dispensing-Machine With Unlimited Funds!
2305	The Self Improvement Crowd Is Not Going To Disappear In The Future. As The World Becomes More Hectic And More Corrupt, The More People Will Want To Look For Ways To Get Ahead, Improve Themselves, Find Themselves, Think More Positively, Set More Goals, Look For More Opportunities, Build Networks, Even Find Something Fun To Do When They Are Old!
2306	These Videos Are Super Cheap And Well Worth So Much More Than You Can Imagine
2307	I Handing You The Very Best Information About The Internet Marketing Industry On A Silver Platter So You Can Begin Ramping In Serious Profits With This Entire Video Training Course That You Can Brand As Your Own With Full Confidence!

2308	You Need To Think Outside The Computer Box And Into The Crazy Realm Of Cyber Space. And We Have Just The Tips To Get You There. We Have The Tricks Of The Trade That Can Generate The Traffic You Need. So Join The Web-Solution And Discover How To Earn Traffic On Your Website.
2309	If A Million Visitors Came To Your Site Today Would They Buy Anything
2310	An Indication That There's No Money To Be Made There Is Based On Whether The Competitive Markets Have Amazing Amounts Of Money Swirling Around Them. It's True That There's Tons Of Competition, But There's So Much Business That You Can Easily Find A Small Corner To Set Up Shop In.
2311	Keys That Every Successful Website Have In Common That Can Practically Guarantee Your Success
2312	The Information Age Can Help Secure Your Market Niche But Only If You Take Action
2313	Use These To Out Pull Your Best Ad And Eliminate Your Money Worries Forever
2314	Step By Step Guide Is Now Your Playbook For Making A Lot More Money Online
2315	Keeping The Masses Fighting For Scraps While They Feast On Our Ignorance
2316	It's Not Uncommon To Hear Complaints Ranging From "Too Much Traffic, Not Enough Conversions" To "There's Not Enough Traffic For My Niche", And Everything In Between.
2317	Everyone's Running Around Telling You They Have The "Secrets" To Internet Marketing And Making Money Online. There Are So Many Hyped-Up "Get Rich Quick" Schemes Floating Around The Internet -- It Drives Me Crazy!
2318	How One Simple Change To Your Offer Can Double And Even Triple Sales
2319	There Are Some Things Government Politics Can't And Shouldn't Try To Solve
2320	BUT... Finally After Being Lied To Over And Over Again Thankfully Someone Made Me Stop And Learn.
2321	Local News: Open House Friday Dec 21st, at the Sewage Treatment Plant from 9am - 5 pm Refreshments Served -
2322	I Really Appreciate Your Time And Readership. Your Feedback Is Invaluable, So If You Have Something To Share, Just Let Me Know. Have A Great Week And Weekend,

171

2323	Every Day We Bring Together An Remarkable Array Of Amazing Products At No Cost. Our Powerful Proprietary Systems And Techniques Scour The Earth, Searching Out An Incredible Range Of Hidden Freebies.
2324	Be Prepared To Sweat A Little To Gain Ultimate Financial Control
2325	But Then You Get That Sinking Feeling In The Pit Of Your Stomach..
2326	Proven Plug And Play Wealth Building System That Produces Cash On Demand
2327	Now... The Choice Is Yours And Your Future Lies Entirely Within Your Own Hands. Just Ask Yourself This Very Simple Question... "Do I Want The Financial Freedom To Live My Life The Way I Want To Live It... Or Am I Happy Just Doing What I'm Doing Right Now?"
2328	Well, It May Be The New Frontier In MLM. OK, When A Personal Marketing Friend Of Mine Recommended This I Asked Him If He Was Nuts! Until He Showed Me Some Sobering Numbers.
2329	Time To Take Control Of Your Earning Potential And Never Feel Dependent On Anyone Again
2330	The Amazing Free Research Tool That Instantly Exposes The Hidden Value Of Any Site. It Lets You Unearth The Treasure Chest In Mere Seconds...
2331	Join The Successful People Who Know Exactly How To Help Make You Profitable
2332	How To Survey Your List, So They Sell Themselves On Your Product Before You Even Create It!
2333	Everyone In Your Organization Duplicates Your Efforts Because They Receive The Exact Same Strategy, Tools, Sources And Materials.
2334	Start New "Feeder" Websites And Blogs Dedicated To Specific Niches And Affiliate Products.
2335	Several Of These Relationships Have Developed Into Lucrative Business Ventures And Income Opportunities In And Of Themselves. It Just Keeps Expanding And Getting Better And Better Every Single Day...
2336	I Can Teach You Plenty Of Great Techniques But Are You Ready To Make That Kind Of Money
2337	If You Are Looking For Ideas On How To Get People To Click - I Suggest Having A Look At Digg.Com And Reddit.Com For Headlines That Have Gotten A Lot Of Clicks.

172

2338	First Off, I Want You To Know That We Are Working Behind The Scenes To Create A Series Of How To Videos That Will Show You Exactly How To Get The Most Out Of Your Store.
2339	Included With Your Purchase Are My 2 Favorite Methods Of Cloaking Your Clickbank Hop Links... One Is A PHP Script The Other Is A Secret HTML Page That Does A Sweet Job. Use Them To Prevent Casual Hijacking Of Your Hard-Earned Commissions!
2340	Entrepreneurs Fall Into The Trap Of Wanting To Do Everything Themselves. Entrepreneurs Are Usually Not Good Delegators. As An Entrepreneur You Should Make A Point Of Investing A Portion Of Your Time To Delegating Responsibilities To Others And Automating Your Business.
2341	I'm A Firm Believer That There's A Lot Of Money To Be Made Online
2342	What Happens When You Live Up To My Promises And Succeed
2343	How To Make Big Ticket Sales With Only 30 Minutes Of Your Time
2344	How To Eliminate Your Prospect's Fear Of Doing Business With You
2345	Getting More Traffic To Your Website Is A Constant Pain So We Came Up With A Valuable Tool That Can Directly Influence Your Business And Success, NOW!
2346	If You Are Interested In Owning Private Label Rights To A Very High End High Quality Training Course Like Many Were Last Week, Then Make Sure You Grab This Course Now At Such A Crazy Low Price And While We're Teaching It Live.
2347	I've Tried Affiliate Marketing, Pay Per Click, Infomercials, Copywriting, Forex, Ebay, List Building, Membership Sites, Multi-Level Marketing, Info Products, Website Flipping, Lead Generation, Blogging, Direct Response, Joint Venturing, Media Buying, Mobile Marketing, Newspaper Advertising, Postcard Marketing, Press Release Marketing, Social Networking On Myspace, Facebook, Youtube, Twitter, Teleseminars, Webinars, Cap Marketing, Ezine Advertising, Magazine Marketing, Small Business Consulting, Forex, Day Trading, And Even Neuro-Linguistic Programming To Name A Few..

2348	Taking The Steps To Become An Entrepreneur Takes Guts That Most People Don't Have, To Make The Effort To Learn About Your Business To Ensure Your Success As Much As Possible Takes Intelligence.
2349	How Were They Able To Keep This Hidden For So Long
2350	Can We All Just Agree To Ignore Whatever Comes After Blue Ray. I Don't Want To Have To Restart My Collection...Again.
2351	Do You Know That You Can Earn MORE Money With This Search Engine Optimization Company Than You Can With ANY Other Traditional SEO Business?
2352	If You're Renting A Home Or Apartment With A Payment As Little As $550
2353	These Are Just Some Of The Overwhelming Responses From My Students. They Are Happy To Share With Me Their Successes For Using The Tools That I Provide For Them. I Wish The Same For You As Well And Encourage You To Grab Your Copy Right Now Because Lack Of Action Limits Opportunity.
2354	Getting Up A Head Of Steam Over This Is Well Worth It
2355	Avoid All Those Smoke And Mirror Garbage Offers And See Why This Offer Is For Real
2356	Those Are Not Ways To Grow A Huge Business. They Never Have Been. We're Not Knocking These Companies, The Way They Run Their Businesses Or Any Of The Choices They Make.
2357	Tired Of Mediocre Marketing Results When This Will Provide Real Solutions
2358	STOP Prospecting Strangers and Buying Useless Leads, Because The Smart Marketers Who Understand The Power & Leverage of The Internet Are Dominating The Industry... Don't Get Left Behind!
2359	Be Ready To Be Blown Away By Both The Quality And Quantity
2360	This Isn't An Old Report You'll Find All The Other Marketers Peddling
2361	The Downside To Affiliate Marketing Is That While You Do Make Some Cash, You're Busy Building Someone Else's Business Instead Of Your Own. You Have To Keep Promoting New Products To Keep The Money Coming In.
2362	You're Here Because You Want To Make A Significant Income Online. Making Money Online Is Easy When You Know How To Do It.

2363	Just Because Someone Puts Down A Few Bucks And Is Now 'Self Employed', This Does Not Entitle That Person To Success.
2364	How To Get Your Own Domain Name And Web Site, Without Paying A Web Hosting Company
2365	I Know I Can Give You This Marketing Stuff But You Need This First
2366	Listen, I Could Spend The Rest Of My Life Trying To Describe The Incredible Cash Markets, Insane Traffic Secrets And Techniques That Will Be Instantly At Your Fingertips.
2367	Your Real Online Journey Starts When You Create Your Own Product
2368	How To Increase The Value Of Any Website Without Risking A Penny Of Your Own Money – Guaranteed!
2369	It's Time For Me To Pass The Torch And Turn You Into A Lead Capture List-Building Machine. It's Time That You Start Forcing People To Join YOUR Opt-In List, So That You Can Create Cash Out Of Thin Air.
2370	A Revolutionary System. One That's Been Refined Over Time, One That Is The Results Of Hundreds Of Hours Of Testing And Tweaking. One That Works Now, Not 4 Years Ago.
2371	How To Build A Money Making Mailing List That Can Then Build Itself
2372	You Earn Multiple Streams Of Monthly Recurring Income As Members In Your Growing Organization Automatically Feed Into The 6 Progressive Level Core-Businesses After You.
2373	Snip Your Content And Post The Short Blurbs On Twitter.
2374	You Don't Need To Be A Web Master To Make Money
2375	How To Close A Customer Who Says I Don't Have Any Money
2376	You Will See The Power Of This Software And You Will See Why Building A Website Is Not Such A Daunting Task Like Most People Think.
2377	A Quick Note About All Those Gurus Out There. Most Of Them Are Gurus Because They Sell Products That Say They Are Gurus. The Truth Is That If They Didn't Call Themselves Gurus, No One Else Would. It's A Crazy Cycle That Only Ends Up Hurting You, The Person Who Needs To Succeed More Than Anything!
2378	When You Find The Light Switch You'll Be Able To Successful Walk Down Any Marketing Path
2379	If You're Working A Day Job Your Job Is Tougher Than This

175

2380	To Conduct A Test Mailing With Postal Direct Mail Is Pretty Expensive. A Small Test Mailing With Snail Mail Might Cost You $10,000 By The Time You're Done Paying For Postage, Printing, Assembling Your Mailing, Labor And So On.
2381	The Basic Structure Of Successful Marketing Copywriting Focuses On 3 Areas: Something I Have Of Interest, Here's Something That Will Do Something Specific For You, And Finally, Here's What To Do Next.
2382	Simply Enter Your Google Adsense ID In Admin And Start Earning Extra Cash
2383	There Are Two Types Of People In The World. Those That Will Fill Out This Free Registration, And Those That Will Still Wonder How They Can Use The Internet For Promotion. We're About To Find Out Which Direction You're About To Take, Change Nothing In Your Life, Or Jump Out Of You Comfort Zone And Live Life!
2384	SO...Before This Starts To Sound Like An ALL OUT Sales Pitch, Let's Get Back To The Story..
2385	Anticipate Any Objections Your Visitors May Have About Your Product Offer. You Must Research Your Target Audience's Needs And Wants.
2386	First Off, Teenagers Of Today Are Very Much Put Off By Pretense. Immersed Daily In A Sea Of Advertising From The Day They Were Born, They Are Hypersensitive To Phony Advertising Claims.
2387	We Hold Nothing Back As We Teach You How To Make Big Bucks Using The Private Label Rights In This Package! Learning How To Monetize PLR Will Help You To Cash In On All The Products In This Powerhouse Membership Site. Never Spend Another Cent On Coaching Again Once You Learn Our Secrets!
2388	Format Each Lesson Of The Mini-Course And Load Them To An Autoresponder
2389	If You Can Send An Email, You Have What It Takes. You Don't Need To Pay For Inventory Or Storage Costs. You Can Promote Or Advertise Products For Free - In Many Different And Creative Ways.
2390	So Simple And Powerful You Think Everyone Would Know How To Use It To Make Money
2391	But For You There Is An Answer – YOU Can Unleash The Kind Of Traffic That Transforms Your Life Completely – You Can Begin Generating A Substantial Income Online.

2392	I'm Ready To Learn All Of The Secret Underground Tips & Techniques
2393	If I Grabbed You In That Special Spot You Know I'd Have Your Full Attention
2394	Stop Kicking A Dead Horse Keeping Your Online Business Broke Day After Day
2395	How Would You Like To Create An Army Of Highly Motivated Selling Machines All Working To Put Cash In Your Pocket? Discover How To Find And Motivate Your Affiliates To Keep Selling Your Products...
2396	In This Tutorial You'll Uncover The Importance Of Tracking, And You'll Learn My Super Easy Techniques So That This Is Actually Almost As Fun As Watching The Money Pour In.
2397	With Affiliate Marketing Becoming So Competitive, Access Our Affiliate Vault For All The Hot, Proven Success Components You'll Ever Need To Become A Top Earning Affiliate, For One Ridiculously Low Monthly Charge...
2398	If You've Relied On Only Living A Simple Lifestyle Maybe It's Time To Take A Smart Risk
2399	Magic Bullet After Magic Bullet. So Many Big Promises. So Few Results. New Products Are Being Released Every Single Week Screaming For Me To Buy Them Otherwise I Will Not Make Money. What's Up With That??
2400	If You Would Like To Access Some Of The Best Network And Internet Marketing Tips You Can Use In Your Network And/Or Internet Marketing Businesses...Tired Of "Theory"...Then You're In The Right Spot At The Right Time, Period.
2401	If You Act Right Now Will Get Instant Access For Only $67.00 Today And When You Decide To Remain A Member For Life (Which I Know You Will) It's Only A Paltry $67.00 Per Month For Brand New Content, Training And Tested Methods!
2402	Successful Marketers First Do Proper Market Research First To Underpin A Profitable Niche With Reasonable Demand And Then Create A Product Around That Demand. This Ensures That Every Product They Come Up With Automatically Sells By Itself!
2403	Maybe It's Time For You To Take Your Own Computer Security Seriously
2404	Why 95% Of The Marketing World Hates To Close A Deal
2405	You Need Very Little Or No Start-Up Capital! (Yes, You Can Get Started For Free Or As Little As $100.)

2406	Still Not Sure About How To Use Private Label Rights (PLR) To Explode Your Online Profits? Or Looking For Ideas To Use The PLR Lying Dormant On Your Hard Disk? Then This Report Is Just What You Need! You'll Discover How To Use PLR To Fast Forward Your Business To The Profit Zone And Leapfrog Your Way To The Top Of The Online Food Chain!
2407	P.S. Right Now You're At A Business Crossroads. You Can Do Nothing And Watch Your Email Marketing Efforts Slowly Lose Their Effectiveness To Spam Filters, White-listing, And Declining Delivery Rates. Six Months From Now Your Business Will Probably Be Doing The Same As It Is Now.
2408	DISCLAIMER: No Part Of This Sales Letter, Names, Aliases Or Association Can Be Copied And Used For Your Own Sales Letter - NO Swiping Allowed.
2409	Create Offline Affiliates To Market Your Product. Have People Sign Up At Your Web Site To Sell Your Products Through "House Parties".
2410	I Know It May Seem Overwhelming And Even A Bit Incredible, Especially If You Are A Beginner, But You Can Really Earn A Full Time Living With A Form Of Marketing Called Affiliate Marketing Where Basically You Get Paid To Promote The Other Peoples' Products And Services.
2411	The Latest Smooth As Silk Drop Down That Transitions Your Visitors Naturally To The Opt-In Without Distracting Them Away From The Flow Of Your Sales Page.
2412	I Know How It Is When You Got So Much Going On It's Hard To Really Spend Time On Your Business, As Much As We Try To Sell The Lifestyle Truth Is You Can Only Have The Laid Back Lifestyle If You Work Hard First...
2413	Who Else Wants Instant Access To 3 Products You Can Set Up Tonight And See Profit From By Tomorrow Morning?' Fill Out The Form Below For Instant Access To 3 Brand New Products With Full Resale Rights Of Course.
2414	Why No One Will Want To Even Think Of Competing Against You In Your Selected Niche
2415	The Right Way To Find A Market Niche That'll Gobble Up Your E-Book Like They're Starving To Death. This Is More Than Half The Battle, And I'll Give You A Quick And Easy Way To Find These Gold Mines Without Spending A Single Penny. All You Need Are The Three Free Tools And The Simple Formula I'll Hand You.

2416	3 Ways To Make A Memorable Contact, Make Eye Contact, Smile, And Give Them A Great Looking Business Card.
2417	I Haven't Just Thrown You In The Deep End As You Will See Exactly How To Build Your Own Powerful Websites So You Can Start Selling Online Straight Away.
2418	Almost Overnight, You'll Shatter Limiting Beliefs, Transform Your World View, And Set A Course For Success. Problems And Difficulties Will Melt Away And You Will See The World In A Totally Different Way.
2419	Let Me Say That The Professional Methods Of Marketing Never Change. It's The Mechanics Of Marketing, The Medium Of The Message That Change:
2420	Why Pay More In Taxes When You Can Legally Keep Most Of It
2421	Selling Information Products Is One Of The Quickest And Easiest Ways To Make A Living Online. Creating And Delivering Digital Content Has A Very Low Overhead, So You Can Get Going With Absolutely Minimal Investment.
2422	How 2 Inferiority Complexed Wallflowers Excited The Curiosity Of Marketing Giants
2423	I Will Show You Where The Visitors To A Website Can Be Matched With Your Product Or Service. Imagine How Much Money You Will Make Knowing Where To EXACTLY Go To Get Your Customers.
2424	This Is An Excellent Technique To Use With Autoresponders, Newsletters, News Groups, And Even In The Forums As Long As You Keep The "Selling" To A Bare Minimum And Provide Value-Added Content In The Story.
2425	You'll Unearth The Sneaky, Diabolical, And Cut-Throat Tactic You MUST Utilize In Order To Profit From Your Subscribers Just 3 Minutes After They Opt-In And It Works Every Time.
2426	And If For Some Reason (Or No Reason At All) You Decide The System Isn't Everything I Promised Send Me Just One Email, And You'll Get A Full Refund. No Questions, No Worries. We Part Friends.
2427	7 Quick Tips For Writing Your Own E-Booklets For Instant Profit Online
2428	Enough Of The Small Talk Let's Get Down To Doing Some Real Business
2429	Ancient Discovery Reveals Marketing Technique Hasn't Changed And Probably Never Will

179

2430	In Order To Be Successful Online There Are 3 Criteria You Need To Master
2431	You'll Learn About What Money Really Is. You'll Come To Understand That Money Has A Life Of Its Own And If You Understand Its Habits; You Can Control It. The Majority Of Bloggers Out There Tell You The Same Thing Over And Over Again.
2432	Remember, Good Quality Backlinks, Like The Ones You Will Be Receiving Here, Are The Key To Getting High Search Engine Rankings Today! This Could Be Just What You Need To Get Those High Rankings You So Desperately Want!
2433	You And I Have Most Likely Never Met In Person. But The Fact That You're Reading This Tells Me A Couple Of Things About You. Most People Simply Don't Have The Guts It Takes To Get As Far As You've Just Gotten. It Also Tells Me That You're Intelligent Enough To Know You Must Keep Learning And Putting What You've Just Learned Into Action!
2434	You Can Work From Home You Can Run Your Business From Your Own Home And Not Have To Deal With The Hassles Of Dealing Employees As Well As The Other Headaches "Dirt World" Business Owners Face Every Day.
2435	How Many Times Have You Wished You Could Have These Types Of Software Scripts, But Just Couldn't Afford Them?
2436	Conducting Surveys Where Everything Is Uncensored Allows You To Uncover Your Prospects' REAL Inner Desires And Wants Like A Magic Wand That Allows You To Magically Produce Only Products That Sell Like Crazy!
2437	Please Excuse My Error. Things Have Been Absolutely Crazy Over Here. I've Been Working Around The Clock And Can Barely Sleep Since I'm So Excited About This Product. You'll See Why Soon Enough.
2438	In Normal Driving You Slow Down When You Reach A Curve But Not In Drift Racing. Using Special Techniques You Barely Slow Down Reminding Me Of How Acceleration And Not Losing Speed Is An Important Part Of My Marketing Approach.
2439	What Promotional Actions Do You Need To Take To Ensure Continued Success?

2440	The Cyber World Holds Even More Competition To Get Noticed Than In Real Life. More And More People Are Using The Net To Broadcast Themselves And Their Service To Those Who May Be Interested. However, The World Wide Web Is So Incredibly Extensive That It Is Easy To Get Lost In Traffic.
2441	You Can Laugh At Money Worries If You Follow This Simple Plan
2442	Not Everyone Is A Trained Copywriter So We've Come Up With This Powerful Tool That Will Help You To Market Your Products And Services With Minimum Effort - It's Called A Swipe File And It Contains Hundreds Of Words You Can Cut And Paste For Your Marketing Campaigns Without Spending Hundreds Or Thousands Of Dollars On Expensive Copywriters.
2443	That Being Said, Over The Next Week I'll Take You Through The Same Learning Process I Used To Train Fledgling New Pilots And Make Them Some Of The Best Fighter Pilots In The World In Just Over 6 Months, And Walk You Through The Entire Process Of Building Yourself A Real Online Business.
2444	You'll Want To Be On Top Of This Before Your Competition Finds Out
2445	How Can Someone With No Product No List And No Affiliates Make Lots Of Money
2446	Squeeze Pages Are Great, But Many People Have Problems With Either Poor Opt-In Rates On Their Squeeze Pages, Or With Actually Setting Up A Squeeze Page And The "Tech Work" Behind It. Most People Are Not Designers, Are Not Tech Wizards, And Just Don't Like Doing All These Little Things. But I'm Sure Everyone Would Love To Have High Opt-In Rates And Big Lists.
2447	Well Guess What? Now There Is An Alternative. For Over 6 Months We Have Been Working On An Ad System That Uses Keywords To Display Relevant Ads From The Clickbank Marketplace On Your Website.
2448	I Hope You See The Value In This Offer And Will Give These Products A Try
2449	I Needed The Ability To Build A Sales Page In A Matter Of Hours And Get A Product Out At Exactly The Right Time Which As Made Me Tens Of Thousands Of Dollars.
2450	A No-Nonsense Way That You Can Pick Up And Put Into Practice Straight Away! But What If You're Broke And Don't Have Money To Invest In The Core-Business? No Problem.

181

2451	Unfortunately For Most This Is Usually A Losing Proposition...Which Is Why You'll Be Ecstatic When You Quickly And Easily Hop From One Insanely Profitable Niche To The Next.
2452	The BEST 3 Words You Need To Use Over And Over Again
2453	Marketing Ideas That Make You Money In Less Than 24 Hours
2454	You Won't Need A Lot Of Time Money Or Even A List To Create A Big Profit
2455	So Let Me Ask You... Are You Effectively Using Reciprocal Link Exchange In Your Daily Marketing Activities?
2456	Spills The Beans On The Inside Secrets To Increase Conversions By At Least 75%
2457	After Serving Many Years As A Master Teacher I've Learned It Pays To Learn From My Students
2458	The Point Is, That's What One Simple Idea Can Do For You. Find Something That Works, That Generates A Little Money, And Then Just Duplicate It. "Roll It Out," As They Say In The Direct Marketing Industry.
2459	Never Again Will You Have To Waste Your Hard Earned Money
2460	Did You Start Your Business To Work Harder Than Your Old Job
2461	I'll Have Immediate Access To The Same Techniques That Have Already Been Proven More Effective Than Using Other Forms Of Advertising.
2462	Need A Dozen New Ideas To Help Take Your Business Into More Profits
2463	Another Technique For Driving People To Action Is Simply To Very Casually Give The Affiliate Links To The Tools Or Information You Used To Accomplish Or Achieve Whatever Result As You Tell The Story.
2464	There Is Absolutely No Better, Faster, More Efficient, Lower Risk Way To Make Money Online Than The Specific System That I Am Going To Reveal To You In This Report.
2465	Do Yourself A Favor And Click The Order Button Below, Secure Your Copy Today, Read It Tonight, And Put The Tricks To Work As Early As Tomorrow.
2466	For More Information Contact The Person Who Gave You This Video
2467	How The Online Marketing World Really Works And How You Can Instantly Benefit
2468	What Can You Bring To This Offer So We Both Win

2469	Why Let Your Fingers Limit Your Own Online Dam Leaking Strategies
2470	This Is The True Story Of How I Lost My Mind Very Late One Crazy Saturday Night...And Decided I Was Going To Give You Some Of My Most Profitable Campaigns. Hands-Off Total Autopilot Income Streams.
2471	How Do You Begin Sorting It All Out And Decide What's The Right Path For You Follow
2472	It All Began With A Chat On Messenger With One Of My Personal Students. She Was Complaining About The Lack Of 'Real' Education On Internet Marketing And That She Would Still Be Trapped In The Vicious Guru Circle If Not For Having Me As A Coach.
2473	Don't Talk About What You Do Save That Till The End
2474	Undoubtedly The Most Incredible Collection Of Power Words, Trigger Phrases, And Action Headlines Ever Assembled. Even Professional Internet Marketers Would Gladly Pay A Fortune To Keep Them For Themselves.
2475	A Glaring Mistake Most Newbie Sellers Make In Writing Ad Copy. This One Could Be Costing You Lots Of Money, So Make Sure You're Not Doing It.
2476	Why Am I Giving Away The Whole Enchilada At Such A Small Price? Here Are Three Reasons:
2477	We Take You By The Hand In Setting Up Your Entire Marketing System
2478	These Marketers Didn't Start Off With These Enormous Lists Either, They Created Products And Services Which Grew Their Lists.
2479	But What If You're Broke And Don't Have Money To Invest In The Core-Business? What Do You Do? Who Can You Turn To? What If All Of That Amounted To A Simple - No Problem?
2480	Why Most Businesses Fail To Have A Master Plan Of Action
2481	All These Products Are Created From The Day The Ideas Were Conceived Up To The Finishing Touches... 100% Original!
2482	Castro Finally Dies At Age 112; Cuban Cigars Can Now Be Imported Legally, But President Chelsea Clinton Has Banned All Smoking
2483	If You Use Spam Arrest Or Other Services Please Whitelist The Following Email Address

183

2484	No Experience? That's Fine. The Best Way To Learn Something Is By Doing It. A Common Problem With Internet Marketing Newbies Is That They Feel They Have To Know Everything Before They Start Doing Anything. That Doesn't Work.
2485	The Key Is To Figure Out What Works And What's Duplicable -- What's Repeatable -- So When You Find Out What's Working, You Can Roll It Out. That's How Fortunes Are Made.
2486	You're Frustrated And On The Verge Of Giving Up...I'm Here To Tell You...Don't Quit. YOUR INCOME Will Only Be Limited In This Market By How Quickly You Can Get Started.
2487	How To Create A Series Of Money Making Reports In Just Minutes
2488	How To Get People Bidding Like Crazy On Websites You Paid Next To Nothing To Build...
2489	Earning Consistent Incomes Is The Most Exciting Event We Solely Focus Upon
2490	Why Search Engines Always Give Dot Coms Better Treatment And Higher Page Listing
2491	Wiggle Free From The Trap Before You Get In Too Deep
2492	Increased And Targeted Traffic Can Definitely Be Achieved By Utilizing Effective And Relevant Link Exchange To Attract Larger, Quality And Targeted Traffic For Your Web Site.
2493	How Many People Clicked On Your Ad Let Alone Actually Read Your Offer
2494	Even If You Know Nothing About Blogging But Just Want To Learn A Fool Proof Way To Generate Thousands Of Dollars Per Month Then You Need To Listen Up As This Will Be The Most Important Webpage You Visit All Year.
2495	Don't Start If You Can't Dedicate At Least One Hour A Week To Your Online Business
2496	Develop A "Dummies" Type Guide.
2497	You'll Find NO Hype NO Affiliate Links NO Sales Pitch And NOTHING To Buy
2498	I Had Trouble Finding The Right Products To Promote. I Couldn't Figure Out How To Target The Correct Keywords That Converted.
2499	Ex- Executive/Insider Exposes Underground Trade-Industry Secrets To Increase Conversions By At Least 75%
2500	I Reserve The Right To End This Offer Forever At Any Time

184

2501	Custom Brand PLR Desktop Wallpapers And Give Them Away To Your Clients So Your Logo Will Be On Their Computer.
2502	There Are A Number Of Good Ideas For A Home Based Business That Actually Work. Affiliate Marketing (Where You Promote Other People's Products) Is A Popular Method Since You Can Start Out Without Having Your Own Website Or Your Own Product.
2503	Each Member Receives The Exact Same Marketing Strategy, Tools, And Free Marketing Sources And Materials.
2504	What Would It Be Worth If You Could Email 50 People About Your Product? What About 100?...200...500 Or Even 1000?! Do You Think It Could Make A BIG Difference In Your Income?
2505	The Real Secret To Making It Big Online Is Not A Myth
2506	New And Existing Businesses Will Either Soar Heavenly Or Spiral Into The Abyss
2507	I Understand I'll Be Getting Access To This Incredible Collection Of Over 15,000 Mini Phrases And Action Headlines That Sell For A Tiny One-Time Investment Of Just $1,226 - $612 - $122.50 - $67
2508	No Selling Of Any Kind, I Don't Even Have To Give Anyone My Phone Number
2509	But They Got Started Anyway, And That Decision Improved Their Lives In Ways Far Beyond The Great Money.
2510	If You've Struggled To Get By In Life, Always Needing Just A Little More Cash, Or Maybe You're Just Sick And Tired Of Wasting Day After Day In A Soulless Job. Then You Need To Read Every Single Word On This Page Very Carefully - You're About To See Exactly What This Devastating Business System Will Do For You.
2511	What It Is And What It Does Determines What It's Really Worth
2512	The Fact Is That Typography Plays A Major Part In Any Design. And If You Have Good Enough Looking Text, You Don't Even Need Any Images. Killer Text Will Spice Up And Make ANY Design Better.
2513	Why A Curious Introvert Is Always A Better Closer Than An Exciting Extrovert
2514	Experts Agree That Putting VIRAL Traffic Methods Into Place Is An Outstanding Tactic To Get More Traffic. After All, Once You Do Your Initial Promotions, The Viral Aspect Takes Over.
2515	Most Online Entrepreneurs Are Failing Simply Because They Don't Know This

185

2516	Don't Forget To Ask For The Order If You Want The Sale
2517	This Isn't Just Some Theory Or Conjecture Either...The 'Modeling Theory' Is Proven Science That Tells Us This Is One Of The Easiest Ways To Learn.
2518	Instantly Put Your Product In Front Of Millions Of Eager Hungry Buyers
2519	Discover Exactly How You Can Become A Good Marketer So That Whatever You Do Will Prosper And Is Almost Guaranteed To Succeed
2520	$30000 In Prizes! Help Us Find The Name For These New Marketing Ideas
2521	Stop Beating Yourself Up And Start Feeling Good About Your Opportunities Online
2522	I'm Looking To Create Opportunity To Those Who Need It. And Research Shows People Often Stop Themselves From Spending $100 Or More, Even When It's In Their Best Interest.
2523	This May Be Your Final Chance To Stop Killing Yourself Working And Fire Your Boss
2524	This Dynamic Shift Is Already Having A Profound Effect On The Way Business Is Being Conducted Online, And Will Completely Re-Shape The Way All Future Online Business Takes Place.
2525	Add The "Tell A Friend" Function- On Your Website, Add The 'Tell A Friend' Function. This Is A Simple Little Button That Allows People To Easily Connect To Your Website And Inform Others About It. In The Cyber World, Word Of Click Is Just As Important As Word Of Mouth. So Make The Most Of This With Social Media.
2526	Swoop Down And Slide Under Your Competitor's Traffic Without Them Ever Knowing
2527	You'll Have A Full 56 Days To Test Everything. Watch All The Videos, Follow The Step-By-Step Instructions, Get Your List Up And Collecting Names For You On Autopilot... And Start Cashing Those Affiliate Checks.
2528	These Are Products People On Your List Are Likely To Buy Anyway! Without A List, That Money Would Have Gone To Someone Else. Don't Let That Happen.
2529	Everything Is Going To Change For You, Starting Today. Imagine Being Able To Make Thousands Of Dollars By Writing Simple Emails That Generate A Massive Unstoppable Flood Of Cash Effortlessly, With NO Room For Error Or Risk Of Failure.

2530	Discover How To Make As Much Money As You Want, Just By Having Some Spare Time, And An Opinion. Your Opinion Is Worth Gold To Big Business…And They're Ready To Pay You Right Now For Your Time!
2531	Every 22 Days, A New Company Outside Of The U.S. Generates A Billion Dollars In Sales For The First Time. Imagine… A Billion Dollars In Sales… Right Under Our Noses. So What Are We All Missing And What Do We Need To Start Doing Right Now?
2532	How Often Do You Hear Yourself Saying: "No, I Haven't Read It: I've Been Meaning To!"
2533	Are You More Invested In What They Want Than They Are
2534	Use Bold Subheadings. Many People Will Simply Skim Through An Article Looking For The Most Important Parts. So Give Them What They Want By Bolding The Important Parts And Using Bolded Subheadings To Split Up The Article.
2535	I'm Not Looking To Become The List Building Guru, I Don't Want To Hang Around With Rich Elitists.
2536	There Is No Shame In Not Knowing Where To Start When You're Smart Enough To Ask
2537	Finally You Can Tell That No Good SOB To Take Their Job And Shove It
2538	The Sad Truth Is That The Majority Of Internet Marketers Have No Rhyme Or Reason On How To Get Traffic To Their Sites! They May Try A Few Things Here Or There, But Only Continue To Experience Failure.
2539	May The Best Man Or Woman Win In The Head To Head Affiliate Marketing Business
2540	There's Always Got To Be A Better Way To Sell Your Product Or Idea
2541	Because The Truth Is, Economic Recessions Or It's Uglier Cousin, Economic Depressions, Are Just The Perfect Opportunities That Anyone With Vision Can Take Advantage Of To Become Not Just Rich - But Filthy Rich!
2542	Are You Really Ready To Experience Some Phenomenal Changes In Your Life
2543	If You Are Able To Produce A Product Or Service That People Want, Why Should You Turn All That Profit Over To Someone Else In Exchange For The Supposed Security Of A Job Or Of An Hourly Fee. At A Minimum, You Should Share In The Profit Of What You Create.

2544	If You Answered Yes To Any One Of The Questions Listed Above... I've Got A Simple Solution.
2545	Looking For Meaningful Revenue And Profit Growth For Your Company? Frequently You'll Find It One Of Four Major Places: Through A Better Selling Approach, Through Better Marketing Methods, Through A Better Overall Growth Strategy Or A Better Business Model.
2546	Nothing Else In The Marketplace Could Possibly Make This Any Easier
2547	It Runs Automatically While You're Out Doing Things You Want To Do
2548	If You Do Not Position Yourself As Someone That Others Look Up To, You Might As Well Pack Your Bags And Go Back To Working 9 to 5.
2549	This Gives Everyone An Equal Chance To Duplicate And Achieve The Same Incredible Results With No Additional Effort Or Investment.
2550	I Thought I Knew It All After 10 Years In This Industry...I Was Wrong, And In Some Cases, DEAD Wrong! You Can Watch It Now And Have It Delivered To You Instantly By Going To The Site Below.
2551	People Are Eagerly Seeking Information, And They Will Gladly Pay For What They Perceive As More Valuable, Reliable Content-Because They Paid For It! I'll Show You Why They'll Pay, What They Are Looking For-And How To Effectively Market Your Own Paid Membership Site That Can Earn You Monthly, Six-Month, Or Yearly Fees. That's Money That Keeps Coming In, Month After Month, Year After Year!
2552	If A Relationship Has To Be A Secret, You Shouldn't Be In It
2553	I'm Releasing This Massive Report Which Exposes The Marketing Language Guru's Use On You To Make You Depart With Your Hard Earned Cash. Once You've Learned This Profit Pulling Language You Can Use Them On Your Own Web Sites, Creating Money On Demand!
2554	How To Avoid Wasting Precious Time Developing The Right Product For The Wrong People
2555	Join The World's Leader And Expert On Creating Automated Money Making Websites
2556	This Marketing Roundtable Discussion Group Is About To Unveil Their Top Strategies

2557	What Exactly Does This Affiliate System Do? In Short, Everything! And It Does It All Automatically With Absolutely No Experience, No List, No Contacts And No Marketing Resources Of Any Kind Required!
2558	PPC Is Not Even Close To Dead, It's Evolved And You Just Need To Grow Along With It.
2559	Editable About Us And FAQ Pages That Can Be Customized In Admin
2560	If You Could Write 10 Great Headlines A Day It Would Take You Over 13 Years To Re-Create This Incredible Collection.
2561	Entry Into A Unique World Of Making Money I Guarantee You Never Even Knew Existed A Unique "Money Making Loophole" That Can Never Be Closed And Is Completely Recession Proof. It's So Simple And Powerful, You Can Have It Running And Making You Money Within Hours Of Setting It Up.
2562	If Reality Is Creative Thought Where Does That Leave You And Your Business
2563	If You Know Your Home Page Isn't Working Why Aren't You Doing Something About It Now
2564	Skyrocket Your Conversion Rates By 20%, 40%, Even 60% And Leave Your Competition By The Side Of The Road Wondering WTF Just Happened...
2565	Go Here To Watch A Video That Explains Everything...And Click On The "Add To Cart" Button To Reserve Your Spot In The Program And Get Started:
2566	Discover Highly Responsive Niche Markets Before Anyone Else Even Knows They Exist
2567	Tired Of Paying Without Any Results - Get Paid For Your Efforts Today
2568	Why Home Remodeling Has Become One Of America's Most Complained About Industry
2569	You'll Discover How To Create Autopilot Income And The Lifestyle Of Your Dreams – Every Aspect Of Social Network Site Building Is Covered In The Video, Audio And PDF Training Materials... From Site Set Up To Traffic Driving Strategies To Our Secret Formula For Niche Domination... All Designed To Help You Create Financial Freedom.
2570	Ready For An Intensive But Invigorating Report That Will Get You Jumping For Joy

189

2571	I'm Sure You've Heard Of PLR (I.E. Private Label Rights) Content Before. But If Not, Let Me Quickly Explain What It Is And Why It's Literally The Fastest And Easiest Way To Start An Online Business.
2572	When You Know Where You Want To Go You Create Your Life
2573	No One Has More Driving Ambition Than The Boy Who Wants To Buy A Car
2574	So We Searched And Pursued Different Opportunities Over The Last Couple Of Years, Looking, Waiting And Working Towards That Perfect Moment Of When It Would All Come Together.
2575	Instantly Gain A Competitive Advantage By Having Affiliates Literally Jumping Out Of Their Shoes To Promote Your Products Instead Of The Competition's. Removes All Excuses Your Affiliates Can Throw At You.
2576	Most People Buy Things They Want Based On Emotions, Then They Justify And Rationalize Their Decision With Explanations In Their Own Mind.
2577	How This Tiny Little Sales Force Can Travel The World Selling Your Products And Services
2578	We Called In A Few Favors And Twisted Some Arms To Get These Products
2579	Action Now Will Repay You For The Rest Of Your Life
2580	Catch And Engage Their Eyes In A Way That's So Unique It's Downright Scary
2581	Add Your Content To A Membership Site.
2582	Why Is It So Hard To Build A Downline When You Don't Know Where To Start
2583	The Most Important Thing Is To Send It To The Right Person
2584	Find Out Why Text Links Outperform Even The Most Colorful Banners And Graphic Ads
2585	Quit Complaining About Your Job And Focus On A New Direction Today
2586	Who Ever Heard Of A Woman Losing Weight And Enjoying 3 Delicious Meals At The Same Time
2587	Are You Having To Sell The Clothes Off Your Back Just To Pay Your Bills
2588	In Order To Help Hundreds Of Thousands Of People Accomplish This We Realized That We Have To Put Our Profits On The Backburner And Make All Of Our Courses As Affordable As Possible.

2589	We've Got A Slam Dunk Email System That You Can Utilize Right Now And Every Week To Email Thousands Of People Without All The Upfront Headaches That So Many People Have Suffered.
2590	Safelists Are Dead. It's Time To Be A Part Of The Cutting Edge And Partner With Marketers With Fresh And Effective Ideas That Offer The Only Site Of It's Kind While Exploding Your Income At The Same Time.
2591	You Have Full International Master Resale Rights To This Book As Well And You Can Sell It For What Ever Price You Choose To.
2592	Who Would Have Thought You Could Earn Such An Incredible Income From So Few Members? Well, You Can -- And What's More, This Really Isn't As Hard As You've Been Led To Believe.
2593	Getting Inside The Mind Of Your Customers To Provide Better Solutions
2594	One Website Caught My Eye. It Was About Becoming And Affiliate Marketer, Selling Other People's Info-Products On The Internet... And It Changed My Life Drastically. I'll Explain How In A Moment
2595	One Little Sentence, One Little Bullet Buried Into Your Ad, Could Be The Overwhelming Reason Why People Must Get A Hold Of Your Product!
2596	Now There's A Cure For Exploding Conversions Into Real Money Making Opportunities
2597	If I Could Help You Accomplish Just ONE Primary Goal What Would It Be
2598	Don't Hesitate... Take A Moment Now To Invest In Your Business So You Can Be Assured Of An Increased Income In The Coming Months And Years Ahead.
2599	The 5 Most Common Techniques Being Used By The Vast Majority Of Home Based Business Owners That Are Practically Guaranteed To Make Your Business Fail.
2600	Discover How You Can Have Your Very Own Fully Branded, Personalized, Attraction Marketing System Like The Top Producers Online, Generating Quality Prospects, Building Your List AND Exploding Your Business Profits With A Lot Less Effort And Money Than You Are Currently Spending.
2601	Why Beginning With The End In Mind Will Help You Create The Perfect Product That Sells

2602	This Is An Amazing Opportunity For You As A Newbie To Get Off The Ground Fast As An Affiliate, Basically Plug In Your Affiliate Link And Start Promoting, And The Best Part It's Free! No Kidding!
2603	Reading This Report Is Your Chance To Completely Bypass Marketing's Frustrating, And Not To Mention Expensive, Trial And Error Stage And Put Yourself Directly On The Fast Track To Success!
2604	Why You May Want To Clone Your Online Presence To Maximize Your Profits
2605	Don't Forget To Be Here On Time If You Really Want This
2606	Then, You'll Get Updated Tutorials Anytime There's A Change In The 'Rules' Or If Something New And Exciting Comes Along.
2607	How To Immediate Create Direct Association Within The Mind Of The Reader
2608	How Would You Like To Know Exactly Where Real Money Making Traffic Resides
2609	How In The World Do I Get Someone To My Website
2610	Record Subliminal Audio With The PLR Affirmations, Reflections, Or Motivating Quotes. Even Record A Personalized Message At The Beginning Of The Track For A Premium Price.
2611	In A Hype Filled Industry Full Of Bloated Promises, Weak Offers, Rehashed Crap, You've Stumbled Upon An Offer That Breaks All The Rules And That Will Quickly And Easily Stuff Your Pockets Full Of Cold Hard Cash!
2612	Build Unstoppable Momentum - With Each Task You Complete Using Action Machine Pro, You Build Up A Momentum That Propels You To Not Only Get More Done, But Get It Done Faster And More Efficiently Than Ever!
2613	Want The Opportunity To Finally Build A Real Long Term Residual Income That Will Pay You For Years To Come
2614	The Second Is A "Surprise Bonus" That I'll Tell You About Shortly. It's Going To Blow Your Mind. It's A Complete Video Training That I've Never Announced Or Even Mentioned - And It's Really Going To Help You Create An AWESOME Information Product.
2615	How To Instantly Spur Demand For Your New Product Or Service

2616	How To Use Squidoo To Make Boatloads Of Profits. The Search Engines Love Squidoo, And It Offers Various Features That Help Maximize Your Income. If You're Not Using It, You're Leaving Piles Of Money On The Table.
2617	Finally! A Quick And Easy Way For YOU To Painlessly Set Up Your OWN Moneymaking 'Mini' Websites... Without Being A Computer Geek, Buying Expensive Software, Or Paying Outrageous Fees To A Webmaster!
2618	Over 90% Of People Attempting To Earn An Income From Internet Marketing Keep Making The Same Mistakes That Will Kill Their Business Faster Than They Can Build It.
2619	The Right Place To Start Creating A Product. I'll Tell You What Types Of Products To Avoid, As They Could Crush Your Long-Term Results.
2620	Want To Enlist Your Own Army Of Virtual Foot Soldiers Roaming The Cyber Streets Of The World Wide Web Recruiting New Members For You With Cult-Like Loyalty?
2621	If You've Ever Dreamed Of Having A Huge List Of Eager And Loyal Subscribers, People Who Will Whip Out Their Wallet Almost Every Time You Send Them An Offer, Then You're In For A Wild Ride Here.
2622	That's Not A Joke, And It's Not A Typo. The 3 Modules Plus The 3 Bonuses Have A Total Retail Value Of $472.00, But You're Getting A Massive 93% Discount On The Entire Package!
2623	Great Options That Beat The Socks Off Of Having Them Move In With You
2624	I'll Show You How You Can Easily Generate A Very Comfortable Recurring Monthly Income, An Income That Could Dramatically Improve The Quality Of Your Lifestyle!
2625	If Someone Like Me Can Become The Next Marketing Mogul So Can You
2626	How To Get Thousands Of Hits To Your Website Without Spamming
2627	I Don't Think There's Anything Else You Can Sell Me After This
2628	Verbal Buying Signs That Telegraph Your Prospect Wants You To Close
2629	By Giving You This Unique On Of A Kind Advantage We'll All Exceed Our Wildest Dreams

193

2630	Simply Enter Your Paypal Email Address In Your Admin Area That's It
2631	What Would You Do If You Just Earned A Million Dollars
2632	What Started As My Hobby Has Turned Into An Incredible Product I'll Be Releasing Soon
2633	I Have Been A Big Student Of Off And Online Marketing For More Than 2 Decades And Have Been A Part Of Several Big And Respectfully Successful Marketing Projects.
2634	Sometimes Taking A Little Breather And Taking A Look At What Has Already Worked For You Will Open Up A Bigger And Better Picture.
2635	Find Your Niche And Create A Product That Will Scare The Hell Out Of Your Competition
2636	YES, What Your Seeing Is Real, I've Probably Lost My Mind But I'm Going To Show You 3 Niches I Am Already Working In.
2637	Have You Ever Wondered What It Would Be Like To Be Able To Sell Your Product Ideas
2638	I Want To Level With You. Right Now In Your Life, You May Not Even Know It, But You Have 2 Possible Futures. You've Got The Same Problems And Struggles We All Have. But At This Point In Time, You Have A Decision To Make. And Whatever You Choose To Do Will Alter Your Life, Perma- nently.
2639	The Beauty Of The Internet Combined With An International Call Package Means I Can Contact You Wherever You Are Just As Easily And Cheaply As If You Lived Next Door To Me.
2640	Hi And Welcome To My Site. OK, I'm Going To Keep This Short And Sweet - I'm Not Going To Bore You With The Usual "Rags-To-Riches" Story Because I'm Pretty Sure You Don't Want To Hear It.
2641	How To Survive An IRS Audit If You've Been A Sloppy Record Keeper
2642	The 4 Simple Stages Of Any Successful New Internet Busi- ness. After Over A Decade Of Experience, And Having Taught Thousands Of People, I Can Confidently Say A New Business Always Has To Start This Way If It's Going To Be A Winner.
2643	Work Like You Don't Need The Money Love Like You've Never Been Hurt And Dance Like Nobody's Watching

2644	Be Being Persistent I've Learned That I'm Coachable. If It Weren't For My Mentors Over The Years, My Business Would Not Be Where It Is Right Now. Now I'm Going To Teach You How To Build A Strong Downline And How To Sponsor More High-Quality Reps Into Your Business Than You Ever Thought Possible.
2645	It's AMAZING How Many People Are Excited For My Private Coaching Program To Open For Registration Tomorrow. I'm Excited To Coach You! Unfortunately...It Also Means I MAY RUN OUT OF ROOM For Everyone Well Before The Training Begins.
2646	Here's A Solid Foundation For You To Build Your Internet Business Around
2647	And That Expensive Membership Still Wouldn't Include The Easy-To-Install Scripts I've Included For Fully Automating The Entire System.
2648	And I Do Guarantee That. If For Any Reason - Or Even No Reason At All - You Are Not Completely Convinced That This Simple To Follow "Just Copy Me And Make Money" Plan Cannot Make You A Very Nice Part Time Or Even Full Time Income, Then You Pay Me NOTHING. More On This In A Second.
2649	Without Targeted Traffic Even The Greatest Website We Be Dead In The Water
2650	The Best Way For Small To Medium Businesses To Attract Traffic
2651	How Would You Like To Play Around In A $250 Billion Dollar Playground
2652	How To Dramatically Influence Sales And In The Process Win Life Long Fans
2653	The Biggest Problems You'll Have With Most Plumber And How _____ Overcomes Them All
2654	A Very Wealthy Person I Know Sells Bolts. That's All He Does. He Sells A Particular Kind Of Bolt -- Specialized Bolts That Need To Hold A Lot Of Weight -- Bolts For Bridges And Big Structures. That's What He Does.
2655	The Powerful Difference Between A "Money Back Guarantee" And A "Satisfaction Conviction"! (You'll Be Shocked At How Strong This Concept Is, And How It Blows Away A Money Back Guarantee!
2656	Speed On The Internet Two Questions That Other Providers Hope You'll Never Ask Them

195

2657	Every Single Day Millions Of People Are Being Exposed To These Products, And They Are Ready To Buy Them. Now, You Can Help People Tap Into An Enormous Market That Is Just Waiting For You To Profit From It!
2658	Learn From The Products Yourself – These Courses Are Absolutely Jam Packed With Information On How To Drive Targeted Traffic To Your Website, How To Make More Money Online, And How To Run A Successful Online Business. Even If You Don't Sell These Products, Just Go Through The Training And Gain A Ton Of Value!
2659	Even The Ugliest Website I've Ever Seen In My Life Can Be Extremely Profitable
2660	Need Someone Willing To Teach You How Not To Work Again
2661	Guaranteed To Go Through Ice Mud Or Snow Or We Pay The Tow
2662	Now Wait A Minute You Just Raised The Bar Of Internet Marketing To A Brand New Level
2663	How To Automate Your List Building Efforts In A Way That Almost Guarantees Your Success - Follow My Secret System And Create A 'Set It And Forget It' System That Sucks In Subscribers Like Moths To A Flame.
2664	I Can Personally Guarantee That You've Yet To See A Product Like This One. I'm Offering You The Chance To Literally Sit Over My Shoulder And Watch Me Create Live Campaigns While Explaining In Step-By-Step Detail.
2665	Note That The Data Provided Are Estimates And Is Meant To Be Used As A Gauge. Though Knowing These Demographic Insights Will Help You Create A Compelling Sales Message As You Now Know Who Exactly You Are Selling To!
2666	A Gift From Me To You My Free Gift To You
2667	How To Close Thousands Of Sales At Once With Teleseminars And Podcasts
2668	One Of The Best Ways To Build Successful Online Businesses Is By Borrowing The Expertise, Credentials, Content And Even Existing Audience Of Others. Do It Right, And Everyone Makes More Money (Especially You).
2669	They Always Talk About How Much Money You Can Make, But Without 'Moving' Products Nobody Gets Paid.

196

2670	What Makes This Different From Other Similar Products? There Is No Shortage Of Other Opt-In Packs And Products And Templates Out There. The Problem With Most Of Them Is That They're Not Created To Actually Increase The Opt-Ins. Just Like Most Other Template Packages For Anything Else Out There, They're Generic And Don't Help To Convert, But Actually Hurt Conversions In Most Cases
2671	If For Any Reason At All You're Not 100% Satisfied With This Product You Can Get A 100% No Questions Asked Refund By Just Emailing (YOUR SUPPORT EMAIL) With A Request For Refund No Hoops To Jump Through No Strings Attached. This Email Address Is Checked At Least Once A Day Monday – Friday 9:00am – 5:00pm. 100% Risk Reversal With Nothing To Loose.
2672	Using Online Forums Is A Great Way To Learn More About Internet Marketing And Generating Long Term, Targeted Traffic And Answering Some Other Members Questions Will Begin To Generate More Clicks To Your Website.
2673	Yes, You Have Been Told Lies In The Past... Clever Tails Of Hope Where Anyone Can Simply "Copy And Paste" Their Way To Wealth Only To Be Left With The Sour Taste Of Failure Lingering In Your Mouth.
2674	How To Put These Powerful Ideas In Motion To Improve Your Bottom Line Profits
2675	SO Before You Click The Link Below To Earn Your Little Credits So You Can Continue Pimping Get Rich Quick Scams Let Me Share A Little Something With You.
2676	That's A Hard Hit Below The Belt Even Though It's True
2677	Be Different. Write Something That Has Never Been Said Before; Take A Different Approach To An Old Idea; Make People Read To The End. This Is What Generates Traffic.
2678	Guaranteed To Go Through Ice, Mud Or Snow Or We Pay The Tow
2679	Clearly Describe The Actions And Tasks You'll Be Taking To Accomplish Your Goals
2680	Don't Fall Into The Mindset That You Are Being Paid For Your Time. Because Then All You Really Have Is A Job. It's A Job Working For Yourself, And That's A Whole Lot Better Than Working At A Company For Someone Else -- Where Your Entire Income Can Be Cut Off At Any Time.
2681	You've Lost If You're Just Trying To Talk Them Into Buying

197

2682	Why Try Rowing Your Own Internet Yacht When Your Crew Is Already Onboard
2683	You Log Into Your Account And Discover You've Made A Couple Of Hundred Dollars While Sleeping Last Night. You Now Take A Long Deep Sip Of Your Coffee And Feel The Warmth Of The Brew Trickle Down To Your Stomach.
2684	You Always Looking For Ways To Generate More Traffic And Clicks That Don't Cost You Arms And Legs While Not Taking Up A Large Portion Of Your Valuable Time?
2685	More Time Online Than You Are Now In Fact We Don't Want
2686	The Truth Of The Matter Is - You Can Do What Everyone Else Is Doing And Try To Make Money In Overcrowded, Competitive Markets.
2687	Can I Ask You To Do Things And Keep Your Word With Me
2688	How-To Ebooks And Guides Are Typically Full Of Tactics That No Longer Work By The Time The Ebook Is Available
2689	What Makes Owning A Business Different From Having A Job Is The You Must Make A Point To Devote A Portion Of Your Time To Building Your Selling Machine, Your Income-Generating Machine.
2690	FREE Report Reveals 5 Secrets To Increase Conversions By At Least 75%
2691	If You've Ever Felt The Strain Of Debt And It's Effect On Your Marriage Stop It Now
2692	Most People Are Too Busy Trying To Make A Living And Not Making Money
2693	Build Your Empire Much Faster. This Is Everything You Need To Duplicate My Success... Including The Most Vital Part Which Is The One Secret You Need To Know And The One Secret You Won't Find Anywhere Else. I'll Tell You All About It In Just A Minute. For Now, Read My Full Story And To See How Quickly This Powerful And Unique System Can Give You The Lifestyle You Never Dared To Dream.
2694	You Can Definitely Become One Of Our Members And Receive All This Wealth If You Are Prepared To Contribute A Few Minutes Of Your Time To A Good Cause. Your Own Financial Welfare.
2695	Isn't It About Time For Someone To Show You How To Get Your Thinking Cap On Straight
2696	A Proven Affiliate System That Generates Instant Profits Without Breaking A Sweat

198

2697	Does That Sound Like You? If It Does, Keep Reading, Because I'm About To Explain The Details Of One Of The Best Work-At-Home Systems You'll Ever Find.
2698	You Must Do Your Business With People Who WANT To Be In Business With You. You Have To Sell Product To People Who LOVE The Product And Want To Buy It. That Only Comes Through Target Marketing.
2699	Why It's Imperative That You Have A Website That Is Instantly Profitable
2700	How To Avoid Having Your Website Unexpectedly Explode Right In Your Face
2701	I Am Not Out To Take Your Money. This Information Cannot Have A Monetary Value Placed Upon It In My Honest Opinion. Yes, For The Price Of A Pizza Dinner You Will Have All Of The Information You Need To Jump Full Force Into Building A Massive, Profit Pulling List... Without Spending A Dime On Traffic.
2702	Everyone Wants Their Life To Be Better What Do You Want
2703	Signing Up Is Not Going To Make You An Instant Success. You Have To Actually Read And Learn The Materials And Put Them To Practical Application.
2704	I Also Want To Make Sure You Truly Understand That Simply Making Money Does Not Mean That You're Successful. Money Is Merely A Natural By-Product Of Success And It Will Flow To You Freely Once You Understand And Apply The Success Principle To Your Life.
2705	This Is One Of The Best Ways To Really Improve Profits
2706	I Used To Feel Guilty Making More Money Than Any Of My Relatives
2707	While It Can Be Quite Lucrative, Running An Entire Business With Employees, Inventory, Partners, Vendors, And Other Associates Can Be A Time-Sucking, Frustrating Ordeal. Imagine Processing Refunds, Putting Out Fires When Partners Spam, Managing Day-To-Day Operations, Overseeing Projects You've Outsourced And All Of The Other "Stuff" That Business Owners Do.
2708	How To Develop A Direct Response Website That Can Pull In Thousands Of Dollars In Orders Every Single Day
2709	Finally... Discover The Secrets To Generating Everlasting Sources Of Traffic Of Targeted, Hungry Buyers To Your Websites Like There's No Off Switch - It's As Easy As Plug-N-Play But Only If You Know How To!

199

2710	You're About To Discover The Secrets To... Drilling Into Niche Markets... Discover All The Hidden Gold Your Competition Leaves On The Table And Scoop Up The Money All For Yourself Like A Kid In A Candy Store Picking The Keywords That Make Money Quickly And Easily.
2711	Now The Decision Is Up To You. Do You Continue Doing What You've Been Doing Or Do You Grab My Report That Will Show You All The Ins And Outs And Share With You In Great Detail On How To Grow Your Business?
2712	If You're In Network Marketing I Can Only Promise One Thing
2713	Ever Wanted To Be First In Line – Here's Your Chance
2714	I Lost My Unwanted Bulges And Saved Money At The Same Time
2715	Your Health And Financial Well Being: More Energy... More Enthusiasm... More Zest For Life. You'll Have Them All When You Discover The Latest Research On Turning Your Web Site Into A "Well Oiled Machine."
2716	The Product Keys Get Sent Via Email To Your Paypal Address. Please Make Sure (Your Email Address) Is In Your Safe Email List So You Get That Email!
2717	Only 1,000 Lucky Action Takers Can Have Instant Access To My Astonishingly Simple System For Creating Information Products In 24 Hours Or Less... Will You Be One Of Them?
2718	It's The Perfect Reference If You're Selling Products Or Services To Regular Consumers, Business Owners, Auction Buyers And Sellers, Marketers, Entrepreneurs, MLMer's, Affiliates, Web Masters, Executives, Opportunity Seekers Investors, Etc.
2719	As You Navigate This Page We Would Like You To Sit Back And Relax And Take A Few Minutes To Listen To What We Have To Tell You... We Believe We Have Exactly What You've Been Looking For.
2720	Dissect A Million Dollar Campaign Right In Front Of Your Eyes
2721	Most People Scrap The Project They Are Working On And Move On To The Next Shiny Object. And They Do This For Years Until They Either Give Up Or They Change Their Mindset.
2722	OK, You Probably May Have Heard The Buzz, Or Maybe You Read My Emails I Sent The Other Day Sending You Where You Can See Some Very Interesting Videos About Ugly Websites Making Great Money.

2723	That's Right, A Incredible Collection Of 47,000+ Powerful Eye Catching Mini-Phrases And Headlines That You Can Grab, Mix, And Match And Use To Create Your Own Ad Copy.
2724	For All You Know You And I Are Just One Of Those People Who Bought Through A Link With A Cookie Stuffed In Our Browser.....And I Am Not Talking About The Tasty Choc-Chip Types...
2725	No Matter How Many Times We Update The Scripts, You Will Receive All Updates And Upgrades For Twelve Months 100% Absolutely FREE.
2726	What Could You Accomplish If You Could Double Triple Or Quadruple Your Day Job Income
2727	You Get Paid Quickly. Some People Will Pay You The Instantly, Others Pay Every Week Or Two And Most Will Pay You On A Monthly Basis.
2728	The Response Was So Overwhelming That An Entirely New Idea Was Born, To Help YOU Generate New Leads For Your Business And Build Your List So Fast You'll Wonder How It's Been So Difficult In The Past.
2729	I'm Not Going To Apologize For Anyone Who Isn't Willing To Work In Order To Succeed
2730	It's All About Finding The One Thing That Works For You And Your Life
2731	They Don't Know Where To Turn, And Have No Idea How To Properly Promote Their Site Without Getting Ripped Off And Going Broke. They Buy Banner Ads, Pay Per Click Advertising, And Run Ads In The Local Newspaper.
2732	What I Do Is I Use Scientific Marketing Methods To Find Out What People Need Or Want . . . To Find Out What People Are Willing To Pay For. "Scientific Advertising" Is The Term Used By The Great Claude Hopkins, The Father Of Modern Advertising Who Basically Invented Direct Marketing About A Century Ago.
2733	7 Tips For Creating More Responsive Headlines Instantly
2734	You May Be Getting In The Way Of Your Own Success
2735	The Right Keyword Density And Word Count For A Beneficial Article. Ignoring These Aspects Will Negatively Affect The Effectiveness And Profitability Of Your Articles.
2736	Translate Into Other Languages To Capture International Visitors.
2737	Risk Free For A Full Year Takes All The Fear And Doubt Away

2738	Many Try To Guarantee This But Have No Way Of Achieving It Because Any Doubling Is Always At The Expense Of Another Member. This Is The Way It's Been For A Long Time Until Now! You Don't Need To Lose Money Anymore Ever!
2739	Obviously I Can't Keep The Price This Low Forever, Because I Don't Want To Reduce Their Value This Way, So I Recommend That You Act Now, Before It Goes Back Up To The Regular Price.
2740	As Much As We Hate Admitting This, We Feel That Even If God Himself Were An Ebay Seller. He Could Not Even Escape The Rare Unreasonable Customers. Therefore, We've Dedicated Our Lives To Doing Right By People, Have The Best Real Overall Feedback Ever, And We Want To Keep It That Way!
2741	Learning How To Uncover Your Prospects' Real Inner Desires And Wants Is Like Having A Magic Wand That Allows You To Magically Produce Only Products That Sell Like Crazy Because You Only Need To Give Your Market What They Want!
2742	Affiliate Marketing Is Still Considered To Be One Of The Most Ideal Ways For Beginners To Start Making Money Faster Online (Although Just Not As Easy As Most Had Been Brought To Believe).
2743	90% Of ALL KEYWORDS Are Simply Too Hard For You To Achieve Significant Ranking In A Reasonable Amount Of Time. That's Why It's So Difficult Breaking Down This Complex, And Time-Consuming Process Into Making Real Money.
2744	Got To Sell Them The Way They Want To Be Sold
2745	Demystify The SEO Ranking Algorithm And Prepare Your Website For Incredible Results
2746	While There's No Cookie Cutter Approach To Marketing Success, You Will Have Access To This Video Series, That'll Allow You To Create A Steady Flow Of Traffic For The Cheapest Possible Price, Thereby Saving You Money.
2747	There Has Been Some Good And Some Bad But I Think The One Thing That Has Been More Eye Opening Than Anything Else Is Just How Much I Tend To Make Things Seem Way Worse Than They Are.
2748	The Upside To Affiliate Marketing Is You Don't Need A Website And You Don't Need Your Own Product. It's Very Easy To Get Going, And Some People Make A Lot Of Money With Affiliate Marketing.
2749	I Finally Found The Business That Is Going To Make Me Rich And Couldn't Get My Wallet Out Fast Enough.

2750	Safelists Flood You With 1,000s Of Emails You Don't Want And Send Your Emails To Others Who Won't Read Them Either
2751	How Often Have You Seen It's Up To You And Now You're On Your Own
2752	Beat The Rush And Be The First To Reserve Your Copy
2753	If You Can't Set It And Forget It Then You're Trying To Reinvent The Wheel The Hard Way
2754	I Not Going To Confess Or Apologize For All The Money You're About To Make
2755	Continually Dropping Out Knowing You Were Never Truly Committed In The First Place
2756	And You Won't Even Have To Wait To Get Paid Because Your Customers Will Pay The Five Dollars Directly To YOU! I Never Touch Your Money!
2757	And You Can Stop Paying Them The Moment You Feel You Don't Want Them To Work For You Anymore. Virtual Workers Understand. They Don't Expect You To Make A Commitment To Hire Them For A Long-Time; Most Of Their Clients Don't.
2758	This Program Was Tailor-Made For Marketing On Your MySpace Page! Anyone Who Participates In Any Custom Online Storage - Photos, Blogs, Forums, Etc., This Is Perfect For You!
2759	If You Had To Hire A Programmer To Create This System For You, You Could Spend Upwards Of $1200 To $1500 Dollars To Have This Put Together.
2760	You Must Use A Valid eMail Address To Receive A Registration Code
2761	Here Are Just A Few Of The Unsolicited Comments From Our Satisfied Customers
2762	A Magic Character You Can Change In Literally 3 Seconds That Can Increase Conversions By Nearly 17%
2763	People Skim And Scam Your Ads Because They Don't Read Them
2764	Create A Hub Page.
2765	Extinction Probably Isn't The Right Word When It Comes To This Kind Of Marketing
2766	Imagine If You Had A System Of Your Own... A System So Powerful You Had To Expend No More Effort Than Simply *Looking* At A Market To Know Instantly Where The Money Was Hiding.
2767	Freedom Is A State Of Mind That Only You Can Enter

203

2768	Use Your Content As A Gift For Long-Time Clients.
2769	You Will Also Learn How To Put Audio Onto Your Website, How This Can Make Your Website More Personalized Which Can Really Help With Sales.
2770	Renowned Master Copywriter Gives You The Goods On How To Easily Create Interesting, Compelling Web Copy For Your Offers.
2771	Why Is It So Difficult For So Many To Put A Price On Freedom And Independence
2772	Proven Word Of Mouth Marketing Techniques That Will Take Your Business To The Next Level
2773	If You Still Don't Have A Clear Vision Of What You Want To Achieve Online We Can Help
2774	Once You Sign Up You'll Have Instant Access To These Valuable Free Internet Tools
2775	Might As Well Grow And Grow In A Very Profitable Way
2776	Run A Paid Teleseminar Training Series.
2777	Don't Worry About Refunds! I'll Tell You About A Company That Handles It All For You, So You Don't Have To Sweat The Details. Set Things Up With A Few Clicks And Fill In A Few Blanks, And You're Off To The Races.
2778	The Internet Has Dramatically Changed The Offensive Line Of Your Playing Field
2779	Push Your Business Over The Comfort Threshold And Build Your Dreams
2780	How To Persuade Your Customers To Buy From You And Close The Sale! I Describe To You How You Can Make Your Sales Copy A Prospect-Murderer, Sending Their Names And E-Mail Addresses Into Your Customer List, By Closing The Sale Effectively!
2781	Yes There Are Scams But More Importantly There Are Some Great Opportunities Left
2782	Hope You Know I Value You As A Subscriber And That I Try To Provide VALUE To You To Grow Your Business. If You Have To Unsubscribe I Understand And Wish The Best For You And Hope To Be Able To Help You In The Future!
2783	With Nothing Held Back Here Is The Automated Profit System You've Been Seeking
2784	We Start By Giving You The Entire Business Building System For FREE

2785	Should An Experienced Traveler Like You Fly With A New Airline Like Us
2786	You'll Quickly Discover You Have Developed New Habits And Beliefs That Will Steer You Towards Your Goals. You'll Finally Blast Through Whatever Obstacles Have Been Holding You Back.
2787	Imagine The Feeling Of Excitement When You Create The Biggest Pay Day Of Your Life
2788	A Small Leap Of Faith Will Teach You Why Machines Must Do All Your Selling For You
2789	It can be a daunting, discouraging task when you're all alone. But with _____ Membership, you're never alone. _____ Membership not only gives you all the pieces to assembling and running your Internet business... It also gives you detailed step-by-step instructions on how to assemble those pieces.
2790	Nice Sheets Fancy Lingerie Burn Candles Don't Save Them For A Special Occasion Because Today Is Special
2791	People Starting Going Crazy When I Test Leaked Just One Part Of This Little Gem
2792	You Can't Help Them Get There Until You Meet Them Where They're At
2793	It Take One Great Day To Lead You To A Great Life
2794	Use Real-Life Situations- Make Your Writing Relatable. Think Like Your Audience When Writing The Articles And You Will Have A Better Chance Convincing Them To Continue To Click Through To Your Website.
2795	Discover How Adding Photo Blogs Can Make Your Site Wildly Profitable
2796	Isn't It About Time Your Business Get Out From Underneath The Rocks And Flourish
2797	Are You Up To The Job And Ready To Work This Deal
2798	Use Your Content To Address Any Objections You've Faced When Selling Your Products Or Services.
2799	The Three Basic Elements To SEO- Keywords, Linking And Content. Consider Keywords, Linking And Content The Three Musketeers Of All Successful SEO. Keep These In Mind For All Your Copy And Content To Ensure The Maximum Traffic Generation Results.

2800	To Start Maximizing Your Sales, Reserve Your Spot Immediately. Get Started By Clicking The Order Button Below. Unlike Most Video Producers Who Make You Wait For Weeks, I Personally Will Make Sure Your Video Is Created And Sent To You Within 24 Hours Of Submission.
2801	A Simple Formula For Selling Anything To Anybody, At Any Time, In Any Country, Online or Offline, Even If You HATE To Sell!
2802	Web Strategies You Need To Keep Your Costs Low And Your Profits High
2803	Iran Still Closed Off; Physicists Estimate It Will Take At Least 10 More Years Before Radioactivity Decreases To Safe Levels
2804	We're Going To Show You How To Put Your Video To You Tube And Other Online Video Sites. This Is A Great Way To Get Traffic To Your Website And Again It Is A Free Method Of Advertising Your Business.
2805	You See, I Wanted To Develop A System That Was So Simple, Anyone Could Follow It. And Not Just Follow It, Actually Earn Money From It. And I Wanted To Make Sure You Could Do It With No Outlay At All, And Get Started Making Money As Soon As Possible. So I Finally Did It, And I Put It All Into One Simple Video Course...
2806	For An Exclusive Group Of People I'm Passing Out The Exact Same Secret Strategies And Adsense I Personally Use To Attain 6 Figures In Adsense Every Year.
2807	Put A Little Piece Of You Into Every Promotional Idea You Create Or Offer
2808	Over 1,700.000 Jobs Were Lost Last Year Is Your Job Next
2809	You See, We Would Much Rather You Be OVER THE MOON With Our Products And Services Rather Than Just "Satisfied." While Most Marketers Will Never Admit That, We Know You Are Clever Enough To Understand The Sheer Importance This Information Holds To Your Business.
2810	If You're Not Seeing Shockingly Good Results By Then, I Don't Want Your Money And I'll Give Back Every Penny To You - With Absolutely No Questions Asked.
2811	How To Avoid Diet Plans That Torture You Cost A Fortune And Leave You Fatter
2812	Give Away A "Free Report" To Boost The Size Of Your Mailing List.

2813	Free Videos Show You How You Can Literally Have An Endless New Stream Of Distributors Knocking Down Your Door, Credit Card In Hand, Ready To Join... Absolutely Free!
2814	We Are Willing To Shoulder All The Risk For You So You Can Concentrate On Generating Profits For Yourself. And We Know That Once You Start Making Money With Our Products, Just Like Thousands Of Our Customers Are Doing Right Now, You Will Come Back For More.
2815	How Far Are You Willing To Go To Land A Sale
2816	It Is A Very Simple And True Working No-Sponsoring System Will Pay You From Day One And Month After Month. It Will Provide You Even More Excitement With Great Confidence Than Any Programs Now Or In The Past.
2817	Think Of Being Paid For Your Time Instead Of Getting Paid For Building A Business. When You First Start Out, You Will Probably Be Paid By The Hour Or By The Job Or By The Project. But If You Are Good At What You Do, More Business Will Come In.
2818	It Never Ceases To Amaze Me How Easy It Is To Make Money Online
2819	It's Pointless To Lament About Lost Yesterdays When One Can Put An Idea To Use Today, Right Now And Celebrate What We've Learned Rather Than Regret. Do 'IT' Now! Don't Wait Until The Car Is Paid Off, Finish School, Lose 15 Pounds, Get Married Or Divorced, Have Kids, Or Wait Till You Retire. Do 'IT' Now While You're Alive!
2820	Don't Let Your Website Wither Away Getting Blown Around Like Internet Tumbleweed
2821	I Just Wanted To Personally Touch Base With You And See What Could Possibly Be Holding You Back From Taking Us Up On The Amazing Business Offer We Spoke About In Detail Within Our Free Report!
2822	You Either Use Internet Marketing PLR Or You Don't. If You Do, This Is Top-Notch Content That Is Written By Someone Who Has Privately Coached Some Of The Top Gurus Online (Me!) -- And It's Cheap. If You Haven't Signed Up Yet, You Either Didn't Read This Page Or You're Crazy. Go Back And Read It And Then We'll Know Which It Is.
2823	If A 12 Year Old Can Do This Why Can't You
2824	Finally! A Book That Tells The TRUTH About The Tricks Used On The Internet To Take Your Money Time After Time... While You Walk Away With Nothing Time After Time!

207

2825	My 4-Year Old Son Asked Me In The Car The Other Day "Dad What Would Happen If You Ran Over A Ninja?" How The Hell Do I Respond To That
2826	If You're Like Some Of Our Students Who Are Ready To Move Much Faster And Have The Time To Do So, You Are More Than Welcome To Go Through The Course Much Faster. The Great Thing About Our Online Course Is That You Set The Pace To Match Your Schedule Just Like The Affiliate Marketing World.
2827	The Money Is Where You Can Feed The Hungriest Crowd - Want To Know Where
2828	Four Quick Questions Will Reveal A Chiropractor's Operating Philosophy. Ask Them, And Save
2829	People Are Running Around Buying Every Ebook, Software, Script Etc, That Promises Them Thousands In Google Adsense Earnings, But They Don't Know How To Use What They Are Buying.
2830	Are You Finally Ready To Have No More Problems Finding Profitable Products, Setting Up Winning Adwords Campaigns, Building Huge Responsive Lists?
2831	As One Of The First 500 Buyers I Understand I'm Also Going To Get _____
2832	You'll Be Able To Eliminate Those Long, Ugly Links And Instead, Have A More Professional-Looking Solution That Entices People To Click On Your Link And Buy.
2833	Doctors: Put An Easy $341,450 In Your Pocket Every 12 Months... Without Doing Anything More Than You're Doing Right Now
2834	What Would It Be Worth To Know That You Were Finally Doing What You Loved To Do, And Were Making More Money Than You Ever Thought Possible? I'll Tell You This Right Now With 100% Conviction... It's Not A Pipe Dream!
2835	You Now Get The Best Of Both Worlds: Quality Content In Record Time. Discover How You Can Effortlessly Stuff Blogs Full Of Posts And Comments That Don't Just Capture Prized Search Rankings... But, Keep Your Visitors Coming Back For More.
2836	If You Sell A Product Or Service It Stands To Reason, As In Any Type Of Sales, That Getting Directly In Front Of A Potential Customer With Your Pitch Is The Only Place To Be.

2837	At Times We Have All Had The Feeling That We Were Spinning Our Wheels And Going Nowhere. This Can Be Very Frustrating And Costly. We Begin Wondering What Am I Doing Wrong?
2838	These Events Are Usually Reserved For The Big Dog Marketers, But I'll Show You How To Get In, And Shoot Up The Ranks, No Matter How Your List Is Now!
2839	Commute To Work Answer To The Boss And Get Paid What Others Think I'm Worth
2840	Why Did The News Revolution Start Yesterday And Your Were Still Missing
2841	Simply Click Below And Please Be Sure To Leave Your Personal Comments
2842	I Came Up With Something That Just Had To Be Created
2843	How To Draw Visitors To Your Web Site By Holding An Online Contest Or Sweepstakes
2844	Originally Created For My Own Use, I've Since Realized This Is The Piece Of The Puzzle I Was Missing, Before I Built Multiple 6 And 7 Figure Cash Flow Funnel Business Models. So I've Decided To Give This Software Away, For A Short Period Of Time, Only To The Most Eager And Ambitious Online Entrepreneurs, As I Am Positive That You Too Will See Results!
2845	After 30 Days You Will Be Billed $97 For A Further Month's Membership
2846	Do You Wish That There Was A Way That You Could Take Your Current Links And Transform Them Into More Professional-Looking Links, Attract More Visitors?
2847	It Makes Me Wonder What I Might Have Accomplished If I Had Thought Of A Wonderful Goal 30 or 40 Years Ago Planting One Idea At A Time, Like Bulbs In A Garden, And Wonder What I Might Have Been Able To Achieve. My Wish For You Is To Plant Your Dreams Earlier And Celebrate Your Achievements Rather Than Losing Hours Of Yesterday!
2848	At The End Of Your 30 Day Trial, You Can Simply Let The Account Go Or Keep Building Your List And Your Profits For Just $17.95 Per Month.
2849	The Was A Simple Question: Can You Replace Your Previous Income While Working Entirely From Home Using Only His Computer And A Pound Your Fists On The Table In Utter Frustration Slow Internet Connection While Being Literally In The Middle Of Nowhere?

2850	You Know It's Real But Still Haven't Been Able To Pull A Decent Profit
2851	There Will Be Higher Chances Your Article Post Will Be Picked Up By Search Engines Based On How Often You Post Your Blog Post.
2852	A Large Majority Of Online Business Owners Are Completely Unaware Of Their Legal Website Responsibilities. If You Aren't Posting Proper Disclaimers And Terms Of Service On Your Site, You Could Be Open To Very Costly Litigation.
2853	How To Enter Any Niche Market And Become A Big Player
2854	This Secret Holds The Keys That Can Change Your Life For The Better Starting Now
2855	Wish I Could Tell You It's Easy But The Truth Is That It Really Doesn't Have To Be Hard
2856	The Secret To Success In The Network Marketing Industry Today Is To Fix The Problems All Marketers Face In Their Businesses.
2857	Create A Role-Playing Activity At A Workshop.
2858	Just Imagine I'm A Genie, And I've Granted You The Wish Of A Life Exactly The Way You Want It. Feel It. See It. Hear It, Taste It, Smell It. Live It. Take A Minute And Do This For Yourself, You Might Be Surprised By What You Discover...
2859	The Business Must Work For You To Free Up Your Time
2860	How To Turn Pennies Into Hundreds To Thousands Of Dollars. This Is One Of The Simplest Yet Most Profitable Methods I've Seen. Many People Are Already Doing It, But Could You Be Missing The Boat?
2861	Pretty Amazing Isn't It? The Best Part In Joining Is In Accessing An Incredible Library Of Information That Is Just The Beginning. Wait Until You See The Power Of What It Can Do To Your Life.
2862	A Brand New Issue Of The Most Controversial, Revealing, And Shocking Newsletter Ever Written For People To Go From Living A Life Of Mediocrity With No Hope, To A Life Of Riches, Total Freedom And Endless Cash!
2863	The Secret Of Online Promotion" - How To Succeed And Earn At Will, By Offering Products That People Have Been Buying And Re-Buying For Decades, And Having Them Come To You, Money-In-Hand.
2864	Isn't It Amazing How Many People Peddle The Same Junk Minute By Minute Day After Day

2865	How To Guarantee Continually Growing Online Traffic To Your Website
2866	Avoid The Tragedy Of Debt Living Check To Check And The Loss Of Freedom
2867	Even The Competition Will Be Hard Pressed To Ensure Your Online Success Like This
2868	Discover My Step By Step Methods To Milking The "Free Traffic" From The Search Engines. (One Of My Students Used This To Make Over $300 This Week... And It Only Took Him A Few Days To Set Up - Its Not Enough To Retire On... But This Little Site Will Make Him Money Day In And Day Out Without Any More Work.) Great For Those On A Budget!
2869	Social Networking Is THE WAY Of The Web These Days...Not Just A Trend, But The Way That The Web Has Matured - Into A Fully Interactive Environment.
2870	Grab This Incredible Package Featuring 5 Powerful And Affordable Business Building Tools To Automate & Improve Your Online Business For A Fraction Of The Regular Price!
2871	Mix Up Your Paragraph Sizes- Short And Long Paragraphs Grab Reader's Attention. No One Wants To Look Down An Article And See 5 Perfectly Shaped Paragraphs- Talk About Boring! This Isn't English Grammar Class After All. You Don't Have To Use The Standard 5- Paragraph Format Anymore.
2872	These Mini-Phrase Headlines Will Inspire And Transform Your Entire Approach To Advertising
2873	It's All About Buying Smart And Not Trading Quarters For Dollars
2874	A Giant Visual Mind Map Outlining Every Single Step, Sub-Step, And Micro-Step For Building A Monster Marketing List - Fast!
2875	You Need To Offer An Endless Variety Of Products To People
2876	Discover The Secrets To Creating A New Life Of Success, Wealth & Happiness And How To Achieve Your Goals & Ambitions Using Simple Mindmap Strategies In Your Day To Day Life For Lasting And Sustainable Wealth Online
2877	Pay Off Your Debts And Improve Your Lifestyle With The Best System
2878	How To Hotwire The Internet While Creating A Deadly Online Money Making System
2879	You Have Magic Within You And We Can Help You Discover It

2880	You See, There Are A Very Specific Set Of Rules, Techniques And Secrets That You Can Implement Right Now That Will Totally Guarantee Your Success For Years To Come, No Joke...
2881	So If You Decide To Invest $197 Today, You'll Have The Chance To Join An Exclusive Community Of Super Affiliates That Pounce On The Competition Day In And Out, And Receive The Lions Share Of The Clickbank Riches.
2882	Step Outside Your Comfort Zone And Provide A Service To Others
2883	Protect Yourself From Being Burned By It Candidates Who Over-Represent Their Skill Level
2884	You're Going To Want To Share This With Your Friends Right Away And Become Their Hero
2885	I Learned A Very Long Time Ago That There's A Lot More Money Selling Shovels Than There Is Digging For Gold! In Other Words, My Interest Is In Showing You The TOOLS You Need To Succeed – NOT In Lining My Pockets By Selling You On My Own Opportunity!
2886	YOU Will Earn A Substantial Income From Home When You Change Your Mindset, And Begin To Duplicate This EXACT 3-Step Success Method, FREE.
2887	I'm Not Sure It's Not Illegal To Scream "FIRESALE" In A Crowded Internet Web Space :- Maybe It Is ... ? Oh Well ... I'll Do It Anyways ...FIRESALE! FIRESALE! FIRESALE!
2888	Is Your Business Is Bleeding Cash Like A Slot-Junkie In Vegas? If You're Still Thinking There's A Heavy-Hitter Who Will Make All Of Your Dreams Of Business Success Come True, You Should Probably Keep Reading.
2889	You Will Be Up And Running Making Money With This System VERY Quickly
2890	The Easy Way To Leverage One Of The Most Popular Websites To Start Your Own Business... Without Having Your Own Website At All! This Is A Billion-Dollar Industry, And It Takes About A Week For You To Get A Slice Of That.
2891	FOUR Ways To Personalize Your Copy And Capture The Readers Attention
2892	Would You Prefer To Own The Fountain Of Youth Or A Backyard Money Tree
2893	Nothing Makes People Desperate To See Something Like Being Told They Can't

2894	How Many Customers Is Your Data Base Losing Ever Day Week Or Month
2895	You Only Need To Worry About Gaining Control Of Your Niche Market
2896	Making A Fortune By Simply Identifying Rising Trends That Only A Few Even Know About
2897	7 Quick Tips For Producing Better Results From Your Ads
2898	Obvious Warning Signs And Immediate Clues To Detect If A Moneymaking Program Or Venture Is A Scam. Scams Abound On The Internet. If You're Not Careful, You Could Lose A Lot Of Money. I'll Show You How To Detect Scams In The Blink Of An Eye And Ensure You Don't Become A Victim.
2899	Help Me Solve This Problem And I'll Give You One Of My Websites As A Gift
2900	But, If You Want An Idiot-Proof, Connect-The-Dots, Follow The Bouncing Ball, Method That Doubles Your Money Every Time You Use It – Grab The Opportunity While It Is Still Available
2901	Not Only Will You Take Your Life Back, You'll Get To Design It And Live It Just As You Please. You'll Watch Your Money Problems Disappear As You Follow These Directions.
2902	Here's To Everyone Who Wants To Quit Working In The Very Near Future
2903	What Should You Be Spending Your Time On That Produces Results
2904	If You Keep Hearing "The Money Is In The List" But Have No Idea What "A List" Is, Or How To Get One... Or If You're Trying To Build A List And Keep Getting Stalled By Opt-Outs And Trapped In Spam Filters, See Our Solution.
2905	When To Buy An Existing Site, And When It's Easier To Just Swipe The Good Parts For Your Own Site...
2906	The Absolute Easiest, Simplest And Yet One Of The Most Effective And Profitable Ways To Get Started On Becoming A Successful Affiliate! (You Wont Believe How Simple And Easy This Is...You Can Be Up And Running In Under An Hour!)
2907	The First 500 People To Say Yes Receive A Mega Bonus Package
2908	Is It True That You're Business Is Willing To Settle For Only $50 A Day
2909	Has Anxiety Stress And Lack Of Self Confidence Created A Miserable Lifestyle

2910	This Proven System Will Help Funnel Money Away From Your Competition's Bank Account
2911	How To Sculpt Landing Page Copy That Whips Your Visitors Into A Buying Frenzy... A Few Simple Tweaks On Your Landing Page Can Easily Double Your Results - And I'll Tell You How.
2912	Pricing Strategies And The Bigger Picture. How Do You Select The Price At Which You're Going To Sell Your Products? By Looking At The Competition Most People Would Reply. There Are However Several More Factors That I'll Discuss With You That Can Allow You To Charge Five Times What Your Competition Is Charging And Still Outsell Them By An Incredible Amount. (It's Tips Like These That Force Me To Limit The Number Of A Product I'll Sell).
2913	We Don't Know Why People Would Waste Their Time Creating A Portal Content Site When A Creating A "Mini Site" Is So Much More Profitable (And So Much Less Work).
2914	My Personal Strategy For Spending Less Than 1 Hour A Day Creating "Lead Generators" That Rush In Thousands Of Active Buyers And Subscribers And How To Easily Scale Up Your System So That You Can Instantly Maximize Your Exposure Absolutely Free!
2915	Pull Up A Chair Pour Yourself A Drink And Mark This Date On Your Calendar
2916	Killer Strategies For Making The Most Of Free Advertising
2917	As We Sail Off Into The Cash-Rich Sunset At High Speed
2918	P.S. Remember, With My "No Holds Barred" Guarantee, You Have Nothing To Lose... Rather... You Have Incredible Freedom And Prosperity To Gain!
2919	Are You're In The Market For Automating 95 Percent Of Your Business
2920	How To Increase The Value Of Any Website By Up To 91% Just By Registering The Domain Name – Plus The Sneaky Trick To Snatching Domains For Just Pennies!
2921	Think About Creating Your Own Product. That Sounds Complicated And Time-Consuming. Actually, It's Not That Big A Deal. You Can Create A Quality Product You'll Be Proud To Sell Really Quickly.
2922	Do People Really Care About What Offering On Your Capture Page
2923	How Many Times Will You Allow Wishy Washy Members To Continually Kick Your Online Tires

2924	The Easiest And Fastest Way To Create An Instant Surge In Orders
2925	Ordering Our Automated Install Solution Will Help You Cut Down The Time Required To Install And Configure Your New Review Blog Down To Minutes And Begin Working On What Makes You Money A Lot Sooner.
2926	You Might Be Thinking, "I Don't Have Time For That. I'm Buried In Paperwork. The Phone Is Ringing All The Time. There Always Seems To Be An Emergency Or Some Fire That Has To Be Put Out." Then Hire Someone To Buy Your Groceries And Pick Up Your Dry Cleaning. Is This Really A Good Use Of Your Time?
2927	As You Know By Now, There Are Three Inviolable Golden Rules, Which Are Responsible For A Staggering 99% Of Marketers FAILING At All To Rank For A Significant Key-Phrase - One With Traffic And Commercial Value And Acceptable Competition.
2928	How To Scientifically Select The Finest Products That Virtually Guarantees Success
2929	The Most Amazing On-Line Money Making System We've Ever Seen. We Won't Get Ahead Of Ourselves Here, But Suffice It To Say That This New On-Line Miracle Allows You To Make Money On-Line, 24/7/365,
2930	Do You Realize That In 40 Years, There Will Be Thousands Of Old Ladies Running Around With Tattoos And Body Piercings
2931	There Are No Complicated Databases For You To Set Up, In Fact It Has Been Designed So That Even A Child Can Use It.
2932	It Is Finally Time For The Internet Playing Field To Be Leveled By Accessing The Truth
2933	I Realize That You May Be A Bit Confused As To What It Takes To Get Targeted Visitors To Your Website And May Not Know Where To Start But I'm Going To Help You Understand…
2934	If You Want To Make Money Online And You Want A Steady Stream Of Contacts To Talk To Then You've Come To The Right Place. Discover An Unbelievably Quick And Easy Tool That Gives You An Edge And A Big Fat Pay Raise Using One Of The Most Visited Sites In The World! With A Few Clicks Of Your Mouse You Can Be Getting Thousands Of Targeted Leads Daily.
2935	I Have To Be Crazy To Miss Out On This Incredible Offer
2936	A Challenge To Women Who Would Never Dream Of Serving Margarine

2937	As Soon As You Have Created And Uploaded Your First Adsense Site, Simply Drop Me An Email To Let Me Know, And I'll Critique It For You, Right Away.
2938	While Some Of You Reading This May Be Accomplished Business Professionals, I'm Assuming That Some Of You Aren't. If You're Like Me, You're An Average Guy (Or Gal) Who Wants To Earn Money, And Would-If You Had The Right Tools To Work With. My Goal Is To Provide You With Those Tools, That Will Let You Literally "Build" Your Own Successful Business.
2939	First Of All, Thank You For Being A Valued Subscriber. I Try My Hardest To Give To You The Most Relevant And Insightful Information That Will Help Further Your Online Marketing Presence.
2940	I Hope This Will Make You Think More Seriously About Your Future
2941	If You Feel I Send You To Many Emails Please Forgive Me For This And Feel Free To Use My Unsubscribe That's Available In Every Email. We Can Part Friends And You Are Always Welcome To Rejoin At A Later Time. I Mean This In The Most Sincere Way.
2942	So What Is The Big Lie That I'm Talking About? It's The Age Old Marketing "Wisdom" That Says "The Money Is In The List". Actually That's Only Half True! You See, The Money Is NOT Just "In The List".
2943	Live A DREAM LIFE. Tropical Vacations, Exotic Cars, Time And Freedom To Do What You Want When You Want. All On Your Terms. (Live The Life You Deserve.)
2944	Keeping Looking For That Pie In The Sky Then Come Back To Us For A Huge Slice Of Reality
2945	How A Senior Citizen Opened Pandora's Box Of Internet Secrets And Made A Fortune
2946	Everything I Sell Can Be Duplicated And Rolled Out To Thousands Of People, Or Hundreds Of Thousands Of People. If I Conduct A Seminar In A Room And Record It, I Can Also Market It And Distribute It Over The Internet To Tens Of Thousands Of People
2947	Need Someone To Point You In The Right Direction Of What Works
2948	Increase Intensity Duration And Frequency And I'm Not Talking About Sex

216

2949	You Need To Uncover What Your Market Truly Wants BEFORE You Create & Sell Your Product Or Promote An Affiliate Product To Them!
2950	Learn Exactly How A Search Engine Marketer Makes Money And Gets Paid. You'll Discover The Best Companies That Pay The Most, And How You Can Even Get Paid Weekly
2951	Every Single Best Selling Novel Or Book Uses This Simple Tiny Trick Guan Teed To Increase Readership By Nearly 40%
2952	Our Internet Marketing Community May Have All The Answers You're Still Seeking
2953	By The End Of Your First Week, You Had It All Down, As If You'd Been There For Years. It's The Same Way With List Building, But With One Big Difference...
2954	Why Is It That 97 Percent Would Rather Buy A Hamburger Than Learn How To Make Money
2955	I Achieved Financial Freedom Without "Getting Rich Quick." And Now, Financial Freedom Means Being Able To Stay At Home And Spend The Day With My Wife And Son. It Means My Wife Doesn't Have To Go Out To Work.
2956	Click On The Cancel Button Right Now To Stay On The Current Page Because I Have Something Very Special For You.
2957	Ask For The Order More Than Once Then Seal The Deal. You Know, It's The First Rule Of Sales In Real World Business, But I Rarely See Marketers Taking Advantage Of It Online. This One Aspect Alone Could Double Your Sales.
2958	Never Forget That In Our Internet Community None Of Us Is Ever As Smart As All Of Us
2959	Updated Techniques, Tools And Technologies To Take Advantage Of The New Internet And Software Advances So You Can Be Amongst The First People To Harness These New Technologies For Your Own Wealth Producing!
2960	When You Become An Exclusive Member You're Getting Everything Mentioned Above
2961	As A Matter Of Fact ... I Want This In YOUR Hands Right NOW Before I Decide To Take It Off The Market Completely. I Know Only The Deadly 'Serious' Will Take Action Right Now To Change Their Life For The Better!
2962	It Wasn't Very Long Ago That I Was In The Exact Same Situation That You Are In Today. I Was Trying My Hand At Everything Looking For The One Thing That Would Enable Me To Make A Real Living Outside Of The Daily 9-5 Grind.

2963	Put On Your Top Hat And Pull Out Your Magic Wand. Now Start Thinking. What You Are Selling? What Solutions Do You Have To Offer? How Can You Solve Problems?
2964	When You Have An Idea, Do Not Stick To It. Try To Destroy It, To Stretch It Apart, Try To Find Other Possible Uses... You Might Find A New And Remarkable Angle.
2965	There Are No Hitches And No Catches... Well Maybe Just One. Upon Completion, I Am Going To Ask You To Send Me Feedback On What You Thought Of The Course.
2966	1:14 A.M. - Caller Reports Hitting An Intruder In The Head With An Axe. Notes That Intruder Was In The Mirror
2967	How To Collect Powerful Testimonials And Endorsements. Testimonials Are Indeed Powerful Components Of Your Sales Letter. They Back What You Have To Say Or Claim. I Don't Know Of That Many Materials On The Same Subject That Show You How You Can Gather Your Own Collection Of Powerful Testimonials That Will Back Your Claims In Your Sales Letter.
2968	How To Find Hot Niches And Attract Niche Traffic To Your Website
2969	When The Masses Come You Better Be Ready To Automate Your Online Deliveries
2970	Check Out Our No Obligation Test Drive From The Comfort Of Your Own Home
2971	Life And Death Is In The Power Of The Tongue - Or The Words That Come Out From It. Did You Know That With Just A Few Simple Words, Marketers Have Generated Millions Of Dollars In Sales In Just A Few Minutes?
2972	This Information Is Specifically Designed For Those In The Following Companies
2973	Does Your Business Model Speak From Your Heart Or Just Your Pocketbook
2974	Former Barber Earns $8,000 In Four Months As Real Estate Specialist
2975	This Is Too Good Not To Take Advantage Of So Do It Right Now Before It's Gone Forever
2976	Never Ever Allow Your Marketing Skills To Over Promise And Under Deliver
2977	Consider Advertising In The Business Opportunity Sections Of These Valuable Publications

2978	Start A $1000/Month Business And Quickly Turn It Into A $10,000/Month Business, Step-By-Step, Without Spending More Time Online Than You Are Now In Fact, We Don't Want You To Spend More Than An Hour Or So A Day On This
2979	By Clicking Over To This Page You've Shown The Curiosity And Motivation Required To Make A Killing On The Internet, And Understand That Using Keywords Is Crucial To Your Success!
2980	The Cost Of Producing Quality Corporate Videos Has Fallen By 64% Over The Last Five Years
2981	Are So Called Secret Offers Really A Secret If Anyone Can Buy Them
2982	Plus, If You Order My (Product) Now, You Can Take Advantage Of My Immediate Download Feature To Begin Reading And Making Money From The Program's Expert Advice And Comprehensive Information In Just Minutes!
2983	Create A Product And A Set Of Bonuses And Watch Your Affiliates Make You Wealthy
2984	I Love This Program. It Is The Only One You Will Keep Forever. I Can't Even Start To Describe Everything You Get With It But Here Is Just A Taste:
2985	You Have A FULL 30 Days To Review My System – If You Don't Like It, No Problem, I'll Literally FORCE You To Take Your Money Back! You Literally Have NOTHING To Risk Or Lose! The Only Thing You Are Risking Is That By NOT Taking Action Now – This Is A Limited Time Offer - You Could Come Back And This Course Will No Longer Be Up For Sale.
2986	This Extremely Rare Opportunity Won't Last Much Longer That Will Instantly Catapult Your Business To New Heights?
2987	Hold On Hear Me Out I'm Not Just Looking For Anyone
2988	Hopefully By Now You Can See How Neglecting To Build A List Is Not Just Leaving Money On The Table... It's Picking It Up And Tossing It Out The Window.
2989	Classified Ad: Miriam, As A Token Of My Undying Love I'm Knocking A $120 Off What Your Still Owe Me
2990	If You Want Dirt Cheap Clicks Which Are Still Available I'll Show You How To Create Super Relevant Simple Sites That Google Loves.
2991	Customers Want And Need This Because They're Tired Of Get Rich Schemes And Scams

219

2992	I Want You To Think Back To The Last 10 Or So Business Opportunity Presentations You May Have Seen... Do You Recall Any Of Them That Had Huge Wealth Claims?
2993	With The Most Common Questions About Resell Rights Answered For You, You Can Stop Getting Confused And Start Making Some Real Cash With It Now.
2994	They'll Probably Laugh At You For Walking Away From The Best Value
2995	She Isn't Wrong. Actually, She Hit The Nail On The Head. I Know Of Many Failed Newbie Marketers Who Have Bought Ebooks, Software, Memberships And Programs But Have Not Made A Single Red Cent. (Sounds Familiar?)
2996	Your Really Owe It To Yourself To Expand Your New Horizons
2997	Cozy Up To Your Target Audience And Watch Them Eagerly Open Their Wallets
2998	Too Many Choices And Far Too Many People Wanting You To Listen
2999	This Helps You Build And Explode Your Primary Business Through Not Only The Power Of Regular Advertising Networks, But Also Puts The Power Of Viral Marketing Right Into Your Hands!
3000	Use Your Contents To Create Landing Pages For Affiliate Products.
3001	No More Backbreaking Garden Chores For Me Yet Ours Is Now The Show-Place Of The Neighborhood
3002	Have You Maxed Out Your Credit Card Just To Stay In Business
3003	Since We Have Had Literally Hundreds Of Questions About How It All Works, We Decided There Is No Better Way To Answer If This Is For You Than By Giving You The Actual Course Overview And Intro Videos That All The Owners Are Seeing!
3004	Anyway, I Hope That You Take Something Away From This Email As I Sat And Thought About How To Get My Point Across For The Last Two Hours. Its 2 Am Now And I Am Still Up Because This Is Important And I Had To Get It Right.
3005	With These Resources You Can Create An Online eCoaching Program, Incorporating These As Part Of Your eCoaching Program As The Backbone Of The Information You Share In Your eCoaching Program And You'd Have Yourself A HOT High-Ticket Offer Ready To Promote.

3006	It's A Great Feeling To Be Able To Spend Time With Your Family, Relax And Read A Book, Or Even Take Off For A Mini-Vacation Whenever You Feel Like It. The Feeling Of Freedom And Getting Rid Of That Habitual Stress Is Worth Whatever It Takes, In My Opinion.
3007	Map Quest Really Needs To Start Their Directions On #5. I'm Pretty Sure I Know How To Get Out Of My Neighborhood.
3008	How Telling A Simple Story Can Continue Making Thousands Of Dollars For Many Months Into The Future.
3009	They Make It Sound So Easy Don't They? Just Build A Web-site And Place Some Ads On It And You Will Earn A Fortune When Your Ads Are Clicked.
3010	Our Program Is Simply More Extensive And More Complete Than Any Other Product Package Out There. Our "Ladder Up-grades" Allow You To Choose Which Products You Want Access To, And What Your Limits Are.
3011	Avoid This Simple Yet Over Used Approach And Begin Charting Increases In Your Own Sales
3012	Setting Up This Link Will Turn Your Website Into A Backend Money Machine
3013	This Opportunity Lights The Way To An Unprecedented Op-portunity. By Using These Secret Methods To Finally Make A Killing Of Your Own Before 99.99% Of The World Even Knows What's Going On.
3014	All You Have To Do Is Give It Away For Free
3015	How One Of The Ugliest Websites Continually Excites Each And Every Visitor
3016	Well If You've Done One Or More Of The Things Above... You're Not Alone. Most People Get Burned Over And Over Again Until They Either Run Out Of Money, Or Get So Frus-trated They Quit Trying Altogether.
3017	We Have More Ways To Make Serious Money Than Appetites For Pure Profits
3018	Don't Forget To Close The Deal Before You Close The Door
3019	The Secret Strategies For Making A Huge Income From Just One Niche... One Niche Can Be All You Need When You Know Exactly How To Milk It.
3020	Anatomy Of An Affiliate Site With A Killer Structure. I'll Show You What Makes An Affiliate Site Sell Like Crazy And Explain Why... With Screenshots And Notes.

3021	And By The Time You're Done Reading This Page You'll Know Exactly What It Is, How Simple It Is To Use, And How Much Money You Can Potentially Earn By Using It.
3022	161 New Ways To A Man's Heart In This Fascinating Book For Cooks
3023	Why High Gas Prices Are Good For Your New Home Business
3024	You Give 100 Percent In The 1st Half And If That Isn't Enough In The 2nd Half You Give What's Left
3025	Is Your Website Really Worth More Than Just $1 A Day To You
3026	Give Yourself A Big Fat Raise And Never Leave Your Home
3027	I'm Going To Reveal To You How You Can Save Thousands Of Dollars And Make Them At The Same Time By Selling This Mothership Of Swipe Files And Personal Development Words That No One Has Ever Seen On The Internet At This Magnitude!
3028	Universal Laws Unveiling The Hidden Secrets Of Success And How It Works Online
3029	A Simple Truth You Should Know About Your Online Prospects. Understand This And You'll Have What It Takes To Beat The Pants Off Your Competition – Leaving Them Scratching Their Heads, Wondering Why.
3030	It's Amazing How Big You Can Build A Company By Giving Away Great Information For Free
3031	Can You Afford To Pass This Up I Don't Think So
3032	A Tool That Allows You To Automatically "Spin" Out Thousands Of Unique Versions Of The Same Article In A Fraction Of The Time It Would Take You To Reword One Or Two Articles Manually!
3033	Don't Audit Life Simply Show Up And Make The Most Of It Now
3034	You Can Conduct A Product Test Or An Ad Test On Google Adwords For $50. And You'll Know The Results In A Few Hours. You Will Then Know Whether To Move Forward With The Product, Or Perhaps To Conduct Some Further Tests, Or Perhaps To Abandon The Effort Entirely.
3035	You've Made More Money In A Few Days Then In An Entire Month In Your Previous Job! Boy Does Life Feel Good!! Within Just A Matter Of Weeks, You Could Be Making Money Like This On A Daily Basis.

3036	Access My Private Collection Of Over 44,500 Unique Eye Catching Money-Making Word Phrases And Action Headlines And Never Run Out Of Ideas For Your Next Ad, Email, Or Product Promotions.
3037	One Small Trick That Will Triple Response To Your Sales Offers
3038	It Was Maddening. Work, Work, Work....And Then Back To Square One. Surely It Had To Be Easier Than This. Other People Were Making It Happen, And I Knew I Was Just As Smart....Or Smarter...Then They Were!
3039	I'm Sure There Is A Point To All Of This. After All, We All Want To Be That Much Farther Ahead In Our Business Than We Are Currently. It's Just Human Nature For Man To Want More And More. It's About The Satisfaction Of Achievement And Of Course The Perks That Come With It, Isn't It?
3040	These Resale And Republishing Rights To Quality Products Will Amaze Your Bank Account
3041	Imagine How Your Family And Friends Will Be Amazed After Your First Successful Launch
3042	If You Are Looking For A Proven System That Will Enable You To Finally Rid Yourself Of Daily Worries And Free Up The Time To Truly Enjoy Your Life Then The Success Principle Is Exactly What You've Been Looking For.
3043	Just Being Able To Talk With A Live Knowledgeable Representative Earned Our Respect And Appreciation. All Questions And Concerns Were Answered Directly To Our Full Satisfaction.
3044	How To Make Money Even When You're Pitching The Wrong Targeted Market
3045	I Want To Give You A Completely Free Copy Of My New Book As A "Thank You" For Being A Part Of My Newsletter.
3046	The Answer Was Obvious. And To Be Honest, We Felt Ashamed For Not Noticing The Amazing Opportunity Earlier And Not Following The Herd To A Place With No Competition, Just A Profitable Untapped Playground.
3047	Don't Give Up And End Up Going Back To Your Day Job Just Yet
3048	Everyone Knows That The Top Links Are Clicked The Most. Imagine, You Place One Simple Line Of Code On Your Site And You Gain Another Chance To Make Good Money From Your Visitors.

3049	Getting The Most Bang For Your Internet Buck Without Breaking The Bank
3050	P.S. Don't Forget, When You Sign Up, You'll Learn About The Mystery Feature That Will Help Bring Your Business From A Crawl To A Run! All You've Got To Do Is Click Here!
3051	How Inviting Are Your Website Walls When Only An Empty X Appears
3052	Use Your Content As A Market Research And Brainstorming Tool.
3053	There Are Much Better Ways Of Successfully Leveraging Your Time Money And Effort
3054	The "E" Word Has Been All Over The News Lately, All Doom And Gloom. It's All About Control, And When You're In Control Of This One Big Thing, You Write Your Own Paycheck Regardless Of The State Of The "E" Word ...
3055	Spend The Next 30-Days Researching The Product You Want To Create Or Market
3056	First, You'll Get The Step By Step Tutorials That Will Unravel All Adsense Mystery And Put You In The Driver's Seat To Certain Adsense Fortune.
3057	You'll Be Getting Both Of These Starting In About 1-2 Weeks Or So, As We Begin Digging Into The Creation Of Your Actual Products... So Keep Your Eye Out For Them!
3058	You Know, Success Is A Choice! And We All Need Mentors To Help Us Make The Right Choices. These Mentors Club Members Are Experiencing The Life Changing Power Of Mentors Club, AND YOU CAN TOO Starting Right Now!
3059	You Will Not See This Kind Of Collaboration Anywhere Else And It Equates To Amazing Opportunity For YOU.
3060	The Most Successful Word Ever Used In The History Of Advertising
3061	Click Here To Learn More About What This Can Do For Your Business
3062	Are You Finally Ready To Learn To Create Sales Letters That Are 100% Certain To Work
3063	IMPORTANT: After Entering Your Name And Your Email Address In The Form Below And Submitting, You Will Receive An Email With A Confirmation Link -- You MUST Also Click On That Link In Order To Receive Your Download Information.

3064	How To Spot A Product That Is BEGGING To Earn You Commissions. This Video Will Show You Which Products Are FLYING Off The Virtual Shelves And Which Couldn't Be Moved With A Forklift.
3065	Wondering Which Of The Dozens Of Different Competing Techniques, Seminars, Ebooks, Software, And Coaching Programs Hold The Key To Your Dreams -- Especially When They All Seem To Contradict Each Other.
3066	Why Your Competition Gets Really Pissed Off Every Time You Apply This Technique
3067	You Won't Pay A Dime For This Bonus When You Sign Up Now
3068	Looking For Money In All The Wrong Places Isn't Your Fault
3069	Anyone Who Is New To Internet Marketing Needs This Information To Succeed
3070	This Has Been Tested To Death And Still Makes More Money
3071	How To Get ONLY The Must Have Tools And Cut Out The Fluff
3072	7 Proven Strategies For Successfully Getting High Rankings In The Search Engines
3073	Psychographic Variables Are Any Attributes Relating To Interests Or Lifestyles. Knowing These Variables Data Helps You Understand Your Prospects Better And Gives You The Ability To Trigger Their Emotional Hot Buttons.
3074	And I Know I Can't Do That For Most Folks If I'm Asking $997 Even Though I Know It's Worth It And Then Some...But Some Folks Just Wouldn't Get The Chance To Do What They Deserve To Do At That Rate.
3075	What Could You Accomplish With Product Longevity That Never Out Lives Itself
3076	Supercharge Your Credibility And Posture Within Your Elected Niche Sphere Of Influence
3077	There's Simply Not Enough Time To Try To Convince You Of Anything Unless You're Hungry
3078	What If There Were Shortcuts That You Can Use To Speed Up Your Marketing Campaigns
3079	Warning, If You're Not Making At Least $_____ Per Month Online Yet, This One Secret May Be All You Need To Get There.
3080	These Will Only Be Around For A Short Time Before The Doors Are Closed Forever
3081	How To Write Your E-Mails So That They Will Be Opened

225

3082	Come September It's All About To Change In The Blink Of An Eye
3083	So, To Top It All Off, I'll Be Giving You Insider Techniques And Strategies On How To Use Other People's Products To Boost Your Adsense Profits Even Higher!
3084	There's Billions Of Dollars Flying Around In Cyberspace Right Now ...All You Have To Do Is Position Yourself In Front Of Some Of That Cash.
3085	In Only A Few Short Months I've Achieved The Ultimate Internet "Fantasy" Of Making A Lot Of Money From A Simple Web Site That Runs Itself Virtually On Autopilot
3086	Turn It Over To The Experts That Can Help You Succeed
3087	Life Is Too Short To Live That Way. Is $67 Worth Escaping To A Better Life?
3088	How A Few Changes Can Turn An Old Product Into A Brand New Shining Money Maker
3089	The "Magic" Of This Is Phenomenon. This Is Turning The World Upside Down, And It Offers Affiliate Marketers A Way To Stack Up The Money Like There's No Tomorrow.
3090	Get Your Viral Report Into The Hands Of Thousands Upon Thousands Fast
3091	Getting Targeted Visitors To Your Web Business Relies On One Thing...Keywords. That's Right, Keywords Are What Drive Targeted, Truly Interested People To Your Website That Will Actually Buy What You Have To Offer.
3092	I Understand That By Clicking The Link Below I Will Be Securing A Spot In An Incredibly Valuable And Insanely Profitable Opportunity NOW And Joining A Select And
3093	You Can Modify All The Text, You Can Add Your Own Images And Graphics, You Can Change The Colors, And More. All The Things Are Already In Place For You, In The Best Locations, And You Can Easily Swap What Ever "Elements" I Have In The Template For Your Own.
3094	This Program Also Allows You To Target Your Offers To The Groups Which Might Best Suit Your Advertising Needs. We Offer Targeted Categories Such As Work From Home, Retire Early, Business Opportunities, Investment Opportunities And Much More. And Since This Submitter Has Been Preloaded With Double Opt-In Leads So There Is Never Any Risk Of A Spam Complaint.

3095	With Our (Product) Coaching Program You Can Find Other New Business Owners Just Like You That Don't Want To Hire A Full-Time Worker Yet, But Would Like To Share One With Others, So It Doesn't Cost A Lot.
3096	Combine Your Content With Interviews With Industry Experts.
3097	Do You Really Want The Lowest Bidding Agency To Handle Your Million Dollar Project
3098	Search Engine Optimization Experts Agree That The Number One Tool In Their Arsenal of Marketing Tactics Is Article Marketing. It Is The Most Cost & Time Effective Way To Build Traffic, Authority And Relevant Links, In The Shortest Possible Time Frame.
3099	I Used To Operate A Web Design Company, And My Minimum Project Fee Was $499! Armed With The Knowledge You'll Be Downloading In Just A Couple Of Minutes You Will Never Have To Pay For Website Design Again!
3100	What Would You Do If You Were Losing Money To My Customers This Very Second
3101	Why You Need More Than Money That Only Allows You To Purchase Stuff
3102	If You Were Like Me And Need Cash - This Is How I Do It
3103	Throw Your Alarm Out The Window And Start Living Life On Your Own Damn Schedule
3104	Have You Ever Heard Of The 80/20 Rule: "80% Of Your Results Come From 20% Of Your Efforts." Well, Traffic Generation Is The Same Way: 80% Of Your Traffic Comes From 20% Of Your Efforts. The Problem Is, Which 20%?
3105	And That Got Me Thinking... Guys Like You And I, What We Need Is A Complete Roadmap. Something That Shows Us How To Make Money Online Quickly And Easily... And Something That Works Almost Instantly... Because Remember, We Already Agreed That Making Money Online Is Easy, Didn't We? We Just Need The Right Processes.
3106	My Jaw Dropped When I Saw What Had Happened... I Yelled For My Wife To Come See, I Couldn't Believe What I Was Looking At! The Cold Hard Truth Is That We've Just Discovered The Solution To Resolve Our Financial Worries Forever And It May Be Of Great Help To You And Your Family As Well.
3107	What Matters At The End Of The Day Is What's in Your Pocket

3108	The Simple 3 Step Formula To Getting Surfers To Pay Attention To Your Pages (Don't Let The Simple Elegance Of This Solution Fool You; It Is RAW Power.)
3109	So, Get Ready For The Shock Of Your Life...Because I'm Not Even Going To Ask A Couple Hundred Dollars For This...
3110	I'm Talking About Having The Ultimate Internet Marketing Business Handed To Me On A Silver Platter. It's The Learning Curve That Prevents So Many People From Achieving Success And The Curve Is Steep. I've Read That Most People Who Come Online, Looking To Make Extra Income, Are Only $500/Month Away From Bankruptcy. It's A Shocking Figure. Just $500 A Month Would Change Their Life! This Is The Answer.
3111	2 Quick And Easy Ways To Promote Your Product. Neither One Of These Will Cost You A Dime. They're Both Easy And Fast. Even Better, They Work Like Crazy...
3112	Boost Your Credibility And Status In The Eyes Of Your Customers And Be Well Respected And Valued In Your Own Niche. (And Be Nominated For The Most Popular Marketer!)
3113	What Makes You Think Anyone In Their Right Mind Will Break Their Back To Promote Any Of Your Products?
3114	How Anyone Can Profit Even In Their Spare Time Doing Something Fun And Rewarding
3115	How To Collect Glowing Testimonials And Actually Get People To Use The Words You Want To Hear In Them.
3116	I Am Handing You An Instant Online Business If You're Ready To Take It
3117	You'll Need To Use A Huge Spoon Or A Really Big Shovel
3118	They Said It Was Impractical And Pure Foolishness Until They Saw This Work Themselves
3119	I Also Have A Few More Bonuses For You On The Inside
3120	You Are Going To Find It Extremely Useful For Your Online Business. It Is An Interactive Book So There Are Lots Of Links You Can Click On To Find Out More Information.
3121	I'm A Strong Believer In Working – But Only IF You're Doing A Job You Love, When You Want To Do It And Can Stop Or Take Time Off When You Want. I Honestly Believe That I'm Living My Life To The Full.
3122	Protect Your Online Reputation And Reduce The Number Of Blocked And Filtered Offers

3123	If You Need To Have Life Breathed Into A Stagnant Internet Business, We Can Get You To The Next Level Together, Faster Than You Ever Thought Possible! And Just To Let You Know. This Is Not A Dilly Dally Hobby. I Take Making Money Online Dead Seriously, And I Will Expect The Same From You.
3124	The Terrifying Fact Is, Even The Successful Entrepreneurs Are Having Problems Getting More Free Time. The Dream Of Working A Few Hours A Day With An Online Business And Spending The Rest Of The Time Enjoying Life Don't Exist Anymore. There's Just Too Many Things To Do And Decisions To Make To Run A Business.
3125	You're Thinking That This Is Just Another Fluffed Up Make-Money Guide Or Some Airy-Fairy Personal Development Course - Just Another Rehashed Product Teaching You How To Use Some Lame System Or Method That We've All Seen Dozens Of Times Before. Well You Couldn't Be More Wrong.
3126	I Realized That My Success Had Nothing To Do With The Latest Marketing Method Or System And Had Everything To With Me And Nothing Else.
3127	How To Make More Sales By Simply Keeping Your Brand Consistent In Everything You Do
3128	Click Here If You Want To Be Notified First Of All Future Special Discount Offers
3129	Why Transactional eMail Is A Great Way To Generate More Revenue Than Traditional Ones
3130	Your Commission Is Normally Around 50-75% Per Product Sold From Your Ads. This Can Also Include Recurring Billing Products That Can Earn You A Commission Every Single Month.
3131	Even If You've Struggled With Generating Real Monthly Online Income In The Past, This Simple To Use Yet Extremely Powerful Program Puts Lazy Recurring Income Easily Within Your Grasp
3132	Earn Over $1 Million In Profits From One Time Cost Of Only $5
3133	Listen, Even If You've Never Made A Penny Online, And You've No Idea Where To Start... This Contains All You Need To Get Started, And Begin Making Money... But Don't Take My Word For It...
3134	Why You'll Want To Get Rich By Doing What You Love Doing
3135	What Do You Get When You Mate A Mammoth List With A Viral URL

3136	No Portion Of This Website Can Be Copied Without Written Permission From The Author
3137	Plus, I Wanted To Make This Affordable For Beginners To Get Their Feet Wet With Advertising That Doesn't Cost An Arm And A Leg....And Of Course To Help Fellow Marketers Who Are Fed Up With Spending A Fortune On Google Ads Like I Was.
3138	Why Is It That There Always Seems To Be Something Missing
3139	I'm Ready To Discover The Simple Step-By-Step System To Generating Passive Streams Of Income Around The Clock. And Of Course I Want To Take Complete Control Of My Financial Independence By Learning The Skills That Will Give Me The Ability To Create A Part-Time Or Full-Time Income Online.
3140	The Power of Two Is Far Greater Than The Power Of One
3141	This Is Total BS When A Marketer Gives Away A Free CD That Costs $25 For Shipping, Or Offers A Free Digital Product, And Then You Are Enrolled In A Monthly Subscription You Didn't Know About...And Worse Yet, Canceling These Subscriptions Is Like Pulling Teeth.
3142	People Call This The Answer To Their Prayers For A Good Reason
3143	Moving Prospects Into Paying Customers Will Become Super Easy With These Simple Ideas
3144	3 Incredibly Simple Ways To Instantly Pump Up Your Muscles Online
3145	Now That You Know Where You Want To Go We Can Start
3146	What's Your 1st Biggest Challenge - Your 2nd - Your 3rd
3147	I Am Going To Hold Your Hand And Spoon-Feed You The Information Step-By-Step
3148	Are You Always Looking For Ways To Generate More Traffic And Clicks That Don't Cost You Arms And Legs While Not Taking Up A Large Portion Of Your Valuable Time?
3149	(Note: Yes, That Is An Affiliate Code And Yes, I Will Get A Commission If You Use It. It Is The Only Affiliate Code Or Affiliate Link In This Entire Course. No Sneaky Stuff Here).
3150	The Quickest Path To Becoming The Next Super Affiliate Starts Here
3151	Then If You're Still Not Convinced That This Is The Easiest, Most Affordable And Lucrative Business Opportunity On The Internet You Can Cancel And Walk Away Without Risk Or Obligation.

3152	Are You Ready To Learn The Truth Even If It Shocks You Into Reality
3153	Wouldn't That Be A Lot Simpler Than What You're Dong Now? Your Sites Are Then Rotated So That A Different One Appears Every Time Someone Clicks On Your Link. How's That For Efficiency?
3154	This Is Not Going To Be One Of Those Guides Where I Try To Upsell You On A Lot Of "Extra" Services. In Fact, I Will Show You How To Start Researching, Writing, And Submitting Your First Articles Today WITHOUT Spending A Dime.
3155	• A Short Four-Word Sentence That Goes Completely Against Everything You've Ever Learned About Sales, Marketing, And Persuasion. Yet, If Implemented … Will Explode Your Online Sales! At First, Most Don't Believe It's True … Until They Use It And Are Amazed At The Results.
3156	Don't Ignore Behavioral Targeting Simply Because It Seems Too Difficult To Organize
3157	If You're Not Living This Kind Of Life If You're Not Having Massive Amounts Of Cash Deposited Into Your Bank Account While Working From Home That's Probably Because You Are Listening To The Wrong People.
3158	Stunning Results That Actually Work In The Real World Of Internet Marketing
3159	The Hook That Irresistibly Forces You Deeper And Deeper Into The Copy
3160	Even The Most Skeptical Mind Will Instantly See The Light And Buy
3161	It's Because We're All Human Beings Made From The Same Glue. We Make Decisions At A Chemical Level And If You Know A Bit About The Psychology Of Your Prospect, Every Single Call You Make Could Potentially Make You Money.
3162	When They Said I Never Dreamed My Life Could Be This Good They Weren't Kidding
3163	I Don't Think I've Ever Seen So Many Inspiring Stories In One Place As This. I Mean, These Guys Have All Been Raving Successes Online And They Are Spilling Their Guts On What They Did To Get From Zero To Millionaires!
3164	If This Happens You Can Quit, Walk Away And Not Pay
3165	How To Really Get People To Read Your Advertising

3166	The Thing That Gets Most People Is They Come Up With Great Idea After Great Idea. They Even Research, Plan, And Analyze The Idea To Death Until Finally....Nothing Actually Gets Started Or Finished. Sound All Too Familiar?
3167	You Will Instantly Gain The Advantage Over Your Competitors By Advertising In Places That Will Generate More Successful Results And Instantly Start Saving Money On Your Advertising Purchases By 'Targeting' The Most Effective Ad Services.
3168	Selling Big Ticket Items Takes The Same Amount Of Work As Working For Peanuts
3169	The Good News Is, They Will Not Search For Another Program After They Have Started With This System Because They Will See Good Results And Great Support. Once They Start Getting People To Sign Up, They Will Keep Going Because They Will See That This System Is The Real Thing.
3170	When You Become An Exclusive Member Of Adsensenewbievideos.Com, I Do Random Site Critiques, But With This Bonus Offer, You Don't Have To Wait For The 'Luck Of The Draw' For Me To Critique Your Site.
3171	You Can Create Text Ads To Be Shown Throughout Our Site. You Simply Create Your Ad And You Will See How Many Impressions And Clicks It Is Receiving While It Is Displayed To Other Members.
3172	Here Are Simple, Clean, And Professional Designs With Main Focus Being On Sales Copy. Again, The Design Doesn't Distract From The Message Of The Sales Copy, And These Kind Of Simple Designs Are Exactly The Kind That Convert Best.
3173	Rake In The Cash With A Brand New Online Power Shovel
3174	What To Look For When Buying Any Type Of Resell Rights Product. Miss This One And You're Most Likely Going To Fail Trying To Resell The Product
3175	If You're Short On Time, Money And/Or Experience You Want A Realistic Way To Succeed, I Urge You To Take A Look At This Amazing New System. I Guarantee You Won't Regret It.
3176	Isn't It Time You Started Planting Your Own Money Tree Orchard
3177	Want To Boost Your Income Quick Smart? Want To Create More JV Partnerships Than Ever Before? Want To Make It Super Easy For Your Partners To Do Business With You?

3178	I'll Show You The Drop-Dead Easy Way To Set Up Your Own Website To Sell Your E-Book Like Crazy. This Single Step Scares Most People Off...But That's Fine, Because That Means More Money For You! You Also Get Seven Website Tips That Are Proven To Increase Your Sales.
3179	Paint A Really Clear Picture Of Solutions And They Will Fill Your Marketing Wallet
3180	Do Something Today To Advance Your Future Before It's Too Late
3181	Have You Ever Been So Close To Success Online That You Could Literally Taste It
3182	If You Don't Know Where You Want To Go You'll Never Get There
3183	How Would You Like A List Building System That Will Explode Your Sales, Signups And Build Your List At The Same Time Without You Spending A Single Cent
3184	It's Written In Such A Concise Compact Format That Just Moments After You Fill Out The Form Below You'll Begin To See Exactly How To Get Your Own Website Up And Running Building Massive Residual Profits.
3185	Do Not Buy This If You Don't Have 60 Seconds To Set This Up
3186	How Write And Publish Your Own Outrageously Profitable Ebook In As Little As 7 Days... Even If You Can't Write, Can't Type, And Failed High School English Class!
3187	Sick Of All The Dishonesty And Tired Of Being Deceived And Cheated
3188	Why Are 1 out of 3 Affiliate Commissions Never Getting Paid
3189	Action Headlines You Can Apply To Any Webpage That'll Earn You Instant Respect And Trust So Your Traffic Snaps Up Your Recommendation And Puts Cash In Your Pocket.
3190	It Normally Is Best To Keep Things Simple. You Want A Marketing System That Automates Your Efforts And Quickly Establishes YOU As An Authority Figure
3191	Looking For New Tools And Ideas To Help Automate Your Business
3192	How To Tell A "Browser" Niche From A "Buyer" Niche... The Difference Can Make You Millions... Separating The Buyers From The Tire Kickers Is A Skill Only The Most Successful Have.
3193	It's OK To Get Angry With God Because He Understands Your Frustrations

3194	I'm Not Going To Get Into The Exhaustive Features Which Are Fully Listed On Their Product's Website, But What I Am Going To Do Is Touch On It's Power, Capability And Flexibility For A Moment By Listing Them Brute Force!
3195	Generate More Buzz And Close More Sales By Using This Simple And Easy Technique
3196	Do It When And Where You Want The Way You Want To Do It
3197	The Key Pillar To Success Online Is Laser Targeting The Exact Audience That's Interested In Buying Your Product In Spite Of The Fact That The Online Business Industry Is Booming.
3198	Did You Do What You Said You Were Going To Do This Week
3199	Discover How To Get Instant Access To My Latest Collection Of Top Quality, In-Hot-Demand Products That You Can Brand As Your Own And Generate Massive Profits From... Starting Today!"
3200	YOU HAVE TO READ THIS Before You Even Consider Joining Any Other Money Making Programs! You Have Just Stumbled Upon The Greatest Online Money Making System Ever And We Guarantee You That This Really Works!
3201	If You Do It Right You'll Find It Really Is Possible To Make A Great Living Online
3202	The 13 Biggest Mistakes You Could Make As The Parent Of A Teen
3203	I'm Getting Sick And Tired Of All These Money Making Scams
3204	Why Not Save Yourself Tons Of Cash And Months Of Frustration
3205	Never Accept A Real Estate Contract That Contains These 5 Words
3206	Perhaps The Most Important Information Ever Released Is Now Within Your Grasp
3207	Rewrite Your Content Or Hire A Rewriter To Repurpose And Reuse Your Content.
3208	This Time Why Not Start Over And Do It The Correct Way
3209	Don't Despair! Because You Are A Past Customer, We'd Like To Extend To You Our Most Valuable And Cost Effective Package, The Ultimate Collection Of Email Tools And 1 Year Of Gold Membership For Just $197.
3210	Great Marketing Just As In Playing Cards You Don't Want To Give Your Hand Away
3211	Never Flinch When Anyone Tells You That You'll Never Make Money Online

234

3212	That's The Beauty Of Doing Business On The Internet, Once You Build Your Internet "Machine" It Just Keeps On Running And Spitting Out Cash And Commissions Everyday, It's Un-stoppable!
3213	It's Never Been Easier At Least Not For Me And I'm A Slow Learner
3214	You Can Embrace This Rare Chance - 100% Risk-Free - To Take Life By The Collar And Let It Know Who's Boss.
3215	Did You Know That You Become The Composite Version Of The People You Hang Around With Most? Studies Have Proven That You'll Become Just Like The 4 Or 5 People You're With All The Time. If They're Broke, You're Broke.
3216	Be Sure To Fasten Your Online Seatbelt Because Here We Go
3217	How To Set Up Your Business For Quick Cash When You Need It, Steady Cash While You Build It, And Massive Profits With Zero Risk!
3218	Totally Automate Your List Building And Recruit Armies Of Loyal Buyers 24/7... Works Like Magic Whether You're A Hardened IM Veteran - Or A Total Newbie!
3219	Who Would Say 'No' To This Offer! We Will Show You How Easy It Is To Do. You Will Not Have To Pick Up The Phone, Chase Prospects Around Like Unwanted Bills, Or Do Any Of The Other Tasks That You Are Always Expected To Do.
3220	You May Now Stake YOUR Claim With "The Internet Land Rush" And Start Making Money TODAY, Without Spending A Single Penny. BUT, You Better Get Started BEFORE IT'S TOO LATE:
3221	With Membership Limited Was It Really Unfair To The Person Whose Spot You Just Took
3222	If You're Still Thinking It Over Then At Least Accept My Free _____
3223	Don't Have To Touch A Thing If You Don't Want To
3224	They Say You Get What You Pay For Our Next Generation
3225	Things You Need To WIN At In Order To Become The Next Guru In Your Field
3226	Perhaps You've Already Fallen Victim To One Or More of These Work At Home Scams
3227	Is Doing Tasks You Hate Really Part Of Being Self Employed

3228	A Direct-To-The-Point Report That Reveals Three Concentrated, Proven, Quick And Easy Ways To Make A Killing Online... So You Can Make Money Within A Few Days (Not Months, Not Even Weeks)!
3229	Why Most People Can't Write Their Way Out Of A Paper Bag
3230	Do You Really Just Want To Be Part Of All Those Scam Promotions
3231	See Behind The Big Picture... Find Out How The Super Affiliates Turn One Product Promotion Into A Lifetime Of Big Income Checks... This Is Where The Real Money Is Online.
3232	Simple And Easy Way To Generate High Quality Articles That Attract Tons Of Traffic
3233	Our Customers Always Bring Us A Smile, Some When The Come, And Some When They Leave.
3234	Only iHogs Are Stupid Enough To Try And Nickel And Dime You To Death
3235	Basically What I Am Doing Is I Am Leveraging Technology To Reach Hundreds Of Thousands Of People -- Entrepreneurs -- Who Are Interested In Improving Their Marketing And Growing Their Businesses. I Am Using The Same Technology, Computers, And The Internet To Distribute My Product.
3236	Don't Get Fooled Again By Thinking This Is The Same Thing
3237	Because The Old Ways Of Marketing Just Aren't As Effective As They Used To Be, And If You Don't Figure Out How To Turn Things Around Pretty Quick, You're Business Is Dead.
3238	I Know That May Seem Incredible To You, Especially If All You Have To Show For Your Surfing These Days Are Sore Cramped Fingers, Gut Wrenching Failure And That Empty Feeling You Get When You Feel You're Disappointing Your Family By Not Giving Them The Luxuries You Hoped Your Online Business Would Provide.
3239	They Are Getting Rich Because They Have Set Up A System -- A Machine -- That Allows Them To Sell And Resell People's Time. And They Are Able To Repeat That Process Over And Over Again.
3240	Educating People From Waste Then Neck Up And To One Side
3241	E-Products Are The Future, Not Only Do You Have A Product That Can Be Replicated Infinitely At No Cost To You.
3242	These Are The Most Powerful And Practical Tools For Starting A Marketing Campaign

3243	I'm Not Going To Beat Around The Bush Here, This Is A Limited Release, There Are Thousands Of Others Reading This Page Right Now, Maybe Even Reading This Very Sentence.
3244	I'm Sure You Realize That This Isn't For The Faint Of Heart. This May Not Even Be Right For You.
3245	Say Goodbye To Stress Forever And Start Eliminating Your Everyday Financial Worries
3246	Splintering Your Marketing Topics Is Crucial To Increasing Sales Conversions And Profits
3247	How You Can Start And End Your Sales Letter Interestingly Without Boring Your Prospect In The Process. Even If It Is A Sales Copy, Your Prospect Wants To Be Entertained. No Questions Asked. Usually, The More Information He Gets, The Better Chances You Have Of Closing Your Sale, Because Anyone Would Know That You Obviously Have More To Offer In Your Paid Product Or Service, And I Show You Do Just That.
3248	YOU And Your Ability To Create A Massive Stream Of Prospects That Are Approaching You (Not The Other Way Around). By Doing This, You Move Products. This Is How You Get Paid.
3249	We help people 'Make More Money' doing things they already love doing. We help them figure out exactly what they really want out of life and keep them focused on achieving results every step of the way. Could you benefit by learning how to make more money doing something you love doing? Lynn and I are personal business coaches and would love the opportunity to work with YOU one-on-one step-by-step, answering your concerns as we work together as a team, focused on your success.
3250	Instant Download! Special $17 Price (Ends Soon) Order Now For A One-Time Payment Of Only $77! $67 $47 $17 DUE TO THIS INSANELY LOW PRICED OFFER THERE WILL BE NO REFUNDS
3251	Discover The Exact Words You Have To Say To Them To Get Them To Open Up Their Wallets And Give You Money.
3252	By Spending A Mere $37 - One Time Payment - Today You Will Be Saving Yourself Hundreds Of Dollars Over The Next Year Alone, And Possibly Thousands Over Your Entire Career As A Website Owner.

3253	Don't Underestimate The Simplicity Or Be Fooled By Other Products On The Market Because There's Simply No Other Product Available Today That Can Match Or Out Perform Our Ultimate Marketing Kit
3254	Make Attractive Promotional Bookmarks To Surprise Buyers With Purchase Of Your Physical Products And Books.
3255	Looking For An Audience Of Highly Targeted Prospects Within The Make Money Online Niche, This Is One Of The Fastest Ways You Can Get The Word Out For Your Offer.
3256	Were You Sleeping In Class When They Passed Out All The Money
3257	Why Settle For Only Pennies Out Of Each Advertising Dollar Spent
3258	The Heartbreaking Truth Is That Most People Just Take A Quick Look, And Then Leave. And It's Not Your Fault! Sure. That Still Means 95% To 97% Of Your Traffic Is Wasted.
3259	Your New Found Expertise Will Even Attract The Top Affiliate Marketers
3260	Create A "What To Look For..." Buyer's Guide To Help People Make Buying Decisions.
3261	Send Your Ad Out To Mass People Daily And Earn Money Too
3262	Just Giving Someone Your Money Does Not Create Success. It's When You And Your Entire Team Can Duplicate, That The Money Starts Flowing Faster Than You Ever Imagined.
3263	This One Piece Of Information Is So Critical To Your Internet Marketing Success That I'm Amazed It's Been Kept Hidden For So Long. If You're Interested In Working From Home And Becoming An Internet Entrepreneur, Then You Need To Read Every Word Of This Short Email.
3264	1 In 14 Adults Have This Disease And Don't Even Know About It
3265	Yet, Why Is It That 90 Some-Odd Percent Of The People Who Go To Those Websites Click Away Without Joining?
3266	You Desperately Want To Prove To Your Friends And Family That It's All Real And Then Rub It In Their Face When Your Living The Good Life. (Admittedly, I Still Do That A Little. LOL)
3267	Are You Willing To Invest 5 Minutes A Day For Your Retirement
3268	You Can Take Our System Out For A Spin And Thoroughly Check It Out Without Risking One Thin Dime.

238

3269	This Means That Our Wits Will Learn To Filter The Immense Bulk Of The Contents Coming At Them.
3270	I Take People's Time And Money VERY Seriously And I Will Not Allow You To Waste Yours Under My Guidance.
3271	You Can Teach An Old Dog New Tricks Especially When They're Hungry
3272	Things Were Getting Tougher And Tougher, I Was Slowly Spiraling Into A Mess Of Debt. And When I Found It, It Was Like A Bolt From The Blue - Like A Gift From Heaven Itself. And It Really Was Exactly What I'd Been Looking For - A Way To Make As Much Money As I Wanted, With Very Little Work.
3273	I'm Always Slightly Terrified When I Exit Out Of Word And It Asks Me If I Want To Save Any Changes To My Ten-Page Research Paper That I Swear I Did Not Make Any Changes To.
3274	You Are About To Discover The 7 Laws Of Buying, And How You Can Use These Laws To Legally Force People To Buy Anything You Want Them To Buy From YOU!
3275	I'll Mail For You If You Put Me On Your Order Page
3276	Now You Can Learn The Secret Of How-To Write Short Powerful Headlines ... Simple Headline's ... That Give Regular People A Lifetime Of Freedom!
3277	Take These 10 Defensive Measures, And You'll Save Way More Than $600
3278	Get The Following Gifts With No Obligation And Nothing To Buy
3279	Summarize Your Offer And Get The Person To Go Out And Take Action
3280	Boldly Go Where No Mouse Keyboard Or Monitor Has Ever Gone Before
3281	50 Spots Are Allocated For My Subscribers And Customers. The (Product) Will Not Be Priced At $1,497 - Or $997 - Or Even $497. Much Lower That That For What You're Getting From The System Today.
3282	How Would Your Life Change If You Could Double Your Money Any Time You Felt Like It? How Quickly Would You Quit Your Day Job? How Fast Could You Erase Your Debt?
3283	Don't Blame Anyone Else But Yourself If You Pass On This
3284	WARNING: This May Finally Open Your Eyes To The TRUTH...And Sometimes The Truth Is NOT What We Want To Hear. Are You Ready? Here We Go:
3285	What If You're Sitting On A Goldmine And Just Don't See It

3286	Strange Ways To Make Money. You'll Be Surprised At How Some Odd (And Fun) Things To Do Can Actually Make Real Money For You.
3287	Create An Affiliate Army That Can Storm Any Niche On The Internet
3288	You Have A Choice To Make Do All The Work Yourself And Most Likely Take 2 Or 3 Or 4 Times As Long To Make A Good Income Or Even Any Income. (Most Fail Because They Get Overwhelmed From Having To Learn How To Do Everything Themselves Or Get Others To Help Do The Work For You And Get Your Business (Hopefully) Making You Money A Lot Faster.
3289	Raise Your Hand If You Think You're Slightly Smarter Than Others Around You
3290	So If You're Tired Of Banging Your Head Against The Wall. Tired Of Failing, Struggling, And Looking Your Wife In The Face Trying To Explain Why Your Credit Card Bill Is About To Explode.
3291	Did You Move Or Are You Hiding Out Under A Rock
3292	Nearly Half Of Working Mothers Are Single Moms Working 2 Jobs
3293	No More Sleepless Nights And Endless Hours Struggling To Squeeze A Few More Lines Of Copy Out Of Your Exhausted Brain -- It's All Been Written For You Already
3294	From A 'Business Model' Does It Really Make Sense To Make A List Of Your Friends And Family, Constantly Make 3 Way Calls To Your Upline, Hand Out Piles Of Audios And CD's.
3295	Be 1 Of Only 200 To Get Residual Income At Zero Cost
3296	Starting Your New Business Takes Much More Than Just An Idea
3297	I Haven't Made Any Wild Claims And I Haven't Tried To Hard Sell You Anything... Because I Don't Have To. I Developed My Own System To Give Myself A Very Comfortable Lifestyle, Which Gives Me Time To Do The Things I Want To Do With My Life, Rather Than Spending Time On Things I Have To Do. And By Simply Copying My Unique System, There's Abso-lutely No Reason Why You Can't Do Exactly The Same. It's Entirely Up To You.
3298	Is It 'Marketing' That Really Makes The Difference In Your Business? Is The Hype Of 'Marketing' Real? How Important Is Marketing To Your Business Really? Is It All A Game And Hype? Or Is There More To It?

240

3299	Undeniably Link Exchange Is The Easiest Way To Improve Your Website Link Popularity, And By Doing So, To Achieve Better Search Engine Positioning And Increase Your Site Traffic.
3300	Your Goal Should Be To Set Up A Business That Provides You With Recurring And Passive Income. That Means You Do The Work Once, And The Money Keeps Coming In Over And Over. Then If You Do More Work, It Means More Money Comes In Every Day, Every Month, All Year Long. It's Like Owning Your Own ATM.
3301	If You Were To Combine The Very Best Features And Benefits From Each One Of Those Business Systems, You'd Come Up With The Finest Product Ever Conceived. Guess What? We Just Did And Are Ready To Share It With You!
3302	How To Add A Web Seal Logo To Your Web Page
3303	The Perfect Product! Information Is The High-Demand Product Of Today And Tomorrow! We Will Deliver Your Information Products... At No Cost To You Or Your Customers For Shipping Or Handling... Instantly Anywhere In The World! Doesn't Have To Be Insured Because It Can't Be Damaged During Delivery! Won't Spoil Or Rust Or Melt Or Spill Or Break!
3304	Gently Remind Them It About The Problem You Can Help Them Solve
3305	How To Never Feel Lost Again On How To Make Money Online
3306	Give Yourself The Gift Of Figuring Out What You Want Out Of Life
3307	You Don't Need To Do Any Cold Calling Or Personal Selling. You Can Be The Shyest Person In The World And Still Be A Sales Superstar. That's The Power And Leverage Of The Internet.
3308	Please Don't Throw Your Hands Up In The Air And Throw In The Towel Just Yet
3309	From Now On All Of Your Financial Responsibilities Shall Be Based Upon A Need-Value Only
3310	How To Choose The Right Tools To Build Your Website To Get The Job Done Right The First Time
3311	Why On Earth Would You Want To Repeat My Early Mistakes
3312	Transform Generic Niche Articles Into A Different Niche By Swapping The Essential Keywords And Tweaking Your Content.

241

3313	What I Learned From Him Wasn't The Entire Internet Marketing "Puzzle", But At The Time It Filled In All The Missing Pieces And Helped Me Transform My Business From A Money Hobby Into A Serious Online Career.
3314	Are You Thinking This Is A Rip-Off If This Software Or This Computer Do What I Need It To Do? If You Buy A Novel By Stephen King Are You Ticked-Off About The Money That Stephen King Is Making Off You At A Whopping $1 Or $2 From You?
3315	There Are Probably More Courses On Traffic Than Any Other Topic, But To Be Honest I Haven't Counted. Unfortunately, The One Thing Most Of Them Leave Out Is That Automation Is The Key To Real Growth, And Knowing That Most New And Even Intermediate Marketers Don't Have The Cash Flow To Fund Or Are Potentially Unwilling To Risk Their Monthly Income On PPC Fighting Google, All We Are Really Left With Are Free Traffic Sources.
3316	And In Case You Haven't Figured It Out Yet, "Buying" Someone Else's Life Experiences In The Form Of A Book Or Consulting Is ALWAYS 100's Or Even 1000's Of Times Cheaper Than Trying To Figure It Out On Your Own.
3317	Get Your Hands On These Never Before Seen Products For Free
3318	Have Your Online Efforts Been Nothing More Than A Tankless Sea Of Hot Water
3319	What If You Could Generate More Targeted Referrals Than You Could Ever Need
3320	Do You Have To Go All The Way Over To The Other Side Of Town, Grab Someone By The Hand And Drag Them Into Your Shop Before They Saw What You Had To Offer.
3321	You Can Find It Here But Only If Your Mind Is Open
3322	Get Smart Is More Than Just A Bumbling Old TV Series
3323	Online Marketing Has Changed The Way People Do Business And Unless You Can Embrace The Knowledge Needed To Meet These Changes,
3324	Here's How You Can Gain Full Lifetime Access To A Constantly Updated Package Of The Latest Resell Rights, Master Resell Rights, Private Label Rights, Source Code Rights Products And Premium Bonuses For One Small Investment
3325	If You're Like Most Marketers, You've Struggled To Get A Sizeable Email List That You Can Advertise To About Your Business.

3326	Great Deals To Be Had If You Know Where To Look
3327	There Are So Many Different Angles You Can Take When Writing An Article. While Some Choose To Write Informative Tips, Others Choose To Write Something Controversial To Really Get The Readers Going. Both Can Work In Your Benefit.
3328	Co-Registration Leads Are Watered Down Names That Have Been Blasted With So Many Offers They Just Tune You Out
3329	This Isn't A Pitch It's An Invitation To See If You're Right Minded
3330	In The Online World, The Exact Opposite Is True. The "Virtual Real Estate" Market Is Booming At An All Time High. People Are Literally Banking Millions Buying And Selling....Or Building And Selling Virtual Real Estate.
3331	I'm Not Charging That Much For The System But The Stuff Worth Your Time Is Pure Lust Building Gold!
3332	Senate Still Blocking Drilling In Anwar Even Though Gas Is Selling For 4532 Pesos Per Liter And Gas Stations Are Only Open On Tuesdays And Fridays
3333	To Carve Out A Beautiful Life As An Internet Mogul...Filled With Freedom, Wealth, And All The Time In The World To Actually Enjoy It. This Is About You. Your Fate, Your Future...Your Freedom.
3334	Let's Get Started On Creating Your Own Information Marketing Empire Today
3335	The Concept Is Really Quite Simple. You Set Up Your Ads Related To Your Websites Content And Appearance. This Takes Just A Few Minutes And Is So Easy A Child Could Do It.
3336	Why It's Important To Choose A Web Host That Won't Ruin Your Reputation
3337	Money You Make Is Equal To Your Motivation To Earn It
3338	Now You Can Deliver Your Digital Products To Your Customer Instantly, Without Burning A Single Calorie. Even With Your Computer Turned Off. Works With Ebay Auctions Like A Charm!
3339	Becoming A Rockstar Super Affiliate Is All About Thinking Differently From The Crowd. So Are You Ready To Conduct Some Real Rock N Roll Marketing?
3340	Website Not Making Money Then Sell Your Time To Someone Else
3341	When I Started Buying My New Toys They Begged Me For My Secret

3342	How Are You Going To Make Some Real Money Online If You Don't Know Where To Start
3343	Increase The Number Of Visitors To Your Website By Over 400%
3344	It's Not The Ones That Got Away It's About The Ones You Caught That Count
3345	Why You Need Automated Internet Tools That Are Highly Productive And Profitable
3346	Learn How To Blast Short eMail And Automate Profit On Demand
3347	A Building Flaw That Can Cost You $10,000 In Resale Value If You Buy From The Wrong Builder
3348	How Do I Say This In A Clear Understandable Human Language
3349	Want To Know How To Create Streams Of Passive Income While You Sleep Work Or Play
3350	Are You Finally Ready To Prey Upon The Search Engine Vaults For Unclaimed Millions
3351	LOOK: Everyone Knows They're Supposed To Test And Track Right? Well, Most Don't Cause They May Not Know How. This ALONE Will Totally Transform Your Business And Get You All The Traffic You Can Find!
3352	How To Use Bartering To Gain An Advantage Over Your Competition
3353	Yes, This Is Brand New And Fresh. This Isn't Lame Crap From 1983 That Smells Like Old Milk. Trust Me, This Is Pure, Uncut, Raw, Organic Awesomeness.
3354	Isn't It Time YOU Experienced The Pride Of Being Successful... Instead Of That Sick Feeling You Get When You Realize That You've Been Lied To Once Again?
3355	They're Divulging Some Critical Information. The Business Is Not Working For Them. They Want To Figure Out What The Problem Is.
3356	SEO Techniques Are A Moving Target Nearly Impossible To Hit, And Even If You Get Lucky They'll Change The Rules Again
3357	You Will Never Make A Real Income Online Without A List! No Matter What Anyone Tells You. I Will Give You The Tools To Make It Happen, Now!"

3358	Well, I'm Not Doing Either, And If You Just Keep Reading, You'll See Exactly How Simple It Is. You See, I Understand Exactly Where You're Coming From. Because I've Been There. I've Sat Where You Are Now, And I've Been Sucked In By All The Crazy Opportunities You See Out There... Probably The Same Ones That Sucked You In Too.
3359	Let Machines Do All Your Selling So You Can Earn $1000 Per Hour
3360	For A Very Brief Time We've Agreed To Share Our Most Elusive And Closely Guarded Secrets. Currently We're Allowing You To Take A Peek Behind The Iron Curtain And See Exactly How To Grow A Huge Downline.
3361	An Often Neglected Mistake That Could Kill Your Sales. I'll Show You How To Turn This Around And Make A Killing In Your Market Instead.
3362	The Fact Of The Matter Is, We Don't Know Everything You're Going To Learn, Because The Biggest Part Of Your Education Here Will Come From The Questions You Ultimately Ask And The Answers You Ultimately Seek To Find.
3363	How You Can Chop The Contents Of This Report Into A Collection Of Unique Articles
3364	You Do Not Need Marketing Skills, Technical Knowledge Or Experience Because The Only Thing You'll Be Doing Is Giving Away Our System By Following Our Strategy And Using Our Pre-Written Ad Copy.
3365	This Is Simple Free And Tremendously Rewarding. If You Take The Time To Review This Like I Did It's Going To Blow You Away As It Did For Me And My Sponsor.
3366	This Gives You Freedom To Do What You Want When You Want. It Expands To How You Live Your Life And What Meaning You Bring To Others (Just Like Turning A Tap).
3367	No False One Time Offers, No Marketing Hype – Just The Solution You Need. And To Make The Decision Even Easier For You – We Provide An Additional Bonus That Will Be Made Available ONLY In This Package.
3368	The "Create Anything" Framework Experts Use To Create Rapport And Sales
3369	Compare Us To Any Other And Find Us A No Brainer
3370	It's Very Important, Because I'm Giving You The Opportunity To Join An Exclusive Group Of Like Minded Entrepreneurs Who Will Possess The Uncanny Ability To Find Profitable Promotions.

3371	Please Take A Moment To Add Your Candid Comments On My Blog
3372	What I Will Tell You Is That It's Possible For ANYONE To Make Money Online With This System, With Much Less Work And Effort Than Anything I've Ever Come Across Before.
3373	Always Add New Content- Are You Constantly Updating And Adding New Content To Your Website? Well You Need To Be To Ensure SEO Success! This Cannot Be Stressed Enough. Content Is What Will Make Or Break Your Site So Make Sure Your Content Is Entertaining, Up To Date And Informative.
3374	Everything Can Change In A Blink Of An Eye But Don't Worry Because God Never Blinks
3375	How Would You Like To Remain Completely Anonymous While Making Huge Profits
3376	Traffic Exchanges Take Hours Of Page Refreshing Drudgery To Earn Even A Sniff Of Visitors
3377	Nobody Should Be Allowed To Have Anything To Do With Advertising Until They've Read This Book At Least 7 Times
3378	So Now You Have It! The Key To The Vault! This System Is The Key To Unlocking Home Based Business Success Like You Have Never Dreamed! So What Are You Waiting For? Click The Button Below To Get Started!
3379	PS: If You've Never Had A JV Partner Before, Then It's Time You Started Building Win/Win Relationships With New Ones. Find Out Why So Many Marketers Are Turning To This Popular Method Of Generating Cash For Yourself.
3380	Looking For Those Missing Secrets That Nobody Else Dare Share With You
3381	Don't Wait Around For Something To Happen, And That's What Most Marketers Do. Take An Active Role In Your Websites, And In Your Business! You Need To Make It A Point Of Always Driving More Traffic.
3382	I Invite You To Be A Member Of My Service Today And Though I Could Charge $200 Per Month In Dues You Will Never Ever Pay That Much...In Fact, You Won't Pay $100...Or Even $50 Per Month...But I Will Have To Charge You Something Or You Wouldn't Take Me Or The Program Seriously... So Here's The Deal... If You Click Here And Sign Up Right Now, I'll Give You Your First, FULL Month For Just $4.99.
3383	Do You Really Have What It Takes To Make A Million Dollars Online 99% Don't

3384	The Richest People Are Usually Not Those Who Do Lots Of Things -- Or Lots Of Things Even Very Well. The Richest People Are Those Who Find One Thing That Works, And Then Just Repeat The Process Over And Over Again.
3385	Just A Real Quick Note - Glad To Have You As A Subscriber And I Will Do My Best To Provide As Much Value As I Can. If You Had Trouble Finding Receiving Your Gifts For Any Reason Then Here Is The Download Link One More Time.
3386	Which Would You Prefer Building A Tiny Hut Or A Sky-scraper
3387	Why You May Turn Out To Be Your Worst Enemy Online
3388	The Ultimate Tool That Allows Webmasters To View A List Of 404 Errors Generated From Broken Inbound Links.
3389	Brand Yourself As An Expert And Start Building Your Own List
3390	This Morning I Woke Up At 5:00am To Finish The Update To This Great New Tool That Will Help You Finally Get The Answers You Need.
3391	Don't Be Surprised If You Laugh At First At How This Works
3392	Holidays Are Just Around The Corner. If You've Been Looking For A Cost-Effective, Painless Way To Energize Your Website And Boost Sales For The Season, Look No Further
3393	You Can Start With A Few Bucks And A Good Idea To Make Lots Of Money Online! I Did, And I'll Teach You How!
3394	Re-Write The Article And Submit It To Newspapers Or Magazines.
3395	How Would You Like To Claim Authorship To This Incredible Product
3396	And I'm Going To Keep The Price Low -- A Lot Lower Then Similar Software -- IF You Will Agree To Share Your Success Stories With Me And Give Me A Testimonial I Can Put On My Website.
3397	First, Like All Of Our Products, If You Don't Love It, You Can Get Your Money Back Without Question Or Hassle.
3398	Free Up Your Creative Efforts By Delegating Tasks To Proven Experts
3399	How To Successfully Joint Venture Your Online Business With Offline Businesses
3400	Knowing Your Niche Demographic Will Help You Create A Compelling Sales Message Because You Know Exactly Who You Are Selling To Based Upon Gender, Age, Ethnicity, Education Status, and Income Levels.!

3401	If We Said NO, There Must Be A Powerful Reason. But If We Said YES We Know You'd Buy.
3402	All That Truly Matters In The End Is That Your Loved
3403	How To Become A Trusted Market Expert Even If You're A Newbie
3404	The Type Of Niche Market You've Selected Is Very Important In Relationship With The Length Of Your Marketing Emails. If You Have A Prospect Who Is Unsure Of Buying From You, Or New To The Market, Or Primarily Interested In Free Informa-tion - Then A Longer Email Might Be Better.
3405	You Will Be Up And Running In A Matter Of Hours
3406	What Do You Need To Do Everyday To Reach Your Goal
3407	What They Think You Should Do Or What Your Customers Want
3408	We Will Be Closing Down This Offer Soon So Act Now
3409	We Tried Everything From Net Stomping To Controlling The Masses To Ebay, Before Finally Settling On Google Adwords We Thought That We Had Finally Found The Secret To Making A Full-Time Living On The Net - But We Were Wrong.
3410	However You Will Also Need To Optimize Your Blog Post URL And Ensure You Tagged Your Blog Post Correctly.
3411	They Could Be Golfing... Fishing... Camping... Gardening... Spending Time With Their Kids... Boating... Relaxing Or Even Sleeping. Or They May Be At Their Job Looking Forward To The Day They Can Fire Their Boss!
3412	Create A Business Card Tip Sheet With Your Contact Informa-tion On One Side And Tips On The Other.
3413	You Can Operate Your Business Anytime And Anywhere You Like, As Long As There's A Computer And Internet Connec-tion!
3414	That's Why It's Critical You Act Now! The Discounted Price Of $27 Will Only Be Good For The Next 100 14 Customers. Once 100 14 Packages Are Sold I'll Up The Price To $47, Then $67, Then $97.
3415	People Don't Know How Much Something Is Worth So Com-municate Value
3416	The Key To Your Success Online Is To Target Your Marketing As Much As Possible. You're Not Looking To Capture Every Online Shopper With A Pulse And A Mouse.

3417	This Is A Limited Time & Quantity Offer Only 100 Will Be Sold! Only 100 99 82 48 42 19 Left. (This Offer Will Be Permanently Removed Once All 100 Are Gone).
3418	The Tactics I Reveal In This Video Will Be Stuffing Your Opt-In Box On Auto-Pilot For Years To Come.
3419	Why Most Savvy Marketers Simply Hand Off Their Products To Affiliates
3420	So How Do You Do All That You Do Without Your Head Exploding
3421	How To Give My Stuff Away For Free While You Make Money
3422	Here's What You'll Receive Once You Own The Super Bonus Package
3423	Nowhere Else On The Internet Can You Gain "Inclusive" Access To So Many Unique And "Must-Have" Marketing Tools! Designed And Programmed In-House.
3424	These Are Absolutely The Best Techniques To Start Making Money Quickly And Quietly
3425	Are You Smart Enough To Avoid These Pitfalls That Plague Your Niche Market Success
3426	The Average Person Can't Find The Volume Of Customers Needed To Succeed
3427	Why Do Good People Continue To Fail Even After The Truth Is Exposed
3428	One Simple Forgotten Piece Of Code Can Decrease Sales by 73%
3429	And What Makes The Money-Wasting Crime Even Worse Is That It Is Now So Easy To Build A List On Autopilot.
3430	Stop Living Just For Peanuts When Bigger Dreams Are More Important To Your Happiness
3431	Have You Joined Other Down Line, Power Line, Forced-Matrix, Or Affiliate Businesses And Been Unable To Get Others To Join Or Recruited Others Only To Have Them Drop Out Because They Couldn't Duplicate Your Success?
3432	I'll Admit This Was Not Really My Cup Of Tea But I Tried It And I Simply Can't Believe The Staggering Numbers, Hits, And Commissions I'm Getting, No Bull!
3433	Access Five Of The Most Powerful Marketing Strategies Without All The Typical Bull Sh@t
3434	Pocket Money Without Doing Anything More Than You're Doing Right Now

249

3435	I Got Rid Of All The Free Stuff ... I Got Rid Of All The "Feel-Good" Stuff ... I Got Rid Of Everything Except What This Guy Told Me To Put Into My Web Site.
3436	What If You Could Simply Flip A Switch And Make A Small Yet Powerful Income
3437	It's All About Reaching That Next Level And Having The Opportunity To Make More Money
3438	1 in 5 Mothers In The U.S. Are Stay At Home Moms
3439	While Everyone Else is Literally Fighting for Their Lives in a Collapsing Economy, You and Your Family Will Thrive and Prosper Like Never Before...
3440	$80,000 In Prizes! Help Us Find The Name For These New Kitchens
3441	The Universal Desire For Realistic Rewards Online Has Never Been Stronger
3442	If I Told You That You Could Make Between $500 And $3000 A Month, Doing Nothing But Sitting In Your Pajamas Typing On Your Computer, From ANYWHERE In The WORLD, Would You Do It?"
3443	If You're One Of The Thousands And Thousands Of People Out There Looking For A Way To Make Money Online, Your Search Is Over... This Is What You've Been Looking For. A Complete, Foolproof Roadmap. It's Simple, And It Works... Fast
3444	Any And All Copywriters – Online Or Offline - That Is Or Even Isn't Worth His/Her Salt Has What's Called A "Swipe File" On HisHer Hard Drive.
3445	Never Worry About Losing Your Hosting Account Due To False Spam Complaints
3446	Once You Learn What We're Going To Teach You, The Sky Really Is The Limit To Your Earnings Potential. Now We Know That Many Of You Love Your Job And Simply Want To Build A Part-Time Income To Supplement What You're Making And For Job Security.
3447	As If All That Isn't Enough... I'm Even Going To Show You My Super Simple Method So You Can Start Building Websites Today Without Any Coding Knowledge Or Special Skills.... Plus I'll Show You How To Make Your Site Do What Its Supposed To - Make Money!
3448	So Now What Do You Do Yeh What Do You Do

3449	YES. I Want To Sign Up For FREE. Click To Get Yours. You Really Have Nothing To Lose By Giving It A Try. Get Yours While It Is Still Free.
3450	Do You Know That You Will Be Shown The Top, Proven, Most Stable Website Promoting Service In The Entire Internet Marketing Industry?
3451	As Long As You Know More Than The Average Person You Are Considered An Expert
3452	My Advanced Methods For Infiltrating And Dominating The Giveaway Events That Can Blast Your List Into The Stratosphere.
3453	Get Access Before These Next 500 Sell Out. After These Next 500 Sell Out, We Will Again Evaluate The Market And May Close This Offer For Ever. This Could Happen In The Next Few Hours Depending On When You Are Reading This Page So Don't Miss Out... Order Now
3454	The Simple 5 Word Phrase That Gets Site Owners Hot To Sell Without Tipping Them Off To Golden Egg They're Sitting On...
3455	A Proven, Foolproof Way To DOMINATE The Search Engines, FLOOD The Internet With Your Message, Get Web Rankings, Drive Unlimited Free Traffic And Generate Qualified Leads Quickly, Easily And Inexpensively.
3456	Increasing Your Search Engine Rankings Is A Long-Term Strategy And You Could See Growing Cash Streams Over Time But You Need To Be Prepared To Wait.
3457	The Truth Is The Best And Biggest Approach Trend Surfacing In Online Marketing
3458	Don't Make Things Hard On Yourself, If Your Site Isn't Open For Business In Front Of A Ton Of Traffic, How Are You Ever Gonna Make Any Money?
3459	You Will Have Everything You Need To Be Up And Running Very Quickly And Easily. Even If You Have Never Built A Website Before.
3460	Getting Someone To Submit Their Email Is Great, But You Also Have To Make Sure They Confirm It (If You Use A Double Opt-In List). So To Help You Do That, You'll Be Getting A Matching "Confirm Your Email" Page Where You Send Your Subscribers To Confirm Their Email. That's Where You Give People Instructions For How To Confirm Their Emails.
3461	If You Want Traffic You're Going To Need To Pull Out Everything You Can To Get People's Attention.

3462	But After Today, You Can Kiss Those Days Goodbye, Because With This New, Tested And Proven-To-Work Affiliate And Link Tracking Software.
3463	I Pay Ghost Writers Every Month So You Can Get Your Hands On Fresh Content Articles By Experts Analyzed In Ready Money Making Niche Websites All For Less Than 5 Cents (Yes Five) Per Article!
3464	But Even When I Say "Hire A Full-Time Worker" We're Talking About A Total Cost Of About $250-$300 Us Per Month. So You Can Certainly Have Someone Help You Part-Time For A Small Fraction Of That.
3465	First, You're Going To Get A Video Training Program That Will Help You Create Your First Information Product." This Program Will Be Taught By The Guy Who Has Done My "Audio/Visual" At My Seminars For The Past 8 Years. It's Going To Be AWESOME.
3466	I Hope That's You... I Really Do. I Want To See You Succeed. I Know How Hard It Is To Get Started Making Money On The Internet. Do NOT Let This Pass You By. Go Ahead And Order Right Now.
3467	Double Your Money Back If You Don't Increase Conversions By At Least 75%
3468	Make Lots Of Money With Your Own Free People Search Website
3469	You've Got The Ugliest Kids I've Ever Seen In My Life (That's What They'll Say If You Get Caught Using The Wrong Photographer)
3470	The Choice Is Yours. You Can't Become Something You Hate In Order To Be Successful. This Model Works For The 8% Who Are Real Salespeople. It's A Disaster For The Rest Of Us ... A Very Bad Business Model.
3471	I Knew I Needed To Build A List But Had No Idea How. I Struggled To Figure Out The Fastest Way To Make A Decent Living From Home But Just Couldn't Seem To Get It Right Until I Accidentally Discovered These Simple Strategies.
3472	Instant Access To Professionally Written Sales Letters That Help You Sell Products
3473	I Want To Wish You Every Success In The World With What Ever You End Up Doing. But Before You Leave, I Really Encourage You Take A Good Hard Look At What You May Be Missing.

3474	You Might As Well Have Never Wasted Your Time In The First Place
3475	When The Time Comes You'll Have More Money Than You'll Have Time To Count It
3476	The Quickest, Easiest Way To Find A Reliable Web Hosting Company To Host All Of Your Domains For Less Than You'd Spend On A Value Meal At The Drive–Thru...
3477	The Best Thing I Did Was To Give This Away For Free
3478	3 Things You Need To Win The War Of The Search Engines
3479	Guiding You Through The Exact Process Of Setting Up Your Niche Website
3480	Each Step In The Core-Business Pay Plan Earns You A Higher And Higher Commission As Your Referrals Progress Through The System Too. So Your Income Will Always Continue To Grow.
3481	If Money Is Tight And You Simply Can't Afford The Expense Of $37 At This Moment, I Understand. I Am Willing To Part With My Ebook For A Fraction Of What I'm Asking For. If You Order Through This Page, You'll Get My Ebook For Only $17.00... That's An Incredible 50% Off The Already Heavily Discounted Suggested Retail Price.
3482	The Most Powerful Emotional Triggers Are: Greed, Fear Of Loss, Money, Promise Of Gain, Desire To Impress, Curiosity, Save Time, Avoid Work, Save Money, Better Health, Vitality, Quitting Day Job, Financial Security, Happiness, Feeling Self Confident, In Control Of One's Life, And Ultimately, Freedom.
3483	Written In Simple, Down-To-Earth Manner That's So Easy And Quick To Read! No Technical Jargon Or High Falutin' Language. Just, Plain, Simple Straight Talk To Show You A Whole World Out There You Don't Even Know Exists Yet!
3484	Imagine the Power You'll Hold In Your Hands When You Use This Incredible Technique
3485	Create An Automated Blog That Auto-Posts A Mix Of PLR Content.
3486	Saddle Up The Internet Horses And Be Prepared For One Hell Of A Ride
3487	Want To Get Paid Really Well For What You Love Doing
3488	Isn't It Time You Get What You Really Want From Life
3489	What Else Do You Really Want To Accomplish Online In Addition To Making Lots Of Money

253

3490	How To Develop A Solid Customer Relationship Now That Will Pay Dividends Forever
3491	Are You Still In A Total State Of Confusion About Making Money
3492	It Is Important To Have Your Site Looking As Professional As Possible So That You Can Make Heaps Of Money With These Quality Products
3493	This May Be Your One And Only Chance To Get Your Hands On This Exclusive Affiliate Series.
3494	What If It Were Easy To Make More Sales Online And Make The Kind Of Income You Really Deserve?
3495	News Flash! Yes, Don't Rub Your Eyes Just Yet - You're Gonna Have The Amazing Ability To Continually Crank Out Kick-Butt Sales Copy Based On A System Ingeniously Crafted By The Finest Copywriters In The World Regularly Valued For At Least $20,000 EACH For A Limited Time Not For $347 But Only $197. A Real Steal Of The Year!
3496	I'm About To Share With "You" A System That Can Dramatically Change Your Financial Future For The Better With Everything You Need To Get On The Fast Track To Financial Success.
3497	The First Wave Of The Internet Opportunity Explosion Has Come And Gone. If You Were In Tune To The Opportunities Of The Day In The Late 1990's AND You Were Very LUCKY You Likely Would Not Be Reading This Right Now. Instead You Would Be Resting Comfortably "On The Other Side" As Some Call It.
3498	I'll Also Be Providing Additional Downloads And Resources In The Members Area. Just Click The 'Buy Now' Button For Instant Access And I'll See You On The Inside!
3499	And You're Ready To Kick Down Those Freakin Barriers And Finally Make Some Real Money Online. Well, Guess What? An Effective Marketing System Doesn't Have To Be Extremely Complicated. Quite The Contrary.
3500	How To Find And Endless Supply Of People Practically Begging You To Buy
3501	It Seems Incredible That You Can Offer These Signed Original Etchings For Only $5 Each
3502	7 Most Powerful Ways To Build A Targeted And Friendly Prospect Contact List
3503	Time Is Short And This May Be The Most Important Thing You Need To Know Right Now

254

3504	Where Do You Feel You're Not Putting Forth Your Full Abilities
3505	Manage Your Store Online Via Your Own Easy To Use Web-Based Store
3506	If You Can't Get People To Read What You Write, You Won't Sell A Thing. The Secrets You'll Learn Are So Powerful, That Even If They Don't Want To... They'll Be Compelled To Read Every Single Word.
3507	3 Easy Ways To Write Your Own Original, Attention-Grabbing Article, Even When You Get Stuck For Ideas. I'll Show You Quick Little Tips On How To Write Articles That Capture Attention And "Hypnotize" People Into Reading Them.
3508	We've Mastered The Art Of Building Businesses... You Now Have This Knowledge At Your Fingertips! You Really Can't Fail This Way, Unless Of Course You Just Don't Take Action.
3509	It Was Everything I Needed At That Point In My Life! I Knew Deep Down Inside Me I MUST Learn To Do What He Was Teaching.
3510	Practical Advice On How To Improve Your Marketing Performance Throughout A Broad Spectrum Of Analyzing Activities Surrounding Your Marketing Campaigns.
3511	Want To See How My Million Dollar Napkin Made A Huge Profit On The Internet
3512	Find Out From Me How To Have Cash Emailed To You Up To 37 Times A Day
3513	Would You Prefer To Talk With Either A Millionaire Or A Billionaire
3514	I Made Sure To Get Up Extra Early (Well, Kind Of ... 9am Is Early For Me!) As I Had A Great Idea For A Blog Post That I Wanted To Get Written And Sent Out To You.
3515	It Requires A Little Work At The Start, But In General It Shouldn't Take More Than About Half An Hour Per 300-Word Article. If You Get 1000 Articles From An Hour's Work... That's A Really Good Investment Of Time.
3516	Would You Rather Have The Golden Goose Or The Golden Egg
3517	Offer Digital Versions Of Your Product As An Upsell On A Branded USB Key.
3518	Instantly Know Which Ads Are Working And Which Ads Are Dead Ducks

3519	Be A HEAVY HITTER And Add 3 Reps A Day Into Your Home-Based Business Using Our Proven System That Has Already Created More Than $12 Million Dollars For People Just Like You"
3520	From Broke To Breaking Even To Profitable Then The Millionaire Billionaire Mindset Kicks In
3521	Tired Of Creating Or Promoting A Product Only To Be Disappointed By Failing To Make Even A Single Sale?
3522	You're About To Eat The Forbidden Fruit. Finally, You Can Find Out, Once And For All, How The Gurus Have Been Lying To You...
3523	Click On The Graphic To Access A Nifty Little Piece Of Software That Will Let You Experiment With Multiple Membership Site Pricing Scenarios, And You'll Begin To Have A Greater Understanding Of Exactly What Is Possible.
3524	When Trust Is Reflective Of Your Service Then You Know You're Going To Make A Lot Of People Very Happy!
3525	Collaborate With Other Business-Minded Individuals And Create Unique Packages And Programs For Sale.
3526	Start Your Trial Membership Today And Gain Instant Access To These Bonuses
3527	Build A Nice Sized Library Of Short Reports And Make A Nice Profit
3528	We Quickly Discovered The Cold, Harsh Truth That The Abundance Of Affiliate Programs Out There Doesn't Necessarily Mean An Equal Opportunity. To Begin With, Most Affiliate Programs Out There Don't Convert Well.
3529	If Your Idea Makes A Million-Dollars For A Company, You Should Be Compensated Based On That, Not On How Much Time You Spent To Come Up With The Idea.
3530	If Hanging Out With The Same Old Group Of Office Ass-Kissers, Day After Day, Year After Year Until You Get Unceremoniously Canned At A Moment's Notice Is Your Idea Of A Party Then, By All Means, Do Nothing.
3531	Joint Venture Secrets That Produce A Slam Dunk Every time They Launch A Product
3532	And As An Additional Feature You Can Even Do Split-Testing To Find The Best Selling Ad Copy For Your Site.
3533	Split Ebooks Into Several Smaller Articles And Blog Posts.
3534	If You Don't Mind Paying Double You Can Join Any Old Time

3535	Even If You're A Jaded Skeptic Prepare To Have All Your Doubts Erased
3536	It's Got To Fit You Instead Of You Trying To Fit Yourself To It Right
3537	Review The Training Materials. Use The Tools To Build Your Own Sales. See For Yourself What Thousands Of Other Online Marketers Are Talking About.
3538	Why This Targeted Audience Is Already Eager To Promote Your Product Or Service
3539	You Deserve A Better Life Once You Follow This Plan Of Action
3540	Here's Your Holiday Sleigh Full Of Incredible Virtual Goodies You'll Enjoy
3541	If You Could Write 10 Great Headlines A Day It Would Take You Over 4 Years To Create This Incredible Collection.
3542	Ozone Created By Electric Cars Now Killing Millions In The Seventh Largest Country In The World Mexifornia Formerly Known As California
3543	When Times Are Bad, People Really Need Training And Continuing Education. And They Will Pay For High-Value Information, Because They Really Don't Have A Choice When The Economy Pulls The Rug Out From Their Current Occupation.
3544	What You're About To See Isn't Just Another Get-Rich, Pie-In-The-Sky Product Promotion. This Is A Proven System That Has Personally Generated One Man As Much As $_____ In Only 7 Days... And Now He's Giving Away His Most Closely Guarded Secrets.
3545	How To Leave Them Hungry And Eager To Do Business With You Again And Again
3546	Bonuses Are Strictly Given To Those Who Use The Link Provided Here Only. To Make Sure That You Got It Right, It's Suggested That You Delete Your Cookies First Before Clicking The Link.
3547	Don't Be Intimidated By The Phrase "Social Networking", It Really Isn't As Hard As It Sounds. In Fact My Videos Make Setting Up, Building, And Profiting From Facebook As Simple As Tying Your Shoes!

3548	If You're Working A Job Right Now, I Can Tell You Without A Doubt That Your Job Is A Heck Of A Lot Harder Than Making Hundreds Per Day With This Course. And You're About To Have Instant Access To This Entire Video Coaching Course At Less Than Cost!
3549	Well Here We Go! It's Absolute Crunch Time Right Now. You Have Got To Get Your Butts In Here Right Now If You Even Want A Shot In The Dark To Win Some Serious Bonuses To-day!
3550	Now I Know You're Probably Asking... What's The Catch? Well, There Is NO Catch. That's Right, I Will Give You The Entire Wealth Building System For FREE!
3551	I'm Going To Define A Set Of Rules For You That Will Take You Right From The Very First Word, To The Last Letter. No Need To Flail Blindly In The Dark Anymore. I Take You Through Each Step To The End Result.
3552	If You Downloaded This Unique Software When I Recom-mended It, But You Haven't Got The Full Package Yet, You Need To Act Now. That Link Bypasses The Opt-In And Gets Straight To The Point. It May Be Your Last Chance To Get Your Hands On It Before It's Gone Forever..
3553	We're Paying Top 75% Commissions On Two Levels And Want You On Our Team
3554	The Money Is There So Start Making The Internet Work For Yourself
3555	What Preventative Actions Do You Need To Take To Ensure Future Success?
3556	Make Them Laugh- Reading Something That Is Humorous On The Web Is A Welcoming Change. If You Can Add Humor To Your Articles, Go For It! This Is One Of The Best Ways To Gain Respect From Your Readers And Convince Your Pros-pect To Click To Your Site.
3557	Your Direct Link To Success Is About To Bite Your Mouse
3558	Are You Only Making Half The Money You Need To Be Profit-able
3559	You Don't Have To Do That Anymore Now That This Is Active
3560	So, What Are The Qualities Of A Great Blog? Well, For Me It's One That Offers Me Something Of Value, Whether That Be In The Form Of Valuable Information, Or Points Me In The Direc-tion Of Free Products Or Services.

3561	It's Entirely Up To You How Much Time Equity You Want To Put Forth To Grow Your Income. YOU Control Your Own Destiny... NOT Your Boss.
3562	I Liked This Guy's Style. He Cared More About His Store's Integrity And The Long-Term Success Of His Customers Than Making A Sale, And Was Even Willing To Ask His Customers To Leave In Order To Demonstrate This Fact.
3563	Former School Teacher Now Makes More In One Day Than He Did In One Year
3564	Notice To All Struggling Affiliates: If You Don't Already Have A Tried And Tested System Currently Piling Cash Into Your Pockets That Can Be Setup While You Watch A Football Game Then Read This Entire Letter Immediately...
3565	Send Email Ads To Paypal Users For A One Time Fee
3566	So When You Have Made The Decision That What You Want Is A Business, Not A Job -- A Business That Can Generate Income For You On Its Own, Without You Even Being There -- Don't Think How Enormous The Task Is In Front Of You.
3567	Capitalize On The Massive Viral Growth The Social Networking Can Help You Achieve
3568	P.S. Don't Fret Another Day Wondering How You'll Find Time To Build Your List. Now You Can Set The Entire Process On Autopilot And Simply Let The Starving Crowds Find You.
3569	Nothing You've Ever Seen Is As Easy Because It's An Automatic Money Machine
3570	Build Your Primary Business With A Private Personal Contact System That Is Easy To Duplicate. Build Residual Income, Build Your Primary Business, And Show Others Exactly The Same Process.
3571	Cheap Or Free Classified Ads Remain A Great List Building Tool For Your Business
3572	Why Limit The Supply? Because Neither You Nor I Want Thousands Of Idiots Barging Into The Secret Guru JV Planning Areas And Screwing It Up! So I'm Only Letting A MAX Of 50 People Have Access. PERIOD.
3573	Grab Your FREE Professionally Designed Fully Automated Profit-Pulling Cash Machine To Start Harnessing The Web's Most Lucrative Opportunities
3574	I'm Sure That You Are Aware Of The Fact That The Online Business Industry Is Booming And Billions Of Dollars Of Product Are Sold Every Year In Online Businesses Alone And It's Continually Rising! So, Is Your Business Profiting?

259

3575	You Can Make A Killing With This Enormous Amount Of Business In Your Pipeline
3576	One Of The Forms Of Traffic That I Used To Put At The Back Of The Line Was List Building Programs... You Know The Ones, There Are Dozens Of Twists, But They Almost All Do The Same Thing: Exchange Your Time And Efforts For Traffic.
3577	Getting All This Traffic For Free Was An Incredibly Rare Event
3578	It's Time Someone Told Me Exactly What I Needed To Do About My Marketing Approach
3579	This Sounds Like A Lot Of Work. But The Truth Is The Average Internet User Can Become Basically Versed Within 30 Days Or Less If They Put Forth An Effort To Learn.
3580	Basically, I Didn't Do All The Things That So Many People Get Suckered Into Doing. Ask Yourself How Many Programs You've Bought In The Past Because You Were Told You Could Make Money With Them. Be Honest.
3581	The Best "Love Life" You Ever Thought Possible. Succeeding With People... Meeting New Friends...Building Stronger Family Ties. Everything Is Covered By The World's Leading Experts On Creating Perfect Relationships.
3582	Read This Powerful Report Before You Generate A Single Lead, Talk To A Single Prospect, Sell A Single Product Or Recruit A Single New Associate Into Your Business.
3583	The Secret Of Making People Like You Even If You're A Jerk
3584	Why Just Grind It Out Working Hard Not Making Any Money
3585	The Truth Is There Are NO Secrets Only A Field Tested Proven Success Strategy
3586	That's Right, A Incredible Collection Of 16,000+ Powerful Eye Catching Mini-Phrases And Headlines That You Can Grab, Mix, And Match And Use To Create Your Own Ad Copy.
3587	If You Can Identify With The Pain And Agony Your Customers Go Through. They Will Try And Buy Just About Anything That Offers Relief From Their Suffering No Matter What The Cost.
3588	Request The Most Talked About eBook This Year And Claim Your Free Copy
3589	If Every Dollar You Spent Turned Into $5 To $10 What Would You Do
3590	I'm Talking About Markets You've Never Thought Of With Millions To Be Made But Only If You're Using The Right Trigger Words, Mini-Phrases, And Action Headlines, That Will Open Your Mind To Unlimited Possibilities.

3591	Without A Leap Of Faith I Wouldn't Be Experiencing Unbelievable Success Today
3592	The Art Of Working Part Time With A Full Time Mentality
3593	Why You Have To Get Rid Of The Expert Mind Set
3594	You'll Discover How To Effortlessly Predict Whether A Particular Niche Is Going To Be Profitable Or Not And Whether People Are Already Spending Money On Offers Within That Niche.
3595	Imagine A Flood Of Hungry Prospects Melting Your Hit Counter Virtually Overnight
3596	But I Said I Was Here To Help. It Is Truly My Desire To See You Succeed And Reach The Kinds Of Profits You Previously Only Dreamed Possible.
3597	It's Never Too Late To Start Growing And Successful Online Business
3598	With The Actions You've Already Taken, Which Ones Have Proven To Be Successful?
3599	NOTE: You Need To Have Adobe Flash Player To View All Of The Videos. If You Don't Have The Application Installed In Your Computer, You Can Get The Plug-In From The Adobe Official Website For FREE. Link To The Application Will Also Be Provided In The Customer Download Area.
3600	The 10 Habits That Keep People Poor And The 12 That Can Make You Rich
3601	Why Speed Is The Name Of The Game For Winners Only
3602	Once You Master Our Proven System For Launching And Growing Your Website Into A Profit Pulling Machine, What's Stopping You From Creating Multiple Membership Sites Across Multiple Niches.
3603	Create A "How-To" Video Course From Your Contents And PLR Graphics. Post Samples Of The Video On Youtube To Promote The Course.
3604	You Will Not Be Hounded Or Pressured To Do A Thing... Because Once You See How Easy Creating Wealth Can Be, Your Only Decision Will Be To Use The System... Or Not.
3605	Access Your Own Complete Profiteering System And Opens The World's Money Vault
3606	This Is An Amazing No-Fat, All Meat Service! It Cuts Through All The Trial And Error... They've Already Been There, Done That, And You Learn From Their Very Valuable Experience.

261

3607	Would You Like To Know The Ways To Make Your Marketing Campaigns To Work Faster
3608	What To Do For Aging Parents When You Don't Have The Money
3609	Revealed: 15 Cheap & Ugly But Brutally Effective Web Traffic Strategies For The Little Guy. If You've Got No Budget, No Computer Skills And No Traffic Then Here Are My Not Brainer "Do It On The Cheap" Instant Traffic Solutions.
3610	Why The Heck Do You Want To Start Your Own Business
3611	Get The Inside Scoop Of Where The Internet Is Heading With The Biggest Opportunities
3612	Act Quickly If You Want Your Link Included Because There Are Only A Couple Of Spots Left
3613	Right And Wrong Farming Methods And Little Pointers That Will Increase Your Profits
3614	What You Have To Do If This Is What You Want
3615	I Believe Our Conditioning Is Partially To Blame. Because We All Want Our Freedom. We All Want Our Time To Spend Freely On Our Terms. And Most Of All We Want Security. But All Our Lives We Are Taught Differently, From A Very Young Age. Do You Think The System Trains People To Be Entrepreneurs? Or Are They Preparing You To Get A Low Paying Job?
3616	Keep The System And Send Me An Email. I Will Gladly Refund Your Full Purchase Price. As A Matter Of Fact I Will Feature You On This Site With Your Testimonial On How Easy It Was To Get Your Money Back. So Far No One, And I Repeat, No One Has Requested Their Money Back.
3617	You Paid The Price To Get There So Dig In And Duke It Out
3618	I Don't Know Any Marketer Making Only $1 A Month Per Member On Their List. You'd Have To Be Extremely Lazy To Average Just $1 Per Month From Your Best List Members.
3619	The Magic Keyword Prefix That Practically Reads Your Prospects Mind... And Blasts You Ahead Of The Competition Like Being Fired From A Cannon!
3620	Change Your Life And Your Lifestyle Starting This Week! Take Control Of Your Financial Future And Start Enjoying The Lifestyle Of Your Choice. Come Stand On The Shoulders Of Giants To See Further Than You Ever Have Before.
3621	It Really Works Because They Know How To Do It Right

3622	Too Many Ebooks Give You Lots Of Ideas But No Few Specific Tips For How To Actually Implement Them. A Surefire Way To Dominate Smaller Niches. Only A Few Niche Marketers Are Using This Powerful Method, So This Could Give You A Tremendous Edge Over The Competition.
3623	Now Just To Be Sure We Are Not Leaving Any Juicy Traffic Tips Out, We Have Created A Blog, Where Store Owners Can Reveal Their Successful Traffic Strategies In A Community Of Buyer List Builders Helping Each Other.
3624	Never Again Will You Suffer From The Pain & Hassle Of Paying Monthly Bills For Your Autoresponder, Mailing List Management, Ad Tracking, Shopping Cart, Refer-A-Friend System & More.
3625	I Can't Let You Walk Away Without Some Cool Bonuses! So Here's What Else You're Going To Get.
3626	You Deserve The Good Life. Live The Life You Desire Not By Selling, But By Giving It All Away. Bookmark This Page And Try Selling People Stuff Online Then Come Back Before You Are Totally Disgusted And We Will Show You A System That Really Works
3627	Reduce Your Risk Of Losing Money On Advertising To Almost Zero
3628	The Truth Is That You Don't Need An Elaborate Website To Make A Lot Of Money
3629	Yes! I Understand If I Am One Of The First 100 Buyers I'm Also Getting _____
3630	You Will Be Able To Publish All The Websites You Want Now And It Will All Be A Piece Of Cake! Now You'll Be Able To Have And Eat Your Cake As Well!
3631	First Of All, As A Thank You For Opening My Offer, I Would Like To Give You A Fun Bonus As My Personal Thank You Just For Joining My List.
3632	Just Skip One Bad TV Show Every Week And See What Can Happen
3633	I Know Because I've Done It, I've Helped Other People Do It, And Once You See How Simple And Easy Our System Makes The Whole Process, You'll Be Surprised, Amazed And Chomping At The Bit To Get Started On Your Own Site.
3634	Never Write Down Something You Don't Want Anyone Else To Read
3635	Why This Is One Of My Favorite Success Stories Of All Time

263

3636	No Other Site On The Entire Internet Offers You Every Tool, Every Resource And Even Personalized One-On-One Help To Get YOUR Business Up And Running FAST. You Can Either Spend Your Time Getting Ready Or Start A Business.
3637	Cash In On Holiday Sales That Make Huge Profits All Year Long
3638	A New Kind Of Offer That Forces Money Into Your Pocket Without Your Permission
3639	Does Your Copy Suck Or Does it Suck In Lots Of Cash For You Quickly And Automatically
3640	No One Likes To Run Their Business With A Dirty List Of Out Dated Email Addresses
3641	I Feel Kind Of Sorry For Some Of The Other Old Timers Who Cling To Their Antiquated Methods. After All, I Know How Hard It Can Be To Embrace Change. Mostly, I Feel Sorry For All The New Surfers Who Are Receiving Horrible Advice Being Tossed About That Will Quickly Kill Their Dreams In No Time Flat.
3642	Billionaires Are Billionaires Because They Think Differently Than Most People. They Have A Different Approach To Life And Business. It's Well Worth 3 Minutes Of Your Time To Give This A Careful Read.
3643	At The End Of The Day What's In Your Bank Account
3644	But The Only Reason That You Could Pass This Up Is That You're Afraid Of Becoming Ultra Successful With Adsense.
3645	5 Tips On Becoming The Person You Most Want To Be
3646	Create A Wiki To Encourage Your Visitors To Collaborate And Contribute To Your Vision.
3647	Learn The Fastest Way To Drive Free Traffic To Specific Pages On Your Website
3648	Ideally You Want To Be Building Your Own Business And Creating Your Own Products Then Other People Can Be Your Affiliates — They Do All The Work And You Get The Money! That's A Smart Long-Term Strategy To Creating A Successful Online Business.
3649	Here's Your Opportunity To Become Rookie Of The Year In Internet Marking
3650	Mind Boggling Ways To Run A Whole New Business Out Of Your Basement
3651	You Will Get A Bundle Of My Top 5 Marketing Software Scripts At The Price Of Less Then Just One Of Them!
3652	The Traits Of Championship Closers And What They Do Differently Than You

3653	It's The Perfect Reference If You're Selling Products Or Services To Regular Consumers, Business Owners, Auction Buyers And Sellers, Marketers, Entrepreneurs, MLMer's, Affiliates, Web Masters, Executives, Opportunity Seekers Investors, etc.
3654	The Simple, No-Brainer Way I Made My First Million Dollars. This Is One Of The Easiest Ways To Make Money On The Internet, And It's Still Going Strong. You Don't Even Need Your Own Product To Sell! You Can Let Somebody Else Do All That Hard Work.
3655	Where Will You Be Standing At The End Of The Day
3656	Do You Really Want To Strike It Rich Or Be Comfortable
3657	Time To Take It To The Next Level. Create Your Own Products And Low A System That Is Completely Fool Proof.
3658	What Have You Been Missing All These Years Without Free Access To This Amazing Secret
3659	Traffic Generators Can Be A Personal Website, A Business Profile, A Blog Site Or Anything Else. The Rewards Of This Traffic Are Twofold. For One, If You Own A Business, The More Traffic Your Can Direct To Your Company Site, The More People Are Going To Buy Your Product Or Service.
3660	If You're Sick Of Missing Out On The Really Big Affiliate Launches You'll Want This`
3661	Exactly How To Find A Market BEFORE You Create A Product. Yes, That's The Key. I Show You How To Do This With Two Free Tools. You'll Be Able To Find "Hot" MONEY-MAKING Markets In A Matter Of Minutes.
3662	The Real Buzz Is All About Getting Paid Immediately And We Mean Instantly
3663	An All Too Common Mistake That Will Suck Your Energies And Time. (This Is One Of The Main Reasons Why Most Projects Fail - Avoid It All Costs)
3664	Post A Free Ad Change It As Often As You Like
3665	My Goal Is My Family's Happiness Everything Else Is Just A Perk
3666	Why Everything You've Been Told About List Building Is Wrong And How To Profit From Other People's Mistakes - I'm Going To Spell Out Exactly Why I Think The 'Experts' Have Got This Horribly Wrong And I'll Give You My Secret Blueprint To Follow Instead.
3667	Click Here To See If You're Losing Money On The Internet Today

3668	76 Reasons Why It Would Have Paid You To Answer Our Ad A Few Months Ago
3669	Be Sure To Get It While You Can Before It's Gone
3670	The Key To Getting A _____ Is Knowing How To _____
3671	I'm Getting Payments Of $47 And $97 Over And Over And Over
3672	If An Internet Marketer Or An Entrepreneur Doesn't Have The Mindset To Invest A Couple Of Dollars In Their Business, What's The Point Of Being In Business In The First Place
3673	You Know Good Advertisements When You See Them; Creative Headlines, Attractive Pictures, Meaningful Ad Copy, Etc. When It Comes To Marketing, There Are Lots Of Ways To Spend Ad Dollars, Including TV, Newspapers, Info Boxes, Mailers, Magazines And The Internet. This Step Is Designed To Help You Make Great Advertising Decisions. It Will Get Your Creative Juices Flowing And Give You Some New, Time And Money Saving Promotions Ideas!
3674	For Your Information Only! You Will Even Soon Be Getting 1 Brand New Report Every Month Packed With Solid Content To Help You Build Your Business! This Report Includes Both Audio And Video Versions And Actual Action Steps.
3675	Now Your Dreams Can Smile All The Way To The Bank Using This Miraculous Idea
3676	Tomorrow I'll Be Running A Pre-Launch Sale For A Very Unique Plugin Package Starting At Noon (EST). The Price For This Plugin Package Starts At Only $7.00 For The First 20 Buyers. After Every 10 Sales The Price Will Increase By 50 Cents. You Already Know That The First People To Get In Quickly Always Get The Best Deals, And It's Not Unusual For The First 50 Sales To Occur In The First Hour. So, The Sooner You Get Here The Lower The Price. I'll Send You An Email Reminder A Few Hours Before Launch.
3677	Come In If You Dare I'm Still Working In My Underwear
3678	Just Having One Product Isn't Going To Make Your Filthy Rich
3679	How Public Speaking Can Help Jump Start Your Business And Expand Profits
3680	There Are In Essence, Three Simple Rules Of Engagement On The Internet To Make Yourself Money. Whether Anyone Wants You To Believe It, Or Decides To Tell You Differently, The Answers Lie Below.

3681	You've Got To Go Where Your Market Is Already Hanging About. If Your Website Is Like A Ghost Town Right Now...You Just Need To Place It In Front Of The Oodles Of Traffic That's Already Out There.
3682	You Don't Have To Be In A Price War With Others
3683	All Your Hard Work In Setting Up Your Email Marketing Becomes Useless If They're Deleted
3684	Don't Be Afraid That Your Life Will End, Be Afraid That It Will Never Begin. Start By Brightening Someone Else's Life This Very Moment
3685	It's Never Too Late To Have A Happy Childhood Because The Second One Is Up To You And No One Else
3686	The Answer Is In Your Mind. It's Your Mindset, Once Again, That Makes All The Difference. It's The Way You Look At Things That Will Make The Biggest Difference In Your Life And Your Business. People Who Run Successful Cash-Cow Businesses
3687	Again, You Might Be Scratching Your Head In Disbelief Thinking Why Is He Willing To Go This Far Due To An Epiphany Of Late Night Of Deep Thinking.
3688	People Can Really Mess With Your Mind If You Let Them
3689	I Didn't Know How To Write Winning Ads Or Even Write Compelling Copy And Emails. I Had No Idea That I Could Simply Spy On The Competition.
3690	Wouldn't You Like To Be Able To Generate Income By Simply Providing Your Honest Opinion? Wouldn't It Be
3691	No One Cares What You Know Until They Know That You Care About Them
3692	Why It's Crucial For Free Product Sales Pages To Use Psychological Triggers
3693	I Must Warn You That You Must Follow All The Instructions Very Carefully
3694	Instead Of Struggling With Dull, Boring, And Lifeless Headlines, You Can Easily Create Powerful Eye-Grabbing Headlines In A Matter Of Seconds! Our Inspirational List Of Action Headlines And Trigger Phrases Will Excite And Inspire Your Marketing Juices With The Full Force Of Niagara Falls.
3695	This Alone Can Be Several Hundred To Several Thousand Dollars A Month, In Addition To The Profits You Make Through Your Ads As You Use The Service.
3696	Major Diet Plans Which Ones Actually Work And Which Ones Leave You Fatter

3697	Information Overload And Failing To Take Action Is The Major Roadblock To Success
3698	Flat Monthly Rate With No Hidden Charges Fees Or Contracts To Sign
3699	Today Is Your Special One Time Offer To Upgrade Your Membership
3700	Sign Up For The (Product) Coaching Program Before It's Too Late. You'll Also Get Immediate Access To Our Online Community Where Others Just Like You're Already Discussing Ways To Immediately Help Each Other So You're Not In This Alone.
3701	Who Are You And Why Do You Care About My Success Online
3702	How To Format Your Sales Letter Like A Champion. I Describe To You How You Should Format Your Sales Letter And Demonstrate My Points By Showing You Some Of Best Case Studies On Champion Sales Letters Which I Have Picked Up Along The Way. Someone Has Already Done It Right, So It Would Make Sense To Follow Something That Is Already Working.
3703	Spend LESS TIME WORKING. Spend More Time With Your Loved Ones. See Your Friends And Family As Much (Or As Little) As You Like Without Worry. Stay Home With The Kids If You Have Some.
3704	There's No Rush Hour To Deal With... Just The Fun Traffic, The Kind That Brings New Buyers To Your Websites. There's No Dress Code... You Can Work In Your Pajamas If You Feel Like It.
3705	I Disagree With Kay Jewelers. I Would Bet On Any Given Friday Or Saturday Night More Kisses Begin With Miller Lite Than Kay
3706	Still Browsing The Net For A Program That's Really Worth Your Time
3707	How Will You Feel When You Can Help Others Make Money
3708	But, The Truth Is, The Biggest Opportunity In Online Training Is Not In Being What's Known As A Subject Matter Expert... That's A Person Who Has The Knowledge And Credentials That Power A Training Program.

3709	Thankfully, I'm Not Going To Ask You For Anything Like Ten Thousand Dollars, Or A Hundred Thousand, Or Any Other Crazy Numbers Like That. No Sir. I'm Not Even Going To Ask You For A Thousand Dollars... ... Not Even $500... If You Go Ahead And Move On This Now, You Get Access For Just $197.
3710	30 Day Blueprint For Success Especially If You're Just Starting Out
3711	What If This Had The Maximum Impact That Changed Your Life Once And For All
3712	Create Dazzling Attention Getting Responses To Each And Every Marketing Campaign
3713	Perhaps The Most Incredible Thing You'll Ever Be Likely To Come Across
3714	If You Don't Want To Make Extreme Amounts Of Money Please Skip This Unique Idea
3715	If You're Lazy Then This Website Is Definitely For You. It's Integrated With The Latest Cutting Edge Technology So It Makes Money On Auto Pilot. Once Setup You Won't Even Have To Do Anything And Still Rake In The Cash Day After Day.
3716	What You Must Never Say To A Site Owner You Want To Buy From. This Common Slip That Can Cost You The Best Deals...
3717	Just Imagine How Many Extra Sales You Could Make, If You Could Leverage Other People's Customers, Right When They've Just Made A Purchase And Are In 'Buying Mood'...
3718	The Products Are Stored On A Host Server And Can Be Downloaded As Many Times As You Wish At Whatever Price You Should Choose.
3719	How One Fool-Proof Traffic Strategy Can Funnel More Traffic To Your Website Than Nearly Any Other Method And Keep It Coming In For Months To Come! The Fastest Method Of Generating Targeted Traffic To Your Website, Instantly Without Spending More Than A Few Minutes Setting It All Up!
3720	If You're Look For Time Tested And Proven eBook Software Which You Don't Have To Be A Rocket Scientist To Use, Then You're In The Right Place. Find Out Why Thousands Of People All Over The World Choose This Product For Their eBook Publishing Needs.
3721	Uncover More Places That You Can Submit Your Video For More Exposure And Traffic

269

3722	Turn Up The Skepticism To Maximum. Clear Your Mind Of All You Were Told About Making Money. I Am Going To Show You Something Truly Remarkable ...
3723	Find Balance In Your Life - Add More Structure To Every One Of Your Days By Purposely Allotting Specific Chunks Of Time For Work, Play, And Growth So That You Avoid The Frustration And Unhappiness That Comes From An Unbalanced Life.
3724	So I Think It Would Be A Very Good Idea For You To Go To This Page And Bookmark It. Visit It Often Looking For More, And Always Be Sure To Open Emails From Me, As I Will Not Be Plugging Stuff To You.
3725	Do You Know That This Service Can Generate You Thousands Of Hits To Your Website Per Month...For The Rest Of Your Life?
3726	If You Just Commit To Start Doing Something Online You Will Be Successful
3727	You Will Also Learn How To Embed That Video Onto Your Website So That Your Visitors Can Watch What You Have Created, On Your Website.
3728	There's More Important Stuff On How To Get The Absolute Most Cash Out Of Each And Every Product As Well As How To Make Your Refund Rate Plummet (An Ever-Present Thorn For Information Product Vendors).
3729	Future Is Either Reliving Your Past Or Your Breaking Your Comfort Zone
3730	What You're About To Read Is Real And Cannot Be Denied
3731	Start By Focusing On Something Small So You Can Actually See And Feel Achievement
3732	I Didn't Know Exactly What I Was Looking For, So I Typed "Make Extra Money" Into Google. And Then Blammo!
3733	You're Not Dreaming When You Take A Sneak Peak At This Unbelievable Offer
3734	They Were All Building Relationships With Every Single Customer They Encountered. They Understood The Lifetime Value Of These Customers, And Knew They Didn't Need Millions Of "Passer-Bys" To Be Successful.
3735	The Enemy In The Mirror Is Much Closer Than First Imagined
3736	Reorganize Your Contents To Create A More Persuasive Sales Letter.
3737	The Real Reason Why Your Buyers Are Far More Important Than Your Product And How To Protect The Relationship With Them.

270

3738	Moving Toward What You Want And Avoid That Which You Don't Want
3739	Have You Ever Wanted To Feel The Rush Of Send Buttons Flooding Your Bank Account
3740	Getting Started Is The Hardest! So I'm Handing You A Special Quick-Start Guide Which Shows You How To Customize & Setup Your Private Label Rights Product Quickly & Easily.
3741	Best Of All, Regardless Of Your Experience, Location, Industry Or Even If You Have Absolutely No Start Up Cash To Spare, You Can Start Making Money With A Single List And A Handful Of Quick Emails. It's Really That Easy.
3742	Gateway To Building Unlimited Leads In The Hottest Market Currently Online
3743	You Can Start Small And Grow Big At Your Own Pace. Start Earning A Couple Hundred Dollars A Month And Grow It To Earn Thousands Of Dollars, Month After Month.
3744	You Just Need To Believe That You Can Make It, It Is 100% Possible, Just Take Action And Make A Start On It Today!
3745	You Get Full International Master Resale Rights To These So You Can Watch Them Again And Again And Copy Them To Produce Your Own Powerful Websites That Sell Time And Time Again.
3746	The Value Of Website Promotion Cannot Be Underestimated If You Wish To Increase Your Website Traffic. Proper Promotion Results In Increased Page Ranking, Greater Website Traffic And Better Search Engine Placement
3747	NLP - The Meaning Of A Communication Is The Response You Get
3748	How Can You Use Your Expertise To Make $10,000 A Month
3749	Make More Money Through Affiliate Programs With Higher Payouts And Higher Commissions
3750	Give Away These Free Reports As A Bonus To Your Customers
3751	There Are Literally Social Networking Sites For Everyone And Everything. For Baby Boomers, For Music Lovers, For Avid Photographers, For Video Gamers, For George Lucas Fans, For Twilight Lovers, And For Every Single Other Fetish In The World.
3752	Save Money By Knowing How Supermarkets Trick You Into Buying Higher Priced Items

271

3753	There Is No Doubt That These Are Frustrating Times. But It Is Not Just The "Economy." The Times Are Also Changing. And The Combination Of A Number Of Individual Factors Have Meshed To Create A Time Of Seeming Instability, Anxiety And Negativity. It's A Good Time To Remember That You Cannot Always Change What Is Happening Around You, But You Can Change How You React To It!.
3754	What Is The Real Reason Why Internet Women Outlive Internet Men
3755	Do You Like What You Are Doing For A Living? Are You Happy With Your Current Job Or Do You Find You Have To Force Yourself Out Of Bed Every Morning Just To Get Ready To Go To Work?
3756	Why Keep Spending Money Just To Help Them Make More Money
3757	If Money Is So Dirty Why Do The Big Boys Want It
3758	Start Creating As Many Social Networking Accounts As Possible. Social Networking Is A Great Way To Get Your Product Or Service Noticed. Set Up A Myspace Page, A Facebook Page, A Yahoo Page And Much More. Ask Your Friends To Add Your Page As "Fans" And Watch Your Traffic Jam Up.
3759	You Don't Need To Get It Perfect You Just Need To Get It Going
3760	I Seriously Want You To Succeed. A Blunt Promise By Gurus, However Since I WAS In The Same Position As You Are Right Now, I Know The Frustration. You Want To Succeed But There Might Be A Thing Or 2 That You Could NOT Understand, So Gave Up.
3761	You'll See A Detailed Walk thru Of My Personal Launch Planner
3762	I Have Information In My Hands That Makes Living Online Amazing
3763	Castro Finally Dies At Age 112; Cuban Cigars Can Now Be Imported Legally But President Chelsea Clinton Has Banned All Smoking
3764	Don't Even Consider Joining These Sites Until Your Read This Powerful Update

3765	The Myth Dispelled Once And For All - Long Sales Letter vs. Short Sales Letter. I Dispel The Myth About The Age-Old Copywriting Question, "Which Is Better? Long Copy Or Short Copy?" Once And For All. Forget What You Read In The Free Articles. If You Would Notice, They Are Mostly Personal Opinions. I Give You The Expert's Advice, Having Written Several Sales Copies That Sell Myself.
3766	One Percent Of Something Is Always Better Than 100% Of Nothing
3767	Are You Fed Up With Making Other People Or Companies Millions Of Dollars? Tired Of Accepting Wage Handouts At The End Of Every Week But Scared To Death You'll Lose Your Crappy Day Job Because Your Boss Is A Jerk.
3768	Imagine The Kind Of Lifestyle You Could Lead With An Extra $2,000 A Month Lifestyle Bonus From Savings Highway! Go On Trips, Take Vacations, Save, Donate To Your Church Or Favorite Charity, Or Just Go On A Shopping Spree... It's Up To You!
3769	How To Get People To Click Your Affiliate Links After Reading Your Page
3770	I've Been Advised To Only Let This Information Go The Most Serious Of Serious Minded Business People At The Extremely Forgiving Price Of Only $997.
3771	The Best Part About It Is That Others In Your Niche Don't Even Have A Clue About It. Only A Select Few Even Knows This Exists Until I Showed Them Where To Look. But Now I Need Your Help.
3772	Play Your Dreams Out In Your Mind And Watch What Happens
3773	We'll Reveal The Exact Web Pages And Tactics People Online Right Now Are Using To Make A Passive Income By Just Putting Up Simple Free Web Pages In All Kinds Of Weird Little Niches.
3774	It's So Simple A 3rd Grader Could Do It. If You Can Read, Copy And Paste, Follow Easy To Understand Instructions And Spare Just 2 To 5 Hours A Few Nights Or Days A Week.
3775	They're Literally Cropping Up In The Dark Overnight Like Poisonous Mushrooms
3776	Stop Wasting Time On All The Things That Don't Make You Money
3777	Becoming A Rockstar Super Affiliate Is All About Thinking Differently From The Crowd

3778	7 Places To Promote Your Ezine And Grow Your Business
3779	Lucky For You, There Are Very Few People In This Business That Understand How To Rapid Fire The Quality Content Needed To Boost Your Profits..
3780	Think About It - If You Could Go Inside The Mind Of Your Customers And Find Out Exactly What They Are Thinking When They Decide To Buy From You, Would That Give You An Advantage Over Your Competitors?
3781	Who Else Wants Outsource Their Traffic Generation Chores, Get Thousands Of Visitors To Their Websites Every Month... And Bank In Hard, Cold Cash Like Clockwork?
3782	There's An Incredible Step-By-Step Business Feeder System That Will Take You By The Hand And Show You Exactly How You Can Easily Create Wealth Without Interfering With You Job Or Your Lifestyle.
3783	Tweak Your Content So It's Relevant To Current Events Or Celebrity Stories.
3784	EASY... Because I Teach You To Craft Offers That Are Unique And Stand Out From Everything Else, Therefore Grabbing More Attention In A World Where We Hardly Have Time To Get The Information We Are Looking For.
3785	I Wanted To Do Something Special For You Today Just To Say Thanks For Remaining One Of My Loyal Subscribers... So, I Got In Touch With My Good Friend And Fellow Marketer, _____, And Convinced Him To Hook You Up With FREE Access To His Now Famous _____ System.
3786	I Can Help You Make More Money Right Now - Can I Show You How
3787	Time To Spruce Up The Old Website And Start Making Money
3788	Could This Finally Be That Magical Moment That Changes Your Life Forever
3789	Electronically Deliverable Products Are Delivered With An IP Secured And Time Expiring Secure Download Links. Recurring Orders Can Be Handled Through 2Checkout And Paypal.
3790	Why I'm Banning Some Marketing Words. The Language You Use In Your Sales Material Might Actually Be Casting A Negative Light On Your Products And Services With Regards To Their Price, So Much So That I Banned Them From My Vocabulary. I'll Show You Why If You Ban Them From Yours Too, Your Sales Can Skyrocket In A Matter Of Days.

3791	How To Simplify The Process And Effectively Create Your Own Winning Sales Copy
3792	You Can Find Your Daily Download Below, But I Want To Let You Know About A Pretty Cool Resource . . . This Shows You How To Make Money Using Simple Tactics, And Things That Take Just A Few Minutes To Set Up.
3793	This Won't Last Long. Thousands Have Received This Same Invitation So Get In Early! Your Free Money-Making Web Site Is Waiting For Your. It's Completely FREE! Just Fill Out The Form Below And Get Started Today!.
3794	How To Tell The Different Between A Resell Rights Product And A Private Label Rights Product.
3795	Understand Your Customer's Mind And You'll Be Able To Offer Them Exactly What They Want
3796	Men Who 'Know It All' Are Not Invited To Read This Page
3797	This Allows You To Become A Tour Guide Of Sorts, Taking A Continuous Stream Of Interested Prospects Through An Education Process - A Process That Does All Of The Selling And Telling For You, So You Don't Have To.
3798	Determine Your Motive For Action To Get The Results You Want
3799	Why Grammar Is Not Everything And What You Should Do About It
3800	Love To Tell You About This Now But I've Got To Pee
3801	Why You Need To Do What You Are Trying To Learn
3802	To Start, Run And Grow Your Own Business, You Need A Lot Of Components, Such As Websites, Hosting, Products, Sales Letters, Autoresponders, Etc. You Also Need The Know-How, Information, Techniques And Guidance.
3803	As Much As We Try To Complicate What Great Service Is...It's Really Pretty Simple: It Is Giving The Customer More Than They Expect...Consistently. You Notice I Said Simple, Not Easy. There Is A Big Difference!
3804	Let One Of Them Take Your Spot If You're Not Serious
3805	I Want To Send You The First 18 Pages Of This For FREE Tried Articles, Squidoo, Free Blogs And/Or Bum Marketing? Feel Confused And Over-Whelmed? Feel Like You're Not Getting Anywhere? This Can Help! Just Enter Your Name And Email. Your FREE Sneak Peek Will Be In Your Email Shortly!
3806	Spin An Article Into A "10 Best" List.

275

3807	Many Of You Love Your Job And Simply Want To Build A Part-Time Income To Supplement What You're Making And For Job Security. So We Always Let Our Students Make The Decision What's Best For Them And Their Family. Some People Love Making Extra Money Part-Time And Others Can't Wait To Tell Their Boss, "I Quit!"
3808	How To Get Other People To Build A List For You
3809	The Strength Of Your Headlines Comes Down To The Science Of Great Ad Writing
3810	You Really Need To Be Properly Educated On How To Make Money Online
3811	The Story You're About To Read Is Graphic And Shockingly True
3812	Discover A Simple Way To Earn Money Over And Over Again
3813	76 Reasons To Pay Yourself The Salary You Truly Deserve Starting Today
3814	Break This Rule, And You'll Shed Blood, Sweat And Tears, Trying For Months (If Not Years) To Rank For A Keyword, And See Absolutely No Results At All, And Scratch Your Head Wondering Why You Never Ever See To Crack The Front Page!
3815	You Begin To Build A "Feeder" Organization By Following The FREE Strategy And Using The FREE Marketing Methods, Advertising Sources, Tools And Materials That Are Provided For You.
3816	Why Retire When You Can Refocus All Of Your Expertise Online
3817	The Biggest Problem In Marketing Today Is Getting Your E-Mails Read. It's Like The Story Of A Tree Falling In The Woods... If Nobody Sees Or Hears It Fall, Then Did It Really Fall?
3818	If You're Ready To Stop Pretending, Keep Reading . . .What You Do Today Will Generate Income For Years To Come...I Am A Firm Believer In The Concept Of "Work Once, And Get Paid Forever" Principle.
3819	What Scares People More Than Creating A Product Is Building A Website! What In The World Is HTML? How Much Does The Software Cost? How Do I Upload Files? Why Isn't It Formatted Correctly? Why Don't My Graphics Look Like The Ones The Pros Have? If You Are A Complete Beginner, It Can Be Very Difficult (Even Using Templates) To Get An Attractive Website In Place.

3820	How You Can Get In On The Action If You Act Fast
3821	When You Recognize Their Interests, It Becomes Easier For You To Develop Ideas For Possible Sub-Niche Products Or Cross-Sells.
3822	Combine All Of Your Work Tasks And Do Them From Home
3823	How Frequency And Familiarity Trigger Respect And Satisfied Life Long Customers
3824	You Are About To Get Access To My Best Network And Internet Marketing Tips That I Use Daily To Increase My Cash Flow Ridiculously...
3825	Learn The Warning Signs If You Suffer From Disappearing Commission Symptoms
3826	What If Will It Work Or Won't It Work Really Didn't Matter And Either Were Successful
3827	The Same Little Leak That Made Him A Millionaire Can Also Make You Very Wealthy
3828	Imagine A Marketing System That Automatically Builds Your Opt-In List For You, Follows Up With Your Prospects, Converts Them Into Customers.
3829	If Your Subject Line Doesn't Get Read Your Work Is All For Nothing
3830	Do You Believe It's Possible To See Yourself Making Sales Every Single Day
3831	How To Create And Start Selling Your Own Information Product In A Week. This Is Definitely The Way I've Made Most Of My Money. You Won't Believe How Easy It Is To Have Your Very Own Product...Even If You Can't Write Or Don't Know The First Thing About Making A Product Right Now.
3832	The Best Part Is Every Single One Of These Products Pays Your Commissions Directly Into Your Paypal Account Immediately When Someone Buys...Even Better — You Can Re-Sell The Report Itself... This Can Be A Gold Mine For You If You Take Action.
3833	It's As Simple As Either You Make Money Or You Don't Have To Pay A Penny
3834	A Great Exercise For An Entrepreneur To Do If You've Been In Business For A While, And If You Think You Have A Business That Can Run Itself, Is To Try Letting It Run Itself For A While. Pretend For Three Months That You Are Dead. Or On A 3-Moth Sabbatical And See What Happens.
3835	How To Add Automatically Updating Content To Your Website For Free

3836	Listen Up If You'd Like To Give Yourself An Online Raise
3837	The Next Page, I Will Give You All The Nitty-Gritty Details About How This Works. Plus, When You Opt In You Will Be Sent Free Video Training About How To Find The Perfect Niche For You. This Application Will Force You To Look Inside Yourself And Your Internet Marketing Business And Honestly Get To The Heart Of The Question..."Are You Worthy To Be My Apprentice?"
3838	No Other Sponsor Will Give You Such An Incredible Offer. No Other Sponsor Will Want To Advertise Your Referral Link, Like I Do.
3839	If You're Not Building Your Bank Account It Will Destroy Your Future
3840	Why Would Anyone Want To Share Their Secrets With The World
3841	Even Though It May Seem Like It Is I'm Not Suggesting You Legally Steal Money Online
3842	Did You Know That Large And Small Companies Are Willing To Pay You To Take Surveys, Participate In Online Focus Groups, Watch Movie Trailers, Go Shopping For Products And Even To Drive Your Car
3843	It's Time To Finally Take Control Of Your Life, Stop Answering To A Boss Who Only Wants You To Work As Hard As Possible To Make Him Look Good. Think About It - In This Tough Economy, Doesn't It Make Sense To Be In Charge Of Your Own Fortunes? I'm Betting You Know At Least One Person Who's Lost Their Job Through This Monster Recession ... Maybe You Even Lost Yours?
3844	This Powerful Book Touches The Heart And Soul Of Proven Fast Track Internet Marketing
3845	Contribute To Forums- One Of The Best Ways To Use Social Media In Your Favor Is To Make A Brief Contribution To Forums In Your Topic Of Interest. Include A Link To Your Website After Offering Incredibly Advice. However, Make Sure You Use Sparingly- Don't Spam.
3846	All The Big Internet Marketers Use An Automatic Income Formula That Convert
3847	Here Are Just A Few Areas That You'll Soon Be An Expert. Whatever Your Definition Of Financial Success, The Sharpest Minds In The Field Are Anxious To Teach You All They've Learned In Growing A Business.

3848	How Do I Reasonably Price The Solution To All Your Money Worries In A Time Of Economic Instability?
3849	Understand And Spot These Scams Before It's Too Late For Your Empty Pocketbook
3850	Do You Know How Valuable Your Realistic Potential Is In Making Money Online
3851	You're Almost Done – Activate Your Subscription! You've Just Been Sent An Email That Contains A Confirm Link. In Order To Activate Your Subscription, Check Your Email And Click On The Link In That Email. You Will Not Receive Your Subscription Until You Click That Link To Activate It. If You Don't See That Email In Your Inbox Shortly, Fill Out The Form Again To Have Another Copy Of It Sent To You.
3852	Do You Think The Checkout Which Was Surrounded With Displays Of Sweets And Magazines Leaving You Browsing Through Them, For The Next 5-7 Minutes Was Pure Accidental?
3853	What If Something So Simple Was Able To Provide You With A Reliable LIFELONG MONTHLY INCOME And It Was Backed By A DEBT FREE INC500 LISTED CORPORATION?
3854	This Past Weekend I Discovered How Telling A Story With A Happy Ending Could Also Make Me A Lot Of Money... With Other People's Products
3855	I'll Show You The Secrets To Online Success Starting Right Now, Not Weeks From Now, Not Even Days From Now, Not Even Tomorrow, But Right Now...
3856	What Does Your Perfect Job Look Like When You Find It
3857	Life In A Democracy Isn't Always Simple Nor Is Running An Online Business
3858	One Fateful Night In My Life Has Given Me A Chance To Affect Your Life In A Massive Way...To Possibly Alter The Course Of Your Life And Resurrect A Birthright.
3859	Build Generate And Celebrate Join Today For The Life You Deserve
3860	Suppose You're Promoting Somebody Else's Product, But That Person Decides Not To Sell It Anymore. What Happens To Your Income? That's Right, It Plunges Off A Cliff. You Ultimately Have Zero Control Over Your Income When You Don't Own What You're Selling.
3861	The One Thing I'm Doing This Year To Make More Money Than Years Past

3862	Join Risk Free Today And I Will Send You A Free Digital Copy Of The Exact Book That First Exposed Me To Success That Changed My Life. Simply Fill In Your First Name And Primary Email Address In The Form Below To Sign Up And You'll Be Forwarded To A Fully Secured Page Where You Can Complete Your Order And Get Started Right Now!
3863	Do You Realize How Much Each New Customer Is Really Worth To Your Business
3864	Did You Realized After It Was Too Late, That You Just Wasted More Time And Money On A Useless Scam?
3865	There Are A Number Of Ways You Can Shift Jobs And Responsibilities Onto Others. You Can Bring In A Partner, Hire Employees, Or Contract Out Jobs To Outside Companies, Consultants And Freelancers.
3866	Most Didn't Have A System Like This To Make Everything Faster, Easier And Practically Hands-Free.
3867	Now You Can Accurately Hit The Nail On The Marketing Head
3868	Figure Out If The Market You Have Selected Is Hot Or Not
3869	Life Isn't Tied With A Bow But It's Still A Gift
3870	You Can Take It For A Test Drive And Begin Making Money From Thousands Of Fresh, New, Unsaturated Niche Market Goldmines.
3871	The 5 Reasons Most People Fail And What You Can Do To Prevent It
3872	What Other Benefits Would You Get If You Got That Outcome
3873	The Problem With Having Clients Is That The Work Has To Be Customized. It Needs To Be Customized To Fit The Particular Needs Of The Client. I Was Still Able To Enjoy Some Of The Duplication And Rollout Benefits When My Direct Mail Packages Worked, But It's Just Not Quite The Same Thing As Having My Own Products That I Own And Control.
3874	And Even That's Just A Scratch On The Surface Of What I'll Reveal To You... You See, Most Of The Money Making Info You Find Online Has The Same Problem: They Don't Show You The Details. They Don't Show You The Things That You Really Need To Know.
3875	Want To Know How I Achieved The #1 Position On Google

3876	DISCLAIMER: Clickbank Is A Registered Trademark Of Keynetics Inc., A Delaware Corporation. (YOUR SITE NAME) Is Not Affiliated With Keynetics Inc. In Any Way, Nor Does Keynetics Inc. Sponsor Or Approve Any (YOUR SITE NAME) Product. Keynetics Inc. Expresses No Opinion As To The Correctness Of Any Of The Statements Made By (YOUR SITE NAME) In The Materials On This Web Page.
3877	All You Need To Do Is Enter Your Name And Email Address Below. If You Don't Know What An Autoresponder Is Or How To Use One, I Have A Video Series To Help You Get Set Up And You Can Use My Pre-Written Letters.
3878	The Crooks And Scammers Are Everywhere And They're Counting On You NOT Knowing Their Tricks!
3879	I Don't Know About You, But If Someone Walked Up And Said They Could Show Me The Way To Live A Life Of Limitless Success And Happiness And Only Asked Me For $1,500 I'd Jump On The Opportunity Faster Than A Rabid Wolverine Tearing Into A T-Bone.
3880	Greatest Gold-Mine Of Easy Things To Make Ever Crammed Into One Big Book
3881	There Will Be Higher Chances Your Article Post Will Be Pick Up Search Engines And Based On How Often You Post Your Blog Post.
3882	Here's What You're Going To Learn And Here's How It's Going To Help You
3883	Give Us 24-Hours And Get Ready To Dramatically Grow Your Business
3884	What Do I Need To Do To Get You To Finally Write Out Your Goals
3885	You'll Gain Incredible Knowledge Even If You Don't Want To Sell These Products
3886	Through Away Everything You Thought You Knew Or Learned About Internet Marketing
3887	7 Easy Steps To Doubling Your Profits By Next Month
3888	How To Be Sure Your Product Will Sell Before You Develop It
3889	You'll Be Really Glad You Did It Today Rather Than Tomorrow
3890	One Question That We Still Keep Getting On The Calls And In Support Is Something That Just Seems To Keep Plaguing People Over And Over Again. How Do I Find My Niche, And Know That It Will Be Something To Make Me Money. Finding Your Targeted Niche Seems To Be A Place Where The Majority Of The People Remain Stuck At.

281

3891	And, If You Don't Know How To Successfully Reap In The Rewards, The Time You Spend Will Feel Like A Big Waste And Leave You Even MORE Frustrated
3892	It's Crucial For Your Well Being To Remain Positive During This Economic Crisis
3893	This Takes Small Amount Of Time Which Will Never Interfere With Your Current Job, Another Business, Or Your Lifestyle.
3894	I Understand That By Submitting My Contact Information Below I Will Never Be Under Any Obligation To Purchase Anything, And that Once I Have Access To These Money Making Secrets They Are Mine To Keep Forever!
3895	Have You Ever Said It's Becoming Impossible To Make A Profit Online
3896	I Just Finished Up A Special Video Where I Recorded Myself Doing Some "Tricky" Search Engine Optimization Tactics On My Computer.
3897	Grab Your Prospects Attention In A Way That Forces Them To Excitedly Read Your Offer
3898	How To Get The Most From Your Free eBook Marketing Campaign
3899	I Understand That By Clicking The Link Below I Will Be Securing A Spot In An Incredibly Valuable And Insanely Profitable Opportunity NOW And Joining A Select And Lucky Few.
3900	P.S. If You're Still On The Fence, Here's An Easy Way To Decide If This Package Is Good For You. Take A Moment To Look Over Each Product Again, And Ask Yourself, How Can I Use The Product In My Business And How Much Money Can I Make Selling It...
3901	Discover 7 Brutally Effective, Secret Video Techniques That Literally Drag Viewers Away From YouTube & Straight Toward Your Website Every Single Time.
3902	How To Get Your Affiliate Marketing Business Off The Ground And Is Really Easy To Follow.
3903	Did That Hurt If It Didn't I Know Missing This Will
3904	Reading This Page Entitles You To Receive An Additional $100 Off. This Coupon Is Limited And May Not Be Available Next Time You Return To This Page. You Can Have Private Label Rights To In Demand Internet Marketing Training Courses That You Can Sell For 100% Profits.

3905	I'm Always Excited To Have The Opportunity To Meet New People And To Make New Friends.
3906	If Your Business Isn't Growing It's Time To Call It A Day
3907	It's Early Afternoon The Palm Trees Are Swaying And My Business Is Hard At Work Without Me
3908	Driving Traffic Is Getting Tougher Every Day. Search Engines Are More Competitive, And Pay Per Clicks Are More Expensive. Free Methods Stink With Links To Sites Nobody Ever Reads.
3909	It's First Come, First Served. That's The Only Fair Way I Can Do It. That's Why I CANNOT GUARANTEE I Can Hold YOUR Seat For Long. When The Registration Opens To The Public It's Going To Be CHAOS.
3910	Making List Building Faster And Easier Through Automation. It's How A No-Name Marketer Like Me Can Keep Up With The Gurus On That List.
3911	Start Experiencing All The Joys Of Life You Deserve! Hear Our Story And Discover The Truth! Simply Complete The Short Form To Watch our Amazing Movie And Get More Information Right Now!
3912	Plus Get The Whole Package Installed So You Can Save A Truckload Of Time & Money.
3913	No Nonsense Common Sense! We Guarantee That This Will Soon Become The New Standard And Others Will Be Panicking And Trying To Copy Our Deal Once They Discover The True Profit Potential This Has!
3914	There Are Worse Things Than Getting A Call For A Wrong Number At 4 AM. Like This; It Could Be A Right Number
3915	Do You Know What Your Plan Is For The Next 6-Months
3916	P.S. - When You Join With Us - You Will Receive Bonus' That Will Blow You Away. They Are Worth Far More Than The Price To Join. Frankly - We Think You Might Be A Little Nutty If You Didn't Take Us Up On It? Seriously - It's That GOOD!
3917	Use These Money Principles To Leverage Your Way Into Financial Security
3918	Something Great Is About To Happen So Don't You Miss Out
3919	What Do You Do When All The So Called Tricks And Techniques Don't Work For You
3920	If You Have Been Searching For The Solution To Your Financial Troubles And You Are Seriously Looking For That Golden Opportunity To Help You Get Your Life Back On Track You Need Look No Further.

3921	People Buy On Emotions And Then Justify Their Purchases With Logic. So The Main Goal Of Your Sales Copy Should Be To Trigger The Emotions Of Your Prospects And Make Them Buy!
3922	Without Skills How Do You Think You'll Improve Your Quality Of Life
3923	It's A Truism In Marketing That There's No Point In Re-Inventing The Wheel. You Can Knock Yourself Out Trying To Convince People To Buy Something Totally New In A Market Where No Money Is Being Spent...Or You Can Stick To The Well-Worn Paths And Make Money.
3924	Important: In Order To Protect Your Privacy, You Will First Receive An Email With A Confirmation Link -- You Must Click On That Link In Order To Receive Your Download Link.
3925	Develop Tiered Packages Or Memberships That Offer Different Content For The Different Tiers.
3926	Here's How You Make Money With This Amazing Viral Marketing System
3927	I'm Always Looking For The Next Best Deal - Are You
3928	So Here's The Deal. We Take Care Of The Tough Part ... Deliver Thousands Of Potential Customers To Your Site And You Convert Them Into Sales.
3929	Once You Know Who You Are Going To Market To, You Need To Make High-Value Products That They Will Want To Buy. However, It's Not Obvious How To Do This Right, Which Is Why I Outline Exactly What To Do.
3930	How To Double And Even Triple The Number Of Credits For The Same Price As The Average Surfers Pays (This Is What I Do When I Want An Instant Boost In Traffic And Don't Want To Pay List Price.)
3931	You Will Also Learn How To Automate The Sales Process So That Your Customer Is Taken To The Download Page After They Have Made A Purchase.
3932	Financial Security Peace Of Mind And A Sense Of Self Worth That Money Can't Buy
3933	Not Only Increases Your Website Traffic, It Also Greatly Enhances The Placement Of Your Website Listing In Most Of The Major Search Engines.

3934	Each One Shares With You Their Piece Of The Puzzle That Will Change Your Life. But We Must Warn You, The Breakthroughs Revealed Are So Awesome, You May Not Be Able To Sleep After Hearing Them. Your Success Programming Will Be So Unrelenting In Wanting To Take Action.
3935	Those Who Have A Dream Of Earning A Lot Of Money From Their Internet Business Would Be Well Advised To Get 'Action Headlines" Immediately And To Start Using It Right Away.
3936	If You Knew Your Website Was Dying A Painful Death Would Continue Business As Usual
3937	They No Longer Laugh When I Say This System Will Make Anyone Wealthy
3938	P.S. Jump Start On The Model That Has Proven Time And Time Again To Generate Profits And Do It In A Simple Way And By Avoiding All The Technical Hurdles And Learning Required.
3939	Secrets To Skyrocketing Conversions Straight From The Lab, Testing, Then Targeting Products That Convert Like Gangbusters. This Is One Of My Most Sneaky Techniques I've Never Talked About Until Now.
3940	If You Are An Entrepreneur In Business For Yourself, You'll Need To Start Out By Doing All The Work Yourself. And Maybe You Will Charge By The Hour. Nothing Wrong With That.
3941	An Alarming Number Of Your Subscribers Never Receive Your Messages ... And Few Of Those Who Get Them Actually Read Them! Here Are My 24 Closely Guarded Secrets For Getting Your Subscribers To Read And Respond To Every Mailing You Send To Them!
3942	Is Your Web Site Experiencing The Same Success As The Bird Flu Epidemic
3943	7 Ways To Instantly Get More Back From Every Promotion
3944	If You Want To Know Why I And My Associates Are Not Concerned About The Economy, How We Are Protecting Ourselves Against The Downturn, And How You Can Do The Same, Go Watch This Video Right Away...
3945	If You Give Away The System According To The Plan That We Provide You With, You Can Earn More Money Than You've Ever Dreamed Possible.
3946	Access A Superstar Cast Of Experts With A Just One Click
3947	Just Think Of What Kind Of Life You Could Have If You Had All The Cash You Needed!
3948	Buy All The Other Tools Out There Then Come Back To Us

3949	Do You Live From Paycheck To Paycheck? Are You Able To Do The Things That Make You Happy? Maybe You Don't Mind Your Job. Heck It Pays The Bills! You Go In, You Put In Your Time And You Get Paid.
3950	If I Describe It In Detail You Probably Wouldn't Believe It
3951	With Our Money Back Guarantee You Really Have Nothing To Lose! Don't Hesitate, Get Started NOW And Take Your First Steps Towards Increasing Your Advertising Revenue!
3952	You Will Discover A Surprisingly Easy Way To Create Up Front Income With No Additional Work Just Surfing To Build Your Business. You Will Be Getting Paid Even Before Anyone Joins Your Primary Business!
3953	When You're Building Lists Of Subscribers On Autopilot, Money Happens Fast. And Once The Bills Are Caught Up, The Debt Is Gone, And You've Taken A Much Needed Vacation Or Two...
3954	No Matter What Your Product Or Service, Chances Are High You'll Find Online Publications That Already Have Subscribers Who Will Fit Your Niche Or Target Audience... And The Right Ad To That Audience Brings The Traffic Stampede!
3955	Google Adsense And Adwords That Will Build Or Destroy All Your Time And Money
3956	As Long As They Can Keep You In The Dark, They'll Be Able To "Push Your Buttons" And Get Money From You... Just Like You Were Their Own Personal ATM Machine!
3957	I Can Hear You Voicing Your Doubts Now. "Gee, I'm About Ready To Pee Myself I'm So Excited About This Opportunity To Join! But I'm Also Scared And Skeptical Because I've Been Ripped Off So Many Times Before Online.
3958	Swipe Files Are Also Commonly Used By Internet Marketers Who Need To Gather A Lot Of Resources Not Only About Products But Also About Marketing Methods And Strategies.
3959	It's Such A Cliché...But Sometimes, It's Inescapable. You Need To Read All Of This And Save A Few Minutes To Digest Because What You're About To Discover Is Absolutely Critical And Mind-Glowingly Powerful.
3960	Become DEBT FREE. Say Goodbye Forever To Those Nasty Bill Collectors. Banks Will Be Fighting For Your Business.
3961	Grab New Opt-Ins By The Hand And Lead Them Straight To The Confirmation Link Before They Can Even Think About Changing Their Minds Or Blowing It Off...

3962	Choose Good Keyword Phrases Instead Of Shaping Words Around Articles, Shape Articles Around Words. Target Your Content Around Keywords Or Ideas. In Order To Find An Angle For Your Article, Consider Using Google Adwords To See Which Keywords Are Most Likely Searched.
3963	This Story, All By Itself Is Worth Ten Years Worth Of Subscriptions To This Private Club. He Tells You Everything, And Will Give You The Knowledge And Tools To Replicate What He Did For Yourself!
3964	Think About It - Whether You Sell Ad Space, Products, Or Develop A Proprietary Technology That You Can Charge A Fee For, Membership Marketing Is A Source Of Tremendous Revenue And It's Just Waiting For You To Tap Into…
3965	I See So Many Newbies Failing Because Of The Lack Of Resources To Pull This Kind Of "Super Affiliate" Trick Off. You've Given The Little Guy The Big Guy's Toys.
3966	Increase Conversions By At Least 75% While You Sleep While Our Proven System Does The Work
3967	Adding Value Done Correctly 1. At Least 80% Of The Marketing Sites I Visit Are Destroying Their Sales By Adding Value To Their Products Incorrectly. Gain This Insight And Stop It Before It Happens To A Product You've Just Put Your All Into Creating.
3968	Life's Going To Suck If You Don't Know What You Want
3969	Are You Creating Websites That Focus On The Flash And Not The Cash
3970	What Would Happen If You Couldn't Stop Making Money Online Even If You Wanted To
3971	How To Create The Simplest Website You've Ever Seen…And Still Sell A Ton. You Don't Necessarily Need A Site Of Your Own For Some Of The Methods I'll Show You; But If You Do, You Can Create A Site With Just A Few Pages (Maybe Only ONE) And Outsell The "Big Dogs" Who Waste Millions On Sites That Under Perform. I'll Even Give You Some Easy-To-Follow Examples Of My Own Sites You Can Copy…Um…"Borrow".
3972	One Simple Trick Forcing Your Web Site To Appear Professional Looking
3973	This Service Will Deliver Highly Targeted Visitors To Your Store Front Through Our Own Marketing Efforts. You Don't Have To Promote Or Display Our Ads On Your Web Pages, To Make Automatic Income Through Us.

3974	When I First Put My Ebook Online, My Goal Was Just To Make A Few Extra Bucks! I Had No Clue You Could Make A Full Time Living Selling Ebooks On The Internet.
3975	If It Works For All Of Us It Will Work For You
3976	If You Would Like To Dominate Your Niche With Prospects And Sponsor More People Than You Ever Thought Imaginable Then You Owe It To Yourself To Get Your Hands On This Video Interview.
3977	The Internet Boom And Virtual Property Values Are Now Sky-rocketing Every Day
3978	7 Insider Tips For Successful Ezine Advertising
3979	We Are Truly Confident In Our Product And We Know You Are Going To Be Elated By The Results It Brings To Your Web-site. That's Why We Are Going To Let You Try It Out For 30 Days, Risk-Free.
3980	How To Cram 8 Hours Of Classroom Computer Training Into One Easy 75-Minute Session
3981	So, I Will Not Be Doing Any Favor By Getting The Sales For You...I Will Only Be Helping Myself...As Simple As That!!
3982	This Is Not Some Long-Winded And Complicated 200 Page Ebook. It's A Short And Straight-To-The-Point, Simple But Very Powerful Money Making System... That Will Make You A Lot Of Money, Very Quickly... Once I Show You How.
3983	Now It's Your Time To Grab A Huge Piece Of The Internet Pie
3984	This Brand New Video Series Will Show You A More In Depth View Of The Features That Cpanel Provides And Shows You How You Can Take Your Website To The Next Level As Well As Protect Your Business.
3985	Envy Is A Waste Of Time Because You Already Have All You Need
3986	Want To Swipe This Automated System To Generate A Com-fortable Income From Home
3987	If You Want A EZ Step By Step Income Making Site Try This Out ASAP
3988	When You Upgrade Your Membership Today, You Get All The 5 Power Components Fused Together With The 10 Video Squeeze Pages You've Just Signed Up For. This Will In Effect, Create An All-In-One Mega Affiliate Business.
3989	You Know – There's Something I Hear A Lot Of, Which Is, "Making Money Online Is Hard" Or "Succeeding Online Isn't Possible Anymore."

288

3990	Yes, The Money Comes In While You're Sleeping, While You're Attending Your Kid's Soccer Game, While You're Shopping Or Away On A Deluxe Vacation! Discover Exactly How YOU Can Do This For Yourself!
3991	Know How To Leverage Your Launch And Build Momentum Into A Deep Frenzy
3992	Bonuses Done Right. Everyone Offers Bonuses For Their Products Nowadays, But I Can Tell You Right Now That At Least Half Of Them Are Devaluing Their Products By Doing So. I'll Show You Why I Know This Is The Case, And How You Can Avoid It Negatively Effecting Your Sales.
3993	Look It's All About Giving You Something Of Value For Free In Order To Gain Your Trust
3994	Everyone Has To Start Somewhere But It Doesn't Have To Be All That Difficult To Get Started
3995	It Was The Best Of Times It Was The Worst Of Times
3996	Start Putting Responsibilities On Someone Else's Shoulders. Make Someone Else Responsible For Doing A Job From Start To Finish. See If That Person Can Do It. If He Can Or She Can, Then That's One Part Of The Business You Won't Have To Worry About.
3997	If You Have The Desire To Build Your Own List, We Will Provide The Rest. To Get Your Free (Product) Account You Need To Show Me Your Commitment By Placing Your Details Into The Form Below.
3998	Here's Exactly How To Get Hundreds, Even Thousands Of Websites Working For You Advertising And Selling Your Product And You Only Pay Them Once They Make A Sale. This Is The Holy Grail Of Traffic Generation!
3999	Stop Thinking That Your "Time Equals Money" If You Would Like To Build An Income Generating Machine That Can Earn You $10,000 An Hour Or More. Instead Of Thinking How Much Your Time Is Worth, Start Thinking "How Much Value Am I Creating?"
4000	Believe Me, I'm No Workaholic And My Monthly Earnings Average Is Far Greater Than Standard.
4001	How Would You Like To Get The Other Two For A Discount
4002	Going Insane Over Losing Your Data Due To An Unexpected Crash Infection Or Virus
4003	How To Test New Ideas And Get Paid To Do Market Research

289

4004	There Are Problems With Your Computer's Security That Regularly Goes Unnoticed. This Can Be Achieved Easily By A Good Hacker. The Problem Is, By The Time You Know Someone Has Entered Your System It Could Be Too Late.
4005	Our Brains Are Used To Doing And Thinking About Things In A Certain Way. We're Used To Having A Boss Breathing Down Our Neck, No Matter How Much We Hate It. So When You Try To Make The Transition Into An Entrepreneur, You Feel Lost. Because It's Just You, All Alone, Hammering Out At Your Computer For Hours On End. But As A Coach Or Consultant, You Get The Best Of All Worlds.
4006	If You Are A Complete Beginner, It Can Be Very Difficult (Even Using Templates) To Get An Attractive Website In Place. And Hiring A Professional To Do It For You Is Out Of The Budget For Most People. But, With Affiliate Marketing, You Don't Need To Build A Website! You Simply Send Visitors To Someone Else's Professionally Designed Site Through Your Affiliate Link.
4007	Automate Your Own Gold Mine With Buyers More Likely To Buy Again And Again
4008	If You're Not Using Facebook Marketing To Drive Traffic And Sales To Your Websites You're Missing Out On A Huge Opportunity. Shockingly, Most People Don't Even Know How Easy (And Free!) It Is To Start Making Money From Facebook Marketing Today.
4009	The Absolute Quickest, Single Method To Grow Your Business At Blazing Speeds (Hint; Your Leaders Do This Technique Daily, But Never Talk About It).
4010	Looking For Effective And Affordable Ways To Drive Massive Traffic To Your Sites
4011	The Answer For Me Was Very Clear....We Find A Way To Get It Done...And Reap The Rewards Well Into The Future!
4012	No Experience, $0 To Start With? Not A Problem. This Package Was Designed To Work For Everyone Who Tries It, You Don't Have To Be An Expert!
4013	The World Is Your Market! (Unlike Most Offline Businesses Where Customers Come Only From The Neighborhood).
4014	Get In The Game And Start Learning, Trying, And Doing Things! You'll Never Make Money Online Sitting There Wishing You Could Make Money. Wishing And Hoping Doesn't Do It!

4015	I Wanted You To See This. I Think The Strategy They're Using To Launch Is Very Smart, I Wish I Can Do The Same! Right Now, It's At The Pre-Launch Where It'll Allow Anyone To Signup For Free.
4016	You Could Use These Persuasive Trigger Words, Phrases, And Action Headlines In Your Sales Copy, Offers, Blogs, Email Marketing, Web Sites, Newsletters, Etc. The Uses Are Absolutely Endless, Timeless, And Amazingly Powerful
4017	If Words Have Little Effect In Marketing Consider Including The Second Longest Word In Your Next Header: HEPATICO-CHOLANGIOCHOLECYSTENTEROSTOMIES And See What Happens.
4018	Which Team Will You Be On? After This, The Field Will Split And Be Divided Into Two Totally Separate Marketing Factions: On One Side, You Have A Team Of Elite Marketers Who Wield The Midas Touch To Generate Money At Will. On The Other, A Team Of Less Than Average Merely Mediocre 'Biz Opportun-ists."
4019	I'm Not Joking - Here's The Secret To Success - The More Sales Pages You Have Out There The More Money You'll Make.
4020	This Was A Real Revelation To Me, And Pretty Soon I Was Making Money. Just A Little At First, As I Experimented, Try-ing To Find Different Ways Of Working. And Not Long After That I Was Making Serious Money... Money Where I Didn't Ever Have To Worry, Or Watch My Spending... Enough Money To Never Ever Work Some Crappy Day Job Ever Again.
4021	Now You Can Own The LARGEST COLLECTION Of Marketing Firepower Ever Known To Mankind, The Same Firepower Used To Create Incredible Irresistible Offers That Helped Mil-lionaires Fill The Vault Of Their Dreams.
4022	Persuade Your Web Site Visitors To Give You Their Email Ad-dress
4023	7 Sure-Fire Ways To Make Money With Joint Ventures
4024	And Doing It At Your Own Pace, At Your Own Place... And You'll Finally Feel Passionate About What You Do.
4025	I'm So Confident This Can Change Your Life, I Want You To Invest In This Right Now Without Having To Think So Hard. However I Can't Price This So Low Forever So...

4026	Earlier This Week, I Let You In On A Really Cool Shortcut That Can Help You Add The Profit-Producing Power Of 3-4 Employees To Your Business Right Now Without Hiring ONE Single Person. If You Missed It, Find Out More Here.
4027	Warning; Use At Your Own Risk Blackhat Tactics That May Get You Banned
4028	There Are People For You And Those That Are With You
4029	These Step-By-Step Setup Videos Contain Information And Training On How To Set Up Your Hosting Account, Register Domain Names, Using Ftp, Installing Pop-Ups, Dealing With Clickbank, Creating Sales Letters And Thank You Pages, Inserting Paypal And 2Checkout Buttons, Dealing With Zip And PDF Files And Many More!
4030	Someone Out There Has The Secrets That Can Make It Happen For You
4031	How To Protect Your Product And Yourself Against Charge-back's, Refunds And Worse!
4032	Why Your Competition Will Be Covering In Fear While You Continue To Earn Vast Fortunes
4033	This Can Be Your Chance To Set Your Own Schedule & Work Whenever You Want To – You Can Work As Much As You Want Or As Little As You Need!
4034	If You're Looking For Time Tested And Proven eBook Software, Which You Don't Have To Be A Rocket Scientist To Use... You're In The Right Place! Find Out Why THOUSANDS Of People, All Over The World Choose This For Their eBook Publishing Needs.
4035	One Of The Most Important Internet Marketing Steps You Can Take
4036	Mostly What I'm Doing Is Creating And Marketing My Own Products And Programs. What I Sell Now Are My Books, Seminars And Coaching Programs That Are Aimed At Showing Entrepreneurs How To Improve Their Marketing -- How To Use Modern 21st Century Marketing Methods To Take Their Businesses To The Next Level.
4037	P.S. I Reserve The Right To Take This Offer Down At Any Time. I've Truly Put Myself On The Line With Some Of The Sneaky Methods I've Divulged This Time.
4038	You Give 100 Percent In The 1st Half And If That Isn't Enough In The 2nd Half You Give What's Left.
4039	Links Inside A Duplicate Content Article Don't Hold The Same Benefit As A Link Inside A Unique Article.

4040	This Amazing Website Sells Itself! All You Have To Do Is Expose People To Your Very Own Site Exactly Like This One And You Will Start To See A Steady Stream Of Income.
4041	Exactly What You Need In Order To Get On The Fast, Exciting And Extremely Profitable Road To Affiliate Success!
4042	Money Is Only A Big Deal When You Don't Have Enough Of It
4043	You See With 'Web 2.0' The Next Generation Of The Internet Allowing More And More User Generated Content It Has Never Been Easier For Savvy 'In The Know' Web Users To Get Free Web Traffic From The Big Search Engines.
4044	The One Thing You Must Do In Order To Make Your Prospect Trust You
4045	How To Survey Your List, So They Sell Themselves On Your Product Before You Even Create It! Grab The Quick Start Action Guide Outlining The Most Important Steps In An Easy-To-Follow Surveying Formats.
4046	We're Going To Put An End To Your Endless Frustration Over Getting Traffic...No Longer Will You Have To Worry About Losing Traffic To Your Competitors. No More Spending Thousands On Useless Learning Materials. No More Wasted Cash On Ineffective Advertising. And No More Hassle And Technical Barriers To Getting The Money You Need To Live The Life You've Been Dreaming Of.
4047	In Fact, By Accepting This Invitation You Are Already Building Your Professional Network And Establishing Yourself As A Trusted Source In The Community. In Addition, You'll Have Access To Easy-To-Use Tools To Attract More Customers.
4048	If The Money Is in The List Why Do So Many People Find It Difficult To Build One
4049	Online Success Really Boils Down To Quality A Product Plus Traffic Equals Sales
4050	4 Article Directories That Will Get You The Most Traffic. There Are Tons Of Article Directories, But Most Of Them Are Useless. So You Should Focus On The Ones That Give You The Best Results. And These 4 Are The Best Among The Rest.
4051	Take These 10 Defensive Measures And You'll Save Way More Than $600
4052	By Now You Should Understand That Affiliate Marketing On The Internet Is Hands Down The Fastest (And Easiest) Way To Earn Honest Money These Days.

4053	P.S. I Want To See You Get The Best Bargain For Your Money, But I Can Only Offer This Low Price For Those Who Are Serious Enough To Take Immediate Action.
4054	Break Even On The Front End Then Profit On The Back End
4055	Be Ready With Material As Talking Points When The Media Or Your Clients Call You.
4056	Let's Not Beat Around The Bush...You Need To Do This. Well This May Be The Best News You've Had All Year And It's On The House.
4057	And After You Will Be Billed The Low Rate Of $97 Month
4058	How Sympathy For An Underdog Instantly Created A Pit Bull Out Of Their Website
4059	Take A Sneak Peak At Successful Marketing From Sea To Shinning Sea
4060	I'm Willing To Work With People Who Are Ready To Take Fate Into Their Own Hands And That Can Honestly Say That They Are Ready To Stop Jumping From One Opportunity To The Next.
4061	Internet Marketing Is A Reality That Is Only Going To Get Bigger And Bigger
4062	The Real Secrets Of How To Build A Responsive List And How Giving Away Freebies Can Double Your Income - Get This Right And You're Going To Blow Away The Competition But Get It Wrong And You'll Be Down And Out Before It's Even Begun.
4063	All These Business Opportunities Looked Like The Exact Thing I Needed - Lots Of Pictures Of Cheesy Guys Leaning On Sports Cars Outside Their Mansions... And More Importantly, They Promised Boatloads Of Cash... Fast. So I Bought It - And Boy, It Wasn't Cheap. Unfortunately It Turned Out To Be Hogwash.
4064	With The Ever Rising Commercial Nature Of The Internet, You Need Something To Stand Out From The Crowd To Build A Subscriber List. Your Visitors Expect To Be Sold Now. They Know The Proverbial "Pitch" Is Coming. That's Why You Need To Give Them Something Of Extremely High "Perceived Value" To Sign-Up For Your Mailing List.
4065	I Don't Have To Convince You How Challenging Creating Your Own Product Is. To Begin With, It Can Take Days, Weeks Or Even Months (Depending On Your Writing Skills) Before You Finally Complete Your First Info Product.

4066	I Wanted To Share What May Seem Like A Little Thing That Can Make A Big Difference In Your Life And In The Life Of Every Person You Know. This Secret To Happiness And Success May Seem Too Simple To Feel Important, But If You Can Truly Understand Its Power, T Can Change Your Life Forever.
4067	This Quick And Easy Guide To Writing Winning Copy Is Presented In Clear Language And Broken Down Into Super-Simple Steps Anybody Can Follow.
4068	Give Up The Impulses Your Have To Quit And Move On
4069	I'm Not Sure How You Found This Letter Today -- Perhaps You Arrived By Referral From A Friend -- Or Perhaps You Are Simply Tired Of The Barriers That Prevent Your Online Success...
4070	Use Your Content As A Promotional Tool For Your Affiliates In A PDF Format.
4071	It Seems Incredible That You Can Offer These Signed Original Etchings
4072	Step By Step Videos Showing You Exactly How To Set Up Your Website To Sell Your Products And Be Able To Automatically Download The Products To Your Hungry Customers.
4073	Now You Can Profit From The Number One Profit Generating Business Online
4074	What's The One Things That You Think Will Get You There The Fastest
4075	You Don't Need To Know Anything About Digital Cameras Or Photography To Make Money With This System, As I Am Prepared To Teach You Exactly What You Need To Do In Order To Get Started Right Away.
4076	And Believe Me That's Exactly What Will Happen I Know Because I've Been There
4077	Did You Know Most Lead Generation Sites Aren't Generating Leads At All? Their Value Adding Attempts To Attract New Subscribers And Promotion Resources Are Failing Miserably, However, The Worst Thing About This Is That Short Term Ad Tracking Won't Tell Them The Full Story. Learn It Here First And Get Streets Ahead Of The Competition And A Bunch Of New Free Promotion Outlets For Your Business At The Same Time.
4078	Here Is A Way To View The Marketing World With Fresh Eyes
4079	What Other People Think Of You Is None Of Your Business

4080	A Picture Is Worth A Thousand Words, Especially On The Net. Putting Alt Attributes On Your Images Can Allow You To Place Relevant Text Around Your Image, Better For Search Engine Indexing. Keep In Mind That Images Are Searched Just As Much As Content Is.
4081	Our Program Pays A Whopping 70% Commission And Converts Like Crazy
4082	But Nothing I Can Say Will Even Begin To Do These Secrets Justice. You Must Go Now IF You Are Ready To Change Your Life.
4083	It's Amazing How Increased Sales Just Got Easier Without You Having To Find Them
4084	The Different Ways You Can Use And Make Money With Resell Rights Product. You'll Discover Some Cool Ways To Make The Most Out Of Resell Rights Products.
4085	A Whole New World Is About To Open Up Changing Lives
4086	Develop A Social Networking Site Discussing Topics Relevant To Your Niche.
4087	As I Mentioned In Our Email Conversation, I'd Like To Ask You A Few Questions To See If What I Have Can Be Of Help To You! What Is The Biggest Problem, Challenge, Or Roadblock You Are Currently Having? -- What Are Some Of The Problems That Those Roadblocks Are Causing? -- What Is The Ideal Outcome Or Result You'd Like To Achieve? -- What Would Solving That Do For You? -- Based Upon What You Just Told Me, The Next Step Is To Join My 90-Day Coaching Program.
4088	How To BAIT The Search Engines In To Ranking You High For VERY Specific Keywords That Will Get You LOADS Of Visitors To Your Webpages.
4089	They Don't Know Where To Turn, And Have No Idea How To Properly Promote Their Site Without Getting Ripped Off And Going Broke. They Buy Banner Ads, Pay Per Click Advertising, Run Ads In The Local Newspaper.
4090	Just Use Your First Name And Valid Email As Your Password - The Click The "Free Instant Access" Button To Enter. (Use The Same Password When Returning. All Information Kept 100% Confidential). All The Next Page A Few Seconds To Load!

4091	You Won't Find A More Complete, Better Structured, Clearer Step-By-Step Guide Than This One For The Price, But In Any Case, You Can Try It For A Full 60 Days And If You Are Not Completely Satisfied With It For Any Reason, Just Contact Me And I'll Refund 100% Of Your Money On The Spot.
4092	Either Way The Choice Is Yours. You Know What To Do. What's The Worst Thing That Could Happen Anyway? It's 100% FREE - You Have Nothing To Lose.
4093	How Hypnotic Language In Your Ad Always Gives You The Selling Advantage
4094	Mess Up Your Tax Return Here are 4 Excuses That Work With The IRS
4095	Do You Really Think The Gurus Are Going To Tell You Their Secrets? Why Would They? They Make Too Much Money Keeping You In The Dark.
4096	If You Aren't Building Lists And Making Money With My System, Then I Don't Want Any Of Yours. I'll Take ALL The Risk, So You Can Feel Comfortable And Confident About Your Choice.
4097	If You Have Ever Been Bamboozled By How Some Affiliates Seems To Effortlessly Rake In Thousands Of Dollars Whilst Most Others Fail To Earn A Single Cent... Then Come Close And Read Every Single Word Of This Letter...
4098	Making Money Online Can Be Like A Juicy Banana Split With Whip Cream Nuts And Cherries
4099	You Are Confirmed And Will Now Be Receiving Membership Notifications For Free Access
4100	For The First Time, New Breakthrough System Reveals How To Increase Conversions By At Least 75%
4101	Money Can Buys A Heck Of An Education And You Need As Much As Possible. Thousands Of Highly Targeted Visitors If You Can Get Them. The More, The Better. You Want Your Servers Straining To Keep Up, And You Want Your Traffic Stats To Look Like Telephone Numbers...
4102	Put Your Affiliate Link On Your Website And Encourage People To Click Through. This Will Act As Another Multiple Income Stream And Enable You To Earn More Money Online On Autopilot.
4103	What Are You Waiting For Now Is The Time To Take That Next Step

4104	Knowing The Business Definition Of "Luck" Can Mean The Difference Between Success And Failure. For Those That Don't Know, "LUCK" In The Business World Can Be Defined As The Place Where Ability And Opportunity Meet.
4105	Eliminate Months Of Failure By Using These Simple Yet Productive Tactics
4106	How Would You Feel If Your Affiliate Commissions Were Stolen By Hijackers
4107	Don't Want To Work Hard But Still Want Money Handed To You On A Silver Platter
4108	How To Connect To Your Audience On A Deeper More Personal Level And Strike It Rich
4109	In Just 3 Minutes You Can Start Sucking Cash Into Your Bank Account And Building A Huge, Profitable List Of Eager And Rabid Customers That Will Make And Keep You Prosperous For Months And Years To Come.
4110	Your Company Would Not Bat An Eye To Pay You That Kind Of Money If It Was Convinced Your New Idea, Or Method, Invention Or Product Was Really Worth That To The Company. Your Company Could Not Wait To Get The Check Book Out And Write You A Check Before You Sold Your Idea To A Competitor.
4111	Is Your Web Site In Danger Of Being Sabotaged By Your Own Customers
4112	Test Tweak And Perfect This Secret To Double And Even Triple Your Sales
4113	Discover A New Approach To List Building That Will Create Hungry Prospects Eager To Receive Your Mail, While Exploding Your Profits And Results Through The Roof.
4114	What's Your Unique Marketing Hook And How Can You Exploit It To The Max
4115	Napoleon Hill Told The "Secret" To Ultimate Success Way Back In 1937's "Think And Grow Rich."
4116	Shine Through- Let Your Voice And Your Personality Shine Through The Pages. Speak Like You Are Talking. Be Funny, Be Creative And Be Witty. Let That Voice Out And Paste It All Over The Pages Of Your Content.
4117	This Is A Very Practical Guide That Reveals Many Workable Ideas To Make An Additional $100-$200 In A Week, Or Even More. A Father Made $5,000.00 In 2 Months Using Its Methods.
4118	My Financial Future Is Finally Changing Upward Where I Want It To Be

298

4119	Imagine Having Everything You Need At Your Fingertips To Create An Incredible "Real" Sustainable Internet Business From Home - With A Personal Coach Helping You Every Step Of The Way...(Sound Exciting?)
4120	This Is Your Chance To Join The Most Exclusive Club Of Entrepreneurs On The Internet Today! A Team Of Likeminded People 100% Dedicated To Assisting Each Other In Achieving REAL Success.
4121	If You're Tired Of Setting Up Sites And Then Spending Every Waking Hour Promoting Them And Hoping They Get Traffic, This Is Definitely For You. Get Over There Now, And Check It Out There Are Some Killer Bonuses For The First Guys Through The Doors. You'll Be Insane To Miss Them.
4122	You Are Getting A Full International Master Resale Rights To These Products So You Can Sell Them On Again And Again For Vast Profits.
4123	Our Goal Is To Help You Create A 4-17 Hour Work Week
4124	You've Heard "The Money Is In The List." In Fact, Every Marketing Expert In The World Emphasizes The Importance Of Building An Opt-In List. The Power Of An Opt-In List Is That It Is A Resource You Can Tap Again And Again.
4125	How I Grabbed The #1 Position On Google Yahoo And AOL
4126	Create A Life Dripping With Success And Prosperity. Once You Truly Put These Methods Into Action You Won't Even Have To Be "Working" And Money And Prosperity Will Be Naturally Drawn To You With Little Effort. The Cold Hard Truth Is That You've Just Discovered The Solution To Resolve Your Financial Worries Forever.
4127	Access Our Private Collection Of Over 49.000 Unique Eye Catching Money-Making Trigger Phrases And Action Headlines And Never Run Out Of New And Eye Catching Ideas For Your Headlines, Ad, Sales Copy, Email, Or Product Promotions.
4128	Would You Write A Testimonial If I Gave This To You For Free
4129	This Will Completely Change The Way You Think About Money Forever
4130	How Are Your Going To Live The Rest Of Your Life
4131	If You Were Truly Happy With Your Income And Your Business... What Drew You To This Website? I'll Tell You What... You're NOT Satisfied With Your Program Or Your Income...

4132	Once In A "Blue-Moon", You Will Be Afforded An Opportunity To Join A Program That Is Created To Provide An Equal And Fair Opportunity For All Members To Reap Significant Rewards Via Team Building, Profit Sharing And Advertising.
4133	I Hope I Have Made It Abundantly Clear That I Do Not Advocate Plagiarism In Any Way, Shape, Or Form And I'm Confident That You Agree With This Sentiment 100%. Especially Now That You Know Just How Powerful The Act Of Leveraging Others' Expertise Can Truly Be.
4134	Exclusive Video Training! We've Been Adding Videos That Show You Step By Step How To Use And Make More Money From The Sites You Have Access To. If You Haven't Joined Yet...You Are Going To Be Missing Out Big Time This Year.
4135	While Most Americans Are Now Hurting For Extra Cash ... Our Affiliates Are Still Living The Good Life With Cash To Spare And That Trends Show No Sign Of Slowing!
4136	The First Step Of Your Financial Freedom Journey Is Knowing Exactly Where Your Money Goes
4137	How To Avoid Information Overload And Lack Of Motivation - Is Information Overload Stopping You From Making Money? This Chapter And Video Will Help You Deal With This Problem So You Can Take A Deep Breath And Finally Say "I Get How This Whole Thing Works" Then Take Action And Generate Some Revenue.
4138	How To Capture The Attention Of Unlimited Customers For Any Online Business You Create
4139	Leverage Their Reputations Contacts Products And Services While Making A Ton Of Money
4140	After Months Of Frustration And Failure, A Friend Explained To Me That I Was Missing The Boat Without A List And I Finally Decided To Devote All My Time & Energy To Building My Own Cash-Cranking Opt-In List.
4141	Use Keywords- Keywords Are Searched Words- Words That Will Get Your Article Noticed On Search Engines. Make Your Keywords Specific And Use Them About 2-5% In Each Article. Any More Than This And Your Article Could Begin To Sound Like An Advertisement, Or You Could Be Black Listed.
4142	How To Build A Profitable Database And Capitalize On Any Targeted Niche Market
4143	It's The Most Appealing And Profitable Solution I've Ever Seen Anywhere!

4144	Unfortunately There Is A Lot Of Hogwash Out There. Many People Attempt To Use Article Marketing And Simply Write About Anything And Everything. Not A Good Idea. Write Something Entertaining, Write Something Informative And Write Something Worth Reading.
4145	The Key To Successful Affiliate Programs That 99% Of Marketers Don't Do
4146	Rewrite Your Content As A Press Release.
4147	Willing To Invest 5 Cents A Day In Your Online Business
4148	When You Think About Your Own Product What Comes To Mind
4149	Build A Successful Business By Staying Connected Cross Promote Online For Maximum Profits
4150	The Rules For Affiliate Success... The Exact Rules That Will Govern All Your Profits, And If You Don't Make Money, It's Because You Broke A Rule. Simple.
4151	Opportunity Where Timing, Knowledge And Intention Would Meet Up With The Perfect Product To Create The Prime Opportunity For Us Each To Achieve Our Dream.
4152	How To Set Up Your 'Traffic Generation' Methods And PPC Campaigns So Your Hard Earned Money Isn't At Risk... This Could Save You From Loosing Money On Advertising. I Even Show You Some Cool Ways To Get Free Traffic
4153	If You're Still Jumping From Program To Program Re Building It Every Single Time And Still Do Not Have An Active Team Nor A Supportive Mentor We Welcome You To Join Our Community. The Potential Is Unlimited!
4154	You'll Soon Understand Why This Offer Must Be Classified As Time Sensitive
4155	Awesome - What More Can I Say? Use This Exact Strategy And Drive More Traffic To Your Membership Website As One More Powerful Tool In Your Arsenal.
4156	You Never Know When It Will Strike, But There Comes A Moment At Work When You Know That You Just Aren't Going To Do Anything Productive For The Rest Of The Day.
4157	The Difference Between A Pup And A Wolf Is The Way They Act When They Get Hungry
4158	If You Do What Every Other Affiliates Are Doing Then Chances Are You'll Get The Same Dismal Results Showing Up On Your Check. But What If You Started Doing What Other People Are Not Doing?

4159	Create A Calendar With Wallpaper Graphics And Motivational Quotes.
4160	If I Could Help You With That What Would That Mean To You
4161	Want Better Things To Do With Your Time Than Working At Your Current Dead End Day Job
4162	Find Out How The Definition For Viral Marketing Has Been Rewritten For You To Milk It For All It's Worth To Build A Monster List, Build Your Down-Line In Any Program On Complete Auto-Pilot, And Get Freight Trains Full Of Traffic
4163	Why The Best List Is The One You Create For Yourself
4164	Once You Become A Master Of Yourself You Will Become The Master Of Everything You Encounter...And Who Better To Help Teach You How To Become A Master Than Your Own Personal Inner Coach.
4165	You'll Never Beg For Mercy When You Learn To Do It Right
4166	This System Runs 24 Hours A Day... 7 Days A Week... Whether You Are At The Office, Sleeping, Having Lunch, Or Enjoying Some Free Time With Your Family. Your Autoresponder Never Sleeps!
4167	Submitter Software Packages Use Obsolete Technology That Most Sites Are Already Protected Against Before You Even Submit
4168	I Knew That I Would Soon Be Getting Out Of There
4169	Program A 365-Day Email Autoresponder As An Automated Self-Guided Email Coaching Program.
4170	LISTEN I Was There Too Promoting Delectable Systems That Promise Instant Wealth
4171	Ideally, I Wanted To Work From Home, Not Employ Any Staff, Not Have Any Overheads, Not Be A Slave To The Business By Working Twelve To Fourteen Hours A Day, Only Work When I Wanted And Make A Lot Of Money. I Wanted It All My Own Way And All On My Own Terms. So What Did I Do?
4172	If Everything You Want Was Free Do You Still Think You Could Become A Millionaire
4173	This Killer Guide Is Your Handy Desktop Companion For Quick-Referencing Any Trick Or Tactic You Need To Fast Blast Your List Up Another Level.
4174	Is It Just Me Or Do You Smell Lots Of Money Around Here
4175	Rubies Sapphires Emeralds And Pearls But What About These Huge Internet Diamonds

4176	Generate Thousands Of Dollars With Powerful, Motivational Words In Marketing, Sales Letters, Copywriting, Personal Development Affirmations & Mantras, Book Titles, Movies, Music, Proverbs, Poems And Quotes That You Can Copy And Paste Saving You Literally Hours In Product Creation And Selling Anything You Want!
4177	Best Of All, You Don't Have To Re-Invent The Wheel. Everything Is Done For You. Just Follow The Simple Step-By-Step Instructions And You Could Be Referring New Members Within An Hour Of Getting Started!
4178	100 Fresh Marketing Ideas I Can Instantly Put In Your Pocket
4179	The Daily Dread Of Having To Work Away At Piecing Together
4180	Why Free Information Isn't Valued As Much As The Same Information You'll Purchase
4181	I Want Nothing More Than To Get That Email From You
4182	You Don't Want A Job. You Want A System, A Machine That Generates Income For You While You Are On Vacation And While You Are Sleeping And While You Are Playing Golf.
4183	So Switch Off Your Cellphone, Grab A Seat, And Hold Tight. This Page Is About To Alter Your Life... Here Comes Your Revelation... I Mean Literally Anybody. I'm Not Kidding Here, Or Just Hyping You Up. It's Completely True. You Don't Need Some Fancy Degree, You Don't Need To Know How To Program, And You Certainly Don't Need To Be A Computer Expert...
4184	As A Matter Of Fact I Do Know How To Make Money
4185	Open The Drapes To The Internet And Experience The Money Hurricane
4186	Isn't It Time To Update Your Website With Some Great New Products
4187	How A Lot Of White Space And A Dynamic Ad Promotion Can Increase Click Customers
4188	Begin GROWING Your Business THIS WEEK With All Of The Tools, Products And Guidance You Will Ever Need... Listen, If You're Really Serious About Starting An Online Business... Don't Let This Offer Pass You By.
4189	All You Do Is Join The Programs Outlined In Your Guide. Send Me Your ID's From The Various Programs So I Can Rebrand Your Guide And Set Up Your Website, Autoresponder And Splash Pages. Then You Surf The Traffic Exchanges For One Hour A Day. That Is All You Do! That Is Your Job.

4190	Social Networking Is A Very Popular Topic Amongst Internet Marketers, And There Is A Very Good Reason For This....It Works! Social Networking Is Unique Because Not Only Is It Free, But It Is Actually A Lot Easier Than People Realize To Get Started, And The Benefits Are Ten-Fold.
4191	Spills The Beans On How Industry Insiders Are Quietly Increase Conversions By At Least 75%
4192	Our System Teaches Our Members How To Drive Traffic -- Quality Traffic To Their High Converting Websites. This Generate Responsive Leads That Convert To Customers And New Distributors
4193	The Closest Thing To Free Money You'll Ever See Filling Your Bank Account Day After Day
4194	Are You Searching For An Honest Way To Make Money From The Comfort Of Your Home? Do You Still Have Too Much Month Left At The End Of Your Money Feeling Drained And Worried About Your Future?
4195	Want To Know The #1 Thing Standing Between You And Success
4196	Here's Your Access To The Internet's Most Revolutionized Money-Making System, Where You'll Learn Step-By-Step How Get Your Online Business Off The Ground & Everything Else In Between To Ensure That You Profit!
4197	Use Your Profits To Re-Invest And Finance The Business Building Process As You Move Through The 6 Steps In The Core-Business Pay Plan. You NEVER Have To Use Money Out-Of-Pocket.
4198	We Have Ordinary, Driven, & Determined People Achieving Amazing Results With Our Unique System. IMAGINE, You Get Taken By The Hand And Trained By Millionaires That Teach You What They DO And Practice Everyday. We Offer Training On Business Basics, Marketing, & Mindset.
4199	P.S. I'm Putting The Final Touches On All Of The Pre-Built Websites, Pre-Written Autoresponders, And Members Area As You Read This...I Know You're Gonna Love It! Get On The Pre-Launch List Now.
4200	You Have The Resale Rights To Sell This Over And Over
4201	You Don't Have To Know Anything Except How To Write And Send An Email. If You Can Do That Then You Can Be Successful. It Really Is That Easy. It's Not About The Technology; It's About Duplicating Proven Secrets.

4202	Imagine That You Are Earning Commission For Each Member You Refer That Upgrades Per Month.
4203	Get Your Free Web Page On The 1st Page Of Google 80% Of The Time
4204	The Only Qualification Required Is That You Must Be Able To Follow Simple Instructions Carefully To Set Yourself Up And Collect All The Money Which Is Available.
4205	The Key To Knowing Where To Find The Answer Is Crucial
4206	Learn How To Control Your Finances Instead Of Letting Them Control You
4207	The Key To This Successful Product Is It's Strong Appeal And It's Exceptional Price
4208	They Are Literally Cropping Up In The Dark Overnight Like Poisonous Mushrooms
4209	The "Magic Price" For Your Information Product. Yep, It Does Work Like Magic, And There's A Tremendously Important Psychological Reason Why. Once You Know This, You'll Get Past The Thing That Kills More New Information Products Than Anything Else.
4210	That's Why You Need To Learn To Brand Yourself - Which Makes You WAY More Attractive As A Leader ... A Big Key To Your Long-Term Success.
4211	It May Sound Contradictory, But Giving Away Some Information Is One Of The Best Ways To Increase Your Info Product Sales. The Simple Fact Is That People Want Information And Are Willing To Pay For It.
4212	The Easiest, Quickest, And Cheapest Way To Accept Credit Cards Online. If You Think You Had To Be A Big Company To Do This, You're Wrong! You Can Accept Credit Cards Within A Few Minutes, And Not Pay A Dime Unless Somebody Buys Something From You.
4213	Are You Spending More Money Than You're Earning Each Month? Are You Struggling To Make Money Online?
4214	How To Instantly Build Your Targeted Prospects' Trust In You And Your Products. You Could Have The Greatest Product In The World, But You Won't Get Any Sale Unless Your Prospects Trust You. I'll Show You How To Establish Credibility In A Flash To Make Tons Of Sales.
4215	Did You Know The Software You Just Bought Could Be Shareware

4216	This May Sound Harsh, But I'm Not Known For Subtlety. I'm Not Going To Sugar Coat Things For You And I'm Just Going To Give You The Honest Facts...
4217	A Fast And FUN Way To Increase Conversions By At Least 75%
4218	An Old Dog Can Learn New Tricks But Only If You Can Bark At This
4219	Build A Site With A Look And Feel That You Control And Own – Allowing You To Choose The Theme, Color, And Graphics... It's Easy To Customize And Create A Site You'll Be Proud Of... A Site That Devoted Members And Enthusiasts Are Thrilled To Tell Their Friends About.
4220	My Name Is Richard RIVO And I'm Always Excited To Have The Opportunity To Meet New People And To Make New Friends.
4221	What Successful Internet Marketers Do To Make A Fortune Even When Their Launches Fail
4222	Thousands Of People Have Used This Autoresponder System To Save Time, Increase Profits, And Boost Efficiency. You Will Have Full Access To This System Free For The Next 30 Days.
4223	Do You Really Need To Be Dragged Over The Coals For This
4224	The One "Universal" Magic Number Of Keywords Required To Pull-In Sales Time And Time Again
4225	Doing The Least Amount Of Work Possible To Get It Working Well
4226	Why Let Your Profits Crash And Burn Because You Didn't Use This
4227	EVERY Step Is Laid Out For You Exactly, And You'll Be Pleased To Know That You Won't Have To Spend A Dime To Use Our System Of Advertising And Automated Duplication.
4228	The Point I'm Trying To Make Is Our Stuff Works Because We Know Where You're Coming From. We're Just Like You. And We Look Out For Our Own.
4229	Compile The Information As A Report With Your Affiliate Links Embedded In The PDF.
4230	A Wonderful Two Years' Trip At Full Pay But Only Men With Imagination Can Take It
4231	You'll Also Get The Hot Seat, Where I'll Review Random Member Sites, To Ensure Maximum Profitability...And Lifetime Access To The _____ Insider...
4232	Tired Of The Daily Grind Ready To Finally Strike It Rich

4233	Give Your Clients Something They Can Really Sink Their Teeth Into.
4234	Want To Discover The Key Secrets That Are Being Kept From You
4235	Insider Techniques And Strategies To Make Your Website Become An Order Pulling Machine
4236	Own This Magnificent Solution Today And Conquer New Grounds With The Power It'll Give You!
4237	Successful Marketers First Do Proper Market Research First To Underpin A Profitable Niche With Reasonable Demand And Then Create A Product Around That Demand.
4238	Bet Your Wondering - 'What's The Catch?'. There Is NO Catch! The Beauty Of This System Is - These Guys Only Make Money When We Make Money. So It's Been Designed To Help You Every Step Of The Way.
4239	I Have An Excuse And Don't Have Time Because I Have Clean The House, Do The Laundry, Pay The Bills, Take Care Of Pets, Schedule Car Maintenance, Do The Shopping, And Take Care Of Your Health, Etc
4240	What Really Happens In The Niche Kingdom And Why You Should Be Concerned
4241	If It's Still Up And Running You'll Need To Click Here Right Now
4242	Modifying Programs And Creating Multiple Niche Products Is Easy. Modify Them To Suit Your Needs, And Dominate One Niche Market At A Time By Creating Niche-Targeted Products Around Them. You Can Create Multiple Streams Of Income And Not Have To Start From Scratch! And Only You Keep The Profits Because You Own The Products.
4243	Record An Audio Book And Sell It On iTunes And Amazon Stores.
4244	Nothing Will Boost Your Search Engine Rankings Faster Than Quality Original Content Plastered All Over Your Website. However, There's A New Technology That All The Major Search Engines Are Now Using Then Goes Out And Compares It Against All The Other Web Pages On The Internet. Find Out How To Profit From This New Technology Right Now!
4245	How To Really Make Money Online Without The Help Of Those Expensive Consultants

4246	But, What They Didn't Realize Is That There's Just So Much Information Here, With So Many Ways To Promote And Use The Products, That Devaluing Wasn't Even Going To Be Relevant Unless I Sold 100,000 Copies Or More.
4247	10 Million Millionaires In Just 10 Years - Will You Be One Of Them
4248	Do You Often Wish That You Could Find A Home Based Business Opportunity That Cuts Through The Hype And Garbage And Presents You With The Genuine Opportunity To Actually Change Your Financial Situation.
4249	Three Free Tools To Learn The Basics Of HTML. Do NOT Let This Scare You. You Don't Have To Be Proficient In Webpage Creation...You Just Have To Know Enough To Do The Simple Things You Need To Do. Don't Worry, I'll Point You In The Right Direction.
4250	Beat Them Down With Methods That Draw Attention And Make You Stand Out Rather Then Using The Same Old Techniques Everyone Else And There Grandmother Are Using.
4251	You'll Want To Do More Than Sit Back And Watch The Money Coming In
4252	This Strategy Can Bring Your Business Into Unimaginable Profits So Quickly In Fact, You'll Lose Your Hair. Doing Joint Ventures Is Probably The Most Important And Profitable Thing That You'll Learn To Do.
4253	60% of Americans Are Living At Or Just Above The Poverty Level
4254	Here Is Just One Reason You Will Want To Stay An Active Member
4255	Anyone Who's Not Serious Enough About Making Money Online To Invest $9.97 Into This Report Isn't Going To Take The Time To Use The Methods Laid Out Anyway.
4256	What Are You Doing To Earn A Living On The Internet
4257	Your Really Are Everything You Need To Be To Get Started
4258	I Know What I Have On My Hands Is A Bombshell That Can Propel You Towards Living The Life Of Your Dreams. Making Six Figures Or More Working From A Beach In Costa Rica.
4259	How The Internet Doctor Stays Healthy While Most Internet Websites Remain Sick
4260	Information Is Great Until It Becomes Too Much That It Overwhelms You
4261	The Income Potential Is A Very Realistic Full Time Or Part Time

4262	The Whole Process Takes Mere Minutes And As You Can See, You Don't Need Any Technical Know How To Pull This Off. You Can Truly Be Generating Sales And Building Your List In Mere Minutes!
4263	Remember That One Of The Most Important Factors For Ranking Highly For Your Search Term Is To Have Lots Of Backlinks Using That Search Term.
4264	Unlike Other Business Feeder Systems, You Don't Pay To Join Anything Upfront. It's Totally YOUR OPTION!
4265	It Is Also True That Eliminating All Debt Equates To A 40% Pay Raise But Without The Additional Taxation.. I Have Been Teaching Folks How To Do This Same Thing For Over 10 Years Both Online And In The Class Room.
4266	The More Backlinks Your Website Has Search Engines Will Raise Your Position And Ranking
4267	I Know This Product Is A Lot Different From What You Usually See From Us, So I'm Not Offended If It Isn't For You.
4268	How To Make Fast Cash With Your Knowledge! No, You Don't Even Need To Write! Just Talk And Make Money!
4269	Before I Tell You More About These Products That Can Really Make You Some Serious Income This Coming Year Let Me Tell You A Little Bit About Who I Am So You Can Understand More Why These Products Can Really Help You Reach Your Income Goals.
4270	Is Time Running Out Sitting Around Hoping You'll Finally Catch A Break
4271	Make Yourself Irreplaceable And Begin Reaping The Rewards You Truly Deserve
4272	Give Me An Extra $100 A Day And I'll Show You Happy
4273	Forge Your Own Profitable Path To Success Online Starting Right Now
4274	This Program Is One Of The Best System For Making Online Income
4275	Are You Committed To Some Of The Dreams That You Would Like To Manifest Once You Are Financially Independent, It's Time To Practice Them. Each Day Give Yourself Five Minutes To Imagine Experiencing All Of The Wealth That You Desire.
4276	I Have Been Subject To The Same Things As You, My Friend. I Have So Much Junk On My Computer, That I Sometimes Don't Even Know Where To Begin Sorting Through It All.

4277	How To Spot Those Quick, Cheap And Easy Fixer-Uppers AND Practically Guarantee Yourself A Hungry Buyer For Your Site Before You Do Any Work...
4278	Marketer Reveals Incredible Launch Success Rate Of Over 66% By Changing Only One Word
4279	Use Your Content For Postcards Or Mailers.
4280	We Think If The Internet Started Pumping Out Good Wholesome, Worth While Money Making Information, Like This, It Will Squeeze Out The 'Rip Off' Artists And Put Them Completely Out Of Business Online.
4281	If You're Interested In Making Money And Improving Your Life, Then Please Pay Careful Attention To This Letter. Here's What This Is About.
4282	Your Score Will Effect Everything You Do Or Purchase From Now On
4283	Why Scour The Internet For Tools And Things That Don't Work
4284	It Hasn't Always Been Easy, And I've Made More Than My Share Of Mistakes... But In The End, It's Totally, 100% Worth It.
4285	How To Quit Your Day Job And Retire In Less Than 2 Years
4286	Amazing How Quickly A Little Success Can Create Such Powerful Positive Attitudes
4287	The Potential Of Doubling Your Profits Is Now In Your Court If You've Got Game
4288	I'm Now In A Position To Share Several Shocking New Develops In Marketing
4289	You Don't Have To Live In Fear Of "What Happens If This Stops Making Me Money?" (Because Sooner Or Later, It Will.) You've Have Lots Of Streams Coming In Because The Amount Of Effort You Put Into Running Your Business Isn't Going To Be Much Different Selling 25 Products Than It Is Selling One Product.
4290	Copy Paste And Email These Premium Reports And Keep 100% Of The Profits
4291	There Was No Question In Any Of Our Minds About The Power Of This Business Model. We Knew That 'Continuity' Was The Name Of The Game. We Also Knew That Now By Utilizing This New Technology.
4292	Wal-Mart: Police Receive A Report Of A Newborn Infant Found in Trash Can. Upon investigation, Officers Discover It Was Only A Burrito

4293	Exactly What Your Affiliate Promotion Website Should Look Like And Where To Go To Get Cheap, High Quality Graphics And Web Design (Your Website Should Look Simple And Easy On The Eyes…That's Great Because It's Both Cheap And Effective!)
4294	This Is Pure Gold And Will Save You Countless Hours Of Frustration
4295	Nothing Like A Good Old Fashion Challenge To See What You're Made Of
4296	Even Santa Has To Have A Game Plan. He Doesn't Shove Any Old Gift Down Random Chimneys – He Builds A Relationship With The Parents Of The Family To Find Out Exactly What Is Required For The Big Day.
4297	If You're Ready To Get Started Just Click Here To Join
4298	Today, In This Information Driven Society, There's An Incredible Demand For Products And Services. People Are Searching For Products That Appeal To Their Needs, Services That Educate Them, Products/Services That Make Their Life Easier, But Make No Mistake, They Want It NOW!
4299	Look The Internet Is Huge The Odds Are In Your Favor When You Leverage Your Offers
4300	The Increase In Opt-In Conversions From This Script Alone Is Worth A Fortune To Your Business... And It's Yours As Part Of This Killer Package.
4301	Do You Think Grocery Stores Lined Up The Most Frequently Purchased Items At The Back Of The Store For No Apparent Reason?
4302	The Internet Is The Great Equalizer Especially For Those Really Ready To Enter This Arena
4303	We Know That You Have Probably Heard This A Million Times But Just Carry On Reading And We Will Prove It To You! Other Programs Never Get Past This Point! Can Other Programs Guarantee To Double Your Money?
4304	We've Even Traveled To Far Away Places Like India And Nepal To Recruit Some Members Of This "Dream Team" Of Personal Change. These Experts Have Already Assisted Tens Of Thousands Of People In Achieving Their Dreams And Distilled Their Latest Knowledge And Research Into A System So Powerful, It Ought To Be Illegal.
4305	7 Motivational Triggers That Make People Buy And How You Can Use Them Today

311

4306	Not Knowing How To Start Your First Online Money Making Business Is No Longer An Excuse
4307	Discover How You Can Instantly And Effortlessly Have Ten Ready Made Online Businesses That Can Save You A Fortune Change Your Life, And Fill Your Bank Account With Tons Of Cash. You'll Never Find An Easier, Sure-Fire Way To Generate Unstoppable Cash Flow Even While You're Sleeping!
4308	A Quick Trick Which Instantly Makes Your Web Site Stand Out In Every Potential Customer's Web Browser
4309	We'll Be The First To Tell You That Success Is Simple. It's Just Not Easy. You Have To Have A Proper Skill Set And Knowledge To Grow A Successful Organization.
4310	You're Million Dollar Game Plan Is Waiting For Your Final Commitment To Action
4311	Now You Can Access The Language Of Millionaires Using The Most Powerful Collection Of Million Dollar Action Trigger Phrases Ever Assembled And Never Before Offered To Anyone, Anytime, Or Anywhere! This Dynamic Collection Will Truly Inspire You To Instantly Create Your Own Professional Headlines, Ads, Email, Promotions, And Any Other Written Or Spoken Form Of Communication That Can Skyrocket Your Responses And Conversions Like Never Before.
4312	If Your Sales Copy Is Faltering, Having A Amazing Video Making Sales And Driving Viral Traffic Would Be Extremely Valuable.. If You're Not Getting As Many Sales As You Want Or NEED, Then You Need To Add Professional Videos Immediately.
4313	People Do Not Change Because Of What They Know But Because Of What They Feel
4314	Learn Exactly What To Say After You've Been Contacted By A Prospective Buyer
4315	If You Have A Digital Camera And You Have Ever Wished That You Had More Money Coming In To Pay Off Debts, Then This Is Definitely The Most Important Letter You'll Read Today!
4316	I've Gone Against EVERY Piece Of Advice I Got And Am Pricing The ENTIRE System (Modules, Videos, Bonuses, Software, All Of It) For Just A ONE-TIME Low Payment Of $197... Yes All Of It For Just ONE Payment – You Pay And You're Done. There Is NO Tricky Recurring Payments Or GIMMICKS To Get You To Buy More.
4317	I Believe Everyone Can Get The Success They Deserve From Using This Superb Opportunity

4318	This Allows Anyone Who's Serious About Creating Wealth From Home, A REAL Product And Business Opportunity That Could Stand Head And Shoulders Above Just About Anything Else Out There.
4319	Don't Compare Your Life To Others Because You Have No Idea What Their Journey Is All About
4320	The Competition Is Fierce And Using These Underground Tactics Will Not Make You Friends. But This Is Not About Making Friends, This Is About Your Freedom.
4321	You See A New Opportunity And You Think It Sounds Great So You Buy A Product Or Start A Program But After A Few Days Those Old Fears Come Back. What If It Doesn't Work? What If You Lose Money Trying It? What If This IM Thing Is All One Big Scam And What Do You Do?
4322	Do You Know Up Till Today There Are Several Reputable (Well-Known) Companies Making Several Millions Of Dollars Monthly By Dropping Cookies Into Web-Surfers Browser?
4323	Why Should I Have All The Fun When I Know I Can Also Help Others Succeed
4324	How A New Discovery Made A Simple Website Spectacular In Less Than 5 Minutes
4325	HERE'S MY TAKE: Regardless Of What New Opportunities Exist, To Fully Seize Any Of Them You Must Build Your Presence Online. And There's No Better Way To Establish Yourself As An Expert, See Daily Sales And Build Your Business.
4326	Use Your Content As Talking Points. When The Media Or Your Clients Call You, You'll Be Ready.
4327	There's No Point Starting A Business If You Don't First Decide Who You Are Going To Sell To. Choosing A Niche Market Is Not Always Easy, But I Can Help A Lot By Simplifying The Process For You.
4328	Like Many, You Might Be Someone That Likes To Get To The Bottom Line. Hey, I Can Understand That. Please Read On For Just A Sec. I Think It's Plain To See With Everything That I'm Offering You...
4329	This Is The Fastest Learning Curve Shortcut I've Seen To Making Serious Sales Online
4330	At The End Of The Day After All Is Said And Done Are You Still Broke
4331	7 Ways To Tell The World About Your Web Site

4332	I Know What You Might Be Thinking By Now! Why Would I Help You Get Your First Few Sales - Its Plain And Simple - I Get Paid When You Get Paid.
4333	Compare & Price Out Every Single Possible Available Site Without Ever Talking To A Broker
4334	This Is Only For The Most Serious Minded Affiliates Who Want To Take These Insider Tactics I'm Showing You And Use It To Your Great Advantage.
4335	Get Out A Piece Of Paper And Write Down One Idea You Believe Is Achievable Then Do It
4336	We've Helped Small Businesses Generate Millions In Internet Sales Over The Past Year
4337	However, When We Sit And Look At What's Taught In This Industry Those Dreaded Failure Numbers Aren't Surprising.
4338	If You Hired A Writer To Write You Almost 9,000 Words That Would Typically Cost You About $250 Or $10 Per 350 Words, Which Is Equivalent To About One Page.
4339	The EXACT Number Of Links You Should Have To Any Site To Boost Search Engine Ranking Without Tripping The Spam Alarms...
4340	The Secret Is Now Out On An Incredible Website You've Got To See
4341	You Can Click Just To Earn Your Credit Or You Could Get Ready For The Tsunami Of People Looking For A Better Way...Have You Seen The News Lately?
4342	I Know What It Feels Like When You Get Rejected And Laughed At. I Know What It's Like To Live In An Empty Apartment Without Furniture And How It Feels When You Can't Pay Your Bills.
4343	Build A Facebook Page, Separate From Your Profile.
4344	Want To Discover A Proven Blueprint For Generating Highly Pre Qualified Leads
4345	While The Free Edition Is Packed Full Of Valuable Features, There Is Even More In The Professional Edition And For A Short Time We Are Allowing You Access To It For A $5 Trial,
4346	Unfortunately Many Fall Back Into Darkness Because They Don't Use These
4347	It's Like Planting A Little Acorn Knowing That It Will Grow Into A Mighty Oak Tree
4348	Want Your Site Automatically Linked And Submitted To Thousands Of Web Directories

314

4349	How Do We Turn Things To Our Advantage? People Are Turning To The Internet For Better Deals. Instead People Are Staying Home Surfing The Internet To Make Some Extra Money To Support Their Families.
4350	If You're Curious As To What "P+T=M" Is -- It Is Product + Traffic = Money. That's All There Is To It... That's What It Takes To Generate An Incredible Income Online.
4351	The Internet Is A Very Powerful Medium, And We Have Been Blessed To Be Here At This Time In History To Tap It For All It's Worth.
4352	The Secret Gold Dust To Sprinkling On Your Product To Convince People To Buy
4353	Why You Should Be Happy To See Lots Of Competition And How To Make Those Same Competitors Thrilled To Send You Their Best Customers And Traffic.
4354	These Pre-Written Emails Create Attentive and Receptive Readers Ready To Click and Buy and Put Your Marketing On Autopilot. In Just 5 Minutes* They Are Ready To Generate More Sales For You Automatically!
4355	These Simple Yet Critical Areas Are Essential To Building A Prosperous Business Online
4356	Suddenly No One Will Be Telling You That You're Crazy Or Wasting Your Time Online
4357	Because You Are Able To Generate More Leads And More Efficiently Manage Your Follow Up, You Will Have More Time To Develop And Test Effective Ad Copy, Spend Time With Family Or Friends, Or Even Develop New Product Lines And Marketing Approaches!
4358	By The Way, Most Of These Headlines Were Enormously Successful For My Clients, Not Because They Were Tested And Tweaked (And Most Of Them Were), But Because They Were Actually Stolen From Other, Equally Successful Ads Or Sales Letters. All "Great" Copywriters Do This. They Steal. They Recycle. They Copy. They Model. They Swipe.
4359	Seriously, Once You Get Down To It, Making Money From The Internet Is No Harder Than Microwaving Your Dinner Or Making A Sandwich. And You Can Do Those Things Right?
4360	This Could Blow The Turkey Out Off The Dining Room Table Forever

4361	Manage the Sales of Your Digital Products on ALL your Web-sites and eBay Accounts from a SINGLE Centralized Location and Automatically Send Your Digital Products & CD's To Your Customers Instantly, Even if Your Computer is Turned Off.
4362	Sign Up & And We Will Show You... The Exact Steps To Add-ing Responsive Leads To Your Marketing Business, Not Only Will You Be Able To Add Names To Your List But You Will Be Able To Make Commissions On Products Sold!....
4363	Well-Meaning Folks Like Yourself Are Getting Absolutely No-where With Their Internet "Business" Because They Continue To Get Ran Around In Circles With All Of The "Sure Shots" From Every Guru-Come-Lately That Promises The Moon. They're Left Scratching Their Heads, Wondering...Where's All The Money That Was Promised?
4364	Network Marketing On The Internet Has Created And Contin-ues To Create More Millionaires Than Ever Before In The History Of The Planet. The Internet Is By Far The Most Power-ful Vehicle For Business Ever Known.
4365	P.S. People Are Telling Me I'm Crazy. Maybe I Am, Since I Spent Thousands Of Dollars And Countless Hours On The Technology. If I Come To My Senses, The Free Version Might Go Away Soon.
4366	Absolute Proof The "Internet Blackhole" Is Stealing Your Cus-tomers, Swiping Your Profits And How It'll Keep On CRUSHING Your Response Rate Until There's Virtually NO-ONE Left To Read Your Email – Unless You Take Action Right Now!
4367	I Have Found Some Great Videos That Will Guide You Through This Whole Process And Show You Step-By-Step
4368	The Best News Is You Don't Have To Figure Out How To Start Or How To Set Anything Up. I Do All That For You.
4369	How You Can Turn Even The Smallest Idea Into A Great And Profitable Business
4370	Actually, I'm Kind Of Miffed That After Bustin' My Butt For So Long That "This" Is What Would Start To Make Me Staggering Commissions, But I'll Take It! Hey, It's Business. My Re-sponse Rates From My Personal Lists Are At 30% And Around 2%-14% For Others.
4371	Why We Need To Blow The Internet Whistle To Everyone Who Will Listen

4372	Applying A Simple Pressure Point That Convinces even Skeptics To Buy Your Offer
4373	Your Solo Ad On Responsive Sites Can Be Seen By Thousands
4374	Stay On Top Of The Hottest ClickBank Products And Dominate Niches Others Don't See
4375	Come On Whose Fault Is It Anyway When Your Own Website Still Hasn't Made Any Money
4376	I Will Not Only Refund Every Single Penny Of Your Money Right Back To You, But I Will Also Double Your Refund So You Get Twice Your Money Back!
4377	Here's A BIG Tip Which You Must Know... To Sell Something Successfully, You Should Always "Sell The Problem BEFORE You Sell The Solution!"
4378	How To Systemize Your Business And Turn Your Prospects Into Raving Fans
4379	Key To Generating Your Own Hot List Of Real Time Leads
4380	Or If You Have Ever Wanted To Be On A Team That Needs You To Succeed, Then This Is It. This Is Your Chance To Earn $1000's Weekly, And You Won't Have To Break The Piggy Bank To Do It.
4381	At This Point There Really Isn't Much Else We Can Say
4382	Social Networking Is Considered To Be The Next Step In The Evolution Of The Internet From A Flat World, To An Interactive World. The Next Step In The Evolution Of Social Networking Is By Bringing All Of The Popular Features From Less Than 5% Of All Internet Sites Having Them, To 100%, Every Website On The Web Now Fully Interactive, Instantly And All At A Simple Click Of A Button
4383	There Are Two Types Of People In The World...Those Who Are Connected To The Internet Through Our Network...And Those Who Have Still Yet To Connect To The Internet For The Very First Time.
4384	The Quickest Way I Know To Increase Conversions By At Least 75%
4385	Your Just 5 Steps Away From Setting Up Your Very Own Money Making System For FREE. To Sign Up Simply Fill In The Box Below And Press The 'Sign Up' Button. You'll Receive An Email Containing Your Login Details.
4386	It Really Doesn't Have To Be A Big Pain In The End
4387	You'll See These Don't Take Very Long And You'll Make More Money

4388	Dirty Methods Of Dominating Any Niche Operation And Stolen Commissions Exposed
4389	Every Once In A While Something Comes Along That's So Valuable You'd Pay Whatever You Could Afford To Get Your Hands On It. Well, This Is One Of Those Times...
4390	I Understand That When You Start Out Online, It Can Be Quite Confusing, How Do I Do This, How Do I Do That.
4391	I'd Like To Show You How We're Bringing In A Small Fortune With This One Tiny Idea
4392	The Problem Is Who Do You Ask For Help And How Can You Assure You Are Doing The Right Things? From Registering A Domain To How To Create Marketing Campaigns. Making Real Money On The Internet Has Specific Rules.
4393	Now Here's A Simple Formula That Shows You Exactly What To Do Step By Step
4394	My Focus Is On Helping Companies Find The Strategy That Best Fits Their Needs And Budget And Then Establishing Goals For Each Marketing Campaign.
4395	Start By Sharing Your Very Best Stuff With The First 20 Sub-scribers
4396	This Is An Exclusive Secret Download Page Only For Your Subscribers
4397	Would You Like To Know How A Simple, Automated System Designed Especially For Beginners Can Put $100-300 A Day Directly Into Your Pocket Starting In Less Than 24 Hours From Right This Minute? If Your Answer Is "Yes" Or Even "Maybe" - Then We Need To Clear Up A Few Things Before We Go Any Farther.
4398	How To Properly Water Your Online Money Tree Each And Every Day
4399	Would You Rather Drink Water From A Slough Or Water From A Fresh Spring? I Mean Water's Water Right? So, Does It Really Matter Where Your Traffic Comes From?
4400	Well You're In Luck... Because This Time You've Come To The Right Place. One Step 4 Income Is A Sensational New Busi-ness Concept That's Revolutionizing The Online Home Business Industry...
4401	There Are Thousands Of Little Inexpensive Virtual Workers Waiting To Help You That Already Understand The Major 'Moving Parts' In An Online Business -- They Can Quickly Help You To Build A List, Get Higher Search Engine Rankings, And Create Content For You That Will Get You Free Traffic.

4402	P.S. Just Make Sure You Get In Within The Next Few Hours To Get The Early Bird Discount Pricing. We Really Are Putting The Price Up Tomorrow So Right Now Is The Time To Take Action And Save Money.
4403	Well, To Be Honest, I Didn't Expect A Lot Out Of This One But Man... I Was Highly Impressed. I Wanted To Tell You About It Right Away. List Building Is Something That's Important To Every Marketer. This Is One Of The Best Guides I've Seen, And It's Refreshingly Affordable. Definitely Check It Out.
4404	I Have Freedom To Travel And Set My Own Priorities Without Being Tied Down To An Office -- But I Also Work Very Hard To Make That Happen.
4405	Never Before Has Such A Comprehensive Collection Of Action Headlines Been Made Available
4406	Where To Find Red Hot Markets With Little Or No Competition
4407	The Ultimate Blueprint For Spitting Out Profitable Websites After Profitable Website
4408	Simple Six Step Process That Can Lead You To The Bank
4409	Well The First Webinar Is Over But There Is Some Really Great News For You... The Good News Is That It Is Going To Continue For 11 More Training Modules Yet. Just Watch For The Emails Giving Details Each Week. We Really Want You To Find The Help You Have Been Searching For, For Far Too Long Now!
4410	Customize Your Name And Affiliate Links With This Proven Follow up Technique
4411	If You Can Follow Simple Directions, Here's How To Increase Conversions By At Least 75% In Your Spare Time And Have Fun Doing It
4412	If You Know Anything About Online Marketing You Know That An Email List Is Probably The Most Important Ingredient For Success.
4413	Complete Collection Of 19 Professionally-Recorded Videos. This Complete Video Series Will Teach You Everything You Need To Know About Finding A Profitable Product To Sell, And How To Promote It.
4414	For Internet Marketers Who Think They've Finally Maximized Their Profit Potential
4415	Take A Sneak Peak At The Most Powerful List Building Tools Used By The Richest Marketers
4416	Don't Delay You Do Not Want To Miss Out On This Opportunity

319

4417	Starting Your Own Website Shows Ingenuity, Intelligence, And A Sense Of Entrepreneurship. I'm Happy To Lend A Hand To Such A Strong Web-Based Community.
4418	Every One Of Them Geared To Make You More Money. To Put It Bluntly, I've Covered Everything. There's No Stone Left Un-turned. You'll Actually See Me Setting Up My Money-Making Systems With Your Own Eyes... And I Mean All Of It. I Haven't Glossed Over Anything, I Haven't Held Anything Back. It's All There, Everything You Need To Make Money.
4419	All Of Your Potential Customers Are Hanging Around One End, Enjoying The Variety Of Stores And Mingling With Each Other While You Sit There Lonely At The Other End.
4420	Travel Is One Of The Top 3 Industries On The Internet And Those Marketers Who Do Not Have Travel As Part Of Their Income Portfolio Are Flat Out Missing The Boat!
4421	This Is The One Strategy That Separates The Haves For The Have Not's
4422	How To Get An Extra 5,000+ Hits Monthly To Your Site - Abso-lutely Free
4423	Here's Your Chance To Lay Your Hot Little Hands On A Proven System That Increases Your Traffic By A Whopping 727% Allows You To Generate Bank Account Deposits Non Stop 24/7 And Makes You Massive Monthly Income Starting From Standing Still.
4424	And It's Not Going To Tell You To Spend Hundreds On This And That... It's Not Going To Ask You To Wait Weeks Until You Start Seeing Money... Heck, With This Stuff You Can Make Money From Day One... Let Me Just Repeat That... You Could Make Money Right Now, Today.
4425	Sorry, I Offer A NO Money Back Guarantee! With My Absolute Rock-Bottom Focus On Saving Your Money, I Cannot Offer Anyone A Money-Back Guaranteed. This Offer Is Only In-tended For Fast Action Takers Who Know A Great Deal When They See It Right In Front Of Them, Like This One Right Now
4426	But With This One, I Went Even Further. If It Doesn't Work For You To The Tune Of At Least $200 A Month, Well, I'm Not Al-lowed To Keep Your Money.
4427	You Have Nothing To Lose Because It Won't Cost You One Penny
4428	How To Make Your Products Stand Out In A Crowded Market-place

4429	With What You Have In Your Hands Right Now You Can Get Started Right Now
4430	How First Impressions Can Make Or Break Your Product Sales And Ultimate Profits
4431	Buy My System Right Now And Put It To The Test For 8 FULL WEEKS.
4432	Are You Still Seeking The Most Powerful Way To Make Lots Of Money In A Hurry
4433	Earn More Hassle Free Profits By Actually Eliminating All Your Mundane Repetitive Tasks
4434	However, Quickly Throwing Up A Website And Hoping To Make Some Money Is One Thing. Building A Profit Pulling Business That Automatically Pumps Money Into Your Bank Account Is An Entirely Different Thing.
4435	If You Think Gas Prices Are High What's The Real Cost Of Losing Online Conversions
4436	Change Your Life And Your Lifestyle Starting This Week! Take Control Of Your Financial Future And Start Enjoying The Lifestyle Of Your Choice. Stand On The Shoulders Of Giants To See Further Than You Ever Have Before.
4437	Rewrite And Post On A Blogger.Com Or On A Wordpress.Com Blog.
4438	A Dozen Dirty Tricks Of New Car Dealers. Some Are Totally Undetectable Unless You Know What To Look For
4439	Again And Again They Keep Coming Back For More And More Just Like Clockwork
4440	I Do It All Live, Unrehearsed, So You Get To See Exactly What I Would Do To Figure Out How To Get A Top Google Ranking For Basically Any Keyword Phrase.
4441	I Will Be Setting Up A Series Of Email Messages In Your Autoresponder That Will Help People Decide To Join My Program From Your Link. It Is Not Hard To Get People To Join Because They Will Be Reading This Information On Your Website.
4442	Why No One Wants To Speak About Or Reveal This Simple Truth
4443	Deodorize Your Web Site And Begin Smelling The Sweet Smell Of Money
4444	We'll Do The Heavy Lifting And Help Leap You Over Your Online Fears

321

4445	Doesn't It Make You Ill Watching So Many People Earn Insane Incomes Online Instead Of You
4446	Now You'll Apply The Same Tactic As Countless Millionaires For Getting Your Mind Power And Influence To Work Building Your List And Your Business In Ways You Never Imagined.
4447	If No Body Ever Told You I Want You To Know That I Care About You
4448	The Best Autoresponder - Free For 30 Days - Pays On 10 Levels
4449	Ok, So My Point Is We All Have Fear. And We All Tend To Freak Ourselves Out To The Point Where We Are Afraid To Take Action Even Though Taking Action Is In Our Best Interest!
4450	What Others Have Yet Discovered Is A Priceless Gift Awaiting Your Acceptance
4451	I Hate Leaving My House Confident And Looking Good And Then Not Seeing Anyone Of Importance The Entire Day. What A Waste
4452	You Can Get Started Today The Big Reason Why People Don't Make Money Is They Never Get Around To It. You Can Set Up A Money Making Affiliate Marketing Business In Just Few Hours If You Get The Right Advice
4453	If You Didn't Do What You Promised To Do I'm Going To Ask You To Donate $100 To Your Favorite Charity
4454	Locating Broken Inbound Links, Then-Links Attempted But Because Of An Error Don't Connect With A Page On Your Site-Is Like An Opportunity To Locate Missing Money.
4455	We Know You're Busy But Can We Have A Few Minutes Of Your Time In Order To Share With You Information About Our List Building Site That Will Help Drive MORE Traffic To Your Site And Businesses?
4456	There's No Telling Where The Next Undiscovered Fortune Resides Until Now
4457	If You Haven't Read This Yet Your Closest Friends Will Be The First To Tell You All About It
4458	How To Save Thousands Of Dollars And Years Of Your Valuable Time
4459	After Months Of Trial And Error (Well, Mostly Error) We Successfully Cracked The Code To Affiliate Riches And Are Now Making More In A Month Than We Could Have Ever Made From Our Part-Time Jobs.

4460	It Does Not Matter What Home-Based Business You Are In Or If You Are Still Searching To Find A Great Company, What I Have To Offer Will Bring Your Business To The Next Level.
4461	Track Clicks On Your Links From Newsletters And External Web Sites
4462	There's So Much Information That It Just Becomes Overwhelming And Too Much To Handle. Ultimately These Programs Just Become Dust Bunnies Resigned To Take Up Space On Your Hard Drive And Do Nothing Else...
4463	The Only Outcome That Makes It Worthwhile For Either Side Is A Successful One.
4464	This Is One Is My Favorite! You Make The Sale One Time And Get Paid Over And Over Again, Month After Month, Year After Year. A Nice, Steady, Predictable Income From Your Site Will Be So Amazing,
4465	Tweak An Article And Submit It On Another Blog As A Guest Post.
4466	Join Now And Become Part Of The Internet Revolution Or Get Left Behind Forever
4467	You Can Then Judge How Everything You'll Learn Can Help Make Your Business Grow Into The Business You Have Always Wanted And Known It Could Be.
4468	You'd Be Very Angry With Me If I Didn't Let You Know About This
4469	Why You'll Be Making A Huge Mistake If You Fail To Click On This Powerful Report
4470	Why You Don't Need To Be 'School Smart' To Make These Secrets Work And How Having A Degree Can Actually Be A Handicap To Making Real Money. All You Need Is A Proven System One That Works For The Average Joe The Plumber Or Jane The Secretary.
4471	It's A Community Of Newbies And Seasoned Marketers Who Work Together To Build Their Online Futures And Their Fortunes. It's Also A TREASURE CHEST Chock Full Of EVERYTHING You Could Possibly Want Or Need To Start And Run Your Internet Business
4472	Promote YOURSELF In MLM Today People Join People Not Some Company Or Product
4473	I've Had Great Success With Ebooks -- They've Changed My Career, My Bank Account And, In General, My Life!

323

4474	For The First Time In The History Of The Internet, People Who Have Never Made Money Are Getting Paid. Getting Paid Over And Over... Again And Again!
4475	Be Sure To Talkback To Me While You're Here. I Always Look Forward To And Enjoy Your Feedback. If You Enjoyed Today's Post, Please Be So Kind To Buzz Us Up On Yahoo! Buzz By Clicking On The "Buzz" Graphic Above.
4476	If You Know How To Do This Your Going To Become Wildly Wealthy
4477	REALLY BIG In A Few Short Weeks By Using A Portion Of The Profits That You Earn Instead Of Money Out Of Your Own Pocket!
4478	I Got A Lot Of Doors Shut In My Face, But Was Able To Get The Attention Of Several Really Bright And Successful Online Marketers. The Information I Began To Uncover Turned Out To Be Pure Gold.
4479	What Do I Get With My Private Label Rights Package: Source WORD Document - So You Can Edit, Extract, Add And Manipulate It As Much As You Wish Of This Juicy Content About A Hot Topic.
4480	Here Are Just Some Of The Exciting Features And Benefits You'll Receive For Peaking
4481	The Best Converting Graphic Proven To Increase Sales By 14%
4482	Make Peace With Your Past So It Won't Screw Up The Present
4483	Mess Up Your Tax Return? Here's 4 Excuses That Work With The IRS And 3 That Don't
4484	7 Innovative Ways Personalization Can Explode Your Profits
4485	Experience Affiliate Marketing You'll Understand Why Being A Product Owner Is Much Better
4486	Hi. I Wanted To Send A Quick Note To Remind You About The Increased Affiliate Commissions Through The End Of This Month, And To Remind You That The Affiliate Team Is Always Here To Help You Achieve Affiliate Success.
4487	The Next Big Thing Is Based Upon A Whole Lot Of Wisdom Backing It Up
4488	You Can Either Keep Doing What You're Doing Right Now And Continue To Get The Same Results...OR... Follow The System And Change Your Life Completely...I Believe This System Is The Key To Many People Just Like You Hitting The BIG TIME...

4489	Marketers Are Going To Be Continually Coming Out With New Products That May (Or May Not) Help You To Make More Money With Google Adsense.
4490	Always Be Ahead Of The Pack. Our Solutions Will Be Updated Constantly As Things Change And You Will Get The Updated Version For Free.
4491	Track Which Links Are Performing The Best Including Cost Per Click
4492	You Can't Afford To Waste Your Time Or Energy On This Kind Of Nonsense
4493	Words Are The Most Powerful Medium That Will Bring Across An Idea That Will Influence, Move The Masses... Or Even Change The World! In Other Words, It Is The Marketer's Most Prized Weapon!
4494	Create A Web-Based E-Course.
4495	Click ON This Link And Get This Powerful Information And Read It Immediately
4496	Now, What If You Could Email 3,000 People At The Click Of A Button...And Do It Again In A Few Days?!
4497	I Believe In Hard Work, Dedication, And Commitment -- And Those Qualities Are Definitely Required For Any Kind Of Business I Know.
4498	Select Any 3 Of My Products And I'll Throw The 4th Selection In For Free While They Last
4499	Something About What He Said Clicked In My Head, A FREE Product That Can Help You Make Sales From The People Leaving Your Site. PLUS - Viral Marketing Built In To Drive Quality Traffic To Your Site.
4500	Only Fools Thought The Great Internet Gold Rush Was Over Before It Really Began
4501	Everybody Knows That Sending A Press Release To The Media Is The Most Effective Way To Get Publicity For Your Website. Publicity Translates To Traffic And Ultimately Traffic Translates To More Sales.
4502	The #1 Mistake Most New Online Business Owners Make Is Picking A Market Without Checking To See If The Market Is Profitable. This Video Will Show You EXACTLY How To Spot A Profitable Market Or An Unprofitable Market Before You Get Started.
4503	Bad Words ... Good Words, The Words That Increase Sales Every Time

4504	Ok, I'm Sure By Now Your Probably Dying To Know Exactly What Happened That Fateful Night. Correct? I'm Still Not Ready To Talk About That Yet, But Soon, Very Soon.
4505	Make Sure The Headline Text Is Larger Than Any Other Text On Your Sales Page
4506	We're Contacting A Few Specially Selected Business Owners Like You For A Limited Time Offer That Will Help To Make An Incredible Amount Of Money Online Using A Totally Auto-mated Hands Off System.
4507	But There's No Reason To Price Out Those That Need It Most
4508	With Your Permission We Would Like To Review Your Web Site For Free And See How We Could Direct More Traffic To Your Site. Email Us Today To Receive Our Report.
4509	I Don't Know Why We Do It But We All Do. We See A Problem And We Start Looking For The Worst Possible Outcome. We Totally Psyched Ourselves Out This Way. I Know I Personally Have Been Stressing Out So Bad The Last Few Months Over So Many Things. Let Me Give You An Example.
4510	How Adding One Simple Letter To Your Headline Can In-crease Sales By Over 325%
4511	In Case You're Wondering, The Reason I Limited It Was To Avoid Overwhelming Our Support Staff. It Was A Strategic Decision To Leave Money On The Table Because I'd Rather Make Sure Our Customers Are Taken Care Of First.
4512	I Really HATE Sitting There Staring At The Screen Trying To Figure Out What I Should Write, And I Have No Idea What's Going To Work The Best...
4513	PS: This Is A Quality Service For Internet Marketers, Network Marketers, Affiliates, And Webmasters. Joining Free Will Get You Started Upgrading Will Boost Your Income To New Heights.
4514	I Have Work To Do And Don't Have Time For This
4515	Your Web Business Relies On One Thing And One Thing First ...Your Headlines. That's Right, Headlines Above All Else Grab And Peak Curiosity Before A Single Word Of Your Mil-lion Dollar Ad Copy Offer Or Email Marketing Campaign Is Ever Opened Or Read...Period! Your Headline Is Crucial To Anything Else You Could Possibly Do Prior To Placing Your Offer Before Them.
4516	How Would You Like To Choose Your Own Wake Up Time

4517	Get The True Story On How To Find Profitable Keywords And Markets... This Isn't Revealed Anywhere Else - I Show You Inside The Secret Methods I Have Used To Locate Thousands Of Profitable Niches Online
4518	If You're Tired Of Worrying About Layoffs, Salary Cuts, Pension Loses And Retirement, Don't Settle For Just Getting Another Job. We'll Teach YOU How To Make $10,000 Every Month Working At Home. YES That's RIGHT
4519	They Want You To Think That It's Some Big Secret That Only A Select Few People Can Understand And Replicate. But It's Not Like That At All... Making Money Online Is No Tougher Than Making A Cup Of Coffee. Because It's Going To Show You Exactly Why It's That Easy To Build A Successful, Insanely Profitable Affiliate Marketing Business.
4520	Looking For B.S. Look Elsewhere Or Continue Reading Something Useful For A Change
4521	If You Want To Want To Spy On My Entire Online Operation It's Going To Cost You
4522	Let Us Teach You How To Build Multiple Niche Lists While You Build A Passive Residual Income At The Same Time. Start Building Your First Quality List With...
4523	The Way I Made My Living Was To Write Direct Mail Packages For Other Businesses And Non-Profit Organizations. Over The Years, My Direct Mail Letters Have Generated Well Over Half A Billion Dollars In Sales And Donations For All Kinds Of Businesses And Non-Profit Organizations.
4524	Why 6 & 7Figure Internet Marketers Shun Pay Per Click Traffic
4525	Where To Score The Quick Sale, The Value Hunters, And The Deep-Pocket Investor... Plus, The Magic Phrases That Get Each Of Them Reaching For Their Wallets...
4526	Took Less Than 3 Minutes Before I Fully Realized The Unlimited Power I Now Had In My Hands
4527	We Have The Opportunity Not To Live Up To Our Greatest Potential
4528	I Hate When I Just Miss A Call By The Last Ring Hello Hello Damn It!, But When I Immediately Call Back, It Rings Nine Times And Goes To Voicemail. What'd You Do After I Didn't Answer? Drop The Phone And Run Away

4529	People Will See Your Splash Pages, Click On The Link, Read This Information, Join Your Autoresponder And Get Your Guide. They Will Soon See How Simple This System Is And How Quickly They Can Start A Real Internet Business That Produces Real Results. They Will Join The Programs From Your Links And You Make Money.
4530	This Is Great For Swapping Ideas, Talking Strategy, And Learning Several Different Methods Of Making Money With Google Adsense.
4531	Innovative And Powerful Home Based Business Building System On The Planet, And Now I Am GIVING It To You 100% FREE!
4532	The Idea Is To Grab The Eye And Make Certain Key Words And Phrases Stick Out In Their Mind.
4533	It's The Finest Blueprint Of How Business Is Done Online If You Really Want To Succeed
4534	What Actions Do You Need To Take To Improve Both Your Business And Personal Life?
4535	It's True. If You Listen To The Typical "Training" You Are Provided When You Start, You WILL Probably Fail. You Won't Get The Fast Start You Need – And You Will Constantly Struggle On A Monthly Basis Keeping Growing And Pulling In The Money.
4536	Clear Your Mind Of All You Were Told About Making Money
4537	You No Longer Have To Spend A Fortune To Get A Graphics Designer To Create Graphics For You And You No Longer Have To Painfully Spend Countless Hours Trying To Design Your Own. I've Done All The Hard Work For You!
4538	If You Want To Learn How To Create A Highly Profitable, Income-Generating Business With Minimum Start-Up Costs, This Guide Will Teach You How. I Don't Leave Anything To Chance; Instead. I'll Teach You From The Ground Up, Each Step Of The Way On How To Create An Income Stream From Sites That Will Provide Profits For Years To Come.
4539	Ready To Start Down A Less Traveled Path And Into A More Rewarding Lifestyle
4540	How Surveys Can Ultimately Increase Interest And Respect For Your Business Ventures
4541	Don't Get Off The Phone Until You Have Their Credit Card
4542	That's What They Want You To Think...So They Can Continue Reaping All The Profits And Making Quick Moves On Emerging Markets.

4543	Find The Best Places And Methods To Submit A Press Release Online
4544	Incorporate Your Content As Part Of Other Products.
4545	Maybe You Are New To The Online Marketing Game. So Give It All Away And Promote Free Giveaway While Making A Lot Of Money From Several Different Sources All At The Same Time. If You Can Copy And Paste You Can Use This System.
4546	This Is The #1 Google Recommended Technique You Must Use To Get Your Site Noticed
4547	Don't Need To Be A Mathematical Genius To Make Money Online
4548	In Just A Minute I'll Share The Whole Story With You
4549	Why Not Play Ball With The Big Dogs For Big Profits
4550	The Simple And Free Trick To Making Your Domains Rank Higher From The Moment You Register Them...
4551	How Many Times Has Your Ebooks Files Or Reports Have Been Downloaded
4552	I Never Dreamed I Could Get Away From My Dead End Job But I Did
4553	Would It Be OK During Our Coaching Sessions If I Make Requests Of You And Hold You Accountable For Them
4554	Who Else Wants To Get Their Hands On The Specific Checklist Of Components Your Home Business Absolutely Must Have In Order To Avoid Being Part Of The 97% Who Fail Miserably
4555	You'll Be So Excited You Won't Be Able To Contain Yourself
4556	How To Make A Huge Profit From The Creative Process Of Others
4557	It's The Difference Between Having A Cup Of Coffee Or Owning The Coffee Plantation
4558	Millions Of People Are Surfing The Web Every Single Second Looking For How To Solutions
4559	Exactly How You Can Use "Blogging" To Drive Massive Traffic To The Websites You Are Promoting Plus What "Blogging" Service To Use And How To Make Sure Your Blog Keeps People Coming Back For More.
4560	Remember, All This Income Potential And Viral Traffic Comes From A Visitor Who Was Leaving Your Site Anyway. And You Can Have This Up And Running On Your Own Site In A Few Minutes

329

4561	How To Beat Your Competitors Selling The Same Product You Are. This Secret Will Make You Stand Out Of The Resellers Crowd.
4562	What Would It Be Worth To You To Wake Up Whenever You Wanted Every Morning, And Know That You Didn't Have To Deal With A Nightmare Commute, Skyrocketing Gas Prices, A Jerk Boss, Or Just A Mindless Idiot?
4563	Insider Reveals Five Quick, Slick & Zero-Cost 'Secret Techniques.' Internet Marketing Is All About Quick, Easy Cash And Project Quick Cash Is Going To Prove Just That...
4564	This Special Report Is Solely Responsible For Helping Ordinary People Get Huge Results
4565	It's Extremely Frustrating To See So Many Fail Online When A Simple Solution Exists
4566	Advertise For Free And Get Paid For Your Efforts At The Same Time
4567	Imagine Having Your Own Internet Money Machine Sitting Quietly In Cyberspace, Faithfully Sucking In Profits Day After Day, Running On Auto-Pilot As You Do Whatever You Damn Well Please.
4568	How Is It Possible To Work So Hard And Still Have Nothing
4569	Copywriters Are Not The Only Ones Who Can Benefit From Having A Swipe File. Authors And Publishers Can Benefit From Creating A Swipe File Of Best-Selling Titles To Give Them Ideas For Their Own Titles.
4570	Listen Carefully And Read Until The Very End Of This Letter Because You'll Knock Yourself On The Head If You Miss The Tremendous Opportunity That Is Laid Before You.
4571	Competition Is As Scare As Finding A Goldmine On A Desert Road
4572	Yes, That's What I Said: Success Depends Upon Consistently Using A System. In Short, Most Sales People Don't Realize The Sale Is The Result Of A Process. Just Let That Sink In For A Moment, Because It's Really Important. Why? Because It Means No Matter What Your Business, You Can Systemize Your Sales Process.
4573	It's With A Deep Sense Of Urgency That I Highly Encourage You To Take Immediate Action
4574	Tired Of Killing Yourself To Make A Few Bucks Every Now And Then

4575	Nothing To Purchase And No Strings Attached Just Pure Gold Content Rich Information
4576	Actually Its For You! I Know Many Of You Don't Like To Read Long Emails And I Don't Blame You. I Don't Like To Either, So I Am Going To Set Up A Special Blog Just For My Subscribers That The General Public Can Not Access..
4577	Why Internet Marketers No Longer Struggle To Write Money Making Sales Copy
4578	We Use Marketing Funnels, Websites, And Technology To Eliminate The Need For Sales Skills...... Yes, The System Sells Itself
4579	We Just Share With You The Truth About What Works And Does Not Work. NO Hidden Agenda
4580	Oh, Did I Mention You Also Get Attractive Recurring Commissions For Every Friend You Send?
4581	Tagging Is An Important Key In Blogging Which Many People Miss Tagging You Blogs Right.
4582	The Quiet Was So Deafening You Could Anticipate The Excitement This Secret Unfolded
4583	When I Was Just Starting Out Online, I Too Was Bamboozled, Lied To And Misled Into Buying And Enriching 'Them'. It Can Be So Frustrating Isn't It? And It Almost Drove Me To The Point Of Giving Up On Internet Marketing Altogether!!
4584	Get The Truth About How To Make Money With Adsense And Content Networks, Learn How To Supplement Your Affiliate Revenue With Highly Targeted Content Pages... I've Used This To Make As Much As $9 Per Click On Some Sites Where I Was Only Paying $0.30 Per Click To Get Them On My Site.
4585	Backend Sales Opportunities That Tap Into The Core Secret Of Increased Profits
4586	An Important Question You Must Answer If You Want To Build An Internet Empire
4587	But It Can Happen In A Very Short Period Of Time...And It Will Happen If You Can Just Get Your Hands On The Right Formula. Like I Said, I've Done It And Trust Me, If I Can Do It, God Knows....Anybody Can Do It.
4588	You Do Not Need To Be Perfect. Or You Would Waste Most Of Your Time. Simply Remember The Main Processes Needs To Be Highly Reliable. Once Again, Perfection Is Not Your Best Companion.

331

4589	Give Me Just 5 Short Minutes And I'll Show You Where To Begin To Finally Make Real Money Before The Day Ends! The Little Guy CAN Succeed!
4590	This Strategy Can Bring Your Business Into Unimaginable Profits So Quickly In Fact, You'll Lose Your Hair.
4591	How Come Only A Few Rocket Their Business To The Stars
4592	If You Build A Nice Downline Then You Will Also Have Many People To E-Mail To On A Regular Basis! It Doesn't Require Any "Advertising Credits" To E-Mail To This Downline.
4593	It's A Numbers Game So Be Prepared To Lose A Few
4594	Now You Can Earn Massive Profits Using The Same Closely-Held Copywriting Secrets That The Multi-Millionaire Online Gurus Use... At A Tiny Fraction Of The Price
4595	Don't Get Me Wrong - I Think Traditional Internet Marketing Is A Great Way To Make Money IF You Are Dedicated And Willing To Spend A Lot Of Time Learning New Skills. But Let's Face Facts - Only 5% Are Making Any Money Online.
4596	It's Definitely NOT Some Flimsy Little Ebook That You're Going To Forget About Overnight... (I Already Know You've Got Enough Of Those On Your Hard Drive!)
4597	A Proven Method Of Weeding Out Visitors Who Are Merely Curious And Not Serious
4598	Solve Your Customer Complaints By Being Quick And Friendly. The Faster You Respond, The More Your Customers Feel You Care About Them.
4599	How To Promote Is The Problem That Most People Run Into. That Is Where My System Comes In. You Don't Have To Try To Figure Anything Out. I Wrote The Website, Splash Pages And Guide That Will Promote The System For You. You Advertise Your Splash Pages And The System Will Do The Rest.
4600	Every Website Using This Incredible Resource Will Want To Keep It A Secret
4601	It Really Isn't That Difficult To Make Money Online - The Real Question Is How Much
4602	How To Avoid Falling Back Into Debt And Start Following A System Toward Real Wealth
4603	The Sneaky Way To Spy And Recruit JVs To Promote Your Ideas
4604	This Guide Tells Exactly What I Do, All The Mistakes I've Made, And How You Can Get Started With Your Own "Very Small Business." I Didn't Hold Anything Back, And Some Of The Information Is Fairly Personal.

4605	Maybe You're At A Point In Your Life Where It Seems Easier To Give Up And "Be Realistic". Or Maybe You're Just Not Sure If You Can Do It. Hey, That's Okay. You're Not Alone.
4606	So Many Fail To Understand Or Even Use This Incredible Tool
4607	Unless You've Got Connections With These Insiders You'll Always Be On The Sidelines
4608	In Fact... I'm So Serious About Getting This Ebook Into As Many Hands As Possible... I'm Willing To Let You Keep 100% Of The Price If You Help Me!
4609	I Know It's Usually Wise To Avoid Problems At All Costs, Especially When Business Is Involved. But This Is One Of Those Problems You Really Want To Attract: It's The Problem Of TOO Many Loyal, Active Paying Subscribers!
4610	C:\> Bad Command Or File Name Go Stand In The Corner
4611	Free To Public School Teachers And Only $6 To Everyone Else
4612	This Is Your Last Chance To Access The Greatest Free Bargain Of A Lifetime
4613	This Is Not A Trial - You Get Full Access To The Entire Program
4614	We Need You More Than Ever Before This Idea Is Released
4615	Why What's Taught In This Industry Doesn't Work For Most People And Never Will And That's A Criminal Shame.
4616	How Would You Like To Post Hundreds Of Ads World Wide With A Click Of Your Mouse
4617	Especially For Men Who Want To Quit Work Someday While They're Young
4618	Use Paypal To Accept Money From Your Website. How To Put Your Product Into Paypal And How To Embed A Payment Button Onto Your Website.
4619	All I Ask Is That You Pay A $1 Admin Fee
4620	We Show People How To Make More Money Right Now Enjoying Life By Doing What They Love To Do, Even If They Love Their Day. Do You Know Anyone Who Would Benefit By Learning How To Make More Money Now?
4621	This Will Automate Your Business So That When You Make Sales, Even When You Are Asleep, Knowing That Your Customer Can Instantly Download What They Paid For Keeping Your Customers Happy.

4622	Hire Someone To Answer The Phones, To Keep Your Appointment Calendar, To Do Your Filing, Your Book-Keeping And The Clerical Work So You Can Focus On The Money-Making Side Of Your Business.
4623	Your Goal Should Be To Set Up A Business That Provides You With Recurring And Passive Income. That Means You Do The Work Once, And The Money Keeps Coming In Over And Over. Then If You Do More Work, It Means More Money Comes In.
4624	Please Don't Get Bent Out Of Shape Over This But It's The Truth
4625	Watch Learn And Apply These Amazing Techniques And See Your Bank Account Explode
4626	Another Common Mistake To Avoid That Can Be Far Worse Than A Bad Product - It Can Kill Your Long-Term Reputation As A Marketer.
4627	It's Important To Keep This Offer Limited In Order To Protect It's Value
4628	Now It's Your Chance To Make Gobs And Oodles Of Money
4629	How To Survive An Iris Audit If You've Been A Sloppy Record-Keeper
4630	You Can See Why They're Not Really Happy With Me. This Is Serious Business...This Could Mean Them Losing Thousands To Their Bottom Line, That Can Be A Hard Pill To Swallow For Some.
4631	The Motivation Behind This Concept Is Not Bad. If We Start Thinking Our Time Equals Money, We'll Probably Get Off Our Butts And Spend Less Staring At The Boob Tube. So If Thinking Of Your Time This Way Gets You Off Your Duff, Then You're Certainly Better Off.
4632	As A New Year Is Quickly Approaching, There's ONE Thing That I See As Becoming Critical To Our Businesses. ... And That One Thing Is To "Become More Transparent" With What We're Doing In Our Online Businesses.
4633	The Real Reason Why Most People Who Try Never Make A Buck On The Internet. This Is Ridiculously Simple, But It's Amazing How Many People Completely Miss It...And Belly Flop.
4634	If You Keep Hearing "The Money Is In The List" But Have No Idea What "A List" Is, Or How To Get One... Or If You're Trying To Build A List And Keep Getting Stalled By Opt-Outs And Trapped In Spam Filters.

334

4635	We Have Decided To Ignore The Conventional Wisdom And Instead Of Going With A One Time Offer And Other Marketing Gimmicks – We Are Giving You The Options Right Here,
4636	You'll Eventually Want To Create Your Crappy Job Because Of This
4637	Undetectable Dirty Tricks New Car Dealers Use Unless You Know What To Look For
4638	Easy Ways To Create Landing Pages That Get Monster Traffic And Do An Awesome Job Of Grabbing Sales... A Landing Page Like That Will Be A Real Asset To Your Business
4639	This Story Sent Major Shockwaves Throughout The Entire Internet Marketing Community
4640	Now You Can Rise Up With The Sun Or Sleep In As Late As You Want
4641	Our Goal Is To Share Proprietary Ideas That Will Save You Valuable Time And Money
4642	We Help People Come To The Place Where They Value Investing In Themselves
4643	Here's How To Increase Conversions By At Least 75% BETTER For Less
4644	Create A Coffee Table Book With Inspiring Images Using PLR Images Or Wallpapers.
4645	Let Machines Do All Your Selling So You Can Earn $10,000 Per Hour
4646	I Look Forward To Teaching Tomorrow Night And I Am Excited About All The Responses Letting Us Know How Excited You Are About This FR*EE Training. Don't Let It Slip By Without Taking Advantage Of Something You Have Been Waiting For And Asking For So Long Now. Talk To You Tomorrow Night.
4647	You Won't Get Rich By Next Friday Or Double Your Money Every Week
4648	This Incredible Headline Collection Includes Everything Someone Needs To Get Their Website Ads Up And Running.
4649	I Could Give You A Ton Of Other Keywords To Search For, But That Would Be Silly To Give Away My Secrets.
4650	How Will You Tie All These Action Steps Into A Successful Action Plan?

4651	Whether You're Trying To Build Your List, Promote Affiliate Products, Push Resell Products, Or Sell Your Own Products, Everything Online Moves At Breakneck Speed, And If You Can't Build Sites Quickly & Easily, You'll Soon Find Your Competitors Leaving You In The Dust.
4652	I Don't Want You To MISS OUT On YOUR Dreams! I Don't Want You To Die One Day, WISHING You Had Done Things Differently. But There's NO Reason, We Can't Set Aside A Small Portion Of Each Day To Focus On Our BIG Dreams.
4653	As Your List Of Prospects Grows, It Becomes More And More Difficult And Time Consuming To Figure Out When You Last Spoke With Which Prospect And Which Information You Send Them.
4654	These Strategies Will Continue To Work For You Long After You've Initially Set Them Up And "Activated" Them, Ensuring That You Are Able To Flood Your Website With Consistent Traffic Every Day, Passively - Effortlessly And At No Cost!
4655	Imagine The Time And Expense Of Trying To Do This Yourself
4656	7 Commandments Of Writing Highly Effective Sales Letters
4657	Plug Into My Marketing System And Sit Back As Commissions Grow Month After Month
4658	The Exact Same Action Plan Used To Create And Sell Products In 25 Niche Markets That Sold Over $3 Million Worth Of Products Online! This Is So Simple Even A Child Can Do It! So Enter Your Email Now And Begin To Earn!
4659	Create Mini Guide Booklets To Inform, Inspire, Or Educate Others.
4660	You Must Look For A Way To Create Something Of Value If You Want To Build A Business And Then Leverage Someone Else's Time To Do The Time-Consuming Chores That Are Interfering With The Time You Must Spend Building Your Business.
4661	One Out Of Every Five Parents Currently Work Two Jobs To Survive
4662	Because Of This "Disappearance Of Sunday" Nobody Was Able To Access The PLR Special Offer No.10 Page Past A Certain Time So There Are Still A Few Packages Left At The "Way Too Low For The General Public" Price.
4663	This Will Help You Avoid Those Nasty Mistakes That Can Cost You Members And Dollars.
4664	Crush Your Competition By Legally Stealing Profits Right Out From Under Them

4665	Okay, I Can Almost Hear Your Mind Thinking, "Why Give This Book Away For Free If It's Bursting At The Seams With Exact Methods, The Secret Strategies And Closely Guarded Tactics You Used To More Than Triple Your Income?"
4666	Yah Right It's So Easy Simply Follow The Step By Step Video And You'll Make Quadrillions
4667	If You've Been In Network Marketing Yourself, You Know It's A LOT Harder Than They Tell You And 97% Of Home Business Owners Actually Spend More Than They Make And End Up Sad, Disillusioned, And Frustrated.
4668	People Today Want Quality Information: If You Can Offer Them Reliable, Accurate Information On Topics That They're Interested In, They Are More Than Willing To Pay. The Service You Provide, By Offering This Information At One Centralized Location, Is Valuable. I'll Show You The What, The Whys, And Most Importantly, Exactly How To Implement Them.
4669	Learn The Warning Signs If You Suffer From Debilitating Light Wallet Symptoms
4670	Just Understand That If You Don't Choose To Have These Lethal Techniques At Your Disposal, The Savvy Few Will Have The Knowledge And Power To Take You Out Of The Game, While Your Left Broke And Confused.
4671	Each Uncharted Step Could Be A Landmine Waiting To Explode In Your Face
4672	What You Must Substitute For Money In Order To Really Be Successful! This Amazing Surprise Will Shake You Up Unless You're Brain Dead! THIS One Concept Alone, Is Worth More Than Anything You Own Now!
4673	We Don't Want To Put This Out On A Mass Scale
4674	I Have No Control Over What People Do Or Don't Do With My Products. So While Your Income Is NOT Guaranteed In Any Way, Your Money Back IS Guaranteed If You Are Not Satisfied.
4675	How To Add A Meta Description Tag To Your HTML Code
4676	If You're Promoting A Home Business Opportunity Or Affiliate Marketing Product, Listen Up -- Because Right Now, I'm Just GIVING AWAY Targeted Traffic That Would Otherwise Go To Waste.
4677	This Ebook Leads You From Point To Point Like A Well Made Map. All You Have To Do Is Follow Each Step And Success Is Assured. It Could Not Be Simpler. It Could Not Be Easier.

4678	As An Online Marketing Business Coach In The Network Marketing Industry. I Enjoy Working With Struggling Entrepreneurs Helping Them Achieve Their Full Potential In This Great Industry.
4679	You're Missing The Big Picture If Your Business Isn't On Autopilot
4680	Most Of The Programs Out There Are Worthless, And Most Of The " GURUS" Are Selling Their Programs And Software To You, So That They Can Make Their Millions Without A Care In The World.
4681	What's So Great About This Is If You Are Willing To Work Hard And Build A Residual Based System In The Initial Phase, You Can Reap The Benefits. If You Look Around You, You Will See Examples Of Residual Income All Over.
4682	All It Takes Is Compiling A List Of People Who Share A Common Interest. You Really Can't Fail This Way, Unless Of Course You Just Don't Take Action.
4683	Press Any Key To Continue Or Any Other Key To Quit
4684	If Only There Was An Alternative That Could Pay Us For The Results We Give Our Advertisers So We Earn The Commissions We Are Due ...
4685	"If Only The Weekend Could Last Forever!" What If Your Work Week Was Every Bit As Exciting As Your Weekend? What You Do Today, Right Now, Sets The Tone For The Rest Of Your Life. Let's Take A Quick Journey Into Your New Possibilities Right Now!
4686	That's Right... For Less Than The Price Of Dinner And A Movie, You Can Be On Your Way To Earning Thousands Of Dollars Every Single Month.
4687	Hit Send And Sit Back While Watching The Orders Start To Fill Your Inbox
4688	If You Are Going The Affiliate Promotion Route, You Should Promote MANY, And Never Keep All Your Eggs In One Basket
4689	There Are Worse Things Than Getting A Call For A Wrong Number At 4 AM. It Could Be A Right Number
4690	It's So Exciting To See Those Instant Payment Notices In Your Mail Box
4691	Let's Face It, The 'Filthy Rich Marketers' Who We Hear About Every Day Have It Made - Hundreds Of Thousands Of People On Their Lists Making Them Lots Of Money!

4692	First, You Need To Take A Step Back, Think About What You Want In Your Life, What You Want To Achieve And Where You Want To Be In 1 Year, 2 Years Or 3 Years Time.
4693	Where Is Your Business Focusing? I've Found That One Of The Most Powerful Practices As An Entrepreneur Is To Spend A Day Away From The Office, Dream A Little, And Envision My Company 1, 3, 5 Years Into The Future.
4694	This May Sound Silly But Not Everyone Online Is Searching For A Business Opportunity
4695	Use Your Content As An Unannounced Bonus For Buying Your Products.
4696	I Hope You Are Having Great Success With Your Marketing Business But If You Are Having Any Struggles I Would Like To Offer My Help To You For FREE.
4697	Frame Every So-Called Disaster With These Words, "In Five Years Will This Matter"
4698	Do You Know What Separates Real Winners From Losers In Online Business? The Winners "Make" It Because They All Use The Most Powerful Universal Marketing Strategies, Key-words, And Headlines Known To Trigger Consumer Action. Knowing Exactly How Winner's Use Keywords And Structure Headlines Is The Secret To Selling Any Product Or Service.
4699	Earning A Six Figure Online Income (Scalable To 7 Figures) Doing What You Love, Is Not Only Doable In A Very Short Pe-riod Of Time, But Actually Much Easier Than You've Been Led To Believe.
4700	This Private Webinar Is For A Select Group. If You Are Seeing This Page, Then You May Be One Of The 500 People Who Will Be Allowed To Be On This Webinar (But Only If You Act Fast).
4701	If You're Struggling To Make Money Online Start With This Idea
4702	Getting Your Content To Rank Higher Than Everyone Else For Free
4703	You See, Once Most People Hear About All These Benefits Of Running Their Own Online Membership Site, They Get All Ex-cited, Jacked Up, And Motivated To Give It A Go...But Then Sadly Most Fall Flat On Their Face.
4704	I Hope You'll Be Joining Us In This Fabulous Marketing Pro-gram
4705	What If I Could Help Map Your Mind Toward Success Inter-ested

4706	Isn't Time You Stopped Fooling Around And Got Serious About Your Life And Your Business? Chances Like This - To Step Into The Company Of Millionaires And Have Them Reveal The Personal Secrets That Made Them Rich...
4707	We Also Know That This Time Of The Year, Time Is Especially Valuable. We All Need Time To Spend With Our Families But We Need To Continue Our Success As Well. We Have Something You Must See That Will Save You Time.
4708	If You're Trying To Start An Internet Business, But Keep Getting Bogged Down By The Complex Technology Required, Then What I Have To Say Will Be Music To Your Ears!
4709	Find New Target Audiences For Your Products Or Services. For Example, If You're Selling Coffee To Stores Try To Also Sell It To Coffee Shops.
4710	Affiliate Marketing Is Just A Fancy Term To Describe Promoting Another Businesses' Product And Then Earning A Commission Every Time A Sale Is Made. Commissions Can Range From A Few Dollars To $1,000's Of Dollars For Every Item You Sell, Making It A No-Brainer Method For Anyone Looking To Create Income Online.
4711	Nice To Finally Tell People What You Think And Turn That Into A Residual Income Stream?
4712	Important: This Is Very Different From Google-Type Search Results Where You Make Pennies Per Click. Clickbank Commissions Can Be Over $100/Sale!
4713	I Want You To Come Back And Tell Me What Happened
4714	Once You're Committed You Will Be Successful And It's As Simple As That
4715	A Simple Trick That Increases Conversions By 6% While More Importantly, Reducing Return Rate By 38%
4716	How To Quickly Determine A Business Problem Everyone Else To Trying To Solve
4717	The True Reason All Of These Giants Of Industry Are Able To Amass Huge Wealth And Success Is For One Very Simple Reason, They Understand And Apply The Success Principle To Their Lives Every Single Day, Just Like I Do And Just Like You Will Once You Join Today.
4718	Ways To Promote Your Web Site While Doing Non Business Tasks
4719	Plus, The Quick Start Action Guide Outlining The Most Important Steps In An Easy-To-Follow Visual Format.

4720	At Any Time, If You Need Any Additional Help Getting Started I Also Provide You With My Personal Email Address! If You Ever Need To Contact Me About Anything You Can Get Expert Advice Directly From Me.
4721	Here's Some Surprising Information That Is Easily Worth It's Weight In Gold
4722	You Must Have Your Own Website, Product, And Rich Content To Really Make Money Online
4723	But What If You Had Your Very Own Membership Site That Was Pre-Loaded With The Most Valuable, Mind Blowing Content That People Would Illegally Sell Their Kidney On The Black Market To Acquire?
4724	I Help People Systematically Attract New Customers That Make Them More Money By Using "The Language Of Millionaires." Do You Know Anyone Who Could Benefit By Making More Money Right Now?
4725	Fast Forward Your Viewing Clock And See How This Idea Can Unearth Some Serious Cash
4726	Think About It: Web Designers, Banks, Insurance Companies, Teachers, Magazine Editors, Realtors, Graphic Designers, Marketers, Travel Agents, Retailers, As Well As Many Other Business Types Need And Use These All The Time.
4727	Special Of The Week _____ Gone Crazy _____ Only $2.25 (Up To 1 Million _____ With This Ad)
4728	After Ten Years Of Only Dreaming About A New Life We Found One Now
4729	Here's A Quick Way To Increase Conversions By At Least 75%
4730	You Should Also Know That I Do Not Condone Get-Rich Quick Schemes. If You Read At Any Other Website That You Can Get Search Engine Traffic Overnight, It Is Simply Not True.
4731	How Do You Intend To Achieve The Salary You Rightfully Deserve
4732	Ten Elements Every Sales Letter Must Include To Avoid High Click Through Rates
4733	Any Time Another Site Picks Up This Article, It'll Just Be Seen As Duplicate Content Anyway.
4734	You Got To Get Yourself Together Before Someone Can Take You Apart

4735	You Will Learn How To Write Your Own Articles Or How To Outsource The Work On A Budget. Also Where To Submit The Articles To Get Swarms Of Hungry Qualified Traffic To Your Website With Their Credit Cards At The Ready.
4736	Stop Wasting Time And Energy On Marketing Techniques That Never Deliver The Traffic Your Site Needs To Survive.
4737	They Don't Call Him Stupid Anymore Now That He's Making All This Money
4738	This Free Gift Just May Be Your New Secret Weapon To Financial Success
4739	You'll Never Again Have To Spin Your Wheels And Run Around In Circles Trying To Get Your Website To Show A Profit. You Won't Have To Settle For Less Than Maximum Results
4740	Go From Great To Good Enough - Spending Too Much Time On A Project/Task Due To Perfectionism Can Almost Be As Unproductive As Putting It Off Completely. You'll Reel In This Nasty Habit Completely By Giving Clear, Specific Time-Limits To Tasks And An Alarm That Acts As A Slap-In-The-Face That It's Time To Move On.
4741	It Is No Secret That Traffic = Money. What Is Hidden From You Though Are The Actual Working Methods That'll Generate You Targeted Visitors. There's A Huge Difference Between Targeted Traffic And Traffic In General.
4742	How To Get Inside Google's Mind And Make Google Reward You With Ultra Targeted Traffic Coming To Your Site. Discover What Google Is Looking For When It Comes To Pleasing Their Customers (Online Searchers), So You Can Secure The Top Rankings In The Search Results.
4743	I Have It. I've Tested It. It Works As Promised. But Even Better, I've Put Their Customer Support Through The Ringer And Will Tell You That My Experience With Them Has Been Top Notch.
4744	If You're A Veteran Or Even A Newbie To Affiliate Marketing, What's More Of A Challenge Is Trying To Ward Off Those Who Try To Hijack Your Commissions By Bypassing Your Link And Replacing It With Their Own.
4745	Most Of The Good Dot Com Domains Are Already Taken But There Are An Unbelievable Amount Of The Very Best Names Still Available And Only We Offer The Opportunity For YOU To Benefit From The Enormous Residual Revenues Being Generated.

4746	If You're Like Me When I Started You're Probably Looking For Freebies You'll Never Use
4747	This Tool Is Packed With Tons Of New Videos And Tutorials To Help You Get A Firm Grasp Of How This Whole Marketing Thing Works So You Can Finally Take A Deep Breath And Say To Yourself... I GOT IT!
4748	Google Recently Introduced A Feature To Its Webmaster Portal That Can Be Like A Metal Detector On The Beach.
4749	Our Marketing Systems That We Have Built For Other Affiliate Programs This Last Several Years Have Been Instrumental In Creating Millions Of Dollars In Affiliate Profits For Us And Our Team Members.
4750	Think Instead Of How To Create Value Create Or Design A Product Or A System Or A Method That Can Be Repeated Over And Over Again -- Because You Don't Really Have A Business Until You Have A System That You Can Repeat And A Machine That Can Essentially Run Itself Without You Evening Being There.
4751	No List... No Traffic... No Tech Experience... No Worries! Need A Turnkey Solution That Includes Free List Building Training, Free Traffic-Driving Training, Free Installation... And Step-By-Step Instructions For Creating A Cash Cow That Pays You On Autopilot.
4752	Wasting Thousands Of Dollars And Hours And Still No Real Sales
4753	I'm Going To Help Facilitate You Getting To The Next Step
4754	Do You Now Understand How Valuable This Can Really Be For You? Huge Advertising Potential, Insane List Building, Large Direct Commissions, And Mind-Boggling Residual Commissions!
4755	It May Be The Truth But Not Necessarily The Whole Truth
4756	Find Someone Who Already Created A Successful Business Willing To Show You How
4757	Get Started Right Now To Receive Your 100% Risk Free Membership
4758	A Little Secret To Increase Your Returns With Ezine Advertising
4759	Do You Ever Wonder What Your Customers Want? Most Business Owners Ask Themselves That Question Daily. I Know I Do And I Bet You Do Too.

4760	This Is How I Have Made My Living In The Technology World For The Last Decade - And Offline For The 10 Years Prior To That.
4761	Enjoy The Freedom To Come And Go As You Please, Spend More Time With Your Family, Playing Golf, Doing The Things You Love, And Hey...You Can Even Work In Your Underwear If You Want! (Just Make Sure Your Web Cam Is Turned Off!)
4762	You Only Want People With Very Specific Interests And Desires. That Way You're Only Sending Them Info About Things You Know Will Excite Them.
4763	The Foundational Principle Of All Successful Business Is Setting Up A Process That Can Be Repeated And Duplicated Over And Over Again. And That's Really The Foundational Principle Of The Marketing Methods And Systems That I Teach.
4764	I Always Knew I Didn't Belong In The Rat-Race. That I Was Totally Under-Appreciated And Under Paid, And More Importantly That My Creativity Was Not Being Fully Utilized. I Had No Passion For What I Did Anymore.
4765	While 'The Masses' Have Been Flocking Around Harassing Their Loved Ones, Total Strangers, Or Whoever Else... A Small Group Of Innovative Networkers Have Quietly Been Making A Fortune Using The Secret Technology I'm Getting Ready To Share With You Today.
4766	The Secret To Total Niche Domination – That Gives You The Training And The Tools To Find Untapped Niche Markets... Where A Boatload Of Cash Waits Like Low-Hanging Fruit Ready To Be Picked.
4767	This Is Typically Where The Fear And/Or Confusion Sets In For People. Don't Worry. For The First Time Ever, I've Broken Everything Down Into Simple Easy-To-Swallow Nuggets That Are Low In Fluff And Pack More Power Than An Extra-Extra Large Triple-Protein Shake.
4768	The Formula Is Unlike Anything Else You May Have Seen Or Tried Before Because What I've Created Is An Actual SYSTEM That Leads You Through Each Step In The Product, From Start To Finish.
4769	You See, Making Money Online Without A Proven Plan Is A Lot Like Trying To Bake A Cake Without A Recipe...You'll Only End Up Making Lots Of Mistakes, A Big Mess And Wasting A Bunch Of Money

344

4770	Honestly, The Biggest Variable To Your Success Has Absolutely Nothing To Do With The Companies, Their Compensation Plan, All The Literature, The Audios And Cads Or Even The Product!
4771	What's It Worth To Have A Niche Millionaire Hand You A Proven System
4772	I Came Across This Secret Code Without Knowing How Powerful It Would Become
4773	You'll Continue Jumping From Business To Business Until You Become Frustrated And Run Out Of Money. If You Sit There And Do Nothing, NOTHING Will Happen!
4774	For The Price Of A Pizza I Got My Head Back On Straight
4775	Why You Need To Break Through Your Comfort Zone And Think Outside The Box
4776	Look Into My Crystal Ball Right Now As I GIVE You The Trends And Predictions (Based On My 10+ Years Of Online Business) That Will Shape The Next 12 Months Of Internet Marketing... And Beyond.
4777	Discover Simple Sales Page Secrets That Can Double Or Triple Your Profits
4778	The Single Most Powerful Word Consistently Used In The Top 43% Of All Successful Ads
4779	Right Now, There Is Already An 'Elite Group' Using This System. The Longer You Delay, The More Money You'll Be Losing Because You'll End Up Having Hundreds Or Thousands Of Competitors. NOW'S THE BEST TIME.
4780	How To Create An Online Business For Next To Nothing Within A Couple Of Minutes
4781	There's No Need To Continue Searching For The Best Way To Work From Home
4782	Use Your Contents As Inspiration For Poetry, Stories, Or Fables.
4783	Let Us Share Our 12 Years Of Experience Of Online Marketing With You
4784	It's Important Always To Explain Why You Are Doing Anything Unusual In Your Advertising And Marketing. If You Are Offering Your Unfinished Product For Half Price In Exchange For Your Customers Having To Wait Six Months For It, Explain Why.
4785	Get Your Teleseminar Transcribed, Then Sell It As An Ebook Or Course.

345

4786	Your Success Will Be Directly Linked To Your Sales Letter And Automating Your Business
4787	The Course Will Guide You And Show You EXACTLY How To Set Everything Up So You Will Be Live Online And Ready To Sell In A Matter Of Hours.
4788	Speed On The Internet: Two Questions That Other Providers Hope You'll Never Ask Them
4789	How To Test This Like Crazy And Convert Prospects Into Buyers
4790	One Popular Method Of Getting Started Is Affiliate Marketing. This Is Where You Promote Other People's Products And Get A Percentage Commission For Each Sale. The Upside To This Method Is You Don't Need A Website And You Don't Need Your Own Product. It's Very Easy To Get Going, And Some People Make A Lot Of Money With Affiliate Marketing.
4791	This Is Integrity Suicide! I'm Sure You've Seen The Hundreds Of Products On The Market That Are Using The Same Products To Throw Into Their Packages As Bonuses. Nothing Says "Cheapo" More Than A Product That Has A Bunch Of Bonus's That 40 Other People Are Offering Or That Can Be Found For Free On Other Websites.
4792	It Rains On The Rich And The Poor And The Good And The Bad. So Start Doing Something That Really Makes You Feel Good About Your Yourself. Contribute Something Of Value To Yourself And Society. Start A Business Based Upon Your Interests And Make It Happen Without Excuses Until Your Achieve Your Goal. Then Set Higher Goals And Accomplish Them Just By Putting One Step In Front Of The Other Until You Arrive At Each Of Your New Destinations.
4793	In Other Words, You Can Always Earn More Money Than You Spend And Can Easily Grow Your Business And Your Income Month After Month Without Going Broke.
4794	Outsourcing And How To Choose 'The Right' Person For The Job (Discover The 4 Simple Rules That Will Save You Money, Time And Months Of Stress.)
4795	Seriously, If You Really Want To Multiply The Benefit You Receive From Your Article Marketing, This Tool And Service Provided By The Good Guys Is Your Best Bet: .
4796	Share The Wealth Now Or The Government May Do It For You

4797	Some Educational Resources Are Not Appropriate In A Class-room Setting Since People Learn At A Different Rate And Not Everyone Needs To Learn Or Know Everything .
4798	Look, There Are Tons Of Great New Products, Offers, Strate-gies, Quick Money Solutions, Etc. Released On What Seems Like A Daily Basis, But For The Next Week I Want To Change Your Focus. Don't Worry About What You Could Be Missing Out On, And Focus On What You've Got Right In Front Of You.
4799	Do You Know That With This Service, Once You've Joined, Will Allow You To Take A Vacation For AN ENTIRE MONTH, And STILL Get Targeted Hits To Your Site Every Day?
4800	Are Your American Dreams Based On Freebies And Entitle-ments Or Self Determination
4801	It's True. You Don't Need Any Special Printers Or Expensive Photography Equipment Because All Of The Pictures You Take Will Be Uploaded Directly To The Internet.
4802	And, Of Course, Because This Is My Full-Time Occupation You'll Have My Full-Time Attention To Ensure That You Achieve The Same Results As Me. I Will Show You Step-By-Step Everything I Do So That You Can Do The Same.
4803	You're Not Going To Find Slick Sales Copy With Hyped Screenshots And Big Bold Fonts On This Page. I've Chosen To Just Put My Offer Inside A Demo Of The Actual Product.
4804	A Great Place To Be And You Get Paid In Cash
4805	Are You Spinning Around In Circles Trying To Figure Out How To Make Money Online
4806	Capitalizing The First Letter Of Every Word In Your Headline Attracts More Sales
4807	Let Us Give You Back Your Time; And Assist You In Creating A Passive Residual Income With Long Term Benefits!
4808	Special Marketing Test! Discover How You Can Get Your Own Copy Of Our 6 Week Home Study Course, Normal Price $697, And The Complete Business Bonuses Worth $1997 For Only $397 And Your Package Will Be Shipped Via Priority Mail To Anywhere In The World.
4809	12 *Hot* Buttons To Press! Discover All The 12 Hot Words You Must Use In Your Sales Letter In Order To Tap Into Your Prospect's Desire And Emotions And Persuade Them To Act Now - Not Later!
4810	You Can Use This Technique Right Now To Sell More Prod-ucts Through Your Affiliate Links.

347

4811	Don't Just Bend The Rules Break Them And Make Huge Profits
4812	I Think We Got Things In The Wrong Order Here... CUT! TAKE TWO! My Brain Must Be A Little Scrambled. I'm Feeling Kind Of Dizzy...Where Are We?
4813	There Probably Isn't A Better Time To Make A Lot Of Money Online
4814	Now Here Is The Greatest Part Of This System... Almost Everyone That Reads This Website And Gets The Guide, Joins The System. Those Who Don't Join Are Very Rare. Unfortunately For Them, They Can Not See The Awesome Profit Potential In This System. It Isn't A Problem For You Though Because Most People Can See The Opportunity They Are Facing And They Will Join.
4815	How To Spot The Killer Niches... There Are 6 Checks You Need To Do... That's All It Is, Six Simple Things That Point Out The Killer Niches To You.
4816	Here's A Fact For You: It's NOT In The Gurus' Interest For You To Make Money. Once You Make Money, You Will Stop Buying Products From Them...So What They Do Is Keep Promoting All These Products...Products That'll Never Give You The 'Whole Picture'.
4817	The Easy Way To Refine A Product For Ultimate Profitability For Free
4818	Success Watches What Everyone Else Is Doing Then Does The Opposite
4819	For Those Of You That Are Gung Ho And Ready To Go -- As In Make Money Immediately, Well, You May Just Want To Kick It Off With The Quick Start Guide Which Will Have You And Your New Profit Pulling Software Up And Running In A Matter Of Minutes!
4820	If 95% Or More Are Losing Money In Their Marketing, Then The Other 5% is Getting Filthy Rich At Their Expense! So The Real Question Is - Why Aren't You?
4821	If You Decide That This Isn't For You, We Wish You Well And Appreciate The Fact That We Had An Opportunity To Present The System To You.
4822	Why The Majority Of Home Based Businesses Have No Clue About Making Money

4823	It's The Coolest Online Membership Area That Creates The Fastest, Never Ending, Fantasy Money Making System With 11 Huge Categories, Master Products, And Spell Bound Software With Resale Rights
4824	P.S. - When You Join With Us - You Will Receive Bonus' That Will Blow You Away. They Are Worth Far More Than The Price To Join. Frankly - We Think You Might Be A Little Nutty If You Didn't Take Us Up On It? Seriously - Its That GOOD!
4825	If You Leave This Page Or Procrastinate, You May Miss Your Spot. If You Act Immediately By Clicking The Order Button Below, I Can Still Guarantee You One Of These Spots... And I'll Get To Work ASAP Making Your _____.
4826	Every Day Millions Of People Are Looking For Ways To Make Extra Money. They Voluntarily Enter Their Names And Contact Information Onto 1000's Of Web Sites Around The World Hoping To Find That One Golden Opportunity.
4827	A Secret Way To Uncover In-Demand Keywords That Buyers (Not Merely Information Seekers) Are Searching For Online. Buyers = Money. If You Know What Buyers Are Looking For, You Could Easily Fulfill Their Demands And Make Money Like Crazy.
4828	There's No Better Combination To Help You Achieve Financial Security Than Attending Distance Learning Classes That Focus On Internet Marketing Education.
4829	If You're Anything Like Me, You Probably Don't Have The Time To Sit Down And Submit Your Links To A Couple Of Hundred Sites A Week PLUS Manage To Get All Of Those Links On Your Own Site Pages.
4830	Teach Your Friends How Not To Be Jealous Of Your New Success
4831	You've Just Stumbled Across The Best Kept Secret On The Internet
4832	If You've Never Built A Website Before, Or Want To Get Up And Running Quickly And Without Hiring A Software Developer, This Report Is For You. We Reveal The Top Cost-Effective, User Friendly Site Building Software Available, And The Best Services You Can Get For Your Money.
4833	A Proven Method Of Increasing The Value Of All Your Products
4834	It Doesn't Take A Genius To Figure Out That With Just 10 Or More Similar Programs, You Can Have A Really Good Income In Thousands Of Dollars Flowing Into Your Bank Account!

349

4835	We'd Like To Give You This Insane Opportunity To Legally Steal All The Secret Data That Has Been Gathered And Compiled By Our Team Over The Past 4 ½ Years. This Confidential Package Is A Result Of Years Of Research And Has Never Been Revealed Before...
4836	Boost Monthly Affiliate Commissions. Your Only 5 Minutes Away From Getting Your Hands On Our Complete All-In-One Turnkey System That Will Help Stuff Affiliate Paychecks Into Your Pocket Like Clockwork... Guaranteed!
4837	I Don't Expect Any Refunds As You Know Exactly What I'm Offering, There's No Blind Sales Letter Here. If However You're Not Happy For Whatever Reason, Just Drop Me An Email And I'll Refund You No Questions Asked. Seriously I Don't Want Your Money Unless You're 100% Satisfied So You've Got Nothing To Lose.
4838	If It Isn't Working Online Sell Your Time To Someone Else
4839	Carve Out Your Slice Of The Internet Pie With 301 Magical Marketing Tools
4840	Do You Struggle To Find Enough Hours In The Day To Get Everything Done. Between The Demands Of A Busy Daily Life, Working To Make Ends Meet, And Facing All Of The Distractions That Come With Being Socially Connected 24/7, The Time You Have To Devote To Making Money Seems To Become More And More Constricted.
4841	Why Stupid Advertisers Try To Fight The System Only To End Up Paying Dearly For It
4842	Are Your Racking Your Brain Relying On The Same Old Stale Pay Per Click Ad Campaigns
4843	Develop Flash Cards For Students Or Parents.
4844	After You Become A Member Of The Core-Business, You Will Feed The Referrals You Generate (From Following The Step-By-Step Strategy) In To The Core-Business Which Progressively Earns You Recurring Commissions.
4845	Content Is King. No Doubt You've Heard That A Few Times, But You'll Be A Content Machine When You're Done With This Tutorial!
4846	I've Lived Through The Crappy Jobs And Hated My Boss... Man, Sitting In Traffic Each And Every Morning To Make It On Time To A Job That I Couldn't Stand. It's So Stressful Isn't It? And Let's Not Forget The Money... Struggling To Pay Every Bill That Came. And All The While Living In Terrible Apartments, Just Wishing I Could Afford Better...

4847	You Get To Work And You're Like Everyone Around You. They Get A Lousy Paycheck. You Get A Lousy Paycheck. They Trade Their Time For Money. You Trade Your Time For Money And Broke The Day After Payday.
4848	Being Stressed Out... That's Scary. Being Broke That's Scary, REALLY Scary Especially With This Crazy Economy, Things Are Gearing Up To Get Even Scarier. So What Do We Do?????
4849	Create A Brand New Idea Without Having To Write A Single Word
4850	So If You Ever Dreamed Of Being Successful In Business You Must Listen Carefully. Did You Ever Wonder Why Some Words Are More Powerful Than Others Or Why Some Words Create Success While Other Words Fail?
4851	If You're Planning On Spending $2,500 On A Diamond Engagement Ring, I'll Send You Home With Either A Ring Worth $4,100, Or $1,000 Cash Still In Your Pocket
4852	The Pot Belly Approach To Successful Marketing Even If The Subject Is Weight Loss
4853	Amazing! Just Point And Click And You Can Be On The Way To Having Kick Butt Sales Letters!
4854	I Strongly Believe That, Given The Right Know-How, Framework And Foundation, Anyone Can Easily Make At Least $10,000 Or More Every Single Month With A Membership Web Site.
4855	What Will You Do With All The Time And Effort You Save
4856	Find Out My Top Secret Weapon That Almost Every "Guru" Tells You To Stay Away From... This Little Trick Helps Me Get Tons Of Traffic For Pennies On The Dollar... And Most Of The Time This Traffic Produces More "Profit" Than The Traditional Methods
4857	Success Is Earned – It Is NOT A RIGHT. It Takes Work - Consistent Work. It Also Takes A Proven Roadmap. Why Try And Reinvent The Wheel?
4858	Here Are The Good News. While People Turn To The Internet For Comfort, Shopping And Opportunity, Doors Are Opened For Clever Marketers. This Is The Time To Market Online. This Is The Time To Get A Piece Of The Pie.
4859	Information You'll Take Seriously For Less Than A Typical Morning Starbucks

4860	It's Time To Finally Take Control Of Your Life, Stop Answering To A Boss Who Only Wants You To Work As Hard As Possible To Make Him Look Good. If You Truly Want To Make A Difference In Your Own Life, This Course Has To Be So Incredibly Easy That Anyone Can Use It Immediately To Make As Much Money As You Want.
4861	How To Capture Email Addresses To Find Your Fortune In The Follow-Up
4862	If You Can't Yet Build A Simple Website You Pretty Much Need To Learn How To Do This Now, Or Walk Away From Internet Marketing Forever.
4863	You Might Be On The Way To Having A Real Business When You Can Leave For 90 Days, And Never Even Have To Check In, And Be Confident That Your Business Will Still Be Running Well When You Come Back Otherwise You Don't Yet Have A Business.
4864	How Branding Increases Your Revenue Benefits Now And In The Future
4865	Here Is Where You Have To Make A Decision...A Critical Decision ... Following The Masses On Google Or Be Among The Smart Idiots That Cash In On My Secret Yahoo "Glitch".
4866	How To Limit And Eliminate Your Risk Of Losing Money On Ads To Nearly Zero
4867	Record The Text As An MP3 Audio Book And Sell The Recording.
4868	Please, No Tire-Kickers, Forum Whiners, Or Habitual Refunders Wanted. For Those Of You Committed To Take Action I Encourage You To Reserve Your VIP Copy Before They Are Gone For Good!
4869	France Pleads For Global Help After Being Taken Over By Jamaica As No Other Country Comes Forward To Help The Beleaguered Nation
4870	How To Write The Perfect Classified Ad That Always Gets The Job Done
4871	I Can't Apologize Enough For The Inconvenience. I Thought I Had Covered All Our Bases By Splitting Resources And Maxing Out Bandwidth, But Apparently I Was Wrong.
4872	If You Simply Make A Commitment To Spend The Same Time You Normally Do In Front Of The TV – Working Our System – We Guarantee You'll Be Earning Money Online In 33 Days Or Less.

4873	Only Those Interested In The Material In The Articles Are Reading The Content. They Will Also Be More Interested To Click Through To The Link (Your Page) And Continue To Read, As Long As You Write And Target Your Articles Properly.
4874	How Even Newbies Can Compete With The Big Guys And Build A List Literally Overnight
4875	We Want Your Business But Only If It Right For You
4876	Take Advantage Of The Highest Profit Commissions Of Any Industry In Today's World
4877	Save Time Money And Effort By Identifying The Best Performing Ads And Links
4878	The Newbie Factor... Let's Face It. You're Not Born With Knowing Everything And How Could You Be Expected To Know It All?
4879	Millions Of People All Over The World Are Making Money Online
4880	Draw Like A Pro Even If You're Artistic As A Ditch Digger
4881	It's Fresh Out Of The Oven And Ready To Be Inhaled
4882	Making A Solid Income Online Really Is Quite Simple When You Are Shown How And You Have The Correct Tools To Make A Complete System I Am Going To Give You One To Save You Well Over $229 Per Year.
4883	WANTED: People Who Want To Do A Joint Venture. Our Product And Your Headline Will Do All The Work! For Our Special FREE REPORT Go Here.
4884	Does A Person Walk Out Of The Dollar Store Spending Just One Dollar
4885	I've Seen Thousands Of People Coming Online To Get A Crack At Making Money. They Read, Try, Read Some More, Try Some More And The Money Never Hits The Bank. I Know, Because I've Been On Every Bandwagon Until I Thought Enough B.S. Is Enough.
4886	Headlines That Turn The Negative Into Positive Cash Flow On Demand
4887	Maybe It's The Way You're Marketing That Keeps You From Becoming Rich
4888	You've Purchased So Many Home Business eBooks Your Head Is Spinning. They All Promised To Make Your Rich And Some Contained Good Information. But Are You Really Making Any Money Yet?

353

4889	Just Imagine Being Able To Set Your Own Schedule And Work From The Comfort Of Your Home. INSTEAD Of Spending Your Days Slaving Away At Your DAY JOB.
4890	Those Who Act Will Benefit While Those Who Procrastinate Will Continue To Fail
4891	How To Find A Starving Crowd Desperate To Buy Your Products And Services Before You Even Get Started
4892	Everyone Wants To Supercharge Their Marketing. You Can Get Started For As Little As $10, And Earn Thousands Monthly Starting Your Very First Month!
4893	Get Your Customers Talking. Adding Value To Your Product Isn't All About Pre-Sales Marketing Buzz Words That Get Your Customers To Buy Your Products Once. Learn The 'Little Something Extra' Method That Substantially Increased My Backend Sales And Repeat Custom, Techniques That I'm Confident Can Do The Same For Any Online Business.
4894	We're Obsessed About Making Your Experience Effortless And Providing You With Excellent Service. In Addition To Our Case Survey, Please Tell Us How We Are Doing Overall By Answering Three Survey Questions. Please Click Here To Take The Survey:
4895	This Great New Tool Makes Promoting Your Products So Much Easier For Everyone
4896	They May Be Searching In Large Numbers But Are They Buying
4897	But I Realize That For Many Of You The Opposite Is True And You've Been Struggling To Make It All Come Together. To Just Make Sense Of It All. The Market Is Pushing And Pulling You Every Which Way.
4898	Be Eccentric Now And Don't Wait For Old Age To Wear Purple
4899	If They Didn't Find What They Wanted At Your Site, They'll Be Tempted To Use The Search Engine To Find What They DO Want. Here's Where It Gets Good.
4900	We Pay Rea; Cash For Leads - Join This Fantastic Money Making Program
4901	You Will Be Able To Have Your Very Own Professional Website With Products Ready To Sell Even If You Have Never Built A Website Before And Know Nothing About It. This Is An Opportunity Not To Be Missed...
4902	To Truly Harness The Power Of This Type Of SEO Strategy, You MUST Exchange Links With A Large Amount Of Other Sites In Order To See Any Type Of Results.

354

4903	How To Quickly Launch A Powerfully Successful Viral Report From Start To Finish
4904	More Than 95% Of The Power Of Any Ad Is What's Seen In The Subject Line
4905	Some Dream Of Success While Others Work Hard At Achieving It
4906	Please Take A Moment To Read This Because It Concerns Your Affiliate Commissions
4907	Create Prints Or Posters With Online Printing Services That You Can Sell On-Demand Without Inventory.
4908	Now For A Very Limited Time You Can Learn How To Do The Exact Same Thing In A Brief Mini-Course I Have Developed. And The Best Part Is It Will Cost Absolutely Nothing Right Now.
4909	You Won't Be Left Holding The Bag Like Those Other Failed Offers
4910	If You Join Us I'll Be Behind You All The Way, Along With Our Whole Team Of Millionaire Mentors. You'll Have A Completely Automated System In Place To Do All The Sales Work For You So You Don't Have To Convince Any Body.
4911	Many People Find The Idea Of Creating Their Own Products To Be A Daunting, Overwhelming And Even Paralyzing Task. I Don't Have Any Good Ideas! I'm Not A Writer! There's Too Much Competition! I Don't Know How To Set Everything Up!
4912	This Is Not An Affiliate Program. You Can Exercise The Full Rights To This Package And Make Your Profits To The Max From Reselling This Package Or Even Sell The Products Individually In Any Format You Desire!
4913	Start Using A Niche Test To Qualify The Best Money Making Topic
4914	The Sneaky Little Secret To Finding Out Details About A Website Owner – Even If They've Set Their Profile To "Private"...
4915	Many People Find The Idea Of Creating Their Own Products To Be A Daunting, Overwhelming And Even Paralyzing Task. I Don't Have Any Good Ideas! I'm Not A Writer! There's Too Much Competition! I Don't Know How To Set Everything Up! These Are Just A Few Of The Valid Reasons Many People Have When It Comes To Not Getting Their Own Products To Sell.
4916	These Are No Ordinary Times And This Is No Ordinary Offer
4917	I Used To Be Desperate Out Of Work And On The Verge Of A Nervous Breakdown

4918	Without A Doubt This Is The Most Powerful Turn Key System You'll Find On The Internet
4919	I Have Three Questions For You. If You're Like 99.9% Of People I Know... Answering These Three Questions Will Give You A Startling Epiphany...One That Will Smack You Upside The Head Harder Than An Anvil Landing On Willie Coyote.
4920	Have You Unknowingly Been Fattened Up For An Internet Marketing Slaughter
4921	You Are Cordially Invited To The Coolest Person On The Net
4922	Grab The Full Private Label Rights To The Newest Products And Do Anything You Want With Them - Put Your Name As The Author, Edit The Contents, Sell And Keep 100% Of The Sales... It's Your Choice.
4923	You Can Go Ahead And Choose The Other Path. The Path That Leads To Success... The Path That's Going To Lead You By The Hand And Help You Achieve Anything You Want To. You Could Have Your First Profitable Sites Up And Running Today. And I Mean Seriously Running... Getting Traffic, Making Money, The Whole Thing.
4924	Why Affiliate Marketing May No Longer Be A Viable Business Model
4925	That All Sounds Amazing Doesn't It? You're Wondering How Much This Is Going To Cost You, Aren't You? Well, You're Right To. We're Getting To A Point Where You're Going To Have To Make A Decision... But Do Me This Favor: Before You Think About How Much It's Going To Cost You, Think About How Much This Will Make You...
4926	Would You Like Me To Show You How To Finally Earn More Of What You Truly Deserve
4927	You're Going To Need To Change Your Telephone Number After Having This Kind Of Success
4928	Often Companies And Entrepreneurs Will Make The Mistake Of Spending A Lot Of Money And Time And Effort To Develop A Product Before Having Any Idea Whether It Will Work Or Not. Don't Do That. Test It First. Test It On The Internet.
4929	Have You Ever Tried To Put Together Something That Came With A "Some Assembly Required" Tag Attached? I'm Convinced This Is Some Kind Of Trick To See Just How Much We Really Want The Completed Product. Surely Someone Somewhere Is Watching And Having A Good Laugh At Our Expense, Right?

356

4930	The Big Secret To Make Quick Sales From New Downline Members (It Really Is Amazing How Few People Use This Surprisingly Simple Tactic. I Am Going To Show You The Exact Method I Use To Get People To Follow Me Into Other Programs.)
4931	When You're Caught Up In A Day-To-Day Struggle To Survive, Your Dreams Fall Into The "Someday" Trap Where You Hide Your Dreams For The Day You Can (Finally!!) Start Working Toward Them. Only That Day Never Comes.
4932	Find Out Exactly How This Whole 'Make Money Online' Thing Works And How You Can Start Making Money Online Fast With Little Or Even No Experience
4933	What To Do For Aging Parents: 4 Options That Beat The Socks Off A Nursing Home ... Or Having Them Move In With You
4934	Rake In An Insane Amount Of Autopilot Recurring Income Online Without Having To Work Harder And Enjoy The Financial Security And Freedom You So Deserve.
4935	The Real Money Comes When You Have A Product To Sell
4936	Its A Serious Question To Ask Yourself - Are You Just Pretending That You Can Have A Successful Business, Or Are You Ready To Prove To Yourself That It Is Possible To Have The Life You Want?
4937	We're All Different People With Different Goals And Different Wants And Desires
4938	Doctors Prove 2 Out Of 3 Women Can Have More Beautiful Skin In 14 Days
4939	If It Worked For Me It Definitely Can Work For You
4940	How The Game Of Article Writing Has Changed And What You Must Do Now
4941	A Shoestring Budget Is Plenty I Am Not Going To Insult Your Intelligence And Say You Will Make A Truckload Of Money Without Spending A Dime. There Are Only Three Things You Absolutely Need To Properly Start An Online Business And You Can Get The Very Best For Ridiculously Low Prices.
4942	Proven Salesmanship Tactics That Prime The Pump Of Your Money Making Offer
4943	Wake Up Every Morning To An Inbox Filled With Orders From A Single Email Promotion
4944	Save Up To 25% Off Everything You Want To Buy Online

4945	How To Find Out Exactly How Much Traffic Virtually Any Keyword Will Deliver You... If You've Ever Gotten Tired Of Putting Up Sites And Hoping They Make Money, This Is For You...
4946	You Won't Be Able To Stop This No Matter How Hard You Try
4947	If Your Pharmacist Goofs, You Could Be Dead. How To Protect Yourself--Takes Just 3 Seconds
4948	How Will Your Life Be Better Easier And A Lot More Fun Knowing This Secret
4949	The Last 6 Months Of My Life Have Been So Wild It's Almost Like Someone Reached Into A Storybook And Pulled It Right Out.
4950	I Hope This Has Been Helpful. Over The Next Few Days I Am Going To Try To Answer As Many More Questions As I Can. I Want To Strike A Good Balance Between Getting This Info To You And Not Inundating You With Emails.
4951	80% Of The Game Is Showing Up And Taking Little Actions
4952	Now You Have An Opportunity To Build A Massive List Of Highly Responsive Buyers
4953	Free Professional Tools & Resources You'll Truly Need To Succeed Online
4954	Use Logos And Slogans For Your Business. They Make It Easier For People To Remember And Identify Your Business.
4955	Keep Posting New Content To Your Website Or Personal Blog.
4956	A System So Easy That You Couldn't Stop The Payments From Coming In Even If You Were Crazy Enough To Try
4957	Harness The Power Of Sales Letters That Created Every Successful Product Known To Mankind
4958	4 Categories Of Work Where You Can Make Money Quickly And Easily! Some Require Special Skills, But There Are Plenty More Available For People Who Want Something Easy And Simple To Do. Find Out What Interests You And Go For It.
4959	When You Get All Your Lies Right Your Lies Become Your Truth
4960	What Actions Have You Already Taken In Starting A Business?
4961	We're Going To Have A Conversation About What's Going To Help You Get There

4962	This Is The Foundational Principle For Building Any Business -- Whether It's On Online Business Or An Offline Business. It's Taking What Works, And Then Setting Up A System And Process For Duplicating It Over And Over Again.
4963	Because Of This They Can't See Their Way Through To The Other Side
4964	Act Fast Because Every Second You Wait The Price Goes Up 25 Cents
4965	Ready Fire Aim In That Order And Get Ready To Open Every Bank Vault
4966	Do You Think You Can Wake Up One Morning And Say, "I'm Going To Be A Doctor!" And You Go Down And Join A Company, Get A Distributor Kit For 50 Bucks, And You're A Doctor? Of Course Not. That's Ludicrous.
4967	Translate The Text And Publish It As A Book In Your Native Language.
4968	How To Get Hundreds Of Business Contacts From Your Own Website, How To Build A Group In A Particular Niche So That You Can Advertise Your Website To Them.
4969	We Help You Build A Monthly Passive Residual Income And A HUGE Mailing List Using Viral Marketing Techniques".
4970	The Magic Of Three Little Letters. I'll Show You Exactly How Those Three Letters Give You An Almost Unfair Competitive Advantage When You're Creating Products...And Those Letters Will Save You Days, Weeks Or Months Of Work.
4971	The Big Hairy Secret That Big-Name Brokerage Houses Don't Want You To Know About
4972	All You Need Is One Product That Works, And That's Duplicable, To Start Generating Those $10,000 And $100,000 Pay Days. And Once You Find It, It's Like Striking Oil. You Just Duplicate That Product And Roll It Out, Duplicate It And Roll It Out. You Just Do It Over And Over Again.
4973	We've Come Up With A Product That Anyone Can Apply To Become Extremely Profitable
4974	Explode Your Commission Payouts With Less Hassle And Work On Your End To Track And Keep Up With Everything.
4975	You Are Getting Everything You See On This Page For FREE
4976	Why Affiliate Marketing Is Really About Stealing And Not About Sharing Commissions
4977	How To Develop New Products, Back-End Profit Centers, Lead Generators And Repeat Business Money Machines In Only Hours.

359

4978	Because It Is SUCH A Great System, That I Know I Can GIVE It To You, And Still Make MORE Money Then I Would If I Was Using Some Other System And Sold It To You For Thousands.
4979	Nobody Should Be Allowed To Advertise Until They've Read This Book At Least 7 Times
4980	It Doesn't Even Take Computer Savvy; In Fact, This Stuff Is So Simple That If You Can Write An Email And Use A Web Browser Then You Can Make More Money Than You Ever Thought Possible!
4981	I Never Realized There Was So Much Stuff I Didn't Want
4982	It's Only Hard If Your Doing It The Old Fashioned And Conventional Ways. If You're Using Some High Level "Common Sense" Then It's Really Not Too Tough.
4983	Sell These Entire Courses As Is...Simply Add Your Name To The Sales Page, Add Your Payment Button, And Upload The Files And You're Ready To Cash In With On Your Very Own Online Businesses. Break It Down Into Separate Courses Or You Can Combine Different Elements Into Several Smaller Courses.
4984	Don't Give Them What They Need Give Them What They Want
4985	Want Your Customers To Get Value From Your Products. This Is Going To Give You The Ability To Add Completely Original Bonuses To Your Products Where Your Customers Will Be Much More Likely To Trust And Buy From A Website That Offers Unique, Original Bonuses And Products.
4986	7 Ways To Tweak Your Web Site Using Words, Not Money
4987	First Of All, You're Like Us. And We're Like You. It's Not Like Some "Guru" Thing Where You're Stuck Hoping Someone Will Help You Out. Heck, You Can Even Pick Up The Phone And Call Us When You Need Something.
4988	I Am Absolutely Sure That A Lot Of Smart Marketers Would Invest This Kind Of Money (Or Even More) In This Package, Just Because They Are Aware Of The Gigantic Return-On-Investment.
4989	Income Disclaimer: I Am Legally Obliged To State The Obvious, I.E. That I Cannot Guarantee You A Multiple Six Figure Income. As In Any Business, There Are No Guarantees Of Any Kind. Work Is Required. I Trust You Appreciate This!
4990	The Zero-Cost Secret To Skyrocketing The Value Of Any Site In 30 Days Or Less!
4991	Nearer To Finding Out The Truth About The 'Gurus' And What They Have Kept Hidden From You.

4992	Another Common Problem That Can Result In Great Products Never Hitting The Market By Avoiding This Easy To Make Mistake During Project Creation, You'll Be Able To Hit The Market With The Right Project At The Right Time.
4993	I'm Encouraging You To Invest Some Of Your Time In Creating An Asset That Will Throw Off Money For A Lifetime -- By An Asset I Mean A Business. By A Business, I Mean A Repeatable Process That Can Eventually Run By Itself.
4994	How Reading My Junk Mail Gave Me A Million Dollar Idea
4995	They Laughed When I Sat Down At The Piano But When I Started To Play!
4996	If Needed, I'd Gladly Pay Twice The Price Just For The Privilege To Shop At His Store Because I Know That I'll End Up Saving Money In The Long Run With A Trusted Resource Like Him At My Side.
4997	Make Sure The Headline Solves The Problem Of Your Web Site Visitor
4998	Find Out Why The Government Is So Eager To Help You Make Money At Home
4999	How To Steal The Deal And Put Your Income On Autopilot Without Lifting A Finger
5000	Most Often People Who Have No Marketing Background Or SEO Background Would Not Bother About Keywords And Would Just Blog About Almost Anything On Their Blogs.
5001	PS: The Price Can Go Up At Any Time. Please Don't Let This Amazing Deal Pass You By.
5002	How Long Will You Tolerate Your Online Failure? Profit TODAY Our Monitors In The LIVE Business Center Are Here 24/7 To Help You Make Money. This System Is Unique. You Get EVERYTHING You Need For Success. Tools Training Traffic And The Complete Worldwide Monitor Network.
5003	How Would You Like To Turn Your Annual Income Into Your Monthly Income
5004	What If The Odds Are Already Stacked Against Your Online Success
5005	Picture In Your Mind The Typical Day You Would Have... What Are You Doing? Where Do You Live? What Kinds Of Toys Do You Own? How Much Time Do You Spend With Your Family? Who Are Your Friends? Want More?
5006	Here Are The 10 Most Embarrassing Things I Saw On Your Website

5007	Advertise Their Links Too. If They're Successful What Does That Mean For You? When You Combine Your Advertising Efforts With Theirs Everyone Wins!
5008	How To Successfully Market Like A Lone Wolf In The Virtual World Of Clueless Show Dogs
5009	Fretting Every Time A New Bill Comes In, Wondering How You'll Ever Have Time Or Money To Do Anything Fun Or Exciting With Your Life.
5010	Quality Content Is Also Going To Keep Your Subscribers Happy. If You Consistently Publish Informative & Interesting Information To Your List, They Will Be More Than Happy To Click Over To Websites Selling Products You Suggest To Them.
5011	What Makes You Think Anyone In Their Right Mind Will Break Their Back To Promote Any Of Your Products? You Need To Have Promotion Tools Pre-Made For Your Affiliates.
5012	In Fact, If You Are Not Completely Satisfied In Every Way, If You Have Not Experienced Anything That Excited You In This Letter Or If You Do Not Think The Guide I'm Providing You Is Worth The Price - Then Frankly I'm Embarrassed To Keep Your Money
5013	Every Profitable Venture Imaginable Remains Hidden Until Started Inside Your Mind
5014	What Is The One Thing You Really Want To Achieve Online
5015	STOP For One Minute. I Know Your Clicking Links Just To Build Up Credits Just To Promote Your BIG BIZ Op.
5016	If You're Unwilling To Invest In Yourself How Do You Expect To Feel Good About Yourself
5017	Who Ever Heard Of A Woman Losing Weight And Enjoying Delicious Meals At The Same Time
5018	Sites Like MySpace, YouTube And Facebook Have Hundreds Of Million Of Users EACH - And Yet You Have To Be ON Their Websites To Use The Social Networking Features.
5019	Make Millions Start With Over Deliver Over Deliver And Over Deliver
5020	The Sneakiest Search Term Trick You Can Use To Get To The Top Of Google
5021	Take Advantage Of This Feature And Turn Your Products Into Viral Marketing Agents That Can Be Responsible For Your Exposure And Source Of Collecting Leads With No Extra Effort On Your Part!

5022	Easily Add Your Own Ebooks And Downloadable Products Descriptions And Prices
5023	How To Turn One Idea Into A Near Infinite List Of Promotion And Product Ideas... You'll Go From Not Knowing Where To Start To Not Knowing Where To Stop.
5024	Sick And Tired Of Those So-Called Secrets Scam Offers Being Pitched
5025	It's Getting Worse When You Can't Even Feel Secure In The Job You Hate
5026	Here's Your Full-Length Video... Learn How You Can Generate Big Paydays With NO List, NO Product, And NO Upfront Cost (In Fact, You Actually Get PAID To Do It).
5027	Automate The Selling Process In Places Where Eager Buyer Wait With Money In Hand
5028	We Are Going To Put You On The Fast Track To A Full Time Income, And If You Follow The Plan, There Is No Reason Why You Won't Start Earning In A Matter Of Days, And Be Positioned To Explode Your Profits In A Matter Of Weeks.
5029	Do You Just Dream About Work Or Are You On To Something
5030	Why Tire Kickers Will Never Experience This Simple Secret To Success
5031	If Your Answer Is No That Should Tell You Something About Yourself
5032	I'd Let You Download My Stuff For Free If I Thought You'd Really Put It To Work
5033	If You'd Like To Take Advantage Of My Experiences And Learn My Techniques, That's Easy. On The Other Hand, You're More Than Willing To Pursue Your Business On Your Own Without My Advice.
5034	I'm About To Hand You The Keys To Your New Niche
5035	You Will See That This Is A Very Easy Site With Few "Bells & Whistles" - It Is Mostly Just Plain Text. There Is Nothing Difficult Here.
5036	If You Think You're Doing Well Enough NOT TO Analyze Your Site Traffic Statistics, In This ALL Mad, Insane and Super Fast, Dog Eat Dog Internet Marketing World, Then I Have This To Say....
5037	Once You Have Learned How To Build A Simple Sales Web Page, The Door Of Opportunity Should Open Wide For You.

5038	What's More... You'll Never Have To Personally Talk To Anyone, Make Phone Calls, Or Chase After Friends And Family. Everything Is Done Online According To Your Schedule.
5039	In A World Of Constant Launches This Free And Valuable Information Is Insanely Rich
5040	PPS: One Last Thing... Not Only Can You Make Money Using These Products, But When You Pick Up Your Complete Package, You Will Be Given Privileged Access To My Affiliate Program.
5041	When Times Are Good, People Need Constant Training And Education. The World Is Changing Way Too Fast To Keep Up Otherwise. We've Entered An Idea Age That Powers A Creative Economy...An Environment That Requires Continuous Learning
5042	Drive Traffic To Your Website Or Affiliate Sites Through Your Affiliate Link Or Links
5043	See How Far I Can Raise The Value Bar For You
5044	Sit Tight And Learn How To Start Stuffing Your Money Bags
5045	How Segmenting Databases Can Actually Improve Sales And Decrease Unsubcription Rates
5046	Are Your Online Earnings Fluctuating So Much You Can't Count On Them To Pay The Bills

"If words are to enter men's minds and bear fruit, they must be the right words shaped cunningly to pass men's defenses and explode silently and effectually within their minds."
- J. B. Phillips

"*The most valuable of all talents is that of never using two words when one will do.*"
- Thomas Jefferson

We hope this "More Than Words" book companion will help you clearly paint your dreams, sell your ideas, and market your messages, propelling each of your ideas and projects toward incredible success.

We truly wish you the very best and look forward to hearing your success stories.

Richard & Lynn Voigt - RIVO
I. M. Education Specialists
RIVO Inc – RIVO Marketing

About The Authors:

Richard and Lynn help clients clarify their talents and develop creative strategies that paint dreams, sell ideas, and market messages. They help everyday people create an action plan that discovers and connects the missing pieces of a client's success puzzle.

Together, they present a unique team-approach with each client, working side-by-side; utilizing their life-long skills and diverse expertise as education specialists, Internet marketers, entrepreneurs, inventors, artists, authors, and life & business coaches,.

Teaching by example, they focus on proven systems, research and development, trends & technology, key domain portfolio acquisitions, video production, self-publishing, along with managing over a hundred of premium keyword websites on behalf of their company, RIVO Inc – RIVO Marketing.

Their life-long mission is to continually uncover brand new strategies, products, and services, networking useful solutions for their clients, online & offline entrepreneurs, small business owners, writers, local artists, models, teachers, and students and marketing professionals.

Feel free to contact them if you have questions or would like to tap into their talents and expertise. They would appreciate your feedback and success stories.

Richard & Lynn Voigt - RIVO
I. M. Education Specialists

RIVO INC - RIVO Marketing
Website: www.RIVOinc.com
Email: support@RIVOinc.com

Want To See What We've Been Up To:

Visit Lynn's Garden: www.WisconsinGarden.net
        view hundreds of great garden video blogs

See Richard's Unique Artwork: www.RIVOart.com
        view over 3,000 original compositions

Watch For Additional RIVO Titles:

The Golden Vault Of Motivational Quotations –
Words of Wisdom From The Greatest Minds & Leaders

ACTION HEADLINES That Drive Emotions – Volumes 1- 6
 Paint Dreams, Sell Ideas & Market Your Message

BABY NAME.me – 21,400+ Baby Names & Nicknames –
For Family, Friends, Pets, Natural & Man-Objects

DOODLE DESIGNS Volume 1 & 2
For Professionals & Kids Of All Ages

DOODLE DESIGN Coloring Book
For Professionals & Kids Of All Ages

IDIOMS – IDIOMS - IDIOMS
6,450 Popular Expressions That Put Words In Your Mouth

The CLICHÉ BIBLE - 8,400 Clichés For Sports Fanatics & Lovers
Of Popular Expresssions

MORE THAN WORDS
5000+ Marketing Phrases That Sell

HYPNOTIC PHRASING
WARNING-This Book Teaches You How To Grab Eyeballs

The RIGHT TO WEALTH
Becoming Wealthy Isn't Hard When You Know How

PERSONAL NOTES:

www.ingramcontent.com/pod-product-compliance
Lightning Source LLC
Chambersburg PA
CBHW051439170526
45166CB00001B/45